Critical Essays on
Louis-Ferdinand Céline

*Critical Essays on
World Literature*

Robert Lecker, General Editor
McGill University

Critical Essays on Louis-Ferdinand Céline

William K. Buckley

G. K. Hall & Co. • Boston

Library of Congress Cataloging in Publication Data

Buckley, William K., 1946-
Critical essays on Louis-Ferdinand Céline / William K. Buckley.
     p. cm. — (Critical essays on world literature)
    Includes index.
    ISBN 0-8161-8841-6
    1. Céline, Louis-Ferdinand, 1894-1961 — Criticism and interpre-
tation. I. Title. II. Series.
  PQ2607.E834Z57 1988
  843'.912 — dc19   88-13109
                                            CIP

This publication is printed on permanent/durable acid-free paper
MANUFACTURED IN THE UNITED STATES OF AMERICA

For my son John

A man would spend the rest of his days in jail if he told what life was really like—starting with his own. —"Homage to Zola," 1933

CONTENTS

PREFACE

To provide both introductory materials and historical overviews has been the rationale behind my selection of items for this volume. I have arranged each chapter chronologically, so that the change in critical reaction to Céline from 1932 to 1988 may be seen in its surprising complexity. Readers will discover that many of the reviews and essays refer to one another. I believe this will give the book an interesting and informative unity.

Choosing representative essays from a vast field of international reactions that span over fifty years has been a difficult task. I have selected reactions of critics from France, Germany, England, America, Canada, and Australia; provided translations of important French comments; and included all of the original essays I received from an open invitation to scholars. Of course some of the more famous and influential reactions to Céline are printed here (e.g., Trotsky, Bernanos, Gide), yet items not easily available to Americans are offered too (e.g., Dabit's review of *Journey to the End of the Night*, *Figaro*'s interview with Céline's wife, and excerpts from Céline's letters).

My general intention has been to provide a view of how our critical world describes Céline's major works. Sometimes the doctor's famous novels impel us to find out more about him. Interviews and biographical materials have been provided for readers who feel such curiosity.

Balance and fairness will, I hope, finally characterize this volume.

WILLIAM K. BUCKLEY

ACKNOWLEDGMENTS

For their kind assistance in locating obscure references, I offer my special thanks to Robert Moran, director of the Indiana University Northwest Library, and to Cynthia Bauer and Tim Sutherland, reference librarians.

For their helpful and instructive suggestions I thank Lewis DeSimone, editor at G. K. Hall; Robert Lecker, general editor of this series; Barbara Sutton, manuscript editor at G. K. Hall, and Janet Zietowski, production supervisor.

Gratitude and admiration is offered to Jóhanna Eríksdóttir Hull for her careful translation of difficult material; and my special appreciation is offered to Wayne Burns, Gerald J. Butler, and James Flynn for the conversations about Céline we have had over the years. I thank Yves de la Quérière for his willingness to listen to my questions about French history.

Céline delivering his speech "Hommage à Emile Zola" at Médan in 1933. Reprinted with permission from Roger-Viollet Agency, Paris.

INTRODUCTION

Céline and the Critical World

"We walked the ruined streets of Paris with Céline's books — under our overcoats!"[1]

I

Born in a Paris suburb at the beginning of the twentieth-century and having lived as a youth among shopkeepers in the famous Passage Choiseul, awarded the Médaille Militaire by Pétain for bravery in World War I, a physician who traveled the world, studied the ills of factory workers, worked among the poor, and wrote novels that ruthlessly criticized the world and changed the course of the modern novel, called a fascist, a communist, a socialist, an anarchist, a pacifist, a racist, a humanist, a paranoid, the father of black humor, Louis-Ferdinand Céline (1894–1961) remains, at this writing, as controversial as he often said he would be. Always the reluctant political celebrity in his remaining days, Céline became Hermit of Meudon and Grand Chronicler of our times, the collaborator amnestied by a Paris court and infamous anti-Semite. "I have become," he said in 1955, "the unmentionable man!"[2] Today it is still difficult to mention his name in polite circles or in the halls of our universities without causing reactions peppered with invectives, dismissals, or outrage. With comic and characteristic irony he described the world's reaction to him this way: "I represent decay, as the greatest writers of the day . . . right, center, left, the torches of the universal conscience, Cousteau, Rivarol, Jacob, Sartre, Mme Lafente and Larengon . . . and a hundred more in America, Italy, Japan . . . have so magnificently written and demonstrated . . . submitting any of my white elephants to the *Figaro immobilier* or the television, or even the corner bar . . . even on a ten-foot pole . . . would be a very risky business, much riskier than murdering three shepherdesses, two retired colonels, and a postman!"[3]

Céline's astonishing impact on the modern novel began with the publication of *Journey to the End of the Night* (1932) and *Death on the Installment Plan* (1936), and it continues with what has been called his World War II trilogy: *Castle to Castle* (1957), *North* (1960), and *Rigadoon* (1969). Throughout his life Céline maintained that France had never

1

forgiven him for *Journey* — no wonder, with its famous attacks on war, love, patriotism, religion, science, economics, politics, and ideals. In all of his works Céline plays havoc with our pretensions, our posturing, our self-congratulations. He skewers all that he sees, even himself, and provides neither political nor philosophical solutions to the cruelty and absurdity in the world. "There is no system by which he [Man] can be trained," he said in *Mea Culpa* (1937): "He always manages to make his getaway from the controls somehow. . . . What an expert he is in doing just that! Anyone who could catch him in the act would be clever! And then, who gives a damn? Life is too short as it is! To talk morals entails no responsibility. That's a pose, a good front to put on. A preacher is on every dunghill."[4] Such declarations still elicit the anger of politicians, religious leaders, modern novelists, university professors, and the reading public. Yet Céline rubs salt into the wound: "I don't believe in mankind," he declares. All is allowed by man "except *lack of faith in mankind.*"[5] Our culture cannot forgive him for his illustration of such statements with trainloads of facts, opinions, and dreams, and the backlash against him led to his definition of the "true life of the true artist" as one "long or short game of tag with prison, before he's 'it' . . . the scaffold, you might say, is awaiting every artist."[6]

The world of criticism has spent more than fifty years in reacting to what it calls Céline's terrifying vision, often explaining it by anchoring it to frozen moments in French political history.[7] Céline's novels wrestle free from such attempts. His voice is the original modern howl from below, echoing up and over the surface of what criticism calls *literary history*.

> I owe the revelation of my genius to the Pigalle station! . . . the Surface is hardly livable! it's true! so I don't hesitate! . . . I ship all my friends off on the metro, correction! I take everybody willy-nilly, with me! . . . charge along! . . . the emotive subway, mine in a dream! . . . destination! in emotion! . . . the metro and its rails, I bend them! I do, I admit! its rails so rigid! . . . I give them a helluva twist . . . all it takes! its style, shall we say! I distort them one certain way, so the passengers, daydreaming along . . . don't notice . . . the sorcery, the magic . . . the violence also! . . . admittedly! . . . all the passengers enclosed, locked in, double-bolted! everybody in my emotive cars! . . . And the whole Surface comes with me! you see! the whole Surface! on board! amalgamated on my metro! all the Surface ingredients! all the distractions of the Surface! by sheer force! I leave the Surface nothing! . . . I make off with it all![8]

This is Céline's explanation of the style *and content* of his novels, and it gives a poetic lie[9] to Sartre's statement that Céline "was able to support the socialist theories of the Nazis" because "he was paid,"[10] to Sartre's ideological definition of the artist in the 1940s: "Against the vague and synthetic notions which were crammed into us day and night, Europe, Race, the Jew, the anti-bolshevik crusade, we had to reawaken the old spirit of analysis which alone was capable of tearing them to pieces." For Sartre, the question was how can one "make himself a man in, by, and for history?"[11] Céline was neither interested in crusades nor in placing himself in, by, and for the abstract march of time. Instead, he scoops up with a very broad shovel all the facts, opinions, and dreams about history, and then flings the whole batch up into the air, up high enough until all of it glows incandescently for the reader against the black backdrop of death.

Critics may turn to Marx's "Estranged Labour" (1844) for their explanations of Céline's vision[12] (alienated labor may "estrange man's own body from him . . . his *human* being" in *Journey*[13]), or they may soon turn to Marx's "On the Jewish Question" (1843) to explain his particular brand of anti-Semitism (especially when one compares Céline's remarks in Hindus's *The Crippled Giant* [1986] with remarks like: "The *political* emancipation of the Jew or the Christian — of the *religious* man in general — is the *emancipation of* the state from Judaism, Christianity, and *religion* in general" or "the power of religion is the religion of power").[14] Yet Céline is no Marxist. There is "no dialectics in the metro!" he said in *Conversations with Professor Y* (1955). Others may turn to Freud for their explanations of Céline's view of the human animal,[15] since *Civilization and its Discontents* (1929) contains such provocative views on sexuality, happiness, religion, communism, and aggression that appear remarkably similar to Céline's writings. Soon critics may use Freud's *Group Psychology and Analysis of the Ego* (1921) to describe Céline's famous scenes of mob *délire*, or his anarchist positions ("love for women," Freud said, "breaks through the group ties of race, of national separation, and of the social class system, and it thus produces important effects as a factor in civilization").[16] Yet Céline is no disciple of Freud, despite his remarks on the famous doctor: "Freud's a great clinical doctor. One of the last I guess of the great clinical school. . . . There's a touch of the novelist in Freud. . . . Enthusiasm is to let yourself go into delirium. Freud certainly did!"[17] Some may quote Darwin to explain Céline's seriocomic remarks on biology: "the big thing is their [Chinese hordes] blood! . . . it's only the blood that counts! they've got the 'dominant blood' . . . and don't forget it!"[18] Yet Céline is no Darwinian. Others point to Rabelais's *Gargantua* to study Céline's blazing vocabulary and realism, to Swift and Defoe for his inflammatory pamphlets, to Artaud for his theatricality.[19] Someone may even quote his remarks on Gandhi to prove his pacifism.[20] There will be those inclined to use Wilhelm Reich's *The Mass Psychology of Fascism* (1933) to support Céline's criticism of society, or to explain Céline's character structure. Reich said: "As a physician I got to know the international working man and his problems in a way that no party politician could have known him. The party politician saw only 'the working class,' which he wanted to 'infuse with class consciousness.' I saw man as a creature who had come under the domination of the worst possible social conditions, conditions he himself had created and bore within himself as a part of his character and from which he sought to free himself in vain. The gap between the purely economic and bio-sociologic views became unbridgeable."[21] Céline might have said the same. Yet one could call Céline a fascist only if the Passage Choiseul could be proved to have fashioned in him what Reich called the "basic emotional attitude of the suppressed man of our authoritarian machine civilization and its mechanistic-mystical conception of life."[22] D. H. Lawrence could be used to explain his view of women, although Céline thought Lawrence spent an inordinate amount of time in *Lady Chatterley's Lover* (1929) romanticizing a gamekeeper's genitals. Marcuse's "Repressive Tolerance" (1965) may help explain Céline's critique of mass culture in *Bagatelles pour un massacre* (1937); linguists are inclined to study his argot; others try to separate the doctor from the artist. Approaches to Céline are, and may continue to be, long, tricky, and contradictory.

The essays, reviews, and comments in this volume reflect the difficulties, adjustments, and frustrations in criticism when it comes to terms with that sheer originality in an author who cannot be nailed down to an ideology or a platitude. The fact is that Céline is completely unique, independent. There is no precedent for *Death on the Installment Plan*, that irrefutable symphony of new sound. Céline is, as Wayne Burns has said about the serious novelist, "alone and on the defensive: finally against all the forces of our mobilized culture, more directly against the critical representatives of these forces." He is an author who expresses his own "difference," his "madness," his genius, in what Céline called his own peculiar *transposition* of reality.[23] "I have no ideas, myself! not a one! . . . the passionate years of youth are spent getting a hard on and gargling ideeaas! . . . I leave *ideas* to the flea merchants! all *ideas* to the hucksters, the pimps, the confusion mongers!"[24]

What we do have from Céline, then, are his complicated feelings [history is an "Epic Dance Hall"; "politics is anger"; man is a "toad swollen with ideals"; love is a "poodle's chance of attaining the infinite"; art is found in the unbounded and energetic "curve" of the female dancer's leg; approach people "through their animality, enjoy it, and not talk about it"; little bits of kindness between individuals will make us "one hair's breadth less filthy" at death than at birth] and, of course, his "invention."

> "You've invented something! . . . what is it?"
> He asks.
> "Emotion through written language! . . . written language had run dry in France, I'm the one who primed emotion back into it! . . . as I say! it's not just some cheap trick, believe me! . . . the gimmick, the magic that any asshole can use in order to move you 'in writing!' . . . rediscovering the emotion of the spoken word through the written word! it's not nothing! . . . it is miniscule, but it is something! . . ."
> "You're so pretentious you're grotesque!"
> "Granted! granted! . . . so? inventors are monstrous! . . . the

whole lot! especially the little ones! *The emotion of spoken language through the written form!* Just reflect on that a bit, dear Professor Y! get your noodle in gear!"[25]

If we do get our "noodle in gear," and decide to ride Céline's *métro émotif* ("emotive subway") locked and bolted in by his style and content, then we discover in his novels an "agonized compassion"[26] for the human being, born out of that "medical, level eye which loves human beings without sentimentalizing Man."[27] We hear a voice that tells the reader to look squarely at himself, at his "lousy soul dancing."[28]

II

On the Continent, early critical recovery from the shockwave of *Journey*'s publication in 1932 can be measured by the Goncourt Academy's deliberations over whether Céline should receive the coveted Goncourt Prize. Dozens of newspapers and journals reported the Academy's discussions and speculated on what led the Academy members to switch their vote from Céline to Guy Mazeline, the author of a novel now long forgotten. Many in Paris hailed *Journey* as a masterpiece, completely deserving of the prize.[29] Others called the book a scandal that deserved to be ignored,[30] while still others suggested *Journey* was too original and powerful for the conservative Academy to handle.[31] *Figaro* boldly announced that *Journey* should be awarded the prize.[32] *Nouvelliste* claimed parents and leagues of decency should resist the book.[33] *Cri du jour* tried giving the controversy a practical explanation, claiming retail outlets did not have pricing arrangements with Denoël and Steele, the publisher of *Journey*, but had such arrangements with Gallimard, publisher of Mazeline.[34] One reviewer summed up the fireworks by describing *Journey* as an "enormous, filthy boulder" that had fallen into the "little garden" of French letters.[35] Rightist and leftist groups alternately condemned and praised the novel;[36] some critics declared the Academy was afraid of public opinion, or that their votes were up for sale.[37] Most likely because of an onslaught of critical opinion, and under pressure from Lucien Descaves — novelist, vocal supporter of Céline, and member of the Academy who eventually resigned in protest — Céline was given the Renaudot Prize by the Renaudot Committee. Giving the Goncourt Prize to novels about World War I had not been without precedent. Henri Barbusse's *Le Feu* (1916) received one, and Céline openly admitted that Barbusse's success influenced his early intentions to begin *Journey*. Overall, French reaction from 1932 to 1939 divided itself into two hostile camps: those in favor of the novel as a scathing portrait of a society writhing in deadly economic policies, and those opposed to the book as a novel that enjoyed exaggerating the ills of civilization. In Germany, reaction over *Journey* was not as heated. Apparently the novel was seen as an example of French "decadence."[38] In England, Céline was seen as an "aged Tolstoy crying out against copulation and the propagation of the race."[39] At first beguiled by Céline's views on imperialism in *Journey* but later flabbergasted by *Mea Culpa* (1936), Russian writers reacted characteristically: Maxim Gorky criticized Céline's "nihilism of despair" and predicted he would become a Fascist;[40] Leon Trotsky wrote what is still one of the best essays on Céline, but concluded his remarks with lamentations over what he called Céline's "hopelessness."[41]

French writers took their assessments of Céline to heart: for Claude Lévi-Strauss, Céline was "at least" far from the "common enemy," although he was not "in the socialist fold";[42] to his friend Eugène Dabit, author of *Hôtel du Nord* (1930), Céline was a kindred soul;[43] to Georges Bernanos, he was an author whom the French should not want crowned by the dull Academy;[44] and for Jean-Paul Sartre, who took a line from Céline's play *L'Eglise* (1933) as an epigraph for the title page of *Nausea* (1938), he was, according to De Beauvoir, the author of the "book of the year. . . . we knew whole passages by heart, and his type of anarchism seemed very close to ours."[45] As one of the finest explorations of the heart of Céline's vision in *Journey*, Trotsky's essay is reprinted here as the best essay from the 1930s. Bernanos has been chosen since he explains more adequately than others why Céline could not be accepted by the commercialized Goncourt Academy or by society at large—although he must, like Gorky and Trotsky, defend himself against Céline's vision with references to an ideology at the end of his review. Dabit is a curious case: still capable of writing a novel that objectively describes the appalling conditions of modern life, and, like Zola, hoping for reform, Eugène Dabit, locksmith turned novelist, is the example of a French realist writer who finds himself caught in the social upheaval of life between the great wars, the novelist who looks back to Zola for inspiration but must reluctantly admit that Céline's "Homage to Zola" (1933) announces a new and more ominous world. Standing in the doorway of the house at Médan, where Zola had once lived, Céline described what many writers had been keeping to themselves—the beginning of an age where optimistic faith in science was no longer possible. "To get the right tone" today, Céline said to Elie Faure, "one must without hesitation, put oneself in a state of nightmare."[46] Dabit reacts to Céline's "nightmare" with eloquent sorrow in his review of *Journey*. I have chosen his review beause he expresses so honestly the pain of the optimist at reading Céline. (After Dabit's death in 1936, Céline dedicated *Bagatelles* to him.)

Critical reaction to *Death on the Installment Plan* was considerably quieter, owing partly to the fact that French Leftists and Rightists could not nail it down with an ideology, partly to the belief that the novel's argot would make it unreadable in the future, but mostly to outrage at the realistic language and content of the book. Most called it an epic of disgust and despair. Robert Denoël, Céline's publisher, felt impelled to write an explanation of the novel, reaffirming Céline's ties with Zola.[47] Both Sartre and Paul Nizan, however, reacted negatively to the book, claiming it was contemptuous of the poor.[48] In general, and before the appearance of his pamphlets, Céline was seen in 1939 as the "diabolical" genius of French letters.

By the 1940s and 1950s, Céline had achieved an international reputation, not only for his first two novels, but also for his anti-Semitic pamphlets. After reading *Bagatelles* and *Death*, André Gide mounted a defense for Céline in 1938. His claims for *Bagatelles* touched off a controversy that has lasted for over forty years: Are the pamphlets exaggerations of style and content for effect? Do they reflect Céline's beliefs? Are they thunderous appeals for peace? Reactions to the pamphlets in the 1940s fashioned these questions and then attempted to answer them by either labeling Céline a collaborator or calling him an idiosyncratic pacifist.[49] Whether *Bagatelles* (reprinted in 1943) or *L'Ecole des cadavres* (1938) or *Les Beaux draps* (1941) do, as Gide suggests with *Bagatelles*, pile jokes up "six stories high," or whether they reflect the temper of the times, is a question that current criticism says can be answered only if all of Céline's works are studied as a whole.[50] Even more influential has been Gide's comment that *Death on the Installment Plan* is "hallucination" that awful reality provokes. This statement, challenged by Wayne Burns in *Enfin Céline Vint* (1988), is still influential on both continents today. In 1941, while Drieu la Rochelle mentions Céline in his cultural survey of France *(Notes pour comprendre le siècle)* and Sartre makes his famous claim that Céline was paid by the Nazis for his pamphlets,[51] the Russian paper *Izvestia* (20 June 1947) reports that American capitalism and Céline are both leading the resurgence of fascist French letters. In England, by 1945, the *Nation* flatly labels Céline a collaborator (160:22–24, 16 June); in Japan, he is the "humanist-pessimist" *(Furansu Bungaku* 1 [March 1949]:41–52). Roussin's original essay and McCarthy's chapter on politics from his *Céline* (1975) are offered here as detailed studies of these problematic years.

Published under the cloud of his flight from France to Denmark, after being condemned by the Resistance, Céline's *Guignol's Band* (1944) is greeted in France with disappointment, since it did not "speak more closely" to the historical reality of the war years in London or France *(Aspects*, 2 June 1945). When the author returned to France to practice medicine in Meudon, after being pardoned in 1951 by a military court in Paris, his *Féerie pour une autre fois* (1952–54) was greeted with silence. With Gallimard's publication of *Professor Y*, however, Céline stirred up his fame once again. Robert Poulet hoped for an end to the conspiracy of silence that then surrounded his work.[52] Francois Mauriac later defended his art against Céline's attack in *Y*,[53] and Roger Nimier (who called for Céline to win the Nobel Prize) supported Céline's assault on the flatness of French fiction.[54] Roland Barthes mentioned Céline in his *Le Degré zéro de l'écriture* (1953), calling the author's argot a "descent" into the poverty of the life described. And after *Castle to Castle* appeared in 1957, critical floodgates opened in France, England, Germany, and Italy, dividing once again into the old camps of Left and Right. Lucien Rebatet calls the portrait of the Vichy government at Sigmaringen in *Castle* "hallucination" (*Dimanche matin* 217 [30 June 1957]:9); Jürgen Rühle sees Céline as driven to fascism from anticapitalist hatreds,[55] and Paul Sérant describes Céline as neither Left nor Right, but a clear pacifist and anti-Semite.[56] Critics in Italy and Denmark hold similar views. George Woodcock's overview essay from *Encounter* magazine is a compact summary of reaction to Céline in the 1940s and 1950s, emphasizing as it does Céline's "collaboration," and "hallucination." Like most critics of these decades, Woodcock calls *Castle* important but second to *Journey*.

From 1960 to 1979, after Céline's last two novels were published — *North* (1960) and *Rigadoon* (1969) — there was an explosion of critical studies, biographies, collections, and translations. Myriads of thematic, linguistic, and biographical pieces appeared throughout Europe, despite Henri Peyre's implied warning in *French Novelists of Today* (1967) that Céline was not worthy of attention. In Paris, Céline's major works were published by Balland; under the editorship of Henri Godard, Gallimard began to issue the Pléiade critical edition of major and minor works (with the exception of the pamphlets); *L'Herne: L. F. Céline* (1972) appeared; Jean-Pierre Dauphin began his comprehensive bibliography with *Calepins de bibliographie: Céline I (1914–1944)*. Five volumes of *Cahiers Céline* appeared in the 1970s, and Marc Laudelout's *Revue Célinienne* began. The *Australian Journal of French Studies* devoted an issue to Céline in 1976, and a Céline library was established in France. Dauphin's *Album Céline* (1977) reviewed Céline's life with photos, Gen Paul's illustrations for *Journey*, and maps of Céline's journey to America and Canada. François Gibault began his massive biography in 1977, attempting to be definitive in three volumes, and in Denmark Helga Pedersen published in 1975 a book on Céline's exile there. Frédéric Vitoux wrote his *Bébert, le chat de L.-F. Céline* (1976), and Patrick McCarthy's critical biography was published by Allen Lane in England in 1975.[57] In Germany, Eva Förster published an 822-page critical and biographical study of *Journey* and *Death*, using quasi-psychoanalytical insights to "open the secrets" of the novels, while Hans Grössel saw an echo of Freud's "death principle" in "Hommage à Zola."[58] In Italy, Paolo Carile analyzed the Italian reaction to Céline's work, and made a plea to study the author apart from his fascist ideology.[59] *Death* was translated in England in 1966 and greeted as the autobiography of a Fascist,[60] while Céline's major works were beginning to be translated into Dutch, Japanese, Portuguese, and other languages.

Numerous linguistic studies of Céline's style appeared throughout the 1960s and 1970s. To name a few: Marc Hanrez's *Céline* (1961) looked closely at Céline's slang and technical terms; Yves de la Quérière's *Céline et les mots: Etude stylistique des effets de mots dans le Voyage au bout de la nuit* (1973) looked at Céline's neologisms; Henri Godard's lengthy "Un art poétique" (1974) explained Céline's "emotive subway"; and Philippe Alméras, in *PMLA*, studied the changes in Céline's language from *Journey* to *Rigadoon*.[61] Thematic studies focused on Céline's belief in the expression of emotion in art (Debrie-Panel's *Céline* [1961], Roux's *La Mort de L.-F. Céline* [1966], and Vandromme's *Céline* [1963]). One critic saw the author as the antirational, antimaterialist, social Darwinian.[62] Freud was used to explain Céline's personality and to reveal how much Céline knew about him.[63] *North* impelled France and Japan to call Céline a "prophet," while *Rigadoon* caused him to be reproached for "faulty chronology."[64] Only a few saw Céline's final novels "essential to understanding our bleak era as was Rabelais to understanding the Renaissance."[65] Tensions and conflicts in interpreting Céline during these decades can best be understood by comparing views found in Rens and Tierney (Canada) and Heist (Germany), both reprinted here. For Heist, the "ingenious gutter singer is dead" in the final novels; for Rens and Tierney, Céline is to be "ranked with Proust," since from *Journey* to *Rigadoon* the narrative has become "historical reality." Merlin Thomas, in what is one of the finest studies in English yet to appear, summed things up by 1979: "Books and articles often allude to disgust, despair, nausea, even lunacy, when referring to Céline, but much more rarely to the fact that he had the most intense and sincere views about what constitutes beauty, grace, delicacy, kindness, humanity."[66]

Céline research in the 1980s continues to focus on *Journey*,[67] the trilogy, biography, language, and the compilation of Céline's letters, minor works, ballets, medical essays, and radio and television interviews. Laudelout's *Le Bulletin Célinien* announced developments in Céline research, and *Études littéraires* devoted an entire issue to Céline. Godard published a comprehensive look at Céline's aesthetics in *Poetique de Céline*, and Perugia published *Céline*.[68]

Recently, the detection of an emerging but still rare and quiet anti-idealistic view of Céline has been possible. Commenting on Förster's Frankfurt School analysis in *Romanstruktur und Weltanschauung im Werk L.-F. Célines* (1978) and Kristeva's psychoanalytical study of the author in *Pouvoirs de l'horreur* (Paris: Le Seuil, 1980), Leon S. Roudiez criticizes "humanist" writers who confront Céline armed with idealistic perspectives: "Those who belong to the literary club, or *la chappelle*, as the French might put it, are bound to repeat the same clichés, evoke the same 'eternal values,' even when clothed in fashionable vocabulary."[69] And in 1984, the *London Times Literary Supplement* reprinted its own 1934 review of *Journey*, which read as a retort to the narrowness and reactionary view of conventional Céline criticism: "If a place be sought for the perspective from which he [Céline] writes, perhaps it is a symptom of what Señor Ortega Y Gasset calls the European revolt against culture, a revolt that he thinks necessary in order that culture may be brought more into the service of spontaneous or biological life, instead of being opposed to it" (21 September 1984). After fifty years, European criticism may be hinting at returning to earlier, and, in many cases, more courageous views of Céline's work.

III

In the United States, the power of Céline's first two novels was felt by only a handful of writers.[70] Trotsky's essay made an appearance in the *Atlantic Monthly* in 1935,[71] and an extremely rare but negative review of *Death* can be read in the *Yale Review* (28 [September 1938]:x). Two reviews from the 1930s are reprinted here because they illustrate common American reactions found well into the 1970s: outright condemnation of Céline (Adams) and grudging respect (Fadiman). The only other American reaction in the 1930s that comes close to understanding Céline's purposes is Robert A. Parker's short preface to his translation of *Mea Culpa* in the now scarce 1937 Little, Brown and Co. volume of the work.[72] "Gone are all traces of the detached objectivity of a Flaubert," Parker wrote, "the 'scientific' naturalism of a Zola." In 1942 W. M. Frohock described Céline's "nihilism" as a vehicle for documenting the "emotional bankruptcy" of modern man.[73] Slochower reviewed both *Journey* and *Death*: he saw "inverted humanism" and compassion in Céline and called him more "underground" than Döblin, Joyce, Farrell, or Dos Passos.[74] Irving Howe's "Céline: Novelist of the Underground" (1948)[75] took a comprehensive look at both *Journey* and *Death*, labeling Céline a philistine with genius. In 1944 Céline is first mentioned by Henry Miller, and it was probably through him that Allen Ginsberg, Kerouac, and Burroughs first heard of the French author.[76] As late as 1964 Miller was quoted in the *Paris Review* as saying: "Céline lives in me, he will live there forever. That's what is important."[77] J. H. Matthews declared that *Journey* is denied "a place among the really great novels" because it does not provide solutions to the problems it exposes.[78] Wayne Burns explored the relationship between Kerouac and Céline in "The Beat and the Dead" (1959),[79] and explained the sentimental imitation of Céline that Kerouac and so many other of the Beats trapped themselves into making.[80] In 1950, Milton Hindus published his *The Crippled Giant*, hardly sentimental in its descriptions of his visit with Céline in Denmark in 1948.[81] It was the first book-length study of Céline to appear in the United States, but as Hindus wrote in the "Postlude," he was uncertain whether it was a work of criticism, a biography, or a critical biography. He was sure, however, that it represented an answer to Céline's anti-Semitism. Today the book remains a valuable description of the collision between two different men: "Céline went into his usual song and dance about his paganism and how he really felt himself a Greek at heart and loved beauty above everything else. I broke in rudely: 'To hell with beauty! What we need is morality, rules of living together. . . .' Céline stuck to his point: 'To hell with morality! I've got plenty of that myself. Give me beauty.' He said that all of art was a translation of the lines of a dancer's leg."[82]

American criticism in the early 1960s quickly gained momentum. Brée and Guiton's *An Age of Fiction: The French Novel from Gide to Camus* (1957) helped to break reactions into two camps: those who would study Céline's "ungrammatical, spoken language as a narrative technique"[83] and those who would generalize about Céline's comments on our modern lives. In 1962, Hindus published his correspondence with Céline, and the whole world of Céline's theory of language and writing was revealed to the American critic, provoking a flood of linguistic studies in the United States.[84] These letters became the basis for most American criticism in the 1960s and 1970s. Erika Ostrovsky used them while comparing Céline to Artaud;[85] W. M. Frohock used them to focus on the "classical formula" of *Journey*, calling the plot of the novel the *"homme traqué."*[86] Reck's *Literature and Responsibility: The French Novel in the Twentieth Century* (1969) devoted a whole chapter to Céline's early novels, used the letters as sources for interpretation, and looked at Céline's "sound" and word order.[87] Thematic studies appeared with Wayne Booth's comments on *Journey* in *The Rhetoric of Fiction* (1961) ("we cannot excuse" him "for writing a book which, if taken seriously by the reader, must corrupt him"),[88] and with John Fraser's characterization of the first thirty-six pages of *Death* as a "prelude."[89] Irving Howe's two-part study of Céline (reprinted here) is often quoted by American critics. His thesis is that Ferdinand is no longer in anguish about a valueless existence.[90] Joseph Heller admits: *Journey* "gave me a direct inspiration for the form and tone of *Catch-22*."[91]

There is a subtle difference between American critical reaction in the 1940s and 1950s and American reaction in the 1960s: novelists and critics of the 1940s and 1950s recognized Céline's compassionate voice, but no such widespread recognition occurred in the 1960s. The fact that a man could express compassion in his life as a doctor and as a novelist, and express compassion for Semmelweis in a medical thesis yet still be a famous anti-Semite in Paris during World War II, was, and still is, a hard pill to swallow.[92]

In the middle and late 1960s American studies were influenced by two major publications: David Hayman's *Louis-Ferdinand Céline* (1965) and Erika Ostrovsky's *Céline and His Vision* (1967). These two studies caused thematic explanations of Céline's novels to remain the dominant characteristic of late 1960s research. Hayman's long monograph is only the second extended look at Céline to appear in the United States (after Hindus's *Crippled Giant*). And although he does speculate on Céline's style, most of the essay concentrates on *Journey, Death, Guignol's Band, Féerie, Normance, Castle,* and *North.* Claiming that Céline tried to convey "disgust and terror by comic means,"[93] Hayman stated that the "view of life in his novels should not be confused with life. . . . his message relates principally to his fears rather than to his knowledge. . . ."[94] Ostrovsky's *Céline and His Vision* was the first book-length study of Céline and his fiction in America. She noted how Céline shattered the status quo of the French novel with his new syntax, but she also intended to go far beyond all other studies to date. By relying on numerous sources in French, and on all of Céline's novels, pamphlets, letters, and essays, the book, as a result, is the best American research can offer until the 1970s. "To understand," she wrote, "to probe beneath the surface of things, even at the price of turning the scalpel against oneself without pity, this is the real quest for Céline, and of his protagonists."[95] Widmer agreed with this view, but he did not concur with Howe and Hayman that *Death* was Céline's best novel;[96] instead, he returned to the merits of *Journey* — perhaps life, he wrote, is "only 'lie, copulate and die.' That remains the innocent truth for a Céline, until proved otherwise."[97]

After the publication of the Manheim translations of *Castle* (1968), *North* (1972), and *Rigadoon* (1974), American criticism in the early 1970s began to explore all of Céline's life and work.[98] Three of the more interesting contributions are Steiner's "Cry Havoc," Fortier's notes on Trotsky's reception of Céline (both reprinted here), and Ostrovsky's *Voyeur Voyant*, the first American biography of Céline.[99] Nettelbeck argued that Céline's work "evolves toward a spirit of regeneration";[100] in *Céline: The Novel as Delirium* (1972) Thiher called *Journey* an "antidote for the evil and destruction" its picaro hero sees. Solomon used the idea of *délire* to explain Ferdinand as a "lucid superseer" in *Death*,[101] and Bettina L. Knapp in *Céline: Man of Hate* (1974) saw destructive hatred in the anti-Semite's novels.

In the middle and late 1970s, historical, linguistic, biographical, and bibliographical studies continued. *Recovering Literature*, the first American journal with issues devoted to Céline, offered criticism and a bibliography (2, no. 1 [Spring 1973] and 3, no. 1 [Spring 1974]). Nicholas Hewitt proposed that the language of the second novel constituted a rejection of Ferdinand's social and ethical world as well as a rejection of the epistolary novel.[102] Charles Krance, arguing that Céline's words plead for reinstating man at the center of existence instead of dehumanizing him with Judeo-Christian or Marxian abstract truths, described the process of how Céline's fiction achieves *"délire"* or *"extasis."*[103] Stanford Luce published his *Glossary of Céline's Fiction* (Ann Arbor: University of Michigan, 1979) that contained some 4,000 nonconventional French words. Robert Soucy studied the French fascist intellectuals of the 1930s and discovered that Céline's *L'Ecole des cadavres* is a work that complains about the "standardization of modern life, that human beings in the modern world are now deprived of individuality and creativity by the standardization of their authentic emotions."[104] Perhaps the most comprehensive look during the 1970s is McCarthy's *Céline* (1975).[105] Anthony Burgess supports the biography, and Céline, in *Harper's Magazine*, as does John Updike in the *New Yorker*. Burgess, Updike, and a chapter on French politics from McCarthy's book are presented here as examples of the kind of criticism that characterized the 1970s. Several book-length studies followed after McCarthy: David O'Connell's *Louis-Ferdinand Céline* (Boston: Twayne, 1976), notable for its calling Courtial the "Don Quixote of Science" and Ferdinand his Sancho Panza, and valuable for recognizing *Professor Y* as Céline's *ars poetica*; J. H. Matthews's *The Inner Dream* (Syracuse University Press, 1978) the first American book to treat sexual themes in *Death*; and Merlin Thomas's book, published by New Directions in 1979. Four essays were published at the end of the 1970s: Kurt Vonnegut's introduction to the 1976 Penguin edition of the trilogy (*Journey* "penetrated my bones, anyway, if not my mind, and I only now understand what I took from Céline and put into the novel [*Slaughterhouse-Five*] I was writing at the time");[106] Busi's "Céline: The Wild Man of French Literature," one of the few American essays to say that Céline's hatreds were more common to general thinking than we want to admit;[107] Solomon's "The View from a Rump" (reprinted here); and Leslie Davis's "Céline and the Débâcle of Idealism,"[108] which saw *Death* as a novel that abolishes ideals and leads to despair.

Critical reaction in the 1980s has been at once comprehensive and peculiar. In 1980, Charles Krance published an annotated French and English bibliography for *A Critical Bibliography of French Literature* (Syracuse University Press, 1980), listing some 200 items from the 1930s to the 1970s. With Stanford Luce, this author published *A Half-Century of Céline: An Annotated Bibliography, 1932–1982* (1983), the first comprehensive and international bibliography in English. Milton Hindus reissued an expanded edition of *The Crippled Giant*, and Luce translated *Professor Y* (University Press of New England, 1986). The [London] *Times Literary Supplement* noted how Céline's letters to John Marks were sold at auction (2 April 1982). Yet Christopher Robinson writes in his *French Literature in the Twentieth Century* that "Bardamu is no more than the extension and distortion of an author's life which is a commonplace of literary creation."[109] *Recovering Literature* printed a detailed study of *Bagatelles* by Gerald J. Butler, who argued that the pamphlet is more of a critique of Aryans than of Jews,[110] and in an essay on Céline's trilogy Butler concluded that Céline's message for us is that "human beings . . . should have real animality above all by having hearts."[111] James Flynn edited *Understanding Céline* (1984), the first anthology of essays to appear in the United States and containing some of the finest criticism in America.[112] In 1985, *Recovering Literature* devoted another of its issues to Céline, notable for its remarkable essay on *Journey* by Wayne Burns and Douglas Eason's strikingly original interpretation of Céline's artistic goals in *Death*.[113] Luce published his *Céline and His Critics* (1984), an anthology of early and late French criticism, and Tom Clark wrote a "novel" about Céline's flight to

Denmark and return to France (*The Exile of Céline* [1986]) using actual names, places, dates, and plot lines from *North*. Yet in 1987 the editor of the *New York Times Book Review* dismissed Céline completely and claimed that Céline's "insanity is *serious*."[114] Finally, Mary Jean Green, in *Fiction in the Historical Present*, again looked at *Journey* in the political context of the 1930s, documenting her thesis that there is no difference between Bardamu's experiences on the front lines and those he has back in the working-class suburbs of La Garenne-Rancy: all of *French* life was a battleground.[115]

In Europe, Céline criticism has been dividing itself into the old camps of Right and Left, and when it does stay center, it brandishes the academic shield of our currently fashionable approaches. In America, the reaction is a little more rough and tumble: it divides itself into plain and simple outright rejection or full acceptance of Céline's world — whether using fashionable approaches or not. Conventional criticism is always tempted to return to those frozen moments in history in order to explain to us and protect us from originality. Many have been trying to prove, for our safety, that the contemptuous, tender voice in Céline's work is characteristic of "fascist fiction." Only by rejecting official or popular critical practices can we hope to go where Céline would like us to be. Allan Bloom claims in his critique of American higher education, *The Closing of the American Mind* (1987), that Céline "offers nothing for our Marxist, Freudian, feminist, deconstructionist, or structuralist critics to mangle"; rather, his work "would help our students make their implicit nihilism explicit";[116] and in one of the finest American studies to appear, Wayne Burns states in the introduction to his *Enfin Céline Vint* (1988): "I can go as far into Céline's fictional reality as my perceptions will take me. . . . to show that Céline's genius carries him to Santayana's 'absolute grotesque reality.' And at the same time I also hope to show that this fictional reality is not dreadful at all; that it is, deep down, as humane and compassionate as fictional reality can very well be — and still maintain its integrity in the face of the rhetoric that is always threatening to engulf it."[117]

In their difficulties, adjustments, frustrations, and new discoveries in coming to terms with Céline's originality, each of the essays written specifically for this volume (all by leading Céline scholars on two continents) attempts, in its own way, to go as far as it can "into Céline's fictional reality," to ride his *métro émotif*.

WILLIAM K. BUCKLEY

Indiana University, Northwest

Notes

1. Quote from a conversation this author had with an ex-model from Paris and friend to French literary circles in the 1940s. She maintained that before and after the Liberation

(ca. 1940–50), Céline's works were secretly admired but publicly condemned. "If you bought a copy of *Journey*," she said, "you hid it from view on the metro to get home."

2. L.-F. Céline, *Conversations with Professor Y*, trans. Stanford Luce (Hanover: University Press of New England, 1986), 29.

3. L.-F. Céline, *North*, trans. Ralph Manheim (New York: Delacorte Press, 1972), 218. Manheim's note to this quote reads: "Uncertain whom Céline means to insult with this name. *Fente* = crack." And: "Figaro Immobilier (Real-Estate Figaro). *Le Figaro litteraire*, a weekly, read as much for the housing ads as for the book reviews and articles" (450).

4. L.-F. Céline, *Mea Culpa and The Life and Work of Semmelweis*, trans. R. A. Parker (Boston: Little, Brown & Co., 1937), 12.

5. "Letter to Elie Faure" [ca. 1934], in *Cahiers de l'Herne* (Paris: Minard, 1972), 74.

6. Céline, *Conversations*, 3, 5.

7. See M. Green's *Fiction in the Historical Present* (Hanover: University Press of New England, 1986). For others see Stanford Luce and William Buckley, *A Half-Century of Céline: An Annotated Bibliography, 1932–1982* (New York: Garland Publishing, 1983).

8. Céline, *Conversations*, 91, 93, 95. "*Pigalle*: metro entrance in the night life district of Paris where Céline lived and worked. His clinic was nearby in Clichy" (translator's note).

9. Céline to M. Hindus, 10 August 1947: "All that have no poetry in this world may expect my dreadful scorn. . . . That gives you some sense of how I look at the world . . ." (Milton Hindus, *The Crippled Giant* [Hanover: University Press of New England, 1986], 116).

10. Jean-Paul Sartre, "Le Portrait d'un anti-semite," *Les Temps Modernes* 3 (December 1945):238.

11. Jean-Paul Sartre, "Situation of the Writer in 1947," in *What Is Literature*, trans. B. Frechtman (New York: Harper & Row, 1965), 225, 217.

12. See Jürgen Rühle, "Die Schriftsteller und der Kommunismus," in *Literatur und Revolution* (Berlin: Kiepenhaur & Witsch, 1960), 356–58; Alfred Kazin, "A Gifted Angry Writer," *New York Herald-Tribune*, Books sec., 1 August 1937; F. Vial, "French Intellectuals and the Collapse of Communism," *Thought* 15, no. 58 (September 1940):429–44.

13. Robert C. Tucker, ed., *The Marx-Engels Reader* (New York: W. W. Norton, 1972), 63.

14. Ibid., 30, 36. See especially Céline to M. Hindus, 10 August 1947, in *Crippled Giant*, 116–17.

15. See F. Balta, "Céline et Freud," in *Céline: Actes du colloque de Paris*, no. 1 (27–30 July 1976):247–58; Henri Godard, "Céline devant Freud," in ibid., no. 3 (July 1979):19–30; J. Charpentier, "Les Romans," *Mercure de France* 240, no. 828 (15 December 1932):610–15.

16. Sigmund Freud, *The Major Works of Sigmund Freud* (Encyclopedia Britannica, 1952), 695.

17. Céline to M. Hindus, 5 August 1947, in *Crippled Giant*, 115.

18. L.-F. Céline, *Rigadoon* (New York: Delacorte Press, 1974), 260. See Tarno Kunnas, *Drieu la Rochelle, Céline, Brasillach et la tentation fasciste* (Paris: Sept couleurs, 1972).

19. See Luce and Buckley, *Half-Century*.

20. "I am a Gandhist as well — hopelessly so — he's the one great man of our time — but completely misunderstood" (Céline to M. Hindus, 20 August 1947, in *Crippled Giant*, 117).

21. Wilhelm Reich, *The Mass Psychology of Fascism* (New York: Farrar, Straus, & Giroux, 1970), xxi–xxii.

22. Ibid., xiii.

23. Wayne Burns, "The Novelist as Revolutionary," *Arizona Quarterly* 7, no. 1 (Spring 1951):13–27.

24. Céline, *Conversations*, 13, 15.

25. Ibid., 17.

26. Wayne Burns, "Immortal Moments in *Journey to the End of the Night*," *Recovering Literature* 13 (Spring 1985):12.

27. Alex Comfort, *The Novel and Our Time* (London: Phoenix House, 1948), 74.

28. Céline, *Mea Culpa*, 6.

29. See Léon Daudet, "L.-F. Céline: *Voyage au bout de la nuit*," *Candide*, 22 December 1932, 6; Pierre Scize, "La Vérité sur Léon Daudet," *Canard enchaîné* 859 (14 December 1932); L. Christophe, "Voyage," *Gazette* 297 (23 October 1932):4.

30. See A. P., "Prix Théophraste Renaudot," *Liberté*, 12 December 1932.

31. See Luce and Buckley, *Half-Century*, 124–38.

32. André Rousseaux, "La Semaine des prix," *Figaro* 340 (5 December 1932).

33. "Les Prix littéraires," *Nouvelliste*, 11 December 1932.

34. "L'Affaire du'Goncourt," *Cri du jour* 266 (17 December 1932):10.

35. Aristide, "Journey," *Aux écoutes* 761 (17 December 1932):27.

36. See P. Almeras, "Towards a Third Reading of *Voyage*," *Bulletin of the Rocky Mountain MLA* 26 (1972):22–28.

37. See Luce and Buckley, *Half-Century*, 131.

38. "Désagrégation spirituelle de la France," *Lu dans la Presse Universelle* 144 (9 March 1934):14.

39. Edward Shanks, "M. Céline's Journey," *London Mercury*, 30 August 1934, 178, 330–36.

40. Maxim Gorky, "Address Delivered to the First All-Union Congress of Soviet Writers: August 17, 1934," in *On Literature* (Seattle: University of Washington Press, 1973), 245.

41. "Céline et Poincaré," *Atlantic Monthly* 156, no. 4 (October 1935):413–20.

42. "Review of Journey," in *Céline and His Critics*, ed. S. Luce, (Saratoga, Calif.: Anma Libri, 1986), 42.

43. Eugène Dabit, "Voyage au bout de la nuit," *Nouvelle revue française* 231 (December 1932):935–37. See also the correspondence between Céline and Dabit in *Cahiers de l'Herne* 3–4 (1972):57–61.

44. Georges Bernanos, "Au bout de la nuit," *Figaro* 348 (13 December 1932):1.

45. Simone de Beauvoir, *The Prime of Life*, trans. Peter Green (Cleveland: World Publishing Co., 1962), 113.

46. Céline to Elie Faure, undated, in *L'Herne* 5 (1965): 48.

47. Robert Denoël, *Apologie de mort à crédit* (Paris: Denoël & Steele, 1936).

48. See De Beauvoir, *The Prime of Life*, 113; Paul Nizan, "Pour le cinquantenaire du Symbolisme," *Humanité*, 15 July 1936.

49. See Luce and Buckley, *Half-Century*, 210–20.

50. A comprehensive discussion of Céline's political ideas can be found in J. Morand, *Les idées politiques de Louis-Ferdinand Céline* (Paris: Pichon & Durand-Auzias, 1972). See also P. Vandromme, "The Spirit of the Pamphlets," in *Céline and His Critics*, 109.

51. Sartre, "Portrait de l'antisémite. See Céline's reply to Sartre: "A l'agité du bocal," in *Oeuvres completes*, ed. J. A. Ducourneau (Paris: André Balland, 1966–69), 3:413–17.

52. *Rivarol* 228 (26 May 1955):13.

53. "Mauriac répond à ses critiques," *Magazine littéraire*, 22 October 1968, 17–19.

54. Roger Nimier, "L.-F. Céline: denonciateur du roman," *Bulletin de Paris* 78 (8 April 1955):8.

55. Jürgen Rühle, "Die Schriftsteller und der Kommunismus," in *Literatur und Revolution* (Berlin: Kiepenhaur & Witsch, 1960), 356–58.

56. Paul Sérant, *Le Romantisme fasciste* (Paris: Fasquelle, 1959).

57. For more publications along these lines see Luce and Buckley, *Half-Century*.

58. Eva Forster, *Romanstruktur und Weltanschauung im werk L.-F. Célines* (Heidelberg, Groos, 1978); Grössel, "Zu Célines Hommage à Zola," *Akzente* 23, no. 5 (October 1977):442–45. For other German studies see Luce and Buckley, *Half-Century*.

59. Paolo Carile, *L.-F. Céline: Un allucinato di genio* (Bologna: Pàtron, 1969), and *Céline oggi* (Rome: Bulzoni, 1974).

60. Alan Burns, "Making of a Fascist," *London Tribune*, 22 July 1966, 14.

61. Marc Hanrez, *Céline* (Paris: Gallimard, 1961); Yves de la Quérière, (Lexington: University Press of Kentucky, 1973); Henri Godard, *L.-F. Céline I* (Paris: Minard, 1974); Philippe Alméras, "Céline: L'Itinéraire d'une écriture," *PMLA* 89, no. 5 (1974):1090–98.

62. Nicole Debrie-Panel, *Louis-Ferdinand Céline* (Lyons: E. Vitte, 1961); Dominique de Roux, *La Mort de L.-F. Céline* (Paris: Christian Bourgois, 1966); Pol Vandromme, *Louis-Ferdinand Céline* (Paris: Editions universitaires, 1963); Kunnas, *Drieu la Rochelle*.

63. Albert Chesneau, "Essai de psychocritique de Céline," *Archives des lettres modernes* 129 (1971):1–96; Henri Godard, "Céline devant Freud," *Actes du colloque international de Paris*, no. 3 (17–19 July 1979):19–30.

64. See Luce and Buckley, *Half-Century*, 263–67.

65. Christian Dédet, "Louis-Ferdinand Céline: *Rigodon* (Gallimard)," *Esprit* 37, no. 381 (May 1969):971–73.

66. Merlin Thomas, Louis-Ferdinand Céline (New York: New Directions, 1979), 236.

67. See Nicholas Hewitt, *Voyage au bout de la nuit: voyage imaginaire et histoire de fantômes* (The Hague: Actes La Haye, 1983).

68. *Études littéraires*, 18, no. 2 (Autumn 1985); Henri Godard, *Poetique de Céline* (Paris: Gallimard, 1985); Paul del Perugia, *Céline* (Paris: Nouvelles editions Latines, 1987).

69. Leon Roudiez, "On Several Approaches to Céline," *Romanic Review* 72 (January 1981):104.

70. A revised version of this section first appeared in *Understanding Céline*, ed. James Flynn (Seattle: Genitron Press, 1984):242–57.

71. Reprinted in *Leon Trotsky on Literature and Art* (New York: Pathfinder Press, 1970).

72. See also Kazin, "A Gifted Angry Writer."

73. W. M. Frohock, "Céline's Quest For Love," *Accent* 2, no. 22 (Winter 1941–42):79–84.

74. Harry Slochower, "Satanism in Céline," in *No Voice is Wholly Lost* (New York: Creative Age Press, 1945).

75. Irving Howe, "Céline: Novelist of the Underground," *Tomorrow* 8, no. 3 (November 1948):53–56.

76. Ginsberg's *Howl*, Miller's *Tropic of Cancer*, and Burrough's *Naked Lunch* all show signs of having been influenced by Céline. Kerouac's remarks on Céline can be found in *L'Herne* 3 (1963):205; for the English version see *Paris Review* 31 (1964):137.

77. Henry Miller, "A Letter on Céline," *Paris Review* 31 (Winter–Spring 1964):137. Alfred Perlès describes Céline's influence on Miller in *My Friend Henry Miller* (New York: John Day Co., 1956). Kingsley Widmer's *Henry Miller* (New York: Twayne, 1963), notes the same.

78. J. H. Matthews, "Céline's *Journey to the End of the Night*," *Contemporary Review* 191 (March 1957):158–61.

79. Originally written for the *Berkeley Review*. Reprinted in Burns's *Towards a Contextualist Aesthetic for the Novel* (Seattle: Genitron Books, 1968). See also Emile Boelens, "Céline et la Beat Generation," *La Revue célinienne* 2 (1979):19–20.

80. See Allen Ginsberg, *As Ever* (Berkeley, Calif.: Creative Arts Book Co., 1977).

81. Hindus, *Crippled Giant* (New York: Boar's Head Books, 1950). For the reprint see n. 9.

82. Ibid., 91–92.

83. Germaine Brée and Margaret Guiton, *An Age of Fiction* (New Brunswick, N.J.: Rutgers University Press, 1957), 164.

84. Milton Hindus, "Louis-Ferdinand Céline: Excerpts from His Letters to Milton Hindus," *Texas Quarterly* 4 (Winter 1962):22–38.

85. Erika Ostrovsky, "The Anatomy of Cruelty: Antonin Artaud; Louis-Ferdinand Céline," *Arts and Sciences*, Spring 1967, 9–13.

86. W. M. Frohock, "First-person narration (Bernanos, Céline, Giono, Sartre, Camus)," in *Style and Temper: Studies in French Fiction, 1925–1961* (Oxford: Basil Blackwell, 1967).

87. Rima Dell Reck, *Literature and Responsibility* (Baton Rouge: Louisiana State University Press, 1969), 191–215. See also Reck, "Céline and Wolfe: Toward a Theory of the Autobiographical Novel," *Mississippi Quarterly* 22 (1968–69):19–27.

88. Wayne Booth, *The Rhetoric of Fiction* (Chicago: University of Chicago Press, 1961), 383. See also Emanuel Kummer, "Wayne Booth et l'auteur implicite de Voyage," *Australian Journal of French Studies* 13, nos. 1–3 (1976):18–24.

89. J. Fraser, "Darkest Journey: Céline's *Death on the Installment Plan*," *Wisconsin Studies in Continental Literature* 8 (Winter 1967):96–110.

90. Irving Howe, *A World More Attractive* (New York: Horizon Press, 1963), 192–206.

91. F. Kiley and W. McDonald, eds., *A Catch-22 Casebook* (New York: Crowell, 1973), 277.

92. See Henri Poulain's review of *Les Beaux draps*, *Petit parisien* 23383 (17 March 1941):2; "Céline cinq ans après," *Pariscope*, (26 January 1965):19–23; André Brissaud's "Voyage au bout de la tendresse," *L'Herne* 3 (1963):226–31; Gilbert Guilleminault's "Un Petit tour aux enfers," *Aurore*, (6 September 1976):10; and François Nourissier's "Admirez Céline, ne le défendez pas," *Point* 387 (February 18–24 1980):121–22.

93. David Hayman, *Louis-Ferdinand Céline* (New York: Columbia University Press, 1965), 40.

94. Ibid., 28.

95. Erika Ostrovsky, *Céline and His Vision* (New York: New York University Press, 1967), 93.

96. Kingsley Widmer, "The Way Down to Wisdom of Louis-Ferdinand Céline," *Minnesota Review* 8, no. 1 (1968):85–91.

97. Ibid., 91.

98. See the bibliography of Céline criticism for the years 1948 to 1969 in *Modern Fiction Studies* 16, no. 1 (Spring 1970):85–100, for comparison.

99. *Voyeur Voyant* (New York: Random House, 1972). Ostrovsky's "biography" is written in a style that tries to imitate Céline. The book is not a chronological treatment, but a free association of ideas, opinions, and feelings.

100. C. W. Nettelbeck, "Journey to the End of Art: The Evolution of the Novels of Louis-Ferdinand Céline," *PMLA* 87 (January 1972):80–89.

101. Philip H. Solomon, "Céline's *Death on the Installment Plan*: The Intoxication of Delirium," *Yale French Studies* 50 (1974):191–203; Allen Thiher, *Céline: The Novel as Delirium* (New Brunswick, N.J.: Rutgers University Press, 1972).

102. Nicholas Hewitt, "Narration and Desolidarisation in Céline's *Mort à Crédit*," *Essays in French Literature* 12 (November 1975):59–69.

103. Charles Krance, "Céline and the Literature of Extasis: The Virtuosity of Non-Genre," *Language and Style* 6, no. 3 (Summer 1973):176–84.

104. Robert Soucy, "French Fascist Intellectuals in the 1930's: An Old New Left?," *French Historical Studies* 8, no. 3 (Spring 1974):445–58.

105. Patrick McCarthy, *Céline* (New York: Viking Press, 1976).

106. Kurt Vonnegut, introduction to *North* (New York: Penguin, 1976), viii, x.

107. *Midstream* (June–July 1976):69–72.

108. Leslie Davis, "Céline and the Débâcle of Idealism," in *1936: The Sociology of Literature*, vol. 1, *The Politics of Modernism* (University of Essex, 1979).

109. Christopher Robinson, *French Literature in the Twentieth Century* (Totowa, N.J.: Barnes & Noble, 1980), 74.

110. Gerald Butler, "Céline's *Bagatelles pour un massacre*: The Expression of a Forbidden Passion," *Recovering Literature* 8, no. 1 (Spring 1980):27–42.

111. Gerald Butler, "The Meaning of the Presence of Lili in Céline's Final Trilogy," *Recovering Literature* 10 (1982):57–63.

112. James Flynn, ed., *Understanding Céline* (Seattle: Genitron Press, 1984).

113. Burns, "Immortal Moments," 5–12; Douglas O. Eason, "Demonic Eschatology, Demonic Grammar," *Recovering Literature* 13 (Spring 1985):37–52.

114. Anatole Broyard, "Writing off the Deep End," *New York Times Book Review*, 21 September 1984, 11.

115. Mary Jean Green, *Fiction in the Historical Present: French Writers and the Thirties* (Hanover: University Press of New England, 1986).

116. Allan Bloom, *The Closing of the American Mind* (New York: Simon & Schuster, 1987), 239.

117. Wayne Burns, *Enfin Céline Vint* (New York: Peter Lang, 1988), 2.

EARLY REVIEWS

All that have no poetry in this world may expect my dreadful
scorn. . . . That gives you some sense of how I look at the world.
— Letter to Milton Hindus, 10 August 1947

[Review of *Journey to the End of the Night*]

Eugène Dabit*

Louis-Ferdinand Céline's book is a kind of feverish journey, slow and painful, a journey in search of the past, in countries near and far: in France, during the years rotted by the war, in Algeria, amid smugglers, in this colony of Bambola-Bragamance! In America with Molly, the dear little whore; again in France, in a sticky suburb; finally in a "sanatorium" directed by a Doctor Baryton. Meanwhile, a series of adventures, some of which are almost fantastic, like the one from the "Mummies' Vault," where Robinson, a war "companion" of Ferdinand Bardamu, the book's hero, supports his dog's life. Here and there are Epinal images[1] in raw tones, others harshly outlined in black shadows; chitchat between mercenary soldiers, workers, shrews, streetwalkers; sordid stories, some real, others imaginary. Impossible to recount such a book. From the darkness that envelops it surge pale, dreary beings, furtive, pursued by bailiff, detectives, policemen, hounded and overcome by fright, cold, fatigue, hunger. Their flight, their gesticulations, their protests will not save them. All their revolts seem in vain. "One has to choose to die or to lie." They want to live. Even as a conquered race. Besides that, they know and despise themselves, and more than despise their masters. They hate, are capable of murder, of nothing else it seems. That is their heroism, their very own! Life rolls on, in waves of amorphous mud, without hope, without light, as does age, disease, misery. "Against the abomination of being poor, one must, let's admit—it's a duty—try everything, get drunk on no matter what, cheap wine, masturbation, cinema."

In *Journey to the End of the Night* several works overlap, are mixed. There is neither beginning nor end. It is true that war is a beginning, death an end. For 600 pages there is confused combat pierced by glimpses of light. Everybody will be defeated. Ferdinand Bardamu, like the others, is made of the dough that fills the masses, and has the same cowardice, panicking terror, desires, violence. All these men are condemned in advance. No one can set himself free. They lack time and force. Death is around them, and not as a bogeyman. It invades them, and we are no

*Reprinted with permission from *Nouvelle revue française*, December 1932, 935–37.
Translated by Jóhanna Eiríksdóttir Hull for this volume.

longer surprised at their fright. And money, religion, morality, disease, and war are death's so many sure allies.

This tragic presence in the night fills the book. We find death on every page, with despair, suspicion, hatred. It is not a matter of literary creation. We hear a continuous appeal, almost unforgettable, heavy, bitter, unrelenting, full of imagery. We can read pages and pages with passion. When we're worn out, we leave them with a troubled and anxious feeling, but pick the book up again and begin to read anew, finding in it the same halting, sorrowful, pitiful voice. It is of very little importance to ask if the author has "had" us, or if he has, with what skill, what spells, neither that mysterious nor new. It is of very little importance to remember other books, to want to explain, to limit this swarming world. One hopes perhaps for some shade, a recess, some silence, and to find again those countries where one can dispute, dream, doze off. Nothing like it is offered. And it is just as well. Here is a work where art, culture, or a god is no longer the concern, where revolt is born not of aesthetic discussions or symbols, but of a cry of protest against the human condition — against what man can do to a multitude of other men, which is a mockery and crime against life.

Note

1. "Epinal images" (*images d'Epinal*) is a popular French expression that usually means "cliched images." In this context, however, Dabit is suggesting that Bardamu is giving us popular opinions, but in new and more brutal ways (editor's note).

Deep into the Night   Georges Bernanos*

Mr. Céline missed the Goncourt Prize. So much the better for Mr. Céline. We did not see, we will never ever see — glory be to God! — Mr. Céline crowned by Mr. Gaston Chérau, that Maupassant from the sub-prefecture, nor even by our dear Dorgelès [president of Goncourt Academy] whom we truly believe has decidedly passed over to the enemy, that is, to the ladies of high society, who have been distraught by *Partir*. Woe betide the nimble rabbits that let themselves be approached by these lady lion charmers, coming close enough to eat out of the hollow of their beautiful hands!

Mr. Léon Daudet was certainly there. We have seen Mr. Léon Daudet[1] six times in our life, no more, we say it, we repeat it, we will maintain it even under horned cap and sulphur shirt, even if convicted of

*Reprinted with permission from *Figaro*, 13 December 1932, 1. Translated by Jóhanna Eiríksdóttir Hull for this volume.

heresy by the Consistory of the good town of Martigues, and Master Maurras, in whom the illustrious critic Mr. Maurice Pujo, alone among the entire French press, has very successfully perceived as prototype of the humble heroes of our books, the abbot Donissan, the abbot Chevance. We have seen Mr. Léon Daudet only six times in our life, but we know him well just the same. We have never doubted the principal movement of his heart, nor that he cherished the memory of his own journey to the end of the night, with someone called Shakespeare. Only, for almost twenty-five years now the spiritual dictator of French nationalism has, under pretext of Hellenism, pretended to nourish this carnivore of crunchy cookie novels pulled all mouldy from Mr. Anatole France's jar, and that would make the darling owl of Athens sneeze with anger. When the author of *The Bacchantes* escaped from his tyrant — God only knows where our charming colleague Pampille finds him again, and his cheeks smeared with what sauces! — would he break his fast again in favor of Mr. Céline? Would he for cause defy the right-thinking men and women of the League, the indestructible men and ladies, or those adolescents, centenarians already, who believe firmly that *Ode to the Battle of the Marne* is, along with the *Ode on the Capture of Namur*, the apex of French poetry, and who establish journals without readers in order to have the right to come and take turns blowing piously into their bronze kazoo. Mr. Léon Daudet defied everything. God bless him!

I have a duty to carry out, certainly not toward Mr. Céline, who seems to be capable of confronting all alone any conjuncture whatsoever, but to a public that runs the risk of being caught unawares by a book no sensible man would recommend to his wife and even less to his daughter. Another time we will leave to those better qualified than us the care of saying what the artist might think of this extraordinary work, comparable as it is to the unfolding movement of the waves in the black night, when at each of the simultaneous throbbings of wind and sea appears and disappears the livid fringe of the foam. Whether this poetic movement passes by unnoticed or not by my contemporaries, is not at all important to me; nor, I suppose, is it of importance to Mr. Céline. I only try to calculate its power, and its bearing — already measurable, by the way, by a certain underground rumbling, and by an unhinging of several usurped glories.

Mr. Céline scandalizes. As for that there is nothing to be said, since God has obviously made him for this. For there is scandal and scandal. The most fearsome of all, the one that costs our species the most blood and tears, is the masking of its own misery. Never has this misery been more urgent, more effective, more skillfully homicidal, with such a character of diabolical necessity, yet never has it been so little recognized. The powerful lord of old could live in an opulence which the debasing of our standards barely allows us to imagine. He remained, through his dominion of the territory, too close to the ground, to earthly people, to his people, to risk showing the idiotic, blissful ignorance, gorged with inquests and statistics of our modern right-thinking people. We claim that the palatine or a boyar who swam in gold, but who meted out justice himself and who on occasion served the poor and touched lepers, knew far more about misery than the petit bourgeois of our country. We claim that millions and millions of men die today without having even once seen the true face of misery, the horrible mud, the sacred face of misery. How can a foreman, whom a vigilant police screens at the gates of our factories, inform us about the proletariat? What the devil can the poor terrorized street walkers of Montmartre or Montparnasse teach us about prostitution? On reading the ridiculous tirades of certain defenders of law and order, we understand very well that their experience of misery is equal to the one a young shopgirl imagines having of high society. How can people like this understand revolution? Tomorrow, like yesterday, will find them busy polishing the leather of the police in the hope that nothing prevails against a well-polished policeman. For us, the problem is not to know whether Mr. Céline's painting is atrocious, but whether it is true. It is. And even truer than the painting is the unheard of language, overflowing with spontaneity and artifice, invented, created from start to finish like tragedy, as far as possible from a servile reproduction of the language of the destitute, but made precisely to express that which the language of the destitute would never know how to express: their childish and somber soul, their somber childhood. Yes, such is the cursed lot, the shameful lot, the reprobate lot of our people and of course, we concede voluntarily that there are more reassuring images of the modern world. For example, the military image: on the right, the Good Poor, gratified by private-first-class stripes; on the other side, the Bad, who are stuffed in jail. . . . Only, any old priest from the slum belt, to whom it happens that Céline's heroes confess once in a while, will tell you that Mr. Céline is right.

We pity those who, after seeing the spectacle of the isolation of the poor, of his frightening exile, are driven to despair rather than compassion, that is, to all the daring, to all the wrath, to all the furors of compassion. Because after all, even under the banner of Order we must get along! Do we want to save the destitute or only reduce their number? In the latter hypothesis we find nothing better than slavery, an institution much more religious than social, by the way, and to which the ancient world, that we hear harped on endlessly, owed much of its glory. But if one, like you and I do, holds to the first one, there is no more urgent need than to remake a Christendom. Except a Christendom, you see, is not remade without a little bit of scandal, and even — as the young Lyautey wrote long ago — without disturbing the wealthy. A Christendom can be remade on the condition that it runs the risks. But the modern world does not appear very ready to run them. So this voyage to the end of the night is not anywhere close to its end — though we will surely see the end. The end of the night is the gentle pity of God, the gentle pity of God to which I once allowed myself to send Mr. Maurras. And merely the name — the devil if I know why — made him wheeze and gnash like a rat caught under a beam — the gentle pity of God — that is to say profound, profound, profound Eternity.

Note

1. Léon Daudet (1868–1942) was a journalist and novelist who renounced medicine for right-wing activities. He helped to found the *L'Action française* and wrote in *Candide* (22 December 1932, 6) that Céline should have given the reader of *Journey* lyrical relief from the novel's portrait of the world (editor's note).

A Quest Without Any Meaning   Donald J. Adams*

This book [*Journey to the End of the Night*], upon its appearance in France in 1932, produced a literary sensation. Critics expressed themselves violently, pro or con, and there was a grand rumpus in L'Académie Goncourt. André Maurois, in reporting upon it for these columns, was more temperate than his colleagues. He announced, "a newcomer of great talent," with "marvelous naturalness in his expression," and conceded that "while not a masterpiece," the book is "very strange and very original." Other foreign critics have differed so widely as to denounce the book as "an insult to the reader" and to proclaim that it often rises to "a real grandeur."

It is puzzling that M. Maurois could write so temperately, for *Journey to the End of the Night* is a book that must produce strong reactions in any reader. That it has power there can be no question; so much can be granted calmly. M. Céline is master of a very vivid naturalism. To add that it is also a very brutal naturalism is to speak in a whisper. Most readers will find *Journey to the End of the Night* a revolting book; its vision of human life will seem to them a hideous nightmare. It does not carry within itself adequate compensation for the bruising and battering of spirit with which one reads it; there is no purgative effect from all these disgusts. If this is life, then it is better not to live.

The story is told in the first person. The narrator is a young Frenchman, whom we follow first through his experience in the war and in a hospital for nervously deranged soldiers. He is then sent off to French colonial Africa, goes from there to the United States, where he works for a time in one of the Ford plants, and then returns to France, where he resumes the study of medicine which the war interrupted, and takes up practice in a poor suburb of Paris. In its general outline, his life is paralleled by the author's own experience, though he denies that the book is autobiographical. He is a physician whose real name is Destouches.

All the people in the book, of whom there are a great many, all its changing scenes, are viewed through the eyes of the narrator, Ferdinand Bardamu. To Bardamu, a blackguard himself, nine-tenths or something more of the human race are blackguards also. He is an underdog for whom it is difficult to have sympathy. One feels that Bardamu will be disappointed if the world does not consistently do him dirt. One knows where to place the blame when he says that "a certain time is needed for people to get to know you and get going and find out the way to do you some harm." M. Céline, his publishers inform us, calls the theme of his book "a quest for love." But Bardamu proffers none himself. Always he takes; he never gives. The quest, if there is one, has no meaning.

We speak of rose-colored spectacles. Bardamu's are a dirty crusted brown, and he never removes them. If he sees children in the street, they must be "rachitic little urchins, picking their noses." When he looks up the length of Broadway, he thinks of a running sore. He sees a group of workmen huddled over a fire, and the smoke that rises from it is a "filthy" smoke. These are but characteristic touches, chosen at random. The book is inordinately preoccupied with the lavatory and with the natural functions of the human body. Bardamu lives on a purely animal plane himself, with the addition of a reflective brain whose deductions are consistently misanthrophic. He sees everyone else as living on the same plane as himself, with but one or two exceptions, and these bewilder him.

"As you stay on in a given place," says Bardamu, "things and people go to pieces around you; they rot and start to stink for your own special benefit." And as one reads M. Céline's book, much the same sort of thing happens.

A Nightmare Journey   G. W. Stonier*

Voyage au bout de la nuit was reviewed at length in these columns last year. It [*Journey*] can be read now in the English of Mr. John Marks's version published by Chatto and Windus. Something of the original has been lost in translation, the colloquialisms have been rather toned down, but on the whole Mr. Marks has done his work adequately and well. The remarkable qualities of Céline's novel will be evident to anyone who reads it now for the first time.

Its importance lies chiefly, I think, in the fact that Céline has summed up a type which has been floating about for some time in fiction.

*Reprinted from the *New Statesman and Nation*, 23 June 1934, 956.

Bardamu, the civilian soldier and underdog, is a type of whom we are all very much aware at the moment. We find him, on a small scale, in the novels of Hemingway, Dos Passos and William Faulkner; even more strikingly, there is the figure of Alan Berg's *Wozzeck*, with its terrifying and almost lunatic yell from the pit. But all of these, except perhaps Wozzeck, are seen from the outside; the underdog, true to life, is always somebody else; he is exhibited. The assumption (flattering to the reader) is that he is the exception and not the rule.

Céline writes in the first person. The result is a narrative which is half picaresque adventure and half personal phantasmagoria. Bardamu, telling his own story, reveals himself as the *successful* underdog; a man with a certain amount of intelligence, considerable vigour, and a cynical and clear-sighted view of his surroundings. He is not, like Wozzeck, submerged; he travels, has mistresses, sets up a small practice as doctor in a suburb. Nevertheless, he is successful only as an opportunist, as a lead-swinger in the army, as his mistress's second choice, as the man with the feeling that he'll get what's coming to him; and he travels from one no-man's-land to another. It is obvious to him that if he had money he could possess the women he wants; but he makes no serious attempt to get money, it is not his role. His ambitions are little more than sexual dreams, visions of America with its marvellous women. . . . He gets to America, but of course has no money, and passes the ranks of women in the hotel lounge on the way up to his room on the top floor.

It is the war, at the beginning of the book, that has fixed his experience. His only hope then was to be captured by the enemy; the scenes of butchery and squalor ceased to affect him except with a greater desire to save his own skin; at night the burning villages lit up the landscape like bonfires, and watching them burn out before dawn was one of his few pleasures. Before the war, he says, we knew nothing. It is that experience, intense and indifferent, that hangs over the rest of the book. The nightmare of the battlefield is repeated wherever he goes—a Paris suburb, the tropics, New York—scenery exploding round him in a squalid splendour as he pokes his way along; everywhere oppression, poverty, brutality and ugliness.

Céline has made of this autobiographical figure a veritable monument of the underdog; swaggering, cynical, active, patient, one of a mass of men. His self-revelation is brilliantly lifelike and complete. For all his jauntiness and cynicism he is a savage and even terrifying figure, when we come to consider him.

The book is long, shapeless, unevenly written, and marred by a belated plot towards the end. These faults, however, affect its real value very little. The final protest of a human being will always be individual and not political; and Céline's Bardamu has the reality which the political underdogs of so many post-war novels inevitably lack. It is an extraordinary testament of the individual.

Novelist and Politician
Leon Trotsky*

Louis-Ferdinand Céline walked into great literature as other men walk into their own homes. A mature man, with a colossal stock of observations as physician and artist, with a sovereign indifference toward academism, with an extraordinary instinct for intonations of life and language, Céline has written a book which will survive, independently of whether he writes other books, and whether they attain the level of his first. *Journey to the End of the Night* is a novel of pessimism, a book dedicated by terror in the face of life, and weariness of it, rather than by indignation. Active indignation is linked up with hope. In Céline's book there is no hope.

A Parisian student, who comes from a family of little men, a rationalist, an antipatriot, and a semianarchist — the cafes of the Latin quarter swarm with such types — enlists, to his own astonishment, at the very first trumpet call, as a volunteer in the army; he is sent to the front, and in the mechanized slaughter finds himself envying the horses who perish as men do, but without mouthing false phrases; after being wounded and bemedaled, he wanders through the hospitals where successful doctors exhort him to speed his return to the "flaming cemetery of battles"; as an invalid, he is discharged from the army; he departs for an African colony and there pines away from human baseness, from the heat and the malaria of the tropics; he makes his way illegally into the United States, and finds employment in Ford's plant; he finds a true mate in a prostitute (these are the genuinely tender pages in the book); he returns to France, becomes a physician to the poor, and, soul-sick, wanders through the night of life among the sick and the hearty, all equally pathetic, depraved, and miserable.

Céline does not at all set himself the goal of exposing social conditions in France. True, in passing, he spares neither priests nor generals nor ministers, nor the president of the republic. But all the while the warp of his tale extends considerably below the level of the ruling classes, cutting across the milieu of little men, functionaries, students, traders, artisans, and concierges; and in addition, on two occasions, it transports itself beyond the boundaries of France. The present social system is as rotten as every other, whether past or future. Céline, in general, is dissatisfied with men and their affairs.

The novel is conceived and executed as a panorama of life's meaninglessness, with its cruelties, conflicts, and lies, with no issue, and no light flickering. A noncommissioned officer torturing the soldiers just before he perishes together with them; an American coupon clipper airing her emptiness in European hotels; French colonial functionaries brutalized by

*Reprinted with permission from the *Atlantic Monthly* 156, no. 4 (October 1935): 413–20. Copyright 1933 Atlantic Monthly Company.

greed and failure; New York, with its automatic unconcern for the man without a checkbook, technically perfected to suck the marrow for human bones; then Paris again; the petty and envious little universe of scholars; the protracted and docile death of a seven-year-old boy; the rape of a little girl; the little virtuous rentiers who murder their mother in order to economize; the priest in Paris and the priest in darkest Africa, both equally alert to sell a man for a few hundred francs, the one an accomplice of civilized rentiers, the other in cahoots with cannibals . . . from chapter to chapter, from one page to the next, the slivers of life compose themselves into a mud-caked, bloody nightmare of meaninglessness. Receptivity which is passive, with its nerves sliced open, without the will straining toward the future — that is the psychological base of despair, sincere in the convulsions of its cynicism.

Céline the moralist follows the footsteps of the artist, and step by step he rips away the halo from all those social values which have become highly acclaimed through custom, from patriotism and personal ties down to love. Is the fatherland in danger? "No great loss, when the landlord's house burns down. . . . There will be rent to pay just the same." He has no use for historical criteria. Danton's war is not superior to Poincare's: in both instances the "patriotic function" was paid in the coin of blood.[1] Love is poisoned by selfishness and vanity. All forms of idealism are merely "petty instincts draped in high-faluting phrases." Even the image of the mother is not spared: on meeting her wounded son "she squealed like a bitch whose pup had been restored. But she was beneath a bitch because she had faith in those syllables she was told in order to deprive her of her son."

Céline's style is subordinated to his receptivity of the objective world. In his seemingly careless, ungrammatical, passionately condensed language there lives, beats, and vibrates the genuine wealth of French culture, the entire emotional and mental experience of a great nation, in its living content, in its keenest tints.

And, concurrently, Céline writes like a man who has stumbled across human language for the first time. The artist has newly threshed the dictionary of French literature. Pat expressions fly off like chaff. And, instead, words that have been excluded from circulation by academic aesthetic and morality become irreplaceable to give expression to life in its crudeness and abjectness. Erotic terms serve Céline only to rip the glamour from eroticism. He operates with them in the same manner in which he utilizes the names of other physiological functions which do not meet with recognition on the part of art.

On the very first page of the novel the reader unexpectedly runs across the name of Poincare, the president of the republic, who, as the latest issue of *Le Temps* reports, hies himself in the morning to open a lap-dog show.

This detail is not a piece of fiction. Evidently this is one of the duties of the president of the republic, and personally we see no ground for objecting to it. But the mischievous newspaper quotation obviously is not intended to serve the ends of glorifying the head of the state.

Yet, ex-President Poincare, the most prosaic of all outstanding personalities of the republic, happens to be its most authoritative political figure. Since his illness he has become an icon. Not only the Rights, but the Radicals deem it impossible to mention his name without pronouncing a few words in pathetic avowal of love. Poincare is, incontestably, the purest distillate of a bourgeois culture such as the French nation is—the most bourgeois of all nations, pickled in the consciousness of its bourgeoisdom, and proud of it as the mainspring of its providential role toward the rest of mankind. . . .

In his memoirs Poincare laments that "during the first six months of 1914 . . . the abject spectacle of parliamentary intrigues and financial scandals passed before my eyes." But war, of course, with a single swoop swept away all selfish motives. *Union sacree* cleansed the souls. This is to say: the intrigues and the rascalities swung inward behind the patriotic scenes, there to assume unheard-of proportions. As Céline relates, the more drawn out the critical resolution at the front, the more depraved the rear became. The picture of Paris in wartime is depicted in the novel by the hand of a merciless master. There is almost no politics. But there is something more: the living substratum out of which it takes form. . . .

Against the background of the "abject spectacle of parliamentary intrigues and financial scandals"—to use Poincare's expression—Céline's novel attains a twofold significance. Not without cause did the well-meaning press, which in its own time was wroth with the public investigation, immediately damn Céline for calumniating the "nation." The parliamentary committee had, at any rate, carried on its investigation in the courteous language of the initiated, from which neither the accusers nor the accused departed. But Céline is not bound by convention. He rudely discards the gratuitous colors of the political palette. He has his own colors. These he has ripped from life, with the artist's privilege.

True, he takes life not in its parliamentary cross section, not on the ruling heights, but in its most prosaic manifestations. But this does not ease matters any. He bares the roots. From underneath the veils of decorum he exposes the mud and blood. In his ominous panorama, murder for the sake of trifling gain loses its extraordinariness: it is just as inseparable from the day-to-day mechanics of life, propelled by greed and self-seeking, as the Stavisky affair is inseparable from the much higher mechanics of modern finance. Céline shows what is. For this reason he appears as a revolutionist.

But Céline is no revolutionist, and does not aim to be one. He does not occupy himself with the goal of reconstructing society, which is chimerical in his eyes. He only wants to tear away the prestige from everything that frightened and oppresses him. To ease his conscience from terror in the face of life, this physician to the poor had to resort to new modes of imagery. He turned out to be the revolutionist of the novel. Generally speaking, that is the law governing the movement of art: it moves through the reciprocal repulsion of tendencies.

Decay hits not only parties in power, but schools of art as well. The creative methods become hollow and cease to react upon human sensibilities — an infallible sign that the school has become ripe enough for the cemetery of exhausted possibilities — that is to say, for the Academy. Living creativeness cannot march ahead without repulsion away from official tradition, canonized ideas and feelings, images and expressions covered by the lacquer of use and wont. Each new tendency seeks for the most direct and honest contact between words and emotions. The struggle against pretense in art always grows to a lesser or greater measure into the struggle against the injustice of human relations. The connection is self-evident: art which loses the sense of the social lie inevitably defeats itself by affectation, turning into mannerism.

The richer and more solid is national cultural tradition, the more abrupt is the repulsion from it. Céline's power lies in that through supreme effort he divests himself of all canons, transgresses all conventions. He not only undresses life's model, but rips her skin off. Hence flows the indictment of calumny.

But it is precisely in his impetuous radicalism of negating the national tradition that Céline is deeply nationalistic. Just as the French antimilitarists prior to the war were most often desperate patriots, so is Céline a Frenchman to the marrow of his bones, a Frenchman who has torn himself loose from the official masks of the Third Republic. Célinism is moral and artistic anti-Poincareism. In that is Céline's strength, but, too, his limitation.

Only because there are numerous and well-paid priests serving the altars of false altruism does Céline turn away from greatness of mind and heroism, from great projects and hopes, from everything that leads humanity out from the dark night of the circumscribed I. It seems almost as if the moralist who is so ruthless to himself had been repelled by his own image in the mirror, and smashed the glass, cutting his hands. Such a struggle may enervate, but it does not break out toward the light's glimmer. Hopelessness ever leads to docility. Conciliation opens the doors to the Academy. There has been more than one previous occasion when those who have blasted the literary foundations ended underneath the dome of immortality.

In the music of this book there is a dissonance pregnant with much meaning. By rejecting not only the present but also what must take its place, the artist gives his support to what is. To that extent Céline, willy-nilly, is the ally of Poincare. But, exposing the lie, he instills the want for a more harmonious future. Though he himself may consider that nothing good can generally come from man, the very intensity of his pessimism bears within it a dose of the antidote.

Céline, as he is, stems from French reality and the French novel. He does not have to be ashamed of his ancestry. The French genius has found its unsurpassed expression in the novel. Beginning with Rabelais, likewise a physician, there has branched, in the course of four centuries, a splendid genealogy of the masters of epic prose: from life-loving belly laughter down to hopelessness and despair, from the brilliant break of day to the depths of the night.

Céline will not write a second book with such an aversion for the lie and such a disbelief in the truth. The dissonance must resolve itself. Either the artist will make his peace with the darkness or he will perceive the dawn.

Note

1. Georges Danton (1759–94) was minister of justice during the French Revolution. Raymond Poincaré (1860–1934), ninth president of the French Republic (1913–20), economist, and leader of the Progressive Republicans, whipped up French patriotism for the war by the power of his oratory (editor's note).

Misanthrope, Twentieth-Century Style
Clifton Fadiman*

The second volume of Louis-Ferdinand Céline's epic of misanthropy has arrived. *Death on the Installment Plan* (somehow, the French *Mort à Crédit* seems an even bitterer title) is a remarkable book, more so than *Journey to the End of the Night*, about which I held and hold many reservations. But, remarkable as it is, I am in all sobriety recommending it only to those who have strong stomachs and non-rising gorges. Of its six hundred pages at least fifty could be poured into bottles and sold as a substitute for nux vomica. To Céline a dog is not a dog, but so much elimination. A Channel crossing calls for three pages of detailed description of the mechanism and effects of seasickness. When one of Céline's major characters commits suicide, the thing is done—really fiendish, this is—in such a way as to inspire in the reader the absolute maximum of repulsion. It's a commonplace that you can't understand Joyce or Swift unless you understand their passion-horror for dirt. The same goes for Céline, and you can't say I didn't warn you.

Death on the Installment Plan must be read (I'll say presumably must be read) as autobiography. If this is not autobiography, exact and unretouched, then Céline is one of the greatest pure romancers in literature.

*Reprinted with permission from the *New Yorker*, 27 August 1938, 56–58. Copyright 1938, 1966 Clifton Fadiman.

The worst part of this horrible and quite wonderful book is that it sounds true. True as death.

It deals with the childhood and youth of Ferdinand, a Parisian slum weed, who sums up his whole life in the statement, "It was having been born that was such a mistake." His father, Auguste, a petty insurance clerk, is given to hour-long rages, howling bouts of cursing, the impotent resentment of a desperate sewer rat against the narrow confines of his sewer. His mother, Clémence, is just as dreadful in a different manner. Lame, ugly, masochistic, she keeps the family alive by selling antiques and lacework, propelling herself continually into frenzies of self-sacrifice. The family dwells in an alley of horrors, amid scenes and characters that shrink Hogarth and Daumier to Kate Greenaway dimensions.[1] Ferdinand grows up amid an environment perceived by the ear as a shriek, by the nose as a stench, by the eye as a quaking morass. Arrived at adolescence, he is not only completely degenerate but has learned to jeer at his own degeneracy. Each job his parents force him to take—whether as messenger boy in a dry-goods firm or salesman for an eccentric silversmith and engraver—reveals to Ferdinand ever-blacker aspects of human viciousness and imbecility.

Against this cloaca of a world, Ferdinand makes no intelligent protest. Céline has an obscene contempt for the intelligence. He would show his teeth if you called him a "social" novelist, and he would be right, too. His misanthropy is so overpowering that it leaves no room for the rebellious impulse. His fury can generate nothing positive, only more fury. In one revealing passage Ferdinand-Céline, recalling his youth, says, with a kind of gleeful snarl in his voice, "Real outrage comes from deeper down, it starts way back in youth, youth battered, helpless, grovelling at the grindstone. That's the true hatred—it kills. There'll be more of it, so far down that it shall spread and be everywhere, spurting out over the world to poison and leave nothing growing on the surface of the earth but malice among men, among the dead." (Céline has recently come out for Fascism.)

The hapless, stinking, terrified little Ferdinand is sent by a kind uncle to Meanwell School in England. This English section is simply extraordinary. The degenerate boys, the goggling idiot Jonkind, the half-mad master and his beautiful wife, the atmosphere of decay in which all are plunged, the violent erotic episode with which the incident explodes—I have never read anything to equal it, and am not sure I want to. But the Meanwell chapters pale beside what follows—Ferdinand's apprenticeship to Courtial des Pereires, a cracked polyhistor, balloonist, and popular scientific journalist. The story of des Pereires, his dishonest schemes, his manias, his bearded wife, his attempt to grow enormous vegetables by "radiotelluric agriculture," his lies and evasions, his streak of genius, his horrifying end, takes considerably more than one-third of the book. It is a story which begins in a mood of hilarity, deepens to hysteria, and blacks out in horror. The whole episode is surely one of the great masterpieces of the grotesque style. The scenes in which des Pereires' poor wife and the lunatic Canon Fleury grovel over his semi-headless, stickily bleeding corpse are unforgettable.

It is hard to judge Céline. For one thing, he has been praised by critics who disagree with each other about everything else. Two antipodally opposed Leons — Daudet[2] and Trotsky — hail him as great. But whether or not he is great, you can't laugh him off. You may try to dispose of him by saying that he is crazy, that he is a mass of neuroses, that his view of the world is so special as to lack meaning. All this may be true, but his two novels, particularly this second one, stick fast in your memory and imagination. His characters are lechers, perverts, and madmen, but they are lechers, perverts, and madmen of stature. You cannot forget them as you can so easily forget, for example, Mr. Faulkner's waxwork horrors. Céline's people and his misanthropy are both disordered, but they struggle up out of genuine experience. They are not constructs. Here are no stage noises, but the very real shrieks of one suffering from a very real disease. The art that springs out of a universal hatred may be a monstrous art, an unclassic art, an unenlightening art, but it is nonetheless art.

Something should be said about Céline's astonishing style. In the French it is a created style, studded with coinages and neologisms, drawing upon all the resources of the rich compost of French argot. It is not at all "naturalistic." In fact, Céline's technique, on the verbal as well as on other sides, is kin to that of the surrealists, though he is solid and serious, whereas most of them are merely playing. The translator, John H. P. Marks, has wrestled conscientiously with what must have been a brutal assignment, but a great deal is lost in the process. Mr. Marks commits the error of depending too largely upon English slang, a popular lingo which to Americans, at least, seems pallid and hesitant. Its soprano tone is directly opposed to Céline's thick, luxuriant, Rabelaisian basso. Mr. Marks pieces things out with Americanisms, but as some of these date back twenty years and the rest are pathetic attempts to catch the accent of our street speech of today, the result is a pretty awful hash. Only a great linguist, James Joyce perhaps, or one of those torrential Elizabethan fellows, could have transformed Céline so as to make him more than merely acceptable in English dress. Mr. Marks does his best, but Céline is too much for him.

Notes

1. Kate Greenaway (1846–1901), English draftsman, painter, and illustrator of children's books (editor's note).

2. Léon Daudet (1868–1942), journalist and novelist, renounced medicine for right-wing activities. He helped to found the *L'Action française* and wrote in *Candide* (22 December 1932, 6) that Céline should have given the reader of *Journey* lyrical relief from the novel's portrait of the world (editor's note).

LATER ASSESSMENTS

I had a right, you'll admit . . . 769 pages . . . to take a breather
. . . oh, not to deliver messages! . . . the "messagiers" are a different
breed, philosophico-addlepated, heaven help you if you mess with
them, if you lose yourself in their waves, urinals, terraces, abbeys . . .
complexes, seaweeds, and complications, you'll never get your bearings
again . . .

—*Rigadoon*

Céline at the End of the Night George Woodcock*

In his recent book, *L'Opium des Intellectuels*, Raymond Aron commented on the ideological inflexibility which is the besetting fault of so many French writers. But, in devoting his study mostly to the Communists and their fellow-travellers, M. Aron developed only one aspect of the problem. For if there is a left-wing orthodoxy in France, deriving from the myth of the French Revolution, there is also a corresponding tradition of right-wing radicalism which draws its heritage from Bonapartism, that bastard child of the Revolution. Here I am not concerned with recent popular demonstrations of the enduring strength of this tendency (shown particularly in Poujadism and in the disputes over Algeria) but rather with the fact that, if many French writers have maintained their allegiance to Communism in spite of the Siberian prison camps and in spite of Hungary, there are others who have maintained just as steadfastly, in spite of defeat and public hostility, the attitudes which almost two decades ago led them to collaborate with the Vichy government. Beside the self-blinding obstinacy of an Aragon[1] one can place that of a Montherlant;[2] each is dominated by a loyalty to his own past that defies reason and admits of no genuine interest.

Indeed, one of the interesting facts about the post-war period in France is the relative scarcity of genuine admissions of error on the part of collaborationist writers who have since regained some of their standing as men of letters. When they do talk of the past, it tends to be in terms of apology rather than confession, and in the case of one interesting recent example, Louis-Ferdinand Céline's *D'Un Château L'Autre*, the tone is acrid with mingled bitterness and self-righteousness. Yet the book is important, not only for its portrayal of the final stages of the Vichy government after it had been driven into exile on the Danube, but also for the light it throws on the attitude of Céline himself, one of the most talented and untypical of the collaborationist writers.

The novels by which Céline gained his reputation during the 1930's, *Journey to the End of the Night* and *Death on the Instalment Plan*, were

*Reprinted from *Encounter* 10, no. 5 (May 1958):70–79.

striking, disturbing, and influential books. By the use of a harsh and colloquial prose — later imitated by such writers as Sartre and Simenon — Céline made his style a manifestation of the nihilistic iconoclasm which he directed, not only at modern society as a whole, but also at his own characters. The latter he showed almost invariably as the prisoners of social necessity, the slaves of moral and physical decay. One of them, the feckless, amoral Robinson in *Journey to the End of the Night*, with his tragic confusion of irresponsibility and freedom, is the prototype of the existentialist anti-hero, of those victims of their own lack of purpose who people the novels of Camus. The narrator of the same novel (an evident self-portrait of Céline) is caught with Robinson and other characters in a web of complicity over a murder which has to be concealed, and their situation becomes a symbol of the way in which all men are tricked by the circumstances of their lives into sharing the responsibility for society's crimes.

We are, Céline suggests, both criminals and victims. Our efforts to stand out as individuals are meaningless; the most massive and at the same time the most hollow of Céline's characters is Courtial des Pereires, the popular-science expert in *Death on the Instalment Plan*, who poses his way through a life of confidence tricks and, when failure and exposure are finally inevitable, commits suicide. Pereires has become his own pretences; the man with another name who exists beneath them is so atrophied that, once the masks are stripped away, he can only cease to exist. For each man in Céline's world, life begins in the daylight of simplicity, and ends in the darkness of age and corruption; this goes on in cyclic repetition for almost as many lives as there are men to live them. In such an existence love has no lasting meaning; a passing passion, a transient warmth can exist between people, but any permanent relationship ends in mutual destruction.

Yet, despite this bitter view of man's condition, the negation of Céline's earlier novels is not complete. Society is bad, life leads into the darkness, but here and there, shining like minor stars, we meet simple, natural people who have somehow remained uncorrupted. They are, it must be admitted, Céline's least convincing characters — Dickensian saints who have given up their lives to tending orphaned children, prostitutes as golden-hearted as those of Dostoevsky — and they are portrayed with that sentimentality which is usually to be found at some level in association with nihilism. But the very fact that they exist is significant; against the society which he hates and the victims he pities, Céline poses here and there his ideal of the individual of gentle feelings and uncomplicated mind — an ideal not far removed from the natural man beloved of the Enlightenment and admired, significantly, by Swift, a writer with whom Céline has much in common.

Many aspects of Céline's writings during the 1930's made it at first seem surprising that he should become a collaborationist. On first reading, his novels seemed to be written by a devoted anti-militarist, a critic of colonialism, a friend of the poor and the humble, who condemned existing society and current standards of morality. But one should not ignore the conservatism implied in the attitude of the man who criticises modern society in favour of a more simple and more "natural" existence. Moreover, as Camus has shown convincingly in *L'Homme Révolté*, and as we have seen in the examples of such British writers as Bernard Shaw and Wyndham Lewis, there is a certain type of intellectual iconoclast whose anger arises largely from his inability to dominate and change his world and who therefore admires the strong man, the dictator-hero who seems able to cut ruthlessly through the tangled knots of social problems. Céline clearly belongs to this type; the very extremity of despair that emerged in his earlier works suggested that in his view life could only be changed, if at all, by some social apocalypse, and it was the apocalyptic element in Nazism that appealed to him. During the days before he became disillusioned with his wartime associates, he seems indeed to have foreseen the paradoxical possibility of a reign of something approaching social justice in a Europe dominated by men who appeared to share his own quasi-Nietzschian contempt for orthodox morality.

Unfortunately, *D'Un Château L'Autre* does not give us a great deal of enlightenment on the reasoning that turned Céline into a collaborator; it is rather the record of the last and disillusioning phase of his association with the Vichy régime. Céline has, indeeed, always been a largely autobiographical writer, relying on direct experience for most of his material, but in *D'Un Château L'Autre*, though it is called a novel on the title page, even the pretence of fiction is dropped to such an extent that Céline, in his own name, is both narrator and central figure.

His account begins in the present, more than a decade after the war's end, when we encounter him, a prematurely aged man of sixty-three, carrying on a medical practice in a Parisian suburb. He is still pursued by hatred inspired by his wartime record; his few patients are the old and the very poor, his books no longer sell, his fellow writers mostly ignore him, and he is so fearful of violence that he lives surrounded by watch-dogs. One day the fever contracted in Africa when he was a young man returns, and as he lies in his bed the past runs through his mind in a half-hallucinatory series of memories. He remembers the long months when he lay in the solitary, scurvy-ridden confinements of a Danish prison after the end of the war, while his jailers tried to force him to confess to unlikely treasons. And from a deeper layer he recalls the days before Germany finally collapsed, when the Pétain government waited in the old Hohenzollern castle of Siegmaringen, while the Free French forces of General Leclerc moved steadily nearer.

Depressing, and at times almost unreadable, *D'Un Château L'Autre* pushes Céline's nihilistic tendencies to the edge of disintegration. The disjointed prose, elliptical and verbose at the same time, grates with an unredeemed ugliness and, by its own lack of genuine flow, underlines the general lack of development in Céline's narrative. The undeveloped form in turn emphasises the unreality of the vision presented. Céline has always been fascinated by the hallucinations produced in states of physical abnormality, and the use of a bout of fever as the framework for the action of *D'Un Château L'Autre* gives both incidents and characters a peculiarly phantasmagorical quality, so that the recollections he presents seem rather the projections of nightmare than the experiences of actual life. It is true, of course, that the events described have their own air of fantasy. There is Abetz dreaming of a glorious return to Paris, to be celebrated by the erection of a colossal statue of Charlemagne to mark the unity of Europe. There is Pétain taking his solemn morning walk along the Danube, with his ministers following in strict precedence, as if they were something more than the rulers of a vanished realm of puppets. There is Céline himself, reproaching Laval for not having found him a suitable post and accepting a phantom Colonial Governorship from a government that has ceased to wield even the shadow of power. But Céline uses and emphasises these elements of fantasy to such an extent that throughout his narrative both men and motives retreat into the evasions of dreams.

The underlying sentiment of the book is certainly not regret on Céline's part for his own attitude during the war. Rather, it is anger at the associates who proved so disillusioning, at the heroes with clay feet, and grievance at the opponents who condemned him. All faith in humanity is ended; the natural man, one is led to conclude, does not exist, and the only beings for whom Céline shows unreserved sympathy are the cats and dogs who share his exile in Siegmaringen and his present isolation in France. They alone, he says in so many words, are innocent.

D'Un Château L'Autre, like *Guignol's Band*, will disappoint those who admired *Journey to the End of the Night*. Yet, just as one can draw from Céline's earlier novels the intellectual attitudes that help to explain his actions during the 1940's, so the tendency to deal iconoclastically with style, character, and every other aspect of the novel, already flourishing in the works of the 1930's, reaches its not unnatural end in the literary barrenness of this most recent work. There is a negative quality in the attitude of the iconoclast which is hostile to true creativity, and Céline's decline can be regarded as a case of the occupational disease which attacks many satirists who find that their progressive loss of positive feeling slowly robs their work of meaning. After all, one must have some hope of redeeming humanity if one is to scourge it with conviction; that hope Céline seems to have had in the past and to have lost completely to-day.

At the same time, I do not mean these remarks to suggest either that we can do without iconoclasts and satirists, or that in the 1930's Céline was anything less than an extremely vital writer who played a great part in awakening French fiction from the stagnation into which it had declined since the death of Proust.

Notes

1. Louis Aragon (b. 1897) was a novelist, poet, and editor of *Les Lettres française.* From Dadaism he turned to surrealism. In 1927 he became a communist. After the fall of France he emerged as the leader of the intellectual Resistance (editor's note).

2. Henry De Montherlant (1896–1972) was a novelist, essayist, dramatist, and member of the Académie in 1961. He had fascist leanings (editor's note).

Céline: Swastika and Cross   Richard Seaver*

In July 1944, barely a month after the Allies landed in Normandy, Dr. Louis Destouches, better known to the world as Louis-Ferdinand Céline, author of *Journey to the End of the Night* decamped from his Paris apartment on the rue Girardon. With him went his wife Lucette, their cat Bébert, and their friend the film star Robert Coquillaud. Their ultimate destination was Copenhagen, where Céline purportedly had secreted some six million francs' worth of gold. But, as was so often the case in Céline's life, he chose the most complicated and most dangerous route. A collaborator—and famous to boot—he was leaving to avoid being "skinned alive." That was logical and rational. But he also chose to flee straight into the heart of the inferno—Germany. That was illogical and self-defeating. Somewhere in the complexity of that decision, lies the key to the enigma of Céline.

As a pretext, or justification for his itinerary, Céline claimed business—a medical congress at Baden Baden—although why, in those light-traveling times, these three people needed twenty trunkloads of goods and possessions, including some strange wares if we are to believe Céline's close friend, Ralph Soupault, has never been amply explained. To quote Soupault's inventory as given in Erika Ostrovsky's *Voyeur Voyant*: "Dr. Destouches was leaving with about 20 trunks, a dozen of which were said to be stuffed full of horseshoes, pickaxes, barbed wire, hatchets, scythes, harnesses, and copper for purposes of trading with the Teutonic farmers. . . ." Considering the amount of baggage Céline did take, one wonders why he left behind at the rue Girardon all sorts of manuscripts, which neighbors and pillaging patriots promptly stole or consigned to the garbage, so that most were lost forever. Whatever the reason—again, it would doubtlessly be some peculiar mixture of the rational and ir-rational—the curiously burdened trio arrived in the summer of 1944 at the sumptuous Park Hotel in Baden-Baden, a hotel filled with faded aristo-crats, and, as Céline notes in *North*, "former reigning princes or Ruhr magnates . . . slightly wounded generals from every front . . . Boche war

*Reprinted by permission from the *Saturday Review* 55, 5 February 1972, 57–59. ©
1972

widows convalescing from emotional shock" by jampacking the Casino pastry shop and downing huge quantities of *babas au rhum*, cream puffs, blueberry tarts, and platters of éclairs, as the whole German army retreated on all fronts and the world collapsed around them. Such is the setting for Céline's first northward stop in Germany, the first station of the cross on what was to become his seven-year calvary.

In *North*, the Park Hotel becomes the Simplon, Coquillaud becomes the memorable Le Vigan, and Lucette, perhaps amalgamated with some of Céline's earlier dancer-ghosts, becomes Lili. The thirty-odd pages that make up the opening, Simplon section of the book are in themselves a little masterpiece describing, from the loser's side, the tone and tenor of the Third Reich in its penultimate days. His description is far more accurate and, I suspect, more cogent than those of most historians. Céline in fact, refers to himself as an "historian," but the term he prefers is "chronicler." It is not only the facts and events of this apocalyptic period, 1944 and 1945, that he is interested in relating, it is also the truths that they reveal, first insofar as they relate to him personally, and second insofar as they relate to the world at large. Céline's method here is only generally chronological, for he wrote *North* in the late Fifties — that is, during the last year or two of his life and roughly a decade and a half after the exodus described. He is nearing the end of his harrowing, frenzied existence, and he knows it — which is, perhaps, why the opening lines of *North* sound more like Beckett than Céline: "Sure, I tell myself, it'll all be over soon . . . whew! . . . *we have seen enough. . . .*"

It is, then, from this vantage point of age and, if not wisdom, certainly experience both varied and hallucinatory that Céline constantly intrudes on the "present" to comment or castigate in the light of subsequent events. "I'm telling you all this every which way," he warns the reader. "The end before the beginning! . . . what does it matter? the truth alone matters! . . . you'll catch on . . . I catch on. . . . A slight effort, that's all! . . . You take more trouble with a modern painting!" This frequent intrusion of the artist into his work, to strip away the illusion he himself has created, and the elliptical style that some critics, in reviewing virtually every book since *Journey*, have cited as proof of Céline's artistic decline are the hallmarks of *North*. And if the style disturbs, Céline is still right: "a slight effort" and the shock disappears; one is immersed in the torrential flow of words, images, dark humor, irascible vulgarisms — unadorned truth as Céline views it. Nothing sugar-coated here or servile excuses for past conduct or opinions, or others yet to come. Céline has made his sty, and he will wallow through it.

From the Simplon, the triumvirate with Bébert the cat still in tow, entrain for Berlin, the city of "smashed shop windows! twisted wreckage!" where "old women, very old, were picking up everything, well trying, making their own piles, little fortresses right on the sidewalk . . . houses of rubble . . . toys, sand, holes, bricks, for loony grandmothers." There, after a Kafkaesque search to find food and lodgings—an impossible quest without proper papers and their papers questioned because their faces have radically changed since the three set out on their grotesque odyssey— and a near-lynching at the hands of some berserk *Hitlerjugend* who mistake them for Allied parachutists-saboteurs, they finally reach Grünwald, on the outskirts of Berlin. In Grünwald they find relative safety in Dr. Harras's underground offices: "An enormous room furnished like New York, but at least sixty feet underground . . . typists too, just like America, cute, in pants. . . ." Harras's real-life prototype was a Dr. Hauboldt, an important medical officer of the Third Reich whom Céline had met in Paris at the screening of a technical film on typhus. "Typhus is my little speciality . . . but I'd been seen at that picture! . . . the coffins I received after that!" (The "coffins" to which Céline refers were miniature boxes sent by the *maquis* to its intended victims.) After a brief stopover at Grünwald, the little group is sent on to Kränzlin, which Céline renames Zornhof, about seventy miles north of Berlin. There, at a little castle, the trio remains for several months, until, in November 1944, they move on to Sigmaringen, an epoch related in Céline's earlier book *Castle to Castle*.

Zornhof is peopled by a motley array of characters: seventy-four-year-old Count-Baron *Rittmeister* von Leiden, "a pure Prussian . . . absolutely degenerate! . . . and paraplegic!"; his daughter Marie-Thérèse; his son, a basket case and epileptic; and his daughter-in-law Inge. Polish and French deportees work the farm, with the help of some alleged Russian deserters and "Vlasovs" ("Bolsheviks the whole lot of them . . . Communist spies!" rants Dr. Harras with perfect logic, since his own paranoia is but a reflection of the rampant national delusion). And, to round out the tableau, there are the *Bibelforschers*—the conscientious objectors—and a contingent of unreformable Berlin whores who work on the roads at nearby Moorsburg.

What is most impressive about Céline's caustic chronicle of that roughly three-month sojourn at Zornhof is his rigorous lack of self-pity. If he is bitter about the French it is mostly because of what Céline saw as the hypocrisy and dishonesty of the do-gooders, "the Stern and Righteous Men" who under the guise of patriotism, loot and kill, or at the very least turn their coats. If "I'd been on rue Girardon . . . what would my eyes have beheld? . . . four Commanders of the Legions of Honor walking off with my furniture!" Or: "The Marshal [Pétain] . . . turned his coat at the right time and got to be king! . . . I know forty million Frenchmen who've done the same, coats, pants, and gats!" Being anti-French, however, did not automatically mean being pro-Hitler: "Harres, the Boche, the hundred percent Nazi, didn't take us for Hitlerites! certainly not! . . . all he asked was that we speak French. . . ."

For Céline, reason had stopped in 1914—he was badly wounded in the early months of the First World War and was classified as 75 per cent disabled—and the ranting had begun. If there is a ranting, querulous tone to much of his work, including *North* ("a lot of people, even pretty patient ones, have said I gripe too much . . . okay, I'll dry my tears!"), Céline could reply, with perfect justification, that he was simply mirroring the time in which he lived. The problem was, he mirrored it too faithfully, too brutally for most. At a time when the world looked about desperately for distractions and various forms of escape, Céline kept holding up a mirror that reflected its ugliness, stupidity, and venality. If that was not enough, he had made the mistake of writing, as his first major work, a master-piece, which could then be conveniently compared, for the next quarter century, to any new work as proof that he was in full decline. Finally, Céline made the crass error not only of turning violently — everything he did tended to the violent — from Left to Right, but of writing and publishing two vitriolic, anti-Semitic pamphlets, which to this day have never been amply explained, not even in Erika Ostrovsky's *Voyeur Voyant*. It was this last, the political commitment, which caused his "downfall" and disgrace, from which he never recovered during his lifetime. But it is also true that, despite all his *words*, no accusation of acts committed were leveled against him. Although Céline was pro-German during the Occu-pation, no one was arrested at his instigation. In fact, reports indicated that he kept to himself knowledge of underground activities taking place in his own rue Girardon apartment house in Paris. And though anti-Semitic, he is known to have broken up at least one august right-wing assembly by making anti-Aryan jibes. The truth is, he was an anarchist in the fullest, most personal sense of the term. "An anarchist I am, was, remain, and I don't give a damn what anybody thinks!"

Political considerations have too long deprived Céline of his due, at least in the postwar period. It is high time that he be judged on the basis of his work alone. The publication of *North* in English, in Ralph Manheim's superb translation, is a literary event of major importance. . . .

Not a "New Book"
Walter Heist*

To thoroughly understand how sterile Céline is on returning from his fascist adventure, you have to know the aim of the New Book series: publication of avant-garde contemporary literature. In the thirties with his *Journey to the End of the Night* and *Death on the Installment Plan*, Céline made an essential contribution to style and even a decisive contribution to the revival of French literature. This early Céline consist-ently belonged, in respect to contents, to the former series which included

*Translated by Jóhanna Eiríksdóttir Hull for this volume from *Frankfurter Hefte*, 30 September 1975, 66–67. Reprinted with permission of *Frankfurter Hefte* Bank für Ge-meinwirtschaft, Bonn, Konto — Nr. 10.113.506.00.

Malraux, Aragon (*The Bells of Basel*) and Bernanos, who were then producing literature's change in trend. The Camus of *The Stranger* and the Sartre of *Nausea* are stylistically indebted to him. (Sartre put a Céline citation at the front of his first novel.) Not to mention Raymond Queneau, from *The Dogtooth* on, and other successors. So when the changing and embittered Céline wants his meaning to contemporary literature compared with that of Malherbe to classical, he has to be understood in a certain way. But should the translation of his *Rigadoon*, his most recent posthumous work, the end of a trilogy which began with *Castle to Castle* and *North*, be included in the Rowohlt series *The New Book*? The failure of judgment is evident.

Condemned to death for collaboration, Céline spent two years in Danish prisons. (He recounts that experience in *Féerie pour une autre fois* [*Fairytale for Another Time*].) The Gallimard publishing house was certainly right to acquire and to present anew to the literary public the great author of *Journey to the End of the Night* and *Death on the Installment Plan* when Céline returned under amnesty in 1951. First, it brought out two yet unpublished works stemming from Céline's most brilliant period, works he had been able to save by his flight: the fragment of a revelation of the military world, obviously of great consequence, *Casse-Pipe*, and the first part of a fresco of the London underworld, *Guignol's Band*. There followed the reprinting of both "classical" novels, *Journey to the End of the Night* and *Death on the Installment Plan*. Only after that did Gallimard dare to present the really new Céline: the two volumes of *Fairytale for Another Time*. The first, in which there is at first sight the old stylistic vehemence and muckraking, nevertheless clearly shows Céline's transformation. It is not the earlier total attack on the absurdity of the world situation, but a grumbling and self-pitying lament about his last days in Paris and his Danish imprisonment. Not until the second volume (*Normance*), in an apocalyptic description of an air attack on Paris, does the great imagination of old reappear. For the last time.

Because then, with *Castle to Castle*, Céline began the trilogy chronicle of his odyssey as an exile traveling through collapsing Nazi Germany, a trilogy now finished with *Rigadoon*. One can hardly imagine a more genuine rendering of the inferno of those months in Germany than Céline's grotesque exaggeration. More than once we feel the claws of the lion, and certainly in his description of the ghostlike activity of the fugitive Pétain government in Sigmaringen (*Castle to Castle*). Or in the bloody-comical description of prostitutes evacuated from Hamburg, a scene set in the seclusion of Brandenburg Province (*North*). Or in the description, rendered with despairing-sarcastic compassion, of the transportation of mentally retarded children through devastated cities of Hanover and Hamburg (*Rigadoon*). On closer examination, however, we recognize much that is formalistic and routine in his present descriptions of catastrophe. In the publisher Paul Nizan's blurb is a citation characterizing the

Céline of 1932: "his ghastly picture of the world. He tears off all masks and veils, smashes all illusory decor." These words, coined for *Journey to the End of the Night*, are no longer true for *Rigadoon* or the two preceding volumes. Here he deliberately chooses which mystification to tear into, disregarding the others. And he has now finally put on a mask himself: that of the misunderstood prey. His force of imagination, well founded in and transcending reality, and which had determined his newness in the 1930s, has subsided. What is left is a formula, or routine, which is certainly still fascinating for wide stretches, but which his overheated emotions ("Afro-Asians should have certain characteristics improved!" "The Chinese in Brest as soon as possible!") do not make any newer or livelier. The ingenious gutter singer of *Journey to the End of the Night*, still going in *Bagatelles pour un massacre*, is dead. In *Rigadoon* there is no more impulse.

In its contents, *Rigadoon* follows *North*, and tells of the return of Céline and his wife and the cat Bébert from Brandenburg province to Sigmaringen. He skips over his experience there, since he has already told it in *Castle to Castle*. The flight to Denmark is the conclusion. What he experienced there he leaves out again, since it was soon to be read in *Féerie pour une autre fois*.

Everything is presented in that same "spoken language" that was Céline's from the beginning. Even though he can time and again give shape to sweeping passages of his "chronicle," and one can hardly imagine a more adequate depiction of the witches' sabbath in collapsing Nazi Germany, Céline's last three books do not belong in a series in which the progressive tradition is represented by Tretjakow, Chlebnikow, and Carl Einstein. If the editors did not want to forego Céline in this context, they could have chosen for the New Book Series the explosive, as yet untranslated *Casse-Pipe*. Of course, to be on Céline's level, they would have to get a powerful German poet (maybe H. C. Artmann) to help the certainly well informed and painstaking, but abundantly boring or spuriously boisterous translator Bökenkamp.

[Review of *North* and *Rigadoon*]   Charles Krance*

North and *Rigadoon* . . . constitute the second and third volumes of what, together with *Castle to Castle*, . . . is commonly referred to as Céline's World War II trilogy. Written between 1954 and 1961 (the year of Céline's death), and originally conceived as sequels to *Féerie pour une autre fois* I and II . . . — which remain to be translated — these novels, like

*Reprinted with permission from the *Modern Language Journal* 61, no. 8 (December 1977):438–39.

all of Céline's fiction, are largely autobiographical: most of the events depicted in this trilogy, which chronicles the narrator's tumultuous meanders through the Götterdämmerung of the Third Reich (Germany, June 1944 to March 1945), were experienced first hand by Céline himself. His account of these "stranger than fiction" peregrinations is, however, anything but an objective document. The focus of Céline's narrative is not on the chaotic events which he experienced, but rather on the experience itself. But here again, Céline's chronicle is much more than a subjective reflection on an experience which, however turbulent, had been so much water over the dam by the time of the writing. Rather, Céline's last two works attest the degree of stylistic perfection toward which he had so strenuously labored in the last, most productive half-decade of his life: a writing which lays itself bare, mercilessly revealing its own vainglorious claims of objectivity and subjectiveness alike.

The double-edged sword of Céline's credo, *noircir et se noircir* (see Erika Ostrovsky, *Céline and his Vision* [New York: New York University Press, 1967], chapter I), which pervades his writings since his first novel, *Voyage au bout de la nuit* (1932), and before that his biography of Semmelweis (1924 [see my "*Semmelweis, ou l'accouchement de la biographie célinienne,*" *L.-F. Céline*, No. 2 (Paris: La Revue des Lettres Modernes — Minard, 1976), pp. 7–32]), was designed for no less a purpose than to cut free the language of French literary prose from its two traditional oppressors: post-Rabelaisian, (neo-)classical restraint, and the truth-seeking introspections of relentless psychological (self-)analysis. With the writer's creative (and, in a special sense, moral) consciousness — and the language which was his vehicle — thus open on either end, the style with which Céline confronted the second (and, in his lifetime, the last) wave of his readers (after his return, in 1951, from exile and imprisonment in Germany and Denmark) was one which, more like a scalpel than a sword, refined his communicative process even further. Incisively, and with a good dose of tragic humor, Céline, in his trilogy, and especially in *North* (in which he reached the pinnacle of his art), methodically subjects his narrator and reader to the same reactions which informed the miasmal experiences of 1944–45 with their hallucinatory quality. Hence, as one of his more perspicacious critics puts it: "l'écriture [célinienne] témoigne du réel *perçu*. Le roman ne décrit plus le monde, il décrit la manière, mieux, il *est* la manière dont le héros en prend conscience" (Frédéric Vitoux, *L.-F. Céline, misère et parole* [Paris: Gallimard, 1973], p. 84).[1] Céline's probing stylus penetrates not only the surface of his text — leaving his imprint of word groups, disarticulated by the unmistakable, aposiopetic three dots, to speak for itself — but also the very bowels of a kind of literary expression which has commonly come to be known as expressive of, and designed for eliciting "gut reactions." As Céline himself said in one of the first interviews which followed in the wake of the polemics surrounding the publication of *D'un château l'autre*

(*L'Express*, No. 312, June 14, 1957, pp. 15–18), "l'histoire, elle est très accessoire. C'est le style qui est intéressant. . . . C'est la façon de [la] rendre qui compte."[2] Now as a chronicler, now as a memorialist, always the novelist qua artist, "l'histoire" — whether history or story — is to Céline what the apple was to Cézanne, or the mirror to Renoir (see *Cahiers Céline 2*, ed. Jean-Pierre Dauphin and Henri Godard [Paris: Gallimard, 1976], p. 69): a pretext for an aesthetic experience. And, like Cézanne with his apple, Céline allows himself the freedom of certain essential distortions, whether on the level of caricature, hyperbole, or syntactic innovations on the one hand, or that of structural organization on the other (for a detailed account of the many painstaking manipulations and revisions which went into the composition of Céline's trilogy, see *Céline, Romans II*, ed. Henri Godard [Paris: Gallimard, 1974], pp. 955–1192). And like Renoir and his mirror, the world enframed by Céline's narrative is a world which reflects a unique, inimitable experience. The genius of the one as well as that of the other is to have transposed that experience onto the medium of expression itself. Thus, Céline's explosive language and style is the very sign of his experience: its full impact explodes, as if by delayed reaction, before the eyes, and in the consciousness, of author, narrator, and reader alike. . . .

Notes

1. "Céline's writing is reality you can see with the naked eye. The novel no longer describes the world, it describes the manner, rather, it *is* the way the hero grasps it" (editor's translation).

2. "History is very accessible. It's the style that's interesting, the way of transposing it [history]" (editor's translation).

GENERAL STUDIES

Interviewer: "Do you still regard yourself as one of the greatest living writers?"

Céline: "No, not at all. Great writers . . . What do I want with adjectives. First you've got to croak and when you've croaked they classify."

—Céline's last interview, the *Paris Review*, 1 June 1961

Céline: The Sod Beneath the Skin   Irving Howe[*]

I

The underground man, both as literary figure and social type, first enters European awareness in the 19th Century. As rebel against the previously secure Enlightenment, he rejects the claims of science, the ordered world-view of the rationalists, the optimism of the radicals. He speaks in the accents of romanticism, but a romanticism gone sour and turned in upon itself. He is tempted neither by knowledge, like Faust, nor glory, like Julien Sorel; he is beyond temptation of any sort. The idea of ambition he regards as a derangement of ego, and idealism as the most absurd of vanities. He hopes neither to reform nor to cure the world, only to escape from beneath its pressures. For he believes — it is the one thing he believes entirely — that the world is intent upon crushing him, and he takes a spiteful pleasure in delaying its victory. That in the end it will crush him, he never doubts.

A creature of the city, he has no fixed place among the social classes; he lives in holes and crevices, burrowing beneath the visible structure of society. Elusive and paranoid, he plays a great many parts yet continues to be recognizable as a type through his unwavering rejection of official humanity: the humanity of decorum, moderation and reasonableness. Even while tormenting himself with reflections upon his own insignificance, the underground man hates still more — more than his own hated self — the world above ground.

He refuses definition, fixity, coherence. Meek and arrogant, dialectically resourceful and derisive of intellect, starved for love and scornful of those who offer it, he lives in a chaos of subterranean passions. Beneath each layer of his being there quivers another, in radical conflict with the first. He can move in quick succession from Satanic pride to abject humility and then recognize, with mocking self-approval, that the humil-

[*]Reprinted with permission from the *New Republic* 149 (20 July 1963):19–22; (17 August 1963):17–20. © 1963 The New Republic, Inc.

ity is no more than a curtain for his pride. Nor need the sequel of exposure end there; it could go on forever. From a conviction of his inferiority he abases himself toward everyone: — toward everyone but the men of ordinary decent sentiments who seem to have escaped the abyss of suffering and are therefore regarded by him as objects of contempt. Yet to say this is also to notice his conviction of superiority, for at heart he is gratified by the stigmata of his plight and regards his pain as evidence of distinction. Gratified, he indulges in a vast self-pity; but this psychic quick-change artist can also be mercilessly ironic about that self-pity. Above all else, he is a master of parody.

The assumption that man is rational, and the assumption that his character is definable — so important to Western literature — are both threatened when the underground man appears on the historical scene. His emergence signifies the end of the belief that the human being can be understood by means of a static psychology, and in accordance with the modernist spirit, he is seen not as a person with a unique ensemble of traits but as a history of experiences that often are impenetrable.

Brilliantly anticipated in Diderot's fiction, *Rameau's Nephew*, the underground man first appears full face in Dostoevsky's novels. Here he assumes his most exalted guise, as a whole man suffering the burdens of consciousness. In *Notes from the Underground* he scrutinizes his motives with a kind of phenomenological venom; and then, as if to silence the moralists of both Christianity and humanism who might urge upon him a therapeutic commitment to action, he enters a few relationships with other people, relationships that are commonplace yet utterly decisive in revealing the impossibility of escape from his poisoned self.

In the 20th Century the underground man comes into his own and, like a rise of pus, breaks through the wrinkled skin of tradition. Thus far, at least, it is his century. He appears everywhere in modern literature, though seldom with the intellectual resources and intensity of grandeur that Dostoevsky accorded him. In France, during the thirties, the half-forgotten writer Louis-Ferdinand Céline published several novels in which he expressed with exuberant completeness the underground man's revulsion from the modern world. And if the underground man as portrayed by Dostoevsky could be taken as the product of an overwrought imagination, now his historical reality is beyond dispute. Author, central character and chorus, he is running the whole show.

Louis-Ferdinand Céline was born under the name of Louis Destouches in Paris in 1894. His life was shaped primarily by his sufferings in the First World War, during which he was severely wounded and had to undergo several operations on his skull. Throughout his remaining years he was tormented by migraine. "My own trouble is lack of sleep," he once wrote; "I should never have written a line if I'd been able to sleep." Working as a doctor in a poor neighborhood of Paris, Céline wrote and published in 1932 his first novel, *Journey to the End of the Night*, in which he picked up the story of his life at the close of adolescence and carried it through his middle years. The book was an immediate critical success, with figures as various as André Gide, Ramon Fernandez and Leon Trotsky saluting its irascible vitality.

Journey to the End of the Night is composed as a series of loosely-related episodes, a string of surrealist burlesques, fables of horror and manic extravaganzas, each following upon the other with energy and speed. While the sort of novel Céline wrote — a wandering first-person narrative, picaresque in structure and expressionist in manner — presupposes an intimate relationship between author and central character, he was describing less the actual events of his life than their hallucinatory echoes, the distended memories of sleepless nights. The material in these novels is frequently appalling, yet the voice of the narrator is not at all what we have come to expect in the contemporary literature of exposure and shock. It is not a voice of cultivated sensibility, nor of moral anguish, and only on occasion does it rise to an unqualified indignation. Céline writes in a tone of cheerful nausea, a tone largely beyond bitterness or protest, as if he had decided to leave behind the metaphysics of Dostoevsky and the emotions of romanticism. Especially important here is the comparison with Dostoevsky, for it suggests how radically the underground man has experienced a change of character. Dostoevsky's underground man trembles in fright and despair before the possibility of nihilism; Céline's no longer regards a valueless existence as anything but a fact to be taken for granted.

The prose of *Journey to the End of the Night* is drawn from Parisian argot, and even those with a command of literary French find it difficult. For just as the hero of his novels is utterly unheroic ("I wasn't very wise myself but I'd grown sensible enough to be definitely a coward forever"), so is the style of those novels the opposite of literary and academic conventions. Fierce, sputtering, brawling, sometimes on the verge of hysteria, it is an "anti-style," a deliberate nose-thumbing at classical decorum. "To resensitize the language," Céline has written, "so that it pulses more than it reasons — that was my goal." As a statement of intention this is far less original than he supposes, but in its very familiarity it fits perfectly with the general impulse of modern literature. Like most modern writers Céline does not hesitate to sacrifice composure to vividness, unity of effect to ferocity of expression. He neither cares about a fixed literary tradition nor worries about such tiresome souvenirs as formal tidiness. His aim is to burst out, to launch a diatribe of a Parisian who is at one and the same time a miserable sod and an outraged man. Psychological refinements, introspective turns of self-analysis, romantic agonies — Céline will have none of these. The underground man who moves through his novels is beyond the Promethean gesture; he looks upon modern society as a blend of asylum and abattoir; so it is, so it must be;

and meanwhile, with a jovial toughness, he acts out the slogan of the declassed and disabused: *Je m'en fiche.*

The "I" of the novel is something of a louse, quite indifferent to the cautions of morality, yet he can lay claim to one virtue: he dislikes lying to himself. Not that he is infatuated with notions about the sacredness of truth. It is simply that in weighing his own feelings he wants an honest measure: he intends to be sincere with himself, even if with no one else. In one of his infrequent moments of contemplativeness, he tells himself: "The greatest defeat, in anything, is to forget, and above all to forget what it is that has smashed you, and to let yourself be smashed without ever realizing how thoroughly devilish men can be. When our time is up, we people mustn't bear malice, but neither must we forget. . . ." Sincerity is one of the few values to which Céline is genuinely — one almost says, sincerely — attached. Not by chance, it is also a dominant motif in modern literature, a token of that "psychology of exposure" through which the 19th Century unmasked itself and the 20th shivers in self-contempt. The triumph of literary modernism is signalled by a turn from truth to sincerity, from the search for objective law to a desire for personal response. The first involves an effort to apprehend the nature of the universe, and can lead to metaphysics, suicide, revolution and God; the second involves an effort to discover our demons within, and makes no claim upon the world other than the right to publicize the aggressions of candor. Sincerity becomes the last-ditch defense for men without belief, and in its name absolutes can be topped, morality dispersed and intellectual systems dissolved. Sincerity of feeling and exact faithfulness of language — which now means a language of fragments, violence and exasperation — become the ruling passion of Céline's narrator. In the terrible freedom it allows him, sincerity is a bomb shattering the hypocrisies of the Third Republic; in the lawlessness of its abandonment, a force of darkness and anti-intelligence.

The dominant motif of the book is undirected flight. From its opening pages, in which the narrator casually volunteers for the army (why not?), he is constantly running from the terrors and apparitions of his world. Céline (or as he now calls himself in the novel, Bardamu) is trapped in the First World War and — unable to think about it — he refuses to take it seriously, even to the point of opposition. The pages describing the war-time experiences of Bardamu, in their reduction of official glory to nihilist farce, are among the most scathing ever composed on this theme. Bardamu prepares to go off to war; Poincaré, President of the Republic, prepares "to open a show of lapdogs"; *Vive la France!* Bardamu learns, soon enough, that bullets whistle and he must run. For a while he serves as runner to a senile, delicate and rose-loving general, and his reward — Bardamu's, not the general's — is that his feet smell. Running for the general, Bardamu comes to a major decision: if he is to survive he will have to stop running for generals and begin running from them. Heroism is for Sundays; meanwhile the Bardamus must exploit the resources of their cowardice. And so he runs: from the army to the rear, from one hospital to another; from France to a fantastic trading post in a rotting African jungle; from the African jungle to the industrial jungle of America, first as a bum and then as a worker on the Detroit assembly lines; from America back to France, where, still running up and down stairs to earn a few francs, he becomes an indigent doctor. The one peaceful spot he finds is a post in an insane asylum. For ". . . when people are well, there is no way of getting away from it, they're rather frightening. . . . When they can stand up, they're thinking of killing you. Whereas when they're ill . . . no doubt about it, they're less dangerous."

Throughout the book Bardamu keeps looking for a strange character named Robinson, his down-at-the-heel and laconic double. Go to the edge of hopelessness and there you will find Robinson: in the front lines, where he proposes a scheme for desertion; in Africa, where he is getting ready to run off with the company's funds; and in Detroit, where he provides tips on brothels. Repeated through the book as a mock-ritual, these meetings between underground man and shameless alter-ego lead to nothing, for here all quests are futile, even one so modest as Bardamu's for Robinson. When Robinson dies there is nothing more to look for, and the concluding words of the book, a virtual manifesto of disgust, are: "Let's hear no more of all of this."

Images of death streak the novel. The African episode is a journey to the death of archaic tribalism, the American a journey to the death of industrial civilization. Backward or forward, it's all the same, "a great heap of worm-eaten sods like me, bleary, shivering and lousy." Céline is obsessed not merely with the inexorability of death but even more with the vision of putrefactions: ". . . Three feet below ground I . . . will be streaming with maggots, stinking more horribly than a heap of bank-holiday dung, all my disillusioned flesh absurdly rotting."

The algebra of our century: flight from death equals flight to death. But is there in this wild and rasping novel perhaps something more, perhaps a flicker of positive vision? Doesn't the enormity of Céline's hatred indicate some hidden yearning for the good which he himself can hardly express? In principle it is hard to deny such a possibility. Céline too has his humanities, and can be lavish with bottom-dog compassion; without some yearning for the good, one might suppose, he could hardly summon the energy needed for so vindictive an outburst against "man's viciousness." But the particular truth about this novel is less ennobling, less assuaging. As a force within the book, this presumptive yearning for good is hard to discover, perhaps because it is buried beneath the debris of disillusion.

Beneath that debris there may well be a misshapen core of moral sentiment, but it can seldom compete for attention with Céline's rich provisioning of symptoms of disorder and sensations of disgust.

II

In *Death on the Installment Plan* Céline returned to his childhood and adolescence in order to complete the record of his experience. An even grizzlier testimony than *Journey to the End of the Night*, Céline's second novel is written in a fitful and exuberant prose, and its tone is one of joyous loathing at having to turn back in memory to the miasma of youth. The misanthropy of the earlier novel ripens into outright paranoia: but with such bubbling energy, such a bilious and sizzling rhetoric, such a manic insistence upon dredging up the last recollection of filth! *Death on the Installment Plan* is a prolonged recital of cheating, venality and betrayal: the child as victim of the world. Still a boy, he learns to hate the whole social order: "It made me choke to think of it . . . of all the treachery of things! . . . All the swinishness! . . . The whole collection of ordures! Yes, God Almighty, I'd had my bellyful."

Two linked motifs control the book: the richest account of retching in modern literature and a profound yearning for solitude. Both are sequels to the running motif in *Journey to the End of the Night*: one runs from the filth and hopes to find a corner of quiet and a bit of peace. When Céline describes retching, he is an absolute virtuoso: "She brings up the lot . . . right into the wind . . . and I get it full in my face, the whole stinking stew that's been gurgling in her throat. . . . I, who haven't so much as a crumb to bring up! Ah, now, yes, I find I have, after all . . . my stomach gives one more turn. . . ." Vomit links with Céline's fruitless effort to disgorge the whole of his experience, as he runs through the darkness of the night. If only he could start afresh, with nothing on his stomach, and be rid of the rubbish of the past . . . but it cannot be done, there is always one more crumb of recollection.

The yearning for solitude is poignantly developed in *Death on the Installment Plan*. All a paranoid ever wants is "to be let alone," a wish that to be satisfied on his terms would require nothing less than a reconstruction of the universe. In one section of the novel, a set-piece displaying Céline's gifts at their best, he describes a stay in an English country-school, where he finds a happiness of sorts through taking long walks with a little idiot boy and an unobtrusive woman teacher; neither of whom troubles him by attempts at conversation. With the dumb and gentle he finds a paradise of muteness; here defenses can be lowered and nerves unravelled. And in this solitude it is also possible to enjoy the modest pleasures of masturbation. The adolescent hero of *Death on the Installment Plan* masturbates systematically, not with the excited curiosity of a youth but with the tameness of an old man. Pleasure can come only from himself, and only when alone with himself. And who knows, perhaps for the underground man as secret sharer of his potency, this is a kind of good faith, an act of sincerity.

There are writers in whose work a literary theme can barely be kept apart from a personal obsession, and psychological illness, through some perverse dynamic, becomes the source of a boundless creative energy. Céline is one of these.

The Nose and the Mound. Céline depicts a severed universe: on one side, he himself, the big nose, and on the other, the world at large, an enormous mound of *merde.* Maestro of bad smells, Céline learns that his nose is the one organ he can trust implicitly: it is the organ that remains sincere, and by it one can know women, cities, nations, destinies. "It's by smells that people, places and things come to their end. A whiff up one's nostrils is all that remains of past experience." His journey to America is a prolonged exploit in olefactory revulsion, climaxed by a visit to an underground urinal in New York, where he is simply awe-stricken — Cortez before the Pacific! — by "its joyous communion of filth."

Forever exposing himself to the multiplicity of *merde*, Céline reacts not merely to the hideousness of our social arrangements but even more, to the very conditions of existence itself, which dictate the stupidity of death, intolerable enough, and the prolonged stench of dying, still more intolerable. In *Journey to the End of the Night* he declares himself "appalled by my realization of biological ignominy," the last two words of this clause breaking forth as the very source of Céline's inspiration. He flinches before the sensual attributes of the least offensive body, and every time he sees a man engaging in the physiological functions he seethes with rage. Lusting after Lola, the sweet American nurse with piquant buttocks, he shudders in his lust: worms will reign over that flesh too. Had Céline lived in the early Christian era, he would have found himself a Manichean sect and spat upon sensual appetite as the taste of the devil. Being a 20th-Century Parisian, he submits to the most humiliating debaucheries precisely from his fury at being unable to avoid decay. Sartre and Camus may be students in the metaphysics of nausea, but what, by comparison with Céline, do they know about its actual qualities? They are more theoretic specialists, while Céline is an empiric master in the art of nausea.

Perhaps we can now understand somewhat better the running motif of *Journey to the End of the Night.* Céline is running not merely from society but from the sight of every living creature, and running, trips over the knowledge that it is from himself he would flee, the self that is alone inescapable. In *Death on the Installment Plan* he often befouls himself as a child, an act which at first seems the physical equivalent of his readiness to abandon self-respect as a luxury too dangerous for this world, but which after a time comes also to signify a recognition that even he is hopelessly implicated in the physicality against which he rages. One thinks of Swift, whose balked sense of purity melts into a fascination with filth, but there is a notable difference: Swift's writings almost always chart a descent from idea to matter, there is a wracking struggle of opposed life-principles — while in Céline, rot is sovereign, and flesh serves as argument for a gargantuan cosmic deception.

The Cheat of Language. Where finally can the compulsion to sincerity, to the last shameless self-revelation, lead but to silence? Céline writes: "I grow foul as soon as anyone talks to me; I hate it when they prattle." Or again: "The very idea made me howl with terror. Having to talk again — oh, Gawd." Anything beyond the reach of the nose is to be distrusted; all talk about human life is mere drivel unless it begins and ends with the breviary: "I am . . . thou art . . . all of us are despoilers, cheats, slobs." But once that has been said and said again and again, once Céline has spent the virtuosity of his rhetoric upon the denunciation of language, what then remains?

Comedy and Nausea. Cut away from its context in the novels, Céline's outlook upon life is narrow-spirited and tiresome. What saves him as a writer is that he so enjoys roaring his invective from the sewers, he makes his nausea into something deeply comic. In *Journey to the End of the Night*, talking about the war, he solemnly observes that "horses are lucky. They go through the war, like us, but they're not asked to . . . seem to believe in it. In this business they are unfortunate but free." During his visit to Africa, after suffering the afflictions of the jungle, he remarks that he is especially misfortunate because, as it happens, he "does not like the country." In *Death on the Installment Plan* his boss, a bogus scientist, launches a typical Célinesque diatribe after having failed in a piece of chicanery: "I'll get them right this time. . . . Their bellies, Ferdinand! Not their heads, but their bellies. Their digestions shall be my customers . . . I'm through with the spirit for keeps! We're onto the bowels now, Ferdinand, the grand alimentary canal."

It is this perspective of comic nausea that accounts for the vividness of Céline's novels. His hatred and fear of abstraction lead him to stake everything on the specific incident. With noisy verbs and cascades of adjectives, he assaults nose, ear, eye, creating a carnival of sensations. But precisely this vividness soon reveals itself as a sign of Céline's limitation as a writer, for it tends to be monolithic and exhausting. Strictly speaking, Céline is not a satirist in the sense that Swift was, despite the remarkable energy of disgust the two writers share; Céline is neither intelligent nor discriminating enough to be a true satirist. His metier is a kind of savage burlesque. The nausea that makes him recoil from experience is linked to the comedy that makes him relish the experience of recoil — beyond that he cannot go.

Philistine and Genius. Halfway, both of Céline's novels begin to lag, for they are really more like a vaudeville, a grab-bag of skits, than coherently developed fictions. In terms of sheer *performance* they contain pages rivalling Dickens, yet once the climax of a skit is known there is seldom much point in waiting either for its conclusion or repetition. By its very nature, the skit cannot be sustained over a long period of time; it is essentially a virtuoso device and virtuosity holds one's attention largely through initial shock or brilliance. This is a technical difficulty, but as always, the technical difficulty reflects a deeper problem in literary intelligence. The opening of a Céline novel is so seductively vigorous in manner and conclusive in meaning that little remains for further development: a mere accumulation of misfortunes, even when rendered with comic genius, becomes enervating unless the misfortunes are controlled by some principle of selectivity, some idea of greater scope than the probability of further misfortune.

One comes at times to suspect that Céline writes from a total emptiness, that his show of energy hides a void, that he is really without any genuine attitude or values. At such points, his novels seem like charades in which the gestures of life are enacted but the content has been lost. Driven by his simplistic ethics and his raging indiscriminateness of feeling to always greater assertions of cynicism, he falls, predictably, into the opposite error of sentimentalism. The novels are choked with emotions, yet the idea of emotion in its fine particularities remains beyond Céline's grasp. When he announces himself in love, it is with an embarrassing callowness. Let a prostitute show him an ounce of kindness or an inch of thigh, and he moons like a schoolboy. Necessarily so; for anyone with so constricted a notion of human feelings will not be able to respond intelligently to even a flimsy instance of them.

The ultimate limitation in Céline's work is a limitation of intelligence. He does not know what to do with his outpourings, except to multiply them; he cannot surmount his brilliant monomania. He is unable to distinguish among the kinds and degrees of loathesomeness, between a speck of dust and a mound of filth. Irritation and outrage, triviality and betrayal grate on his nerves almost equally. Except on grounds of racial incompleteness, it would be difficult to quarrel with Céline's description of 20th-Century experience; but there is something exasperating, at times even stupid, about a writer who roars with the same passion against nuisance and disaster. So overwhelmed is he by his demon of dirt, so infatuated with the invective he sends hurtling through his pages, he seems unable to think—and in the kind of novels he wrote, thought can be postponed but not dismissed. For all his authentic sense of affliction and all his gift for comedy, Céline remains something of a philistine, a philistine blessed with genius but a philistine nonetheless.

Shortly after the appearance of *Journey to the End of the Night* there

appeared a striking critical essay by Leon Trotsky praising the novel—
"Céline walked into great literature as other men walk into their own
homes"—and predicting that Céline "will not write a second book with
such an aversion for the lie and such a disbelief in the truth. The
dissonance must resolve itself. Either the artist will make his peace with
the darkness or he will perceive the dawn."

Trotsky's timing was a little off, and what he meant by "the dawn"
need not concern us here. Céline did manage to write a second novel with
the same attitudes as those in *Journey to the End of the Night*, but
essentially the prediction of Trotsky was correct. In 1936, by now a famous
writer, Céline took a trip to Russia and shortly thereafter wrote a little
book called *Mea Culpa* in which, together with some shrewd observations
about the Stalin dictatorship, he indulged himself in a wild harangue
about the inherent beastiality of mankind. Apart from the humor and
inventiveness of his novels, Céline's reflections served only to reveal the
radical limitations of the kind of modern novelist who presents his
intellectual incapacity as a principled anti-intellectualism.

There now begins a visible disintegration of Céline as both writer and
person. In 1938 he published an appalling book entitled *Trifles for a
Massacre (Bagatelles pour un Massacre)*, a dreary tract in which he
blamed the Jews for everything from the defeat of Napoleon to the rise of
surrealism, the corruption of the French language and the Sino-Japanese
war. Among those he denounced as "Jewish" were Cézanne, Lenin,
Montaigne, Stendhal, Vatican officials and Mrs. Wallis Simpson, all
"representatives of our great culture [who lie] on all the pallets, in all the
garrets of the official Jewish brothel. . . ." André Gide, reviewing the
book, took it to be a satire on the assumption that it was impossible that a
writer of Céline's gifts could mean what he said; but now it seems obvious
that Céline did in fact mean what he said. What is possible, of course, is
that he was suffering from some kind of mental derangement; but this is
rather different from satire.

During the Second World War, Céline played a dishonorable role,
living at peace with the Nazi occupation forces and expressing admiration
for the Vichy collaborators. (See the preface to *Guignol's Band*, a late
fiction that has almost no literary value but some pathological interest.)
After the war the French government accused Céline of having been a
collaborator and he, self-exiled to Denmark, offered the sad reply that he
had merely been an "abstentionist." Tried by the French authorities *in
absentia*, he was convicted, sentenced, but not required to serve his time
in prison. During the last decade of his life—he died in 1961—Céline was
allowed to return to France, where he lived in semi-retirement, a lonely
and embittered man. Young readers in the late fifties and early sixties who
have come to admire Beckett, Genet and Burroughs seem hardly to know
that behind these writers, both as predecessor and possible influence,
stands the disheveled but formidable figure of Louis-Ferdinand Céline.

His career, like that of Ezra Pound, is a classical instance of how a writer suffers in his purely literary work when his powers of mind are unequal to his powers of imagination. From the depths of the underground man's soul Céline brought forth all its effluvia, so that the world could see what was simmering there. His two novels, in all their brilliant imperfection, seem likely to survive the sickness of their inspiration. But at the end, unable to transcend the foulness which was his authentic and entirely legitimate subject, he made "his peace with the darkness." And not he alone.

Other Types of French   Henri Godard*

It must be because Céline's popular and slang lexicon is in itself very strong, and because the long-lasting taboo against such usage made it more striking, that we were less aware of the diversity of other types of French that coexist in Céline's prose. The slang has so bewitched us that, as far as language is concerned, we have hardly spoken of anything else; for instance, the sudden and sporadic appearance of "literary," archaic terms that clash with the rest. But if we experiment by enumerating all the words on one page that do not come from popular slang, we will be surprised to find them almost everywhere as numerous and diverse as the slang. Céline's language is really defined just as much by his rounding up of vocabulary from all sources as it is by the choice of slang, though slang is the center into which the rest is plunged.[1] A whole series of effects, felt as the most Célinien, was born out of the collision of these vocabularies or from the division of the discourse among them. These vocabularies have to be distinguished and identified with regard to the genre or speech to which they belong, to activities to which they are tied, and to more or less extended communities of which they are the natural "language." Before analyzing and interpreting, the first task to be undertaken is an unraveling of the threads that are intertwined in this prose, which we tend too much to believe comes entirely from popular and slang French.

These other types of French that Céline uses can be distributed along the two axes, synchronic and diachronic, in relation to which all language is defined. On the one hand, we find in Céline's novels echoes from various kinds of people with whom he happened to associate, and discourses, oral or written, that he was involved in at one time or another, whether as listener or reader, or as an active participant. On the other hand, we also find traces of memory from distinct moments in the history of the French language. But Céline takes the precaution of periodically bringing back

*Reprinted with permission from *Poétique de Céline* (Paris: Gallimard, 1985), 82–99. Translated by Jóhanna Eiríksdóttir Hull for this volume. © 1985 Editions Gallimard.

the proper timbre of French in general, mixing in scraps of other languages, and even makes us grasp again, by fits and starts, the power and limits of the language itself, while making place for notations that are strange to him.

In all language at a given time, there coexists under the artificial uniformity of the written scholarly form, like currents in the same ocean, innumerable language practices tied to activities and to groups that only encounter each other on occasion, but that identify each other and recognize that they belong together. The diversity of Céline's experience familiarized him with a greater number of these practices than was known to the average speaker, and he makes a point of making them all appear, at least in sample form, in his novels. Thus we encounter a whole series of distinct "languages" that every French reader identifies in passing. Lacking the power to use the words or even exactly to understand them, the reader knows at least which type of reality is in question, and, correct or not, he gets some idea of their meaning. Each of these types of French that Céline gathers together is confronted at the popular and slang center of his language, and nothing is more natural for letting them pass in review than to group them according to the way they react at that center. In this confrontation there are language types, which, while remaining themselves, more or less blend in, and others that detach themselves from the center, and indeed curse it.

We do not pay enough attention in Céline to the number of words that are neither popular nor slang nor go in the other direction. The general impression of his popular French is actually the effect of a mixture that is very wittingly measured out. The slang that intermittently gives some tone to popular language is counterbalanced by the ordinary, and for this reason unnoticed, written French, which is the one we are the most used to reading. No doubt, this eases our reading. The exclusive use of popular words, supposing that they still exist, would, as with slang, quickly become too much. If we scrutinize a page of Céline line by line, we will usually discover an important portion of words that upon reflection have nothing popular about them, but belong to the most current written French.

Many of the words that come from the languages of vocation, activity, or specialized life-style have a double reason to spontaneously put themselves in orbit around the nucleus of the Célinien language. On the one hand, the people who are in these trades and activities are often the same ones who speak popular French. On the other hand, within this particular vocabulary—which itself sometimes qualifies as slang in the broad sense of the word (a trade's operations, implements, habits, etc.)—it is often difficult to distinguish between technical terms properly speaking and their slang substitutes.

In our course through the novels we easily find the trace of those worlds that Céline has gone through in succession and that are endowed with a particular language. *Death on the Installment Plan* evokes a whole series by itself: the trade talk of the boutique, with its shelf assistants,[2] its dispatches, its Parisian shipments, its messengers, its calicots [drapery assistants], its apprentices, the nightmare of the scroungers, unsold articles, returned articles; the Commission with its representatives from the outside (the slobs), its traveling salesmen with their sleepy heads, its young men who make the scene, visiting the town, defending themselves in such trade, with, as a nightmare, the off-season, when they do not even get one order, when one refuses the merchandise even on ninety days, when the only thing left for them to do is to close their notebook and to change their line of work. There are various branches of specialties of artisans, which the profane reader hardly knows exist: chain makers, timpanists, the makers of accessories for window display, velvets, plaques. There they are, bosses, shop foremen, head workers, those paid by the piece, by the hour, or by the gross, careful not to mangle their hands. Both Ferdinands's apprenticeships provide an opportunity to enter into vocabularies that were even more particular: that of the cloth trade (pinning up the pattern, binding [*comète*], apprentices [*taupins* — math students in Standard French], Bergame velvet, shavings from beveling, curls of satin, filed cuff or lapel, etc.), and that of engraving craft (rings to be adjusted to size, the skill of resetting little gems, profiling fretwork, watermarks, cuttings, precelles, gadgets, etc.). So many terms, of which we more or less guess the meaning, cannot be completely elucidated except by reference to technical manuals or by asking the people who use them. Céline, whose scheme is anything but documentary, does not worry at all about glossing these trade lexicons, as does for example Zola. Neither does he make a point of marking the technical character of these words with quotation marks, or more accurately, he does it so irregularly that the sign loses its value. Avoiding whatever would differentiate these words, he tends to integrate them into the language which he has in common with the reader. If it seems to Céline that the words speak on their own, if for example on account of their root, or by sliding into context as slang does, they give an indication that allows the reader to get some idea of their meaning, Céline makes them virtually enter into general usage without adding anything. He enriches this usage.

Among the other lexicons of this kind, we could cite, the one that would be only natural for Céline to have gleaned, especially in *Casse-Pipe*, is that of the Army, and more particularly the cavalry, with its designations of units, rank, buildings, rites, practices (the post exercise, [*le Rapport*], written order, [*la Décision*], motive, etc.). Mixed with this lexicon is the vocabulary of horses and equitation, which is perpetuated well beyond this novel, for example in *Castle to Castle*, where Céline has come to speak of " 'attack!' yes! . . . 'attack' the cavalry term!,"[3] or the page in *North* devoted to the way the Rittmeister mounts Blouette.[4] The vocabulary of boats and navigation (types of boats, verbs designating maneuvers: to lay a plank over to the quay [*border à quai*], to lie at anchor, to get the ladder ready [*parer l'échelle*], to pull hard at the oars, to strike sail, to drive [*drosser*, as when the wind or current drives a ship onto the shore], etc.) is always ready to reappear when the story brings the narrator or characters back to a harbor or to the quays, but not only on these occasions. These words are so integrated into Céline's vocabulary that he uses them outside of their ordinary places more or less metaphorically. Thus he describes the passengers on uncle Edward's tricycle as "pulling hard at the pedals and by the tackle."[5] The bride, Henrouille, notices Bardamu "stranded [*en pantaine*] on the sidewalk."[6] And when Céline himself suddenly becomes aware: "I expatiate . . . I leave you *en pantaine*."[7]

With what could be called technico-scientific vocabulary, we enter into an intermediary zone. It is partly that of one of the little inventors who spin around Courtial, or of the workers and technicians who in each field use these words daily at the same time they handle the things. We only have to take a look at the page that evokes perpetual-motion machines of the two secondhand dealers from the Porte de Clignancourt or the story of the railroad accountant.[8] But the vocabulary is also and above all scholarly, and in this regard it is by definition separate from popular language and slang.

However, it is not separate in the same way as the literary or philosophical vocabulary we will examine later. However rare and complicated the technico-scientific word is, it responds to a need. Everyone understands that science cannot do without proper terms, as precise as possible, and therefore that it draws on foreign roots or particular forms. The use of scientific terms does not normally proceed from a desire to move away from commonplace or vulgar language. From the point of view of plurivocalism, there is a difference, at least of modality, that has to be taken into account.

In his novels Céline prefers to unfold this vocabulary around the character of Courtial. It is, by the way, when he was at *Eurèka* and from his association with Marquis-Graffigny that Céline must have taken it, or at least picked up its flavor. We find in *Death on the Installment Plan* a thousand echoes of the vulgarizing encyclopedism of the Marquis.[9] From the explosion of the car with "lengthened fusibles" to the polyvalent cottage, to the perpetual-motion competition, to that of the submarine diving bell,[10] to "radio-telluric" agriculture, to astronomy, etc., we can go on endlessly just enumerating the sectors in which Courtial assumes a competence of knowledge, and Céline a competence of vocabulary. But the pleasure he takes in manipulating it is not limited to this character or this novel. The gasmasks in *Guignol's Band II* provide yet another occasion to return to this vocabulary, and later still the explosions (the firebombing *la pyrogénie*)[11] at the bombarding of Montmartre in *Fairy Tale for Another Time*, or, in *Castle to Castle*, the submarines with "catapults by hydrolysis" the admiral is on the lookout for in the apparition on the Danube.[12] This sector of the Célinien lexicon also calls for a study, which will be no less instructive and pleasant than the others. It would require the collaboration of a lexicographer and of one, or more likely several, scientific specialists, not in order to clarify the exact meaning of the terms, which in most cases is not important to the reading, but in order to determine at each turn the degree of suitability and aptness — that is to say, very often of unsuitability and of inaptness — of the use of these terms in context. Readers with a scientific background must derive an extra pleasure from following in these numerous passages, the offhanded way with which Céline mixes, by means of the lexicon, the strangest and the most distant fields of science. He knows he is addressing a public that is for the most part capable of recognizing a word as "scientific," but incapable, with some exceptions, of appreciating its accuracy, or its plausibility, or even simply placing it (is it a chemical, an electrical, or a thermodynamic term?). And he uses these terms more for their connotative than for their denotative value. Finally, each reader according to his knowledge senses or measures a parodic or satirizing intent, which could show that such usages are ill-based or altogether hairbrained. Such a judgment is more useful than an evaluation of Céline's references or borrowings from the subfields of science. We would be better able to judge the plurivocalic and stylistic impact of this vocabulary if we knew in each case whether a word has its meaning in its context, or whether there even is a meaning, some meaning, hardly any, or none at all.

We must make a special place in this erudite vocabulary for a series that for good reason is represented in abundance: the medical lexicon, which also stands in contrast to the popular and slang background by evidence of its scientific character, but in a special way. Neither Céline nor we confront it as we do other scientific words. For Céline it is not a matter of using this vocabulary in a slapdash fashion.[13] It stems from his vocation, from his competence, and his belief in the power of medicine to diminish suffering. This science and its words touch the reader's body, touch that from which he derives pleasure, pain, and by which death comes to him. The comedy that these words can convey is never the same as that of the others, and they are quickly loaded with cruelty. Céline has a whole specific usage of medical vocabulary.

His own pains, the aftereffects of his wounds, his stay in Africa and his incarceration in Copenhagen, his own medical practice as much in historical time from a certain point, as in that of the narration — everything lends itself to the use of this vocabulary. And Céline, who could talk about the same thing in more general and less technical terms, did not deprive himself of the advantage he could take of medical terminology. Without anyone thinking whether they should be surprised — but we still have to analyze the phenomenon — he multiplies in his prose the number of terms we know but encounter only in altogether different contexts. All imaginable series are made to contribute: terms from anatomy, names of organs, of symptoms, of sicknesses, of types of illness, of medical intervention, medication, etc. These are most often words that, because of their origin, strike us above all by their rarity. But Céline does not fail either to use in their technical sense, sometimes indicated by quotation marks, certain words that belong to the common vocabulary as well as to the technical vocabulary of obstetrics, words such as *version* ["translation" in common vocabulary, "the change of position imposed on the fetus to facilitate birthing" in obstetrics], of *siège* ["seat or chair," or "siege" in common vocabulary, "breech as in breech birth" in obstetrics], *incomptable*, "uncountable" for a pulse [too weak to take], *constater*, "to observe" in common vocabulary, "to certify" [that death has occurred] in medical-legal terminology (a branch present as such in the lexicon of the novels), or even *matières* "contents" [as in a table of contents] or "feces."

Even in the passages where these terms are the most numerous, they never reach the point of transforming the text, even a little bit, into an anatomical, clinical, or therapeutic discourse. These words are no more there for their own sake than the slang, specialized languages, or scientific vocabulary. They are one of the resonances of the orchestration.

With regard to vocabulary, the categories enumerated above, and others on the same level, we can expect the prominent display of certain recurrences, some circumstantial, others as traces of preoccupations or obsessions. We should also pay attention to the sometimes deliberate choice of "dated" terms. The vocabulary of medicine, in particular that of nosology and therapeutics, is more developed than the others. Without doubt certain of the terms used by Céline were already out of use in his time. But he himself chooses sometimes, occasionally by making corrections, terms that are no longer those of the medicine of his time. It is not insignificant that he corrects *"vieillarde cancéreuse"* [cancerous old woman] into *néomateuse*.[14] Even the description of pain, which itself does not change, can become outdated or lost. One of the most remarkable of Céline's commentaries on the lexicon during the course of the novel is directed at a case of this type. "Excruciating pains . . . the term is no longer in the dictionary 'excruciating.' . . . However, it was a rich term, it evoked the raw, tore away. . . . it stayed in your ear. . . ."[15] In regard to language, Céline makes fire out of all kinds of wood. A word can be of erudite origin, its usage principally reserved for medical discourse. But this takes nothing from the possibilities offered by its signifier ("raw") or by its signified ("to tear away," derived from *ex-*), which will also be lost to language if it becomes outdated, even in the case of a technical usage where it would always be possible to pick it up again.

In casting himself in turn as patient and doctor, Céline makes us admit that this medical vocabulary is as natural to him as popular language and slang. But what is its place in relation to them? Some of the first critics were indignant or astonished at the mixture. How could a medical doctor write in such a vulgar manner? Now the question is rather how a writer who has chosen popular speech as the basis of his language can join with it words from a specialty that novelists who write in conventional language avoid or reduce to a minimum. Popular French is really neither more nor less distant from the medical vocabulary than is written French. There is at least with popular French a territory of encounter or confrontation that written French does not have, the one of body parts and functions that written language disregards. The lexicon of obscenity and scatology, which easily accompany slang and popular speech, has its counterpart in Céline's prose in the medical names of these parts and their functions: *verge* [penis], scrotum, rectum, anus, etc. Without entering into a study of the dialogue that takes place between these series, we can make the preliminary remark that the medical words are certainly in opposition to those of obscenity and scatology, but not in the same way as are literary or philosophical words. If medicine resorts in each case to a term appropriate for it, then it is in the name of therapeutic efficacy that supposes a diagnostic precision and accuracy to the least detail of anatomic designation. In forging a term and in using only it, medicine opposes all terms at the disposal of nonconventional language for the same referent, but it has a justification in reality that is hardly to be contested. After we realize this opposition, we can better appreciate the game Céline plays with innumerable figures of speech. Whoever wants to convince himself can look at pages 213–19 of *Fairy Tale for Another Time, I,* where Céline addresses the reader at length about the cancer of the rectum that perhaps awaits him, and where repetition of the second person makes all escape impossible. *Rectum* is there, along with *tumor, providence bénigne, caillot* [clot], *prélèvement à chaud* [emergency operation to remove something during a crisis] *in vivo,* etc., in order to speak scientifically and impersonally of the implacable reality of the thing. Around them there are other words, charged with reminding the reader that this reality could well be, if the case arises, his own. These are some of the slang equivalents of the rectum: *trou* [hole], *cul* [ass], *fias,* [butt], *oigne* [asshole], *pouët* [buns], etc. A word in the middle of the passage, anatomic in itself, and humorous because of the deformation, can be seen as the point of intersection of both series: the medical and the slang. It is *anu* that achieves the impossible, opposing the intolerable with the ultimate defense, laughter.

In March 1936, while there was talk of censoring Céline's forthcoming novel, he declared to the journalists, "I'm not called Boylesve. I would never decide to write that my buddies strangled each other passionately while kissing deliriously. . . ."[16] Things are more complicated than that. Because we also find in Céline some words that in themselves — by their register, or because they are associated in the form of clichés, or because they create metaphors in a certain tone — belong beyond question to traditional vocabulary, or rather to "literary" convention. It would be in vain to want to inspect all the ways this language appears in his prose. The following examples, which can be found in all of Céline's novels, regardless of their date, are only given to define the layer of vocabulary called "literary," with the intent of marking its presence in his language. It begins on the elevated fringe of the written language, made of words that are less used because they double other ones that are equally correct and more widely understood. Verbs like *fustiger* [flay], *importuner* [bother], *ourdir* [hatch as with a scheme], *regimber* [grumble or balk], *dilacérer* [tear to pieces, rip apart], nouns like *cohort, phalange, sujétion, promptitude*, and adjectives like *suprême, sublime, ultime* [ultimate], are enough to give an idea of the first stage of this research. We would find the syntactic equivalents in the usage of the *passé simple*, or in turns of phrase such as "his hair became all light," or "it was a place for dreamy thought." One step further and we come to words that are "poetic," either because of the thematic value of the realities they designate (chasm, abyss, shadow, gloom), or because they are "noble" equivalents, once mandatory in poetry, to common words (mire, waves, skiff, firmament, lyre, missive). This "literary" vulgate is also made of automatisms in which the metaphor is transformed into cliché: the dark day, the unchained elements, the unleashing of the storm, the night draws to a close, the sun shines, the fragrant flowers, the vertiginous depth: all expressions that are found, literally, here or there in Céline.

What we want to know, of course, is what he does with them, whether these words are perceived as voluntary or involuntary usages, and how they are inserted into context. As we shall see, they are there as so many virtual effects of plurivocalism. But we have to begin by picking out of the text those words that sometimes pass by almost unnoticed, so trapped are they in a web the preponderance of which remains popular French and slang.

There still remains to be distinguished in these novels a lexicon of abstraction, the relative importance and in general the specificity of which has to be measured case by case. A tendency to "philosophize," if not toward philosophy, a taste for "general ideas," is always perceptible in Céline, especially in the letters to certain intellectual correspondents such as Elie Faure, or in his speech, "Homage to Zola." This tendency surfaces in the novels in the form of maxims, particularly in the *Journey to the End of the Night*, but also in words disseminated all through the text, because this thought has its language, that, lacking even remotely defined notions, is made of words the abstraction and generality of which suggest profundity. Here it is no longer a matter of vulgar words but of high sounding words: life, man, happiness, destiny, society, history, etc. More important, Céline most often outdoes their pretension to philosophical status by writing them with a capital letter. This proliferation of capital letters is a minor but not negligible aspect of Céline's language. In his case any word, even one not belonging to the traditional vocabulary of reflection, is capitalized for emphasis as soon as the referent it designates leaves the domain of that which we can grasp by hand or eye. The phenomenon is found in other writers as well, in Artaud, for example, or in Flaubert, whose manuscripts cause editors the same problems in this regard as Céline's.[17] Once the writing tic is manifest (the elimination of certain capital letters in the manuscripts of the texts printed under Céline's and his secretary's control shows that there is not always a deliberate choice) for the reader of the novels, the capital letter increases the philosophical resonance of the words it begins, or even provides one, reinforcing a certain tone. Céline is the first to use these means to characterize — and set at a distance — the discourse of certain pompous or sententious characters (the father or Courtial in *Death on the Installment Plan*). But it remains for us to evaluate all the cases where he uses them on his own account as a narrator. This research would be connected to ideological study by its emphasis on the display of the words most designated for attention on this level, but would above all study the language the writer selects and the results he derives from his choice. Furthermore, after having recognized the existence of this abstract vein, we need to know how it is combined with the rest, in particular with popular language, which from this point of view has perhaps to be distinguished from slang. The latter has little to do with the high-sounding words, but that does not mean that popular language ignores or is repelled by them. As concrete and full of imagery as it most often is, popular language still talks occasionally of *life, destiny, happiness*, etc., but within boundaries that Céline doubtlessly surpasses so well that even the words that were a part of it end up being out of place.

These literary and philosophical lexicons are linked to a tradition, and are easily spotted. There is one last lexicon, which is more difficult to define, and that has not been identified yet in Céline's language — it plays, however, an important role. It refers less to texts than to an oral discourse; it is defined less by its object than by a tone. Everyone can feel what there is in common in calling a boy *impish, cunning* or *cowardly*, or saying that a young girl *sings ravishingly*, that a man *is a charmer* or *"what a superior mind!"* or speaking of *ladies' sentiments*, of *certain serious habits*, of *hillevesees* [nonsense], or *to be up to mischief*. These words and turns of phrase, which all appear, among a hundred others, in the vocabulary of the narrator, are those of the people of whom it used to be said that they had "some education," or even that they were "members of high society" [*du monde*].

This vocabulary certainly is a world [*monde*], even if it is difficult to specify its contours. We would have to strive to refine its characteristics and tendencies in order to explain the plurivocalic effects they produce. But first we must at least provide signposts by inspecting some of the linguistic forms it takes and by linking it to the characters of the novels who are its speakers, in this case mostly women.

For reasons that perhaps have to do with world view or ideology, this vocabulary contains a remarkable proportion of adjectives, beginning with a series of which the repeated final vowel ends by sounding a little like its fundamental tone: *badin, gandin, gourgandin, mutin, coquin, gredin, mâtin, taquin, chagrin* [jocular, dandy, womanizing, roguish, knavish, rascally, cunning, teasing, despondent], etc. But also: *charmant, exquis, adorable, espiègle, allègre, ravissant, futé, preste, guilleret, gracieux, malicieux* [charming, exquisite, adorable, impish, cheerful, ravishing, crafty, nimble, perky, gracious, malicious], etc., on the one hand; *commun* [common], *grossier* [crude], *malfaisant* [evil], *méprisable* [despicable], *malhonnête* [dishonest], *insolent, criminel*, etc., on the other. These words and all those that follow are to be found without exception in the mouth of the narrator. This abstract vein can be followed across other word categories: nouns (a pretty little face, the elite, an infamy, an enchantment, a character, tricks, [human] beings, munificence, etc.), and among them a particular series of abstract nouns used in the plural (delicacies, sumptuousnesses, graciousnesses, etc.); in addition, this particular French has its favorite turns and figures: exclamation, hyperbole (such a woman is *so supple! the most supple! suppleness itself, what suppleness!*), the concession with reservations (a severe punishment surely, fair enough, I admit it, but just), and the euphemism that weakens derogatory labels in order to make them terms of affection (knave, rogue, rascal, scoundrel). It has its threshold of familiarity (fun, skirt-chaser), its own curses (*mâtin* [sly dog]!), and its insults (hooligan! simpleton! boor! coward! odious character! scoundrel!) This is a language in which one can designate or qualify, if not every individual, thing, or circumstance, then at least those individuals with whom those who speak this language have anything to do, the things with which they are familiar, and the circumstances in which they might find themselves.

Céline himself situates this language when he speaks of "*bel usage* [good usage or social graces], or of "good manners,"[18] because this language is inseparable from politeness. It is in words the equivalent of *savoir-vivre* in behavior. To the division between that which is done and that which is not, corresponds that which is said and that which is not, and, in both cases, there is still the matter of how. It all goes back, it seems, to a certain milieu and a certain epoch, the Parisian bourgeoisie before 1914. This language is above all the one used by the customers of secondhand stores and lace shops of the Choiseul Passage, who are also the strollers of Avenue du Bois. There is a memory that surfaces at least three times and gives at once the tone, a representative sample of those who speak this language, and an indication of circumstances in which it became known to Céline as a child: "the flower fights from before the war. . . . Avenue du Bois, which it then was! officers! purebreds, stamping! and what baby carriages! what lady customers! what a brawl of carnations! lilacs! roses! that the evening after the fight you had a yard-thick layer of petals on the Avenue! from the Étoile to the Port Dauphine! you could say: the rich nation! . . . officers, pretty women and flowers! . . . true roses, true azaleas, narcissus . . . and all the lady customers from the 'Passage' . . . our customers . . . Mom recognized all her guipures, her little veins, her tulles, her 'mob caps' . . . all her things 'all handmade' . . . with those refinements that no longer exist. . . ."[19]

When, in 1960, a young filmmaker comes and offers to transpose the *Voyage* to cinema, Céline advises him to film a prologue, and what he suggests for it are the same women strollers, talking this time, and the same flower fight.[20] In *North*, when the old Prussian Countess wanted to show her Parisian habits, the same memory appears, in the middle of some others.[21] This resurgence is not by accident. The language of good manners is surely that of those women, their milieu, and their epoch, one of the aspects of the world that in 1914 tumbled into the past. The Passage and the Avenue du Bois are surely the places where we can imagine the young Ferdinand recording their conversations. Thirty years later, in the Germany of the Apocalypse, he does not tire of rehearing snatches of it from the mouths of some "escapees" from that time: Madame Bonnard, Madame von Seckt, Countess Tulff-Tcheppe, etc. It is no accident either, if the foreign women on the one hand, and Ferdinand's mother on the other, are linked to these evocations, and to the language from which it is inseparable. Because, if these natural *porte-parole* [spokeswomen, literally carriers of the word] are women from a certain Parisian bourgeoisie, their language is also that which can be used as a password to be adopted, or merely tolerated, by this milieu. No better means for the petty bourgeois who wanted to distinguish themselves from the people, than to make this language of good manners their own, thanks to the context their activity provides them. Everything supports the supposition that it was Ferdinand's parents who relayed this language to him, each one in his own register. Of all of Céline's types of French, it is one of the most representative and among those that play the most with the dominant popular and slang characteristic of his language.

As the most accentuated mark of a literary language, Céline's archaisms have until now been mainly studied in opposition to this dominant characteristic.[22] To use a word that has left contemporary usage, to give contemporary reality the name of a reality several centuries past, is to demonstrate knowledge of texts past, and thus to leave the language of the present, made to express life nowadays, that popular language and better yet slang wants to be. Seen then as an effect of research and of rarity, the archaism is opposed to the fiction of spontaneity tied to oral and popular language. If we take this language to be the natural language of the narrator, and not only the center from which he has chosen to draw most often, we are led to look upon the archaism as a breach in convention and a revelation, both of desire for contrast and elegance, and, unknown to Céline, of his deepest tendencies. But if we take a diachronic point of view, then the archaism appears as the witness of the language's past. Symmetrically, the most recent infatuations and trials are also present in Céline's text in the form of fad words and neologisms. To associate words no longer in use with those that have just come into use, and indeed are not yet in use but only trials, is, in this perspective of language history, to want to hold both ends of the chain at the same time.

In *Journey to the End of the Night*, the archaisms only existed as traces. In *Death on the Installment Plan*, they were often associated with the Legend of King Krogold and thus justified. They flourished without any such justification under Céline's pen during the years just before the war.[23] The tone of the prewar novels is given in *Guignol's Band*, where some pages take on the allure of pastiche, for example, the one that gathers together words or constructs such as *valiant exploits, no one fails nor concedes without finding himself covered with bruises, except a touch of love, a twinge of mercy, a sojourn to be endured, appear in court* [*comparoître* – dated spelling], *may he perish a thousand deaths and then be resurrected to a thousand pains, as tenacious as boiling pitch*, etc.[24] Or again: *courteous estimate, a miraculous trill of a flute (which) bursts forth, minstrel, trouveres, baladin* [a wandering entertainer], etc.[25] But without going this far, we can by simple reading of the four last novels easily gather an ample harvest of archaisms of all kinds: of orthography (in which he shows a predilection for the *y*: *cy, joye* [*joie* in Modern French], etc.), of forms (*fol*), of words (*oyer* [to listen], *choir* [to fall], *gésir* [to be laying down], *béer* [to gape], *oindre* [anoint], to keep to the verbs), of turns of phrase (*force baisers* [heavy kisses], *bouter hors* [to push out]), and finally of grammatical usages.[26] As examples of the latter we will cite two that interfere with other sectors of Céline's language: to the popular usage of the negation reduced to its second term, *pas*, corresponds the archaism of negation with the lone *ne* (*as, ne le sais-je!* [ah, don't I know it!]). But archaism and popular language both expand the use of the prepositions à and *de* beyond the normal. Moreover, it is clear enough that Céline's archaisms, are, on the one hand, constantly mixed, sometimes inextricably, with markings from very different types of French, and, on the other hand, far from worry about authenticity or pertinence (see, for example, the constructions quoted above: *no one fails or concedes* and *tenacious as boiling pitch*). The point is not to recover a state of language in its truth, but to evoke it, and then only by approximation.

In spite of certain appearances, this state is less the Old French of the Middle Ages than that of the Renaissance and of the sixteenth century. These spellings, these words, these turns of phrase, are in effect those of the poets Céline quotes: Christine de Pisan, Charles d'Orléans, perhaps more than others Villon, whose turns of phrase Céline echoes in passing, but also Louise Labé, Marot du Bellay, without counting Nostradamus. Céline could have become familiar with this sometimes "home-cooked"

Old French from the children's magazines of his epoch, which affected the style of the Middle Ages.[27] He could have found it again in the volume of *Historians and Chroniclers of the Middle Ages* published in 1938 by the Bibliothèque de la Pléiade.[28] But the note Céline sounds by intervals is above all the one that brings back to our ear the best known poems of the fifteenth and sixteenth centuries. This note is not only linked to words and turns of phrase, but to certain particularities of word order and rhythm as well. Céline does not invoke Villon's name in vain. When he writes in *Bagatelles pour un massacre*, "the master of the genre, without contest, is Villon,"[29] the genre in question is the transposition to the written of "living, spoken" language. But at the same time that he found in Villon a distant model of his work in this field — without taking thematic conjunctions into account — Céline has acquired from Villon and some others a taste for an old form of French. It is the one for which Julien Gracq proposes the beautiful name of "between-two-tongues."[30] Existing midway between the sometimes radical strangeness of Old French and the familiarity of modern French, Céline's archaisms never really pose a problem of comprehension. The contemporary reader perceives them in passing without having to stop and translate. At the most he occasionally hesitates slightly; the meaning, instead of settling, keeps a slight waver, as with certain words from slang or from specialized languages. Sometimes with the aid of the context, of the root of the word or of its form, we grasp enough meaning to be able to continue, and what we lose in precision, we gain in an opening up of another field, in this case, our language's past. There is in it a fringe that is half obscured, and yet half lit, or which can light up and revive. This is where Céline's archaisms come from.

In itself the archaism in a literary text is a stylistic trait, the trait of writing in a restricted sense of the word, as well as of language. It creates effects of contrast with the context, of parody or ambiguity, and those by Céline have already given rise to various interpretations on one level or another to which we shall return. But what is inseparable from language is the taste one might have for it, and the pleasure it can give the writer as well as the reader.[31] Readers who disregard this between-two-tongues, or who do not take to it, lack an auditory waveband necessary for completely hearing Céline.

At the other extreme, Céline needs the most present of presents. The same attention to movements of words that led him to record the supposed obsolescence of *excruciant* [excruciating] is found in the attention paid to noting the appearance and the vogue of other words, while he writes each novel. Thus *North* and *Rigadoon* conserve the trace of the ephemeral *scoubidou*, launched in 1958 by a song,[32] of *coexistence*, *suspence*, and *abstract*, which draw Céline's attention in the vocabulary of 1958–61. It is not that he has become so caught by the contagion that, without realizing it, he writes the words he hears on the radio, around him, or reads in the press. Each time he uses them, he knows the reason. They are underlined, between quotation marks, or commented on: "Here we are joggling on these platforms with plenty of invisible persons . . . coexistence is said nowadays . . . go ahead then, coexistants! . . ."[33] There is in Céline someone who, just as he picks up a word that French has dropped, is always ready to capture in flight new words that are a part of the language, if only for a time.

Notes

1. Just as Saint-Simon (it is Montherlant who makes the comparison) "lards" his style "with archaisms, trivialities, technical words, invented words, inaccurate terms: there is not a French writer who has carried farther the art of making his own language for himself alone. His [Saint-Simon's] natural style is not properly speaking artificial. It is only conscious, affectionate and deliberate" (*Textes sous une occupation*, in *Essais*, Bibliothèque de la Pléiade, p. 1511). Let us note that in the first edition of this collection (Gallimard, coll. blanche, 1953, p. 187), Montherlant had, without elegance, let slip Céline's name in the following sentence: "His language is to the language of the court that which the language of a Céline is to popular language: it is this and not this" (an omission that made the passage unintelligible). It is true that, politics apart, Montherlant is more sensitive to Céline's style to the artifice than the meaning of the language. (See in 1935 the note "Service inutile" in *Essais*, p. 613, n. 2 (cf. 610). For Montherlant, in this field the whole value is in the exactness of the reproduction. Céline continues to be evoked concerning Saint-Simon and archaisms, this time by Julien Gracq (see below, n. 31).

2. In these pages, the underlined words or expressions are from the text of Céline's novels. They are only given here as examples, and for this reason, they are without references. I keep the quotation marks which Céline used around some of them, at least sporadically.

3. *D'un château l'autre* (Paris: Bibliotèque de la Pléiade, 1957), pp. 34–35.

4. *Nord* (Paris: Bibliotèque de la Pléiade, 1960), pp. 579–80.

5. *Mort à crédit* (Paris: Bibliotèque de la Pléiade, 1936), p. 568.

6. *Voyage au bout de la nuit* (Paris: Bibliotèque de la Pléiade, 1936), p. 372; "en pantaine" means one that has lost its sails and yards.

7. *D'un château l'autre*, p. 214. Céline's novels offer many other examples of these specialized languages. As soon as the story he tells gives him an occasion, Céline does not fail to amuse himself with words from these vocabularies for the initiated (included in *Guignol's band*, that of esotericism and a certain orientalism).

8. *Mort à crédit*, p. 933.

9. On the character and knowledge of Raoul Marquis, as well as on *Eurêka* and Céline's collaboration on this *revue*, see the note to *Mort à crédit*, Vol. I, pp. 1378–85.

10. This diving-bell competition gives rise to one of the pages with the greatest technico-scientific density of the novel (p. 944).

11. *Féerie pour une autre fois* (Paris: Gallimard, collection blanche, 1952), II, p. 288.

12. *D'un château l'autre*, p. 129.

13. This even when he pretended ignorance. "His 'sycosis' as he called it," he wrote regarding Gorloge's skin disease (*Mort à crédit*, p. 663). *Sycosis* is indeed the name of a skin disease. The usage Céline makes of these medical terms is very complex and merits study for its own sake. Thus when he uses in its specialized sense a word which belongs also to the general vocabulary, he sometimes indicates it by quotation marks ("you take away their 'tension' [medically you take their blood pressure]," *D'un château l'autre*, p. 4); sometimes he plays on ambiguity ("I love to touch the exquisite place, it's medical," *Féerie pour une autre fois*, I, p. 45).

14. *D'un château l'autre*, p. 61 and variation *a*.

15. *Féerie pour une autre fois*, I, pp. 222–23.

16. Note to *Mort à crédit, Romans*, Vol. I, p. 1398.

17. See C. Gothot-Mersch, édition of *Bouvard et Pécuchet* (Gallimard, Folio Collection, 1979), 425–426.

18. *Féerie pour une autre fois*, I, p. 270; II, p. 223. Cf. Cascade's words in *Guignol's Band*, I, p. 127: "Shit! . . . It's the end of good manners! Bitchiness in boots!"

19. *Féerie pour une autre fois*, II, p. 151.

20. "Le Voyage au cinéma," in *Romans*, Vol. I, p. 1114.

21. *Nord*, p. 541.

22. For *Journey to the End of the Night* see J.-L. Boissieu, "Quelques effets 'littéraires' ou archaisants dans *Voyage au bout de la nuit*," in Y. de La Quérière, *Céline et les mots*, Chapter IV, pp. 66–78. For the three last novels, A. Montaut, *L'Ambiguité de la subversion formelle chez Céline*, Chapter II, pp. 82–127.

23. In particular in the correspondence with Théophile Briant (for example in a letter of 9 December 1938) and in the pamphlets. On this last point see Ph. Muray, *Céline*, p. 148.

24. *Guignol's band* (Paris: Gallimard, collection blanche, 1952), I, p. 25.

25. Ibid. p. 137.

26. There is a description and a systematic classification of these archaisms in A. Montaut, op. cit., pp. 85ff.

27. Note to *Mort à crédit, Romans*, Vol. I, pp. 1392–93.

28. In June–July, 1944, when Céline is being held in Baden-Baden, this volume was, along with Ronsard's poetry, among those he asks Karl Epting to send to him (F. Gibault, *Céline*, Vol. III, p. 27).

29. *Bagatelles pour un massacre* (Paris: Denoël, 1937), p. 218.

30. "Novempopulanie," *Nouvelle Revue Française*, September 1980, p. 8.

31. In this regard we must quote another text by J. Gracq in which, in spite of the ending which is something of a witticism, he shows himself sensitive to this meaning of "idiom" in Céline: "Twice at a century's interval, Saint-Simon (and more rarely) Chateaubriand, we see *idiom* for an instant burst the congealed crust of language. An abrupt, budding [*verdissant*: greening] vocabulary, from an uncured speck of hide, which still smells of the feudal pig-wallows and offshoots of Old French. Almost all other writers have written by the book. Perhaps afterwards we must count Céline, but it is often less a debacle of the written language than an accident of flushing everything down the drain [*tout-à-l'égout*: a sewer system in which the excrement goes directly into the pipes]" (*Lettrines*, José Corti, 1967, p. 152).

32. *Rigodon* (Paris: Bibliotèque de la Pléiade, 1969), p. 718 and n. 1.

33. Ibid., p. 832. For *abstrait*, see *Nord*, p. 466, *Rigodon*, p. 850. For *suspense*, *Rigodon*, pp. 799, 855.

Louis-Ferdinand Céline's Novels: From Narcissism to Sexual Connection

William K. Buckley*

> "Ah, Ferdinand . . . as long as you live you will aways search for the secret of the universe in the loins of women!"
>
> *(L'Eglise).*

> . . . the female mystery doesn't reside between the thighs, it's on another wave-length, a much more subtle one
>
> *(Castle to Castle).*

"The psychoanalytic concept of narcissism," says Russell Jacoby in his study *Social Amnesia* (1975), "captures the reality of the bourgeois individual; it expresses the private regression of the ego into the id under the sway of public domination. . . . it comprehends the dialectical isolation of the bourgeois individual—dialectical in that the isolation that damns the individual to scrape along in a private world derives from a public and social one. The energy that is directed toward oneself, rather than toward others, is rooted in society, not organically in the individual. . . . The mechanism of this shift is not the least the society that puts a premium on the hardening of each individual—the naked will to self-preservation."[1] This *naked will* to self-preservation, this *hardening* of oneself is an apt description of most "protagonists" in our modern novels.[2] These terms are an especially good description of Céline's main character in his first two novels: the young Ferdinand.

Still creating their storm of interest and influence after fifty years, Céline's *Journey to the End of the Night* (1932) and *Death on the Installment Plan* (1936) are good examples of modern novels that use a narrator who expresses his hardened feelings over both his narcissistic and crushed ego-ideals, and over his careful love choices. Ferdinand, like so many in modern fiction, is a character who has withdrawn his libido from the outer world because his contact with that world has brought mostly economic and emotional disaster; and, in defense, he has directed his libido to his ego. Major American scholarship on Céline has not explored the sexual behavior of Céline's characters as closely as it needs to do. Of course there have been important discussions of Céline's views on sex by many. McCarthy gives us a rather negative assessment of the author's views in his biography *Céline* (1975),[3] as does J. H. Matthews in his book, *The Inner Dream: Céline as Novelist* (1978).[4] In comparing Céline's views on sex to Baudelaire's views in *Journaux intimes*, McCarthy claims that

*Reprinted with permission from *Studies in the Novel* 18, no. 1 (Spring 1986): 51–65. Revised version.

Journey shows women as "predatory" (p. 69), that Céline suggests "women need to destroy men, because there is a link between female sexuality and cruelty" (p. 69), and that, in the final analysis — because of the behavior of Musyne and Lola — "sex turns out to be disgusting" (p. 71) for Ferdinand, reflecting Céline's personal view that the male loses himself in orgasm with a woman because he is "weary" to have done "with himself" (p. 70). J. H. Matthews offers an equally negative view of sex in *Death on the Installment Plan*. He points to several episodes in the novel which support his point that sex "brings no consolation of any kind, no sense of release. It is a heightened form of terror. . . . Ferdinand's sexual contacts revitalize the cliché that represents sex as a form of death and likens the ecstasy of orgasm to dying" (p. 77). Gorloge, who early in the novel invites the young Ferdinand to engage her in oral sex, and her theft of a jewel from the young boy's pocket; Gwendoline, the sex partner Ferdinand meets after crossing the Channel, and whom Matthews calls the *vagina dentata*; Nora's desperate actions with Ferdinand at Meanwell College; the astonishing scene between Antoine and Gorloge to which Ferdinand and his friend Robert are voyeurs: all these scenes are examples of what Matthews calls Céline's linking of violence and eroticism. Matthews further maintains that even masturbation is "marked by terrorism" in this novel (p. 79), especially when the boys at the English boarding school cruelly beat and masturbate the retarded Jongkind for getting penalties during a soccer match. Therefore since at "no time in his life has Ferdinand felt capable of trusting women enough to love any of them," masturbation becomes the "significant feature" of his early life (pp. 79–80). "It is a direct expression of his profound need to change his destiny in a world ruled by violence and predatory sexuality, where [Ferdinand] is alternately victim and pariah" (p. 80). I agree with Matthews that in most of these scenes "tenderness has no place" (p. 77). One could argue, for example, that Gorloge's seduction of the little Ferdinand is an example of emotional exploitation born out of the economic brutalities which exist between the classes in Paris. But Antoine's attempt to copulate with Gorloge, using butter, while Ferdinand and Robert look on and laugh, is an illustration of common but secret sexual hilarities. Ferdinand's laughter in this scene, and our mix of laughter and uncomfortable surprise, is to free us from pompous judgment, to suspend our surprise in humor — much as Chaucer does in his tales on sex. Furthermore, I believe that Ferdinand's experience with Nora, as I will show, is the exception to what Matthews and McCarthy call the predatory nature of sex in Céline's novels. In fact, his feelings over Nora are very exceptional indeed, for they begin Ferdinand's emotional education, his learning to see women as affirmations of beauty and life.

In her *Céline and His Vision* (1967), Erika Ostrovsky sees Céline as debunking sex, but for a very special reason: "Céline tends to blacken most descriptions" of sexual gratification, but in a "spirit of mockery," because the author "finds the business of 'I lo-o-ve you' vulgar, heavy-handed, and

cheaply sentimental."[5] As a result, she says, Céline intends to show us that
eroticism is also "quite frequently linked to violence" (p. 53): witness
Hilda, the sixteen-year-old, who waits for troop trains in *Castle to Castle*,
Frau Frucht, addicted to sexual perversion, in *Castle to Castle*, Ferdinand's escape from a brawl with women on board the *Bragueton* in
Journey, or Céline's comment in *North* that the more cities burn the more
crazy for sex women become.[6] Ostrovsky is quick to point out, however,
that Céline can also be quite positive about sex, can even see sex as
regenerative. She points to the author's descriptions of Lola, Molly,
Madelon, and Sophie in *Journey*, Nora in *Death on the Installment Plan*,
and Virginia in *Pont de Londres* — all characters reflecting, perhaps,
Céline's comment in a letter to Eveline Pollet: "I love the physical
perfections of women almost to the point of madness. It's a truth I reveal
to you. It governs all the others."[7] Moreover, Ostrovsky comments on
Céline's astonishingly positive description of Sophie in *Journey*, that "if
anywhere in Céline's work there is a glimpse of hope and beauty, of sun
and joy, it is in the sight of such women . . . only the physical perfection of
a woman, an animal, a gesture, can offer affirmation or a momentary
respite from horror" (p. 125).

Wayne Burns and Gerald Butler go even further in their positive
estimations of Céline's treatment of sex. In his essay *"Journey to the End of
the Night:* A Primer to the Novel," (from James Flynn's *Understanding
Céline* [Seattle, Washington: Genitron Press, 1984]), Burns says that
"Through loving the woman's body — Sophie's, Tania's, Molly's, even
Madelon's — [Ferdinand] comes to love the woman herself. Much as Céline
would have disliked having Ferdinand compared with Mellors (Céline
once described *Lady Chatterley's Lover* as 'a gamekeeper's miserable prick
for six hundred and fifty pages') Ferdinand's attitude towards women is
essentially Lawrentian in that he comes to the woman herself through her
body" (p. 86). Burns also reminds us of Céline's long "lyrical description"
of Sophie in *Journey*.[8] In his essay "The Feeling for Women in Céline and
His American Counterparts," (also from *Understanding Céline*), Gerald
Butler not only maintains that Céline's view of women is one of adoration
when compared to the way women are seen in Miller and Kerouac, but
also "that it is *not* true," as Julia Kristeva claims (in her chapter on Céline
entitled "Females Who Can Wreck the Infinite," from her book *Powers of
Horror: An Essay on Abjection*)[9] that Céline's fiction "shows all women as
of only two kinds: desexualized and delightful on the one hand and sexual
and terrifying on the other, so that beauty is what wards off the sexual" (p.
142). "Sophie," Butler says, "is both sexual and, in her sexuality, a miracle
of delight for Ferdinand" (p. 142). Her "presence and Ferdinand's reaction
to it is enough to give the lie to the 'heroism' of Robinson that is the
epitome of that bitterness and 'sense of superiority' and 'heaviness' that the
world. . . . teaches" (p. 156). And in his essay "The Meaning of
the Presence of Lili in Céline's Final Trilogy,"[10] he says that Lili is "put

forth in the novels as a guiding light for humanity," that even "her animal qualities, in the positive sense that Céline gives to 'animal' " (and here Butler means Lili is on the same "wave-length" as animals—she tunes in only those who are helpless) "do not detract from her comparison to a heroine from Dickens, for Lili's 'heart' does not exclude the 'animal' but seems to be profoundly connected with it. If that is so, then all the sexuality of human beings that Céline does not at all present in these novels in a favorable light is not an expression of animality in the sense that Lili is like an animal. Rather, the implication, the message for human beings is that they should have real animality above all by having hearts, as Lili does" (pp. 183–84).

These are the important discussions of Céline's view of sexual feeling. My intention here is not to discuss Dr. Destouches' views on sex and love, interesting and shadowy as this topic is turning out to be. (See, for example, Céline's own definition of love and sex in Marc Hanrez's *Céline* [Paris: Gallimard, 1961].)[11] Rather, my intention is two-fold: first, to describe how the young Ferdinand came to feel that women are regenerative, worthy of trust, and beautiful (how he learned about what Ostrovsky, Burns, and Butler are calling the *positive* aspects of sexual experience); and second, how the older Ferdinand came to realize that the sheer naked force of his will and the hardening of his heart would not help him be less narcissistic, would not help him gain sexual satisfaction. My goal is to open a more detailed investigation into those scenes of Céline's novels which describe modern sexual behavior, to look more closely at the sexual needs, desires, and secrets of Céline's characters.

In *Death on the Installment Plan*, young Ferdinand, already hardened to real connection from his brutal experiences in Paris as the son of a mother and father who want him to be a success, retains an erotic fantasy for Nora, the wife of an English school master. He has been sent by his parents to Meanwell College, in England, in order to learn English so that when he returns to Paris he will start his business career off on the right foot. Badgered by an embittered and humiliated father, watching his mother work herself to death in their lace and furniture shop, and seduced by their female customers, Ferdinand is a tight-lipped adolescent, unable to connect with anyone, and full of childhood memories that are violent and sad. He is a classic self-preservative personality. And in this novel his masturbation preserves gratification in fantasy. He compliments his fantasies for Nora this way: "I can still see her. . . . I can bring back her image whenever I please. At the shoulders her silk blouse forms lines, curves, miracles of flesh, agonizing visions, soft and sweet and crushing. . . . The kid that came around to lap me up had his money's worth on Sunday night. . . . But I wasn't satisfied, it was her I wanted. . . . Beauty comes back at you in the night . . . it attacks you, it carries you away . . . it's unbearable . . . I was soft in the head, from jerking off on visions. . . . The less we had for meals, the more I masturbated. . . ."[12] Ego regresses into id under the power of parental domination, fantasy masturbation, and the sheer weight of poverty at the bankrupt English boarding school. Ferdinand's ego-libido creates Nora as his "object-choice." In one scene he masturbates with a school friend, while thinking of Nora, and, as the angry narcissist, fuels his mild sadism with attacks on sentimentality in love. *At the same time,* however, his attack on sentiment exhibits a deep desire for real connection, and this is what gives this novel a complexity rarely found even in our best modern British and American fiction.

> We did each other up brown . . . I was ruthless, I couldn't stop, my imagination kept winding me up . . . I devoured Nora in all her beauty. . . . I'd have taken all her blood, every drop . . . Still it suited me better to ravage the bed, to chew up the sheets . . . than to let Nora or any other skirt take me for a ride. . . . To hell with all that stinking mush! . . . Yak! yak! I love you. I adore you! Sure, sure! . . . Why worry, it's a party. Bottoms up! It's so lovely! It's so innocent! . . . I'd wised up when I was a kid! Sentiment, hell! Balls! . . . I clutched my oil can. . . . You won't catch me dying like a sucker . . . with a poem on my lips. (pp. 239–40)

When Nora does, at last, come to Ferdinand's room, out of her own mad loneliness and lack of connection to her husband, and abruptly flattens him out with her caresses, giving him, as Céline says, "an avalanche of tenderness," young Ferdinand does surprisingly well in responding. In bed with her he is beginning to reject, I believe, his narcissism — if only for a moment:

> I try to soothe her pain, to make her control herself . . . I caulk wherever I can . . . I knock myself out . . . I try my best . . . I try the subtlest tricks . . . But she's too much for me . . . She gives me some wicked holds . . . The whole bed is shaking . . . She flails around like crazy . . . I fight like a lion . . . My hands are swollen from clutching her ass! I want to anchor her, to make her stop moving. There. That's it. She's stopped talking. Christ almighty! I plunge, I slip in like a breeze! I'm petrified with love . . . I'm one with her beauty . . . I'm in ecstacy . . . I wriggle. . . . On her face I go looking for the exact spot next to her nose . . . the one that tortures me, the magic of her smile." (p. 266)

In feeling "love," and in "looking for the exact spot" which tortures him, Ferdinand replaces his fantasy of Nora with her reality. Unfortunately Nora "breaks loose" from Ferdinand, and runs from the school to make her way to a bridge, where she will jump into a river to her death, a "nightgown fluttering in the wind" (p. 267). This whole scene is charged with the helpless desperation of human behavior. "I knew it," says Ferdinand, "she's off her rocker! . . . Dammit to hell . . . Could I catch her? . . . But it's none of my business . . . There's nothing I can do . . . The whole thing is beyond me . . . I listen . . . I look out through the hall door . . . to see if I can see her on the waterfront . . . She must be down by now . . . There she is again . . . still screaming . . . 'Ferdinand! Ferdinand!' . . . her screams cut through the sky . . ." (p. 267). It is Céline's intention, as Wayne Burns has pointed out, "to make the reader hear cries he has never heard before; to make him realize that there is no end to these cries (in either time or circumstance), for they are cries which cannot be remedied by religion or philosophy or morality — much less by the paltry palliatives of social reform or even social revolution."[13]

Ferdinand does go after her, but feels helpless and endangered as he stands on the bridge with the retarded boy both he and Nora had been taking care of at the school. We hear more of her pleas as she "flits" like a "butterfly" from one street lamp to the next. Sirens and whistles blow, rescue squads arrive, but nothing has helped. She is a "little white square in the waves. . . . caught in the eddies. . . . passing the breakwater!" (p. 268). It is Céline's intention, as he later has Ferdinand say in *Journey to the End of the Night*, "to go deeper and hear other cries that I had not heard yet or which I had not been able to understand before, because there seems always to be some cries beyond those which one has heard."[14] This need to hear the "cries" of humanity is not the impulse of a narcissist, for he is not, as Freud says in "On Narcissism: An Introduction" (1914), "plainly seeking" himself "as a love-object."[15] Nor is Ferdinand seeking a Nora as males would seek women to "save," those who would fulfill the male's desire to believe that "without him she would lose all hold on respectability."[16] Even though Nora's behavior could trigger the *narcissistic* impulse in Ferdinand to rescue her, "justified by her untrustworthy temperament sexually and by the danger to her social position" (as Ferdinand might say it), it does not do so, neither in fantasy nor in reality.[17] For there has been no "skill in argument" to win Nora, to save her from Meanwell College, no real seduction on Ferdinand's part. In fact, his *self-preservative* impulse remains defiant and hostile after her death, for he fears he will take the rap for it. Freud has it that "the attitude of defiance in the 'saving' phantasy far outweighs the tender feeling in it, the latter being usually directed towards the mother. . . . in the rescue phantasy, that is, he identifies himself completely with the father. All the instincts, the loving, the grateful, the sensual, the defiant, the self-assertive and independent — all are gratified in the wish to be *the father of himself*. . . . When in a dream a man rescues a women from the water, it means that he makes her a mother . . . his own mother."[18] Yet Nora is not rescued. The drowning is no *phantasy*. And Ferdinand, after hearing Nora's cries and feeling he was sure to get caught and blamed, runs back to the school to wake Nora's old husband out of his own torpor. The scene we see then is painful: the old man, drunk on the floor, making masturbatory gestures with the flesh on his stomach; and Ferdinand, observing, and finally giving up, leaving to pack his bags for Paris "at the crack of dawn" (p. 269).

Despite the suicide, both Nora and Ferdinand had freed themselves, momentarily, from their environments, fixed as they were to their economic realities: Ferdinand to his petit-bourgeois Paris background and Nora to her bankrupt English middle-class. Without moralizing or sentimentalizing their encounter, Céline shows us Nora and Ferdinand achieving a moment of difficult tenderness. "It seems very evident," Freud says in "On Narcissism," that "one person's narcissism has a great attraction for those others who have renounced part of their own narcissism and are seeking after object-love."[19] As an adult, Nora has rejected part of her narcissism, and a kind of vulnerable, nervous, but tender compassion remains. She is no Madame Gorloge, who *orders* Ferdinand to take his clothes off and make love to her. "She grabs me by the ears . . . She pulls me down to mother nature . . . She bends me with all her might. . . . 'Bite me, sweet little puppy . . . Bite into it!' " (p. 180). Ferdinand *plays* "the ardent lover," and charges into her, as he had seen Antoine do when he and Robert were spying on them, "but much more gently" (p. 181). "She squashed me against her tits! She was having a hell of a good time . . . It was stifling. . . . She wanted me to work harder. . . . to be more brutal. . . . 'you're ripping me apart, you big thug! Oh rip me' . . ." (p. 181). Ferdinand did not have to play the "ardent lover" with Nora; nor could their lovemaking be called "ripping." She was not, as he characterized Gorloge, a "vampire" (p. 181). She was a "mirage of charm" (p. 241). Neither was Nora a Gwendoline, Ferdinand's "Greasy Jone" (p. 212), the English fish and chips girl he meets on the docks before finding Meanwell College. "She kept repeating her name. She tapped on her chest . . . Gwendoline! Gwendoline! . . . I heard her all right, I massaged her tits, but I didn't get the words . . . To hell with tenderness . . . sentiment! That stuff is like a family. . . . She took advantage of the dark corners to smother me with caresses. . . . We could have done our business, we'd certainly have had a good time . . . But once we'd had our sleep out, then what?" (pp. 212, 214). "Anyway I was too tired . . . And besides, it was impossible . . . It stirred up my gall . . . it cramped my cock to think of it . . . of all the treachery of things . . . as soon as you let anybody wrap you up. . . . That's all I had on my mind in the little side streets while my cutie was unbuttoning me . . . She had the grip of a working girl, rough as a grater, and not at all bashful. Everybody was screwing me. O well . . ." (p. 215).

Rather, when Ferdinand sees Nora for the first time, he is astonished at his reaction to the *gentleness* in her face: "the special charm she had, that lit up on her face when she was speaking. . . . It intimidated me . . . I saw stars, I couldn't move" (p. 224). Ferdinand's narcissism is under attack by such powerful gentleness, tenderness, and charm because it is responding to it, needing it, and weakened by it in its self-preservative inner life. For all through the Meanwell College scene, Nora will be tending to the needs of a helpless retarded boy. And even though Ferdinand's young narcissism is interested in the idealized Nora — the Nora

of his dreams, the picture of her which helps him adjust to his bitterness —
he still responds, physically to *her*, and not to her manipulations, as he did
with Gorloge and Greasy Jone. This is especially remarkable when you
consider Ferdinand's characterization of himself earlier in the novel:
"you'll never know what obsessive hatred really smells like . . . the hatred
that goes through your guts, all the way to your heart . . . Real hatred
comes from deep down, from a defenseless childhood crushed with work.
That's the hatred that kills you" (p. 144). Even more remarkably, it may be
said that Ferdinand gets a bit of compassion from Nora, learns from her, as
he too walks with the retarded boy Jongkind, who "whines like a dog"
after Nora's death.

> I got to get the brat home . . . I give him a poke in the ass. . . .
> He's worn out from running . . . I push him . . . I throw him . . . He
> can't see a thing without his glasses . . . He can't even see the lamp
> posts. He starts bumping into everything . . . He whines like a dog . . . I
> grab him and pick him up, I carry him up the hill . . . I toss him into his
> bed . . . I run to the old man's door. . . . He blinks a little, his eyelids
> flutter . . . He don't know from nothing . . . 'She's drowning! She's
> drowning!' I yell at him. I repeat it even louder . . . I shout my lungs out
> . . . I make motions . . . I imitate the glug-glug . . . I point down . . .
> into the valley . . . out the window! (pp. 268–69)

Ferdinand's heart and naked self-will are now less hardened to women,
and to those who are victims of biology.

In *Journey to the End of the Night*, Ferdinand, as an adult, is the
eloquent spokesman of revulsion from European colonialism and modern
warfare, the voice of revulsion from our traditional beliefs in brotherhood,
marriage, and love. He does not believe in our modern love, which is, for
him, a "poodle's chance of attaining the infinite" (p. 4). His travels in the
novel from the front lines of World War I, to Paris, to New York City and
Detroit, to Africa, and back to Paris, have given him an anti-idealistic
view of human behavior. "The great weariness of life," he says near the end
of the novel, "is maybe nothing but the vast trouble we take to remain
always for twenty or forty or more years at a time reasonable beings — so as
not to be merely and profoundly oneself, that is to say, obscene, ghastly,
and absurd" (p. 416). His first relationship with a woman in this novel is
with Lola, an American nurse who believes in the existence of the soul and
in patriotism, and it is a relationship characterized by a weariness because
Ferdinand believes only in survival after coming home from the war. The
understanding between them is of the body and not the heart because the
hardened heart cannot be trusted during war time. At first he accepts Lola
for what she is, and this is even more a step forward for his self-
preservative personality, even less narcissistic than his relationship with
Nora, for he no longer needs to see the female body in idealized images: "If
I had told Lola what I thought of the war, she would only have taken me

for a depraved freak and she'd deny me all intimate pleasures. So I took good care not to confess these things to her. . . . she hadn't only a fine body, my Lola, — let us get that quite clear at once; she was graced also with a piquant little face and grey-blue eyes, which gave her a slightly cruel look, because they were set a wee bit on the upward slant, like those of a wildcat" (pp. 49–50). When Ferdinand does admit that he is not going back to the front, Lola leaves him, furious at his lack of ideals, and returns to New York. But when Ferdinand arrives in New York, he meets Lola again: "she inquired after my genital lapses and wanted to know if I hadn't somewhere on my wanderings produced some little child she could adopt. It was a curious notion of hers. The idea of adopting a child was an obsession with her. . . . what she wanted was to sacrifice herself entirely to some "little thing." I myself was out of luck. I had nothing to offer her but my own large person, which she found utterly repulsive" (pp. 216–17).

"Really, it's a pity, Ferdinand," Lola says, "that you haven't a little girl somewhere. . . . Your dreamy temperament would go very well in a woman, whereas it doesn't seem at all fitting in a man . . ." (p. 217). This is an interesting description of female narcissism, to which Ferdinand responds with some of his own. Lola's attitude toward Ferdinand is cool, but now she has found a way to object-love: through a child she could possess the ideal of what she thinks Ferdinand should be. The desire Lola has for Ferdinand is not based on a need to tend him, nor is the desire Ferdinand has for Lola based on a need to protect her. There is, therefore, no *anaclitic* object-choice here. Rather, Lola looks at Ferdinand as a lover who should be what she wants him to be. And Ferdinand looks at Lola as a source for adventure in America. Her body to him was an endless source of joy because of its "American contours" (p. 49); she is "a type" that appeals to him (p. 193). Only when Lola gives him money and he takes off for Detroit to work in the Ford plant, do we see a strong and more radical change in Ferdinand's desires for women. The mechanisms involved in a new object-choice — Molly, the Detroit prostitute — are now *more* anaclitic than narcissistic, more dependent than independent, and not so much concerned about being with an "American type." And although Ferdinand's relationship with Molly shows remarkable similarities with Freud's description of male love for the *grande amoureuse* (especially when Freud describes the childhood experiences, the mother-complex, and youthful masturbatory practices of those who have "love for a harlot"),[20] I believe that the following remarks show Ferdinand freeing himself of narcissistic self-absorption, and combining, if only for a time, his feeling of sex *and* tenderness, despite the fact that he is eventually fonder of his longing to "run away from everywhere in search of something" (p. 228).

> I soon felt for Molly, one of the young women in this place, an emotion of exceptional trust, which in timid people takes the place of love. I can remember, as if I'd seen her yesterday, her *gentleness and her*

long white legs, marvellously lithe and muscular and noble. . . . (p. 227, emphasis added)

"Don't go back to the works!" Molly urged me, making it worse. "Find some small job in an office instead. . . . Translating, for example; that's really your line . . . you like books. . . ." She was very sweet giving me this advice; she wanted me to be happy. . . . if only I'd met Molly. . . . Before I lost my enthusiasm over that slut of a Musyne and that horrid little bitch Lola!" (p. 228)

At the end of the Detroit chapter, we begin to understand the causes of Ferdinand's narcissism, and his possible solutions for his troubles:

Molly had been right. I was beginning to understand what she meant. Studies change you, they make a man proud. Before, one was only hovering around life. You think you are a free man, but you get nowhere. Too much of your time's spent dreaming. You slither along on words. That's not the real thing at all. Only intentions and appearances. You need something else. With my medicine, though I wasn't very good at it, I had come into closer contact with men, beasts, and creation. Now it was a question of pushing right ahead, foursquare, into the heart of things. (p. 239)

No longer do we have a character at the mercy of narcissism — like the young Ferdinand — because the narcissist would never want to plunge "into the heart of things." Rather, the adult Ferdinand sees conventional love (i.e. ego-centric romantic love) as doomed to fail in a world where so many people have to scrape and crawl just to get by in a world where Nature's lessons are hard to swallow. "To love is nothing, it's hanging together that's so hard. . . . All our unhappiness is due to having to remain Tom, Dick, and Harry, cost what it may, throughout a whole series of years" (p. 335). And near the end of *Journey,* when Ferdinand visits a bistro for some cheap fun, living, as he says, a "capitalist's existence without capital" (p. 360), we hear him comment with irony and compassion on a female singing group from England, who are bawling out their little songs of love: "They were singing the defeat of life and they didn't see it. They thought it was only love, nothing but love; they hadn't been taught the rest of it, little dears . . ." (p. 361). Ferdinand finally realizes that conventional love, the kind we see today everywhere in American culture, richly narcissistic as it is, fails to help anyone — especially him.

What *would* help he tries to describe for us at the end of the novel, after seeing the death of his friend Robinson at the hands of a romantic lover. Ferdinand says about himself that he is just "a quite real Ferdinand who lacked what might make a man greater than his own trivial life, a love for the life of others" (p. 501). This "love for the life of others" is not at all narcissistic, and it is the kind of love which the young Ferdinand began to achieve when he took Jongkind back to the school the night Nora died, and when he banged on the door to tell Nora's drunken husband that she was dying. It is the kind of love which would allow death to be

> imprisoned in love along with joy, and so comfortable would it be inside there, so warm, that Death, the bitch, would be given some sensation at last and would end up by having as much fun with love as every one else. Wouldn't that be pretty? Ah, wouldn't that be fine? I laughed about it, standing there alone on the river bank, as I thought of all the dodges and all the tricks I'd have to pull off to stuff myself like that full of all-powerful resolves. . . . A toad swollen out with ideals! (p. 505)

But Ferdinand dismisses even these ideas as hopelessly idealistic for a man like him.

What *does* help him are not resolves, but what he finds in Sophie, the Slovak nurse who works at the lunatic asylum with him. In his relationship with Sophie, I believe, we see a man nearly free of narcissism. For Sophie is a women "who still from time to time caught me to her, her whole body strong with the strength of her concern for me and tenderness and a heart full also and overflowing and lovely. I felt the directness of it myself, the *directness of her tender strength*" (p. 507, emphasis added). Male narcissism could never feel the directness of *tender strength* in a woman's body, the kind of strength Ferdinand now finds that he desires to have not only for himself, but also for women. It is this tender strength in a woman's body, this sex-tenderness and a full heart, which can ease the hardened heart and cruel naked self-will of a man.

I have been looking at scenes which show Ferdinand as an individual seeking meaning and sexual fulfillment. Yet there are other kinds of scenes in Céline's novels which do not emphasize individual sexual action, but rather mass sexual action. These scenes are astonishing in their impact, and they need further study — for they show Céline as a keen observer of herd psychology. Questions, therefore, remain to be answered.

For example, what is the function of Céline's *délire*[21] and exaggeration in the episode from *Death on the Installment Plan*, where, in the Bois de Boulogne, Ferdinand and Mirielle make love in public, and an orgy of sexual chaos moves and surges a crowd up to the Arc de Triomphe, where they are routed by "twenty-five thousand" policemen (pp. 35–39)? Or what is the meaning of that scene in *Guignol's Band*, where Virginia and Ferdinand are swept up in chaos of orgy, violence, and delight in the night club, where people are copulating in a jumble of arms and legs? There are similar scenes of mass, violent delight in *North* and *Castle to Castle*. Are these "little narcissistic eccentricities," as Céline labels his writing in *Guignol's Band*? Or are they scenes which tell us to: "Palpitate, damn it! That's where the fun is! . . . Wake up! Come on, hello! You robot crap! . . . Shit! . . . Transpose or it's death! I can't do any more for you. Kiss any girl you please! If there's still time!"[22] Perhaps these mass scenes expose the flimsiness of even our most sophisticated ideas about love, or perhaps they speak of what Céline thought to be some ancient longing in sex, the "quite bestial act" of it, as he said.[23] Ferdinand (and later Céline himself in his World War II trilogy) are both swept up by such sights and crowds in every one of the novels — as if this author, as a physician, wants us to understand that he sees impulses which repeat themselves on a huge scale, as if all of human life is joyously trapped into having such feelings out of the sheer biological surgings of the species, as well as out of our small motivations, brutalized as they are by war and stupid economies. Witness this description from *Castle to Castle*, where in a railway station, Céline's favorite locale for the mob's sexual *délire*, we see that:

> sadness, idleness, and female heat go together . . . and not just kids!
> . . . grown women and grandmothers! obviously the hottest ones, with
> fire in their twats, in those moments when the page turns, when History
> brings all the nuts together and opens its Epic Dance Halls! . . . you've
> got to have phosphorus and hunger so they'll rut and sperm and get with
> it without paying attention! pure happiness! no more hunger, cancer, or
> clap! . . . the station packed with eternity![24]

Are these scenes of mass erotic action in direct conflict with Ferdinand's lessons about tenderness? Or do they, then, in their juxtaposition with Ferdinand's raptures, for example, over Sophie, show us the value of individual, sexual tenderness in the face of "History"?

More comment is also needed on the intriguing relationship between what Ferdinand enjoys about women (their astonishing bodies, their compassion and intelligence, their ability to have orgasms, and their "wave-lengths"), and what Céline says about sex for men ("it allows a guy a few seconds delirium which permits him to communicate with her").[25] How do we square Céline's striking portraits of what women have to offer men with this statement from *Rigadoon* (1969):

> all our theater and literature revolve around coitus, deadly repetition!
> . . . the orgasm is boring, the giants of the pen and silver screen with all
> the ballyhoo and the millions spent on advertising . . . have never
> succeeded in putting it across . . . two three shakes of the ass, and there
> it is . . . the sperm does its work much too quietly, too intimately, the
> whole thing escapes us . . . but childbirth, that's worth looking at! . . .
> examining! . . . to the millimeter! fucking . . . God knows I've wasted
> hours! . . . for two three wiggles of the ass![26]

And lastly, careful analysis is needed on the relationship between what we see as the positive aspects of sexuality in Céline, what Burns calls "the essentially Lawrentian attitude" Ferdinand gains in coming to the woman, and Céline's personal comment that "(coitus is delirium): to rationalize that delirium with precise verbal maneouvers seems to me silly."[27] Perhaps Céline sees deeper than my critical phrase "positive aspects of sexuality" — a "precise verbal maneouver" if ever I could invent one. Just how deeply and broadly Céline sees can be detected as early as 1916, the

date he wrote a poem for his parents in his early twenties, while traveling
to Africa. Even at this early date we see that Céline's vision of sexuality is
much like the "town crier's," who remains perched in a minaret:

> Stamboul est endormi sous la lune blafarde
> Le Bosphore miroite de mille feux argentés
> Seul dans la grande ville mahométane
> Le vieux crieur des heures n'est pas encour couché—
>
> Sa voix que l'écho répète avec ampleur
> Announce à la ville qu'il est déjà dix heures
> Mais par une fenêtre, de son haut minaret
> Il plonge dans un chambre, son regard indiscret
>
> Il reste un moment, muet, cloué par la surprise
> Et caresse nerveux, sa grande barbe grise
> Mais fidèle au devoir, il assure sa voix[28]

This indiscreet glance, which plunges into a bedroom, and yet
remains mute, frozen with surprise, is a remarkable description of our
reaction to the sexual scenes we see in Céline's works, to the young
Ferdinand's sights of sex behavior in *Death on the Installment Plan*, and to
the eventual mature view of sexual behavior in the later novels. For as an
author, Céline continues to sing that our odd sun rises, despite what he has
seen either in or out of his *délire*, and no matter how many times "History
brings all the nuts together and opens its Epic Dance Halls." At every
reading of his novels, Céline continues to plunge us "into the heart of
things."

Notes

1. Russell Jacoby, *Social Amnesia* (Boston: Beacon Press, 1975), p. 44.

2. Works by Dickens, Hardy, Lawrence, Joyce, Woolf, Forster, Sartre, Döblin, Musil,
Faulkner, Hemingway, Fitzgerald, Miller, Kerouac, Roth, Mailer, Kesey, Pynchon, and E.M.
White all contain protagonists who are particularly narcissistic.

3. Patrick McCarthy, *Céline* (New York: Penguin Books, 1975).

4. J. H. Matthews, *The Inner Dream: Céline as Novelist* (New York: Syracuse Univ.
Press, 1978).

5. Erika Ostrovosky, *Céline and His Vision* (New York: New York Univ. Press, 1967), p.
53.

6. Ostrovsky, p. 54; Matthews, p. 136.

7. Letter to Eveline Pollet, February 1933, *L'Herne*, No. 3, p. 96.

8. *Journey to the End of the Night* (New York: New Directions, 1934), pp. 475–76.

9. trans., Leon S. Roudiez (New York: Columbia Univ. Press, 1982).

10. James Flynn, ed., *Understanding Céline* (Seattle, WA: Genitron Press, 1984).

11. Sexual gratification is "a bonus which nature gives to coitus and reproduction: it
allows a guy a few seconds' delirium which permits him to communicate with her" (Marc
Hanrez, "Céline au magnétophone," *Le Nouveau Candide* [November 23, 1961]), p. 14.

Quoted from Ostrovsky, p. 198. Love is "feeling, it's an act, my God! quite bestial — and, naturally, bestial it has to be! Warding it off with little flowers seems to me crass. Bad taste, precisely, is putting flowers where none are really needed. . . . You go into a delirium (coitus is a delirium): to rationalize that delirium with precise verbal maneouvers seems to me very silly" (Hanrez, *Céline*, p. 275). Quoted in Matthews, p. 75.

12. Translated by Ralph Manheim (New York: New Directions, 1966), p. 239. It should be noted here that Céline's *points de suspension* are retained in these quotes. I have used four periods when omitting one or more sentences.

13. Flynn, ed., *Understanding Céline*, p. 41.

14. Translated by John H. P. Marks (New York: New Directions, 1934), p. 265.

15. Sigmund Freud, "On Narcissism: An Introduction (1914)," J. Richman, ed., *A General Selection from the Works of Sigmund Freud* (New York: Liveright Publishing Corp., 1957), p. 112.

16. Freud, "A Special Type of Object Choice Made by Men (1910)," P. Rieff, ed., *Sexuality and the Psychology of Love* (New York: Collier Books, 1963), p. 52.

17. Freud, p. 52.

18. Freud, pp. 56–57.

19. Freud, "On Narcissism," p. 113.

20. Freud, "A Special Type of Object Choice Made by Men (1910)," pp. 51 and 54–56.

21. See Allen Thiher's *Céline: The Novel as Delirium* (New Brunswick, NJ: Rutgers Univ. Press, 1972).

22. Céline, *Guignol's Band* (New York: New Directions, 1954), pp. 4–5.

23. See footnote eleven.

24. Translated by Allen Thiher, footnote 21, p. 186.

25. See footnote eleven.

26. Céline, *Rigadoon* (New York; Delacorte Press, 1969), pp. 195–96.

27. See footnote eleven.

28. Translated by Karen Rake and W. K. Buckley:

> Stambul sleeps beneath the pallid moon.
> The Bosphorus shimmers with a thousand silvery fires.
> Alone in the great Mohammedan city
> The old town crier has not yet gone to bed.
>
> His voice, magnified by the echo,
> Announces in the city that it is already ten o'clock.
> But through a window from his high minaret
> His indiscreet glance plunges into a bedroom.
>
> He remains a moment — mute — immobilized by surprise,
> And nervously caresses his imposing grey beard.
> But, loyal to his duty, he steadies his voice

The poem was signed and dated "L. des Touches, Ngobonbong, 28 August, 1916," and a copy was sent to his parents 29 August. "Gnomography," *Cahiers Céline 4. Lettres et premiers écrits d'Afrique, 1916–17,* ed. Jean-Pierre Dauphin (Paris: Gallimard, 1978), p. 79.

Louis-Ferdinand Céline: Creator
and Destroyer of Myths
Erika Ostrovsky*

Céline has elicited so much critical commentary—especially in the past decade—the corpus of interpretations devoted to him is so rich and varied, that one might well ask what still remains to be said. Yet his work, by its extraordinary complexity and vitality, constantly inspires, even demands, new explorations. Among these, the treatment of myth elements in his fictions suggests itself as a fecund although (to date) insufficiently used approach. This essay, while necessarily limited in scope, will attempt to make at least an initial incursion into that challenging domain.

At the very outset, however, a clarification is mandatory: the analysis of myth elements here will not deal with factors immediately visible, such as the use of characters, situations, or sites from mythology or the re-creation of ancient myths in modern form (as found in the works of many contemporary French writers, for example, Anouilh, Butor, Cocteau, Giraudoux, Sartre, and Wittig). True, mythological figures do at times appear in Céline's fictions (Charon, the Minotaur, Jupiter, Neptune, Venus, centaurs, and sirens), and, on occasion, the author claims the title of mythographer or creator of legends. But these phenomena are only of minor interest for the present undertaking. Matters far less evident and thus—characteristically—much more fundamental in Céline's writings are those that are based on his recognition of the plight of modern man who lives in a desacralized world, yet feels a profound (though hidden) nostalgia for legend or myth.[1] This nostalgia, also observed by one of the great specialists in the field—Mircea Eliade—translates itself, according to the latter, into what he terms "mythological behavior"[2] manifesting itself in a variety of ways in our lives dominated by the profane.[3] Since, however—and this is essential for the purposes of the present analysis—this "mythological behavior" finds its essential expression in the domain of the imaginary, it demands, for its discovery and analysis in literature, the study of myth patterns that are evident in some aspects of a fiction and follow specific models with which specialists of mythology are well acquainted.

Three of these patterns, representing a choice determined by the richness of the material found in Céline's major fictions as well as by their importance in any consideration of myth structures, will furnish the principal areas of exploration in this essay: (1) Initiation; (2) The Modalities of Time; and (3) Cosmogony and *Eschaton*.[4] It must immediately be added, however, that, although Céline's *adherence* to myth patterns is of great interest, his *subversion*, truncation, or suspension of them is just as fascinating and speaks equally of the author's profound originality. Both as

*This essay was written for this volume and appears here for the first time with permission of the author.

creator and destroyer, Céline remains here — as elsewhere — one of the most innovative of contemporary French writers.

Our point of departure will be Initiation — the point of departure par excellence. Traditionally, the pattern it follows consists of a certain number of motifs and stages: separation of the novice or candidate for initiation from his birthplace, native soil, or the maternal domain; segregation in a place both distant and unknown; crossing of a threshold; encounter with a guardian, guide, double, or spirit; trials (frequently in the form of torture); symbolic death (mutilation, sacrifice, circumcision, subincision[5]); a night journey or visit to the underworld/otherworld; a radical transformation in his mode or level of being; the acquisition of a different name; the revelation of a fundamental truth or mystery; the triumphant return of the initiate, now in the possession of important secret knowledge; the transmission of this knowledge to the community.

Even when seen by itself, this list of motifs and phases in the initiation scenario already reveals many striking parallels with the itinerary of *Journey to the End of Night* (whose very title, of course, suggests the motif of the night journey): the protagonist, Bardamu, like the traditional neophyte, is separated from his native world (Paris, the Place Clichy) and will proceed to a series of distant and unknown places (battlefields, Africa, America); he crosses the first threshold (represented by the image of an empty space obscured by rain but also — perhaps even more powerfully — through stylistic means such as a brutal change of rhythm, the suspension of punctuation, a different lexical register); he encounters a guide or double (Robinson) who will appear at every important turning point, or crossing of another threshold, in the novel; Bardamu undergoes trials, torture, and mutilation, as well as a radical change in his mode of being. Most important of all, a fundamental truth is revealed to him. This occurs in two stages: the first marks his passage into adulthood (which, in the traditional initiation, introduces the neophyte both to death and sexuality) and is here expressed in the famous sentence: "One is as virgin to Horror as to sensuality";[6] the second, after this loss of virginity and the progressive discovery that occurs throughout the novel (in a pattern repeated several times), is summed up in the formula: "The truth of this world is death."[7]

It is at this point that Céline's fiction ceases to adhere to the mythological model and its subversion begins. After having explored and left the "Other World" (at the exact center of the novel), the initiate, Bardamu, does not return triumphant, although in possession of important secret knowledge. On the contrary, he remains a stranger, an outsider, fixed in a pose of failure at the conclusion of his long night journey. And the transmission of the fundamental truth acquired (usually the final stage of the initiation scenario) is completely reversed, for *Journey to the End of Night* ends in an appeal for silence: "Let's speak no more about it."[8]

While the Initiation pattern illuminates many aspects of Céline's early novels (for one could, space permitting, trace similar parallels in

Death on the Installment Plan and *Casse-pipe*[9]), a much more dramatic (although related) scenario is applicable to the later works, from *Le Pont de Londres* onward: that of the shaman. The mythological model in question contains the following elements: illness, seizures, possession, disintegration of personality, as signs of vocation, of being chosen; tortures (even involving the symbolic dismemberment of the body or its reduction to a skeletal state); manifestations of furor, heat, trance, ecstasy; ascension or levitation; astral voyages or descents into hell; extraordinary powers in the realm of poetry, prophecy, medicine; visionary states; a prodigious memory; the discovery of a new language; communication with animals, especially birds; the transmission of illuminations to the members of the tribe.

It will certainly have become apparent to those who know Céline's works well, how many parallels can be found between these attributes and those of the narrators (and their companions or doubles) in his later fiction, such as Sosthène de Rodioncourt and Mille-Pattes in *Le Pont de Londres* or Jules in *Féerie pour une autre fois*. The first enters repeatedly into trance states; the second is, in effect, reduced to a skeletal shape and performs vertiginous acts of levitation at the *Touit-Touit-Club* (a place whose very name suggests, among other things, the sound of a bird-call); the third, whose body has undergone dismemberment (he is a double amputee) ascends to the top of the Moulin de la Galette (an image of the *Axis Mundi*?) and directs an infernal round. Descents into hell occur quite frequently in Céline's last trilogy and are represented by entry into subterranean labyrinths, tunnels, room no. 36, and bomb craters, or assemblies of monsters and demons in *From Castle to Castle*, *North*, and *Rigadoon*. The protagonists of these novels also manifest others of the shaman's unusual powers: that of prophecy (for example, the "extra-voyant" narrator of *From Castle to Castle*); of poetry (such as the writer-doubles of almost all the narrators); of communication with animals (the cat, Bébert, chief among them) and especially with birds (the role of "bird-charmer" had already been attributed to Sosthène and will revert to the narrator at the end of Céline's last novel, *Rigadoon*); of medical skills (which make the protagonist of almost all the later fiction a witch doctor or medicine man, in the truest sense of the word).

In this case, as in the previous one, it can be seen that the subversion of the mythological model (as powerful as adherence to it) operates at the moment of the scenario where the triumphal stage usually begins. Thus, ascension inevitably ends in a fall or a derisive failure — for Mille-Pattes as well as for Jules. (Of course, this pattern had already been prefigured by the grotesque end of Courtial des Pereires' balloon in *Death on the Installment Plan*, but it becomes more dramatic in the later works.) Ecstasy, if it occurs at all, leads to nothing (as in the case of Sosthène); the discovery of a new language is limited to that of an apocalpytic Esperanto or the sign language of cretins; the transmission of an illumination to the members of the tribe either ends in disaster or never takes place at all.[10]

Let us now proceed to the second stage of our itinerary: the Modalities of Time. According to mythological thinking, there are two kinds of time: profane time — linear, chronological, irreversible — which leads to degeneration, decreptitude, and death; the time of origins, of absolute beginnings — primordial, auroral, infinitely recuperable — characterized by strength, purity, perfection. For modern man, who considers himself defined by history, it is the former that dominates, creating a profound sense of anguish that is the result of his "fall into time"[11] and the temporal flow that leads, inevitably, toward death. It is this kind of time that is so powerfully evoked in a passage of *Death on the Installment Plan* (a work whose very title translates this obsession): "Ah! it's really terrible . . . how one loses people along the way . . . pals one never sees again . . . never . . . who've vanished like dreams . . . it's all over . . . gone . . . then one will also be lost . . . in the dreadful torrent of things . . . of days. . . ."[12] An attempt, overwhelming in its futility, to halt the flow of time, follows this pronouncement: "A mad desire took hold of me . . . to jump into the fray . . . to block their path . . . to stop them in their tracks . . . so they wouldn't move at all anymore! . . . so they'd stand still! . . . once and for all! . . . So I wouldn't see them leave anymore!"[13] But the "dreadful torrent of . . . days" cannot be halted nor turned from its course. One cannot be cured of the ravages of time. At most, one can attempt to nullify it by projecting oneself out of the temporal. Bardamu had already expressed this wish in his cry: "To leap out of Time!"[14] and had momentarily succeeded by various forms of escape — the cinema, voyages, eroticism, delirium. But they provided only a short respite and rapidly gave way to an awareness of temporality and its accompanying anguish. It is of no avail either to circumnavigate the globe and to visit the "other world." For once one stops running, "one picks up the thread of the days again, the way one has left it dragging here, filthy, precarious. It waits for you."[15]

If, according to mythological thinking, the return to the Origin is the only way to kill the dead time that leads to death and if, by ritually returning to the beginning of the world one can re-create the paradisial state which preceded our fall into time,[16] then in Céline's fiction, any attempt to break the temporal flow fails in the final analysis. At most, what remains is a nostalgia, an unslated thirst for such a state and some frenetic attempts to attain the Time of Origins (i.e., a Golden Age when a strong, pure race of supermen peopled the earth). The latter seem to lead to the monstrous pronouncements made by the narrators of the pamphlets that coincide (both temporally and historically) with Aryan myths and the racist theories of the Nazis.[17]

The only true means of escaping linear and destructive time (according to nearly all mythologies) is by a repetition of the act of creation — or cosmogony. Such an act is possible for the creator of fiction even if it is impossible for his creatures. First of all, because any construction (in this case, that of a book) is a repetition of the act of Creation, an absolute beginning and, as such, a way of restoring the initial instant, the plenitude of a present without any trace of history. Second, because the writer (and the reader) can move outside of historical and personal time and gain access to an ahistorical and transpersonal dimension: the time of the imaginary that contains all the liberty lacking in the temporal realm of living — a time that is expanded or contracted and where one can, once again, experience all things with the same intensity as when they occurred at the very first instance. The writer can also refuse linear time in his fiction and, by means of structures, suggest a world sheltered from the ravages of chronological time. In his early novels, Céline seems to have undertaken this task by a relatively simple chronological reversal of episodes or of entire works (such as *Journey to the End of Night, Death on the Installment Plan, Guignol's Band*, parts 1 and 2). In his late works however, fictional time itself is expanded or contracted; it even exists simultaneously (for example, in *Rigadoon* where, in numerous passages, verbs in the past, present, and future tense are found in the same paragraph, even in the same sentence); it is exploded, winds back upon itself, and finally becomes so chaotic that it no longer seems to exist at all. It is then no more the representation of a leap out of time but the very annihilation of time itself. This state of nothingness, this regression or return to the amorphous and to original chaos, is the point where what one could term *Endzeit* rejoins the *Urzeit*[18] that figures in all the myths of the End of the World.

This brings us to the last stage of our exploration: Cosmogony and *Eschaton*. Traditionally, the order of these two terms would be reversed, for the *eschaton* supposes the total destruction of the cosmos and its return to chaos — to the primordial *massa confusa* — in order to subsequently permit the renewal or absolute regeneration of the world. Whether it is a question of the diurnal and nocturnal cycle, the round of the seasons, or the Great Year of the cosmos, the pattern remains the same.

In the case of Céline's fiction, the eschatological phase is, of course, the most evident. According to most critics, he is an "apocalyptic" writer, the destroyer par excellence of an existing (literary) universe, a specialist in the reduction to zero. He himself reinforces this impression by the pronouncements of many of his narrators: "I am the thunder, the cataclysms,"[19] one of them says; "I write the opera of the Flood,"[20] another adds. All of this might lead one to think that the mythological model would constantly be subverted or sabotaged and that, in his works, cosmogony would never follow the *eschaton*. It will be seen, however, that even this subversion would be subverted by Céline on occasion.

Naturally, readers of Céline are well aware of the fact that the stages of the destructive phase are painted in great detail and occupy the predominant place in his fictions and that, from *Journey to the End of Night* to *Rigadoon*, an apocalypse of human origin is taking place. All the motifs of the *eschaton* are present: destruction by fire due to criminal acts of war; floods of all kinds, often tragic but at times comical—such as the deluge of vomit during the Channel crossing in *Death on the Installment Plan* or the flooding of toilets in *North*; the reign of demons and the resurrection of the dead, in *Death on the Installment Plan* or in *From Castle to Castle*; the ruin of entire civilizations and the destruction of humanity as a whole, in the last trilogy and especially in *Rigadoon*. Not only on the mimetic but also on the stylistic level, this annihilation is reflected. The latter is expressed by the fragmentation of the novels' structures, the atomization of syntax, the deluge of words, the chaotic nature of fictional time and space.

However, and this is most important, the subversion of the mythological model—exceptionally—does not take place at the moment when Céline's life and work come to an end. For, if one closely examines the second part of *Rigadoon* (from the moment the narrator suffers a head wound),[21] one sees that a transformation takes place and a turning point has been reached: the end of the world allows a new creation to take place. The first indication of this is that the "infernal music" that has pursued the narrator ever since the initiatory head wound inflicted during World War I (described also as "excruciating noises," "the opera of the Flood," "the small song of Death") undergoes a metamorphosis the instant the final head wound is suffered during World War II. The music now heard is: "A song! . . . magnificent! as magnificent as the panorama . . . a song like a symphony for this ocean of ruins . . . crazy ruins . . . 'waves of little flames' . . . pink . . . green . . . and small crackling bouquets . . . the souls of the house . . . far . . . very far away . . . dancing. . . ."[22] Noises have changed into a "magnificent song," "a symphony"; the Flood image has given way to that of the "ocean" and of the "wave" (symbols of birth and becoming); the harsh and brutal colors of destruction have become tender tints of "pink" and "green"; flames have changed into flowers; the round of demons and witches has been transformed into a dance.

From this moment on, a sense of calm and peace will reign; a pause occurs that is neither emptiness nor absolute ending, but rather a time of rest before something takes place. This something, ushered in by inexplicable laughter (the laughter of creation), is the birth of a new world. In the beginning, the seeds of primordial life appear, breaking forth from the original and most primitive substance—clay (or mud)—in the form of creatures existing on the simplest level, beings in a larval state, animallike, functioning on a preverbal level: the "little cretins" with whom "everything is possible" and "everything begins again." Together with the author-*accoucheur* we witness the birth of new life which, truly, arises from its own ashes.[23]

Thus, not only does cosmogony follow the *eschaton* but, in the last part of *Rigadoon*, there is a brief yet extraordinary passage in which one sees a kind of garden of Eden where the narrator and his wife (resembling the first human couple) are surrounded by fabulous birds that eat from their hands (in the presence of Bébert, the cat) as trusting as the animals at the dawn of creation, before the Fall.[24]

This renewal out of the void takes place not only on the level of mimesis, however. Céline, after having submitted literary style to eschatological action, assures us (parodying Genesis of Judeo-Christian mythology) that "In the beginning was emotion" and to re-create style from the base of emotion. And, although the narrator of his final work announces that "each creation carries within itself, with itself, its birth as well as its end,"[25] we might add that each end (and this is substantiated by all his novels) carries within it its own birth or rebirth. And, although the title, *Rigadoon*, contains the image of a target riddled with bullet holes (and thus, of death), it contains at the same time a reference to creation through dance, by dancing.[26]

Thus, Céline, in the work completed at the moment of his death before entering into absolute silence, gives us a brief glimpse of dawn at the end of cosmic night.

Notes

1. Céline himself expresses this nostalgia in a number of his minor works, notably in *La Naissance d'une fée* (a "ballet" resembling a fairy tale—a genre that has its roots in myth) or in the "ballets mythologiques," *Scandale aux abysses* and *Foudres et flèches*. It is also evident in the episodes of *Death on the Installment Plan* that deal with the legend of King Krogold, a legend to which the author repeatedly alludes in later works (especially in the recently published *Maudits soupirs pour une autre fois* [Paris: Gallimard, 1986]). For a more complete treatment of this matter, see my "Céline et la légende du roi Krogold," *L'Herne*, no. 5, (1965):201–6.

2. The French term used by Eliade is "comportements mythologiques". *Mythes, rêves et mystères* (Paris: Gallimard, 1959), 29, 31.

3. Eliade affirms that these "comportements mythologiques" can be seen in our modern world in such behavior as initiations into fraternities; secret societies; worship of various idols—stars of film, fashion, sport, politics, even comic-strip heroes and popular cult figures; utopian theories; and political myths.

4. The Greek term *eschaton* is used to denote the end of the world, rather than apocalypse (related solely to Judeo-Christian mythology).

5. An operation ritually performed, in some societies, to produce a person both masculine and feminine, symbolizing the primordial unity of an androgynous being. It could be suggested (although this may be going rather far) that the change of name (or assumption of a pen name), undertaken at the time of his initiation into writing, turning Louis-Ferdinand Destouches into Louis-Ferdinand Céline, is a parallel act, since a feminine name (Céline) is added to the existing masculine one (Louis-Ferdinand).

6. "On est puceau de l'Horreur comme on l'est de la volupté" (*Voyage au bout de la nuit*, in *Romans de L.-F. Céline* [Paris: Gallimard, 1963], 17); hereafter references to *Voyage au bout de la nuit* and *Mort à crédit* will be to *Romans*.

7. "La vérité de ce monde c'est la mort" (ibid., 200).

8. "Qu'on n'en parle plus" (ibid., 493).

9. Titles of all works by Céline which have been translated to date are given in English in the text; all others are left in French. For the sake of consistency, all translations from the works of Céline are my own.

10. At most, one could state that the author-shaman discovered a new language, a new style (claims constantly made by Céline and born out by critics) and that he transmitted the contents of his insights or visions to the members of the tribe (of readers and critics).

11. Also the title of a collection of essays by E. M. Cioran, *La Chute dans le temps* (Paris: Gallimard, 1964), which treats this notion with great profundity.

12. "Ah! c'est bien terrible quand même . . . comme on perd des gens sur la route . . . des potes qu'on reverra plus . . . plus jamais . . . qu'ils ont disparu comme des songes . . . que c'est terminé . . . évanoui . . . qu'on s'en ira soi-même se perdre aussi . . . dans tout l'atroce torrent des choses . . . des jours . . ." (*Mort à crédit*, in *Romans*, 883).

13. "Il me montait une envie farouche . . . d'aller sauter dessus finalement . . . de me mettre là devant . . . qu'ils restent pile . . . qu'ils bougent plus du tout! . . . Là, qu'ils se fixent! . . . Une bonne fois pour toutes! Qu'on les voye plus s'en aller!" (ibid., 884).

14. "Sortir du Temps!" (*Voyage au bout de la nuit*, in *Romans*, 361).

15. "On retrouve le fils des jours comme on l'a laissé à traîner par ici, poisseux, précaire. Il vous attend" (ibid., 237).

16. A notion that also preoccupies Eugène Ionesco (see his *Journal en miettes* and his novel *Le Solitaire*).

17. For Aryan myths and Nazism, see especially A. Sérant, *Le Romantisme fasciste* (Paris: Fasquelle, 1960). For a discussion of political myths in general, see Mircea Eliade, *Aspects du mythe* (Paris: Gallimard, 1963), 221 ff.

18. *Endzeit* or end of time; *Urzeit* or time of origins, of absolute beginnings.

19. "Je suis la foudre, les cataclysses" ("cataclysses," a word coined by Céline, gives an *argotique* turn or a derisive flavor to the term "cataclysm") (from an unpublished manuscript of *D'un Château l'autre*).

20. "Je fabrique l'opéra du Déluge" (*Mort à crédit*, in *Romans*, 526).

21. *Rigodon*, in *Oeuvres de L.-F. Céline* (Paris: Balland, 1969), 5:423–24.

22. "Un air! . . . somptueux! somptueux comme le panorama . . . un air je dirais symphonique pour cet océan de ruines . . . ruines folichonnes . . . 'houles de flammèches' . . . roses . . . vertes . . . et petits bouquets crépitants . . . les âmes des maisons . . . loin . . . très loin . . . dansantes . . ." (ibid., 425).

23. The enormous "bubble" (the result of a bombing) that is described as "three to four times as high as Notre-Dame" could be considered a representation (or, at least, a parallel) of the Sacred Mountain or the Center of the World which appears in numerous mythologies. It is there that the "little cretins" and Bébert, the cat, find (food) the source of new life. See ibid., 452–57.

24. Ibid., 497–98.

25. "Au début était l'émotion." This phrase is repeated in numerous pronouncements by Céline when explaining his stylistic innovations. "Chaque création porte en elle-même, avec elle, avec sa naissance, sa propre fin" (ibid., 389).

26. *Rigadoon* (French: *Rigodon*) has two meanings: (1) *faire rigodon*, in French army talk, is to hit a bull's eye in target practice; (2) the *rigodon* is also an old dance form based on a pattern of two steps forward and two steps backward, thus remaining in one place. It

should also be noted that Céline's dual preoccupation with death and dance is evident throughout his works. His enduring fascination with dance, dancers, and even a dancing god constitutes a thematics of beauty, creation, and life that is diametrically opposed to his predominant vision of ugliness, destruction, and death. For a treatment of the dancing god and related matters, see also Erika Ostrovsky, *Céline and His Vision* (New York: New York University Press, 1967), especially 183–201.

Louis-Ferdinand Céline:
An Introduction
David O'Connell*

In the last twenty years, Louis-Ferdinand Céline has emerged and, in the opinion of most major critics, joined Proust as one of the two greatest novelists of the twentieth century. This change in his literary fortunes is one of the most interesting stories in modern literature, and is understandable if one remembers that Céline's work was surrounded by what amounts to a conspiracy of silence by French (mostly leftist) intellectuals from the end of World War II until about the mid-sixties. Having been accused of collaborating with the Nazis during the war, it took almost twenty years for his name to be cleared. Once it became apparent that despite his vocal anti-Semitism of the late thirties he had not been a Nazi collaborator during the Occupation, there was no way to stop the frustrated and widespread desire of younger Frenchmen to read Céline and to know more about his life and work.

Louis-Ferdinand Destouches was born on 27 May 1894 in Courbevoie, a suburb of Paris. His father worked for an insurance company and his mother, to make ends meet, ran her own retail establishment, a soft goods store in the Passage Choiseul near the Place de l'Opéra on the Parisian Right Bank. Beginning in 1899, the family lived at the same address as Mme Destouches's store and young Louis, an only child, attended local schools before being sent by his parents in the years 1907–9 for protracted stays in both Germany and England in order to learn the languages of these two countries. In his mother's thinking, such knowledge would eventually come in handy in the lace business. This early exposure to foreign languages and cultures was unusual for a young French boy of this period, especially for one from his less than privileged petit bourgeois social class.

After his return from aboard, he took odd jobs during 1909–12, working for various small businesses in his neighborhood. Although he later claimed that the desire to study medicine had come to him early in life, he still did not attend school through these adolescent years. Not long after reaching the age of eighteen, in 1912, he joined a cavalry regiment

*This essay was written for this volume and appears here with permission of the author.

and attained a rank equivalent to that of sergeant by the time the war began. He was seriously wounded in the arm while carrying out his duties at the front in Flanders and was operated on shortly thereafter. Fearful that army doctors would take the easy way out and remove his arm, he insisted on being treated without anesthesia. Thus he kept his arm, the loss of which would have impeded his later medical career. Awarded the Médaille Militaire for his bravery in battle, he was sent back to Paris to rest and recuperate. His disability for the arm injury and damage to his ear drums was rated at 75 percent, so there was no chance of his being sent back to the front.

A year later, in May 1915, he was assigned to the French consulate general in London, where he worked in the passport office. During the year that he spent there, he married Suzanne Nebout, a French bar girl working in one of the local nightclubs that he frequented, but he did not register the marriage with the French Consulate. When he left London a year later, having been definitively released from military service, he left his wife behind. In search of adventure and to earn a living, he spent the next year in West Africa working as a trader in the bush for a French forestry company. His stay in the Cameroons was shortened when, due to ill health caused by the harsh climate, he had to return home. Back home in France in May 1917, he seemed ready to settle down. Taking accelerated course work, he completed his baccalaureate degree in 1919. Enrolling at the medical school of the University of Rennes in that same year, he completed his medical degree in 1924 and, in the process, married Edith Follet, the daughter of the school's director. The marriage to Nebout was disregarded under French law.

With his doctoral dissertation, entitled *La Vie et l'œuvre de Philippe-Ignace Semmelweis* (1818–65) (*The Life and Works of Philippe-Ignace Semmelweis*), published by the medical school, and good connections in the medical profession thanks to his marriage, he seemed to have a bright professional future ahead of him. But this very perspective, a bourgeois life of privilege, did not appeal to him. On the contrary, he felt restricted by it. For this reason, he left his wife and daughter in 1925 to take a job as a doctor with the League of Nations. Thanks to this new post, he was able to travel to Geneva and Liverpool, and even back to West Africa. He also made a trip to the United States, Canada, and Cuba that lasted more than two months in 1925 and that took him to a number of cities, as well as to Detroit, where he took a particular interest in the social, psychological, and medical problems of assembly line workers in the Ford plant located there. These wanderings continued until 1928 when he finally settled in Clichy, a dreary working-class suburb of Paris. Divorced in 1926, he spent the next ten years there, the first three in private practice and, beginning in 1931, as an employee of the local town clinic.

It is at this point, at the age of about thirty-two, that Céline began to write. He devoted most of his free time during the next four years to the composition of his first novel, *Voyage au bout de la nuit (Journey to the End of the Night)*. Its publication in 1932 was by far the major literary event of the year. As Leon Trotsky, a great admirer of the book, but much less so of Céline the man, put it: "Louis-Ferdinand Céline walked into great literature as other men walk into their own homes".[1] The novel is a startling one to read, its bitter pessimism affecting readers in a powerful way even today, more than a half-century after publication. It is impossible to be indifferent to *Voyage* and, by extension, to its author.

Léon Daudet, at the time a member of the Goncourt jury and an ardent admirer of the novel, sought to have *Voyage* awarded the prestigious Goncourt Prize. The other members of the jury were frightened, however, by the idea of awarding the prize to such a bitterly pessimistic work. Thus, as a matter of simple politics, the award went to the now totally forgotten and insignificant writer Guy Mazeline for his novel *Les Loups (The Wolves)*. Instead, and as a kind of consolation prize, Céline's first novel was awarded the Renaudot Prize.

Voyage opens with young Ferdinand Bardamu talking with his friend and fellow medical student, Arthur Ganate. The point of view of the novel, from the beginning, is that of a first-person narrator. Bardamu sees a parade passing by and, in a fit of patriotism, decides to join the army. From here we follow him to the front and then back to Paris where he convalesces. This section of the novel contains some of the strongest antiwar passages ever written. In the process, it attacks the stupidity of professional military men, the cupidity and mendacity of politicians, the plundering and exploitation of civilians behind the front lines, and the docility with which the average citizen accepts his fate. After this, Bardamu goes off to Africa where he works in the bush for a French company. Here we see colonialism at work, with black natives being systematically exploited by the whites as well as by each other. Although the narrator clearly feels that the natives are inferior to whites, he still displays sympathy for their woes, since the white colonials are only creating more problems for them. At the end of this section, as during the previous section in France, the hero lapses into a state of delirium brought on by the stress of living. Delirium to Céline is an escape from the stressful reality of modern life, and it is only through delirium that he escapes from Africa.

When he awakens, he is in New York, and from here his travels will take him to Detroit, where he falls in love with Molly, a local whore, and works in a Ford factory. While in the United States, he comes in contact with modern, unrestrained capitalism and the worship of money and material comfort as reflected in modern American life. At the same time, he sees how people at the bottom of the social ladder live in comparison to the rich. Here, in Detroit, he meets up again with a certain Léon Robinson, his alter ego, whom he had already met in other stressful situations, at the front in France, in Paris, and even in Africa. Partly in order to get away from Robinson and partly to put his own life in order, Bardamu leaves the United States and returns to France where he decides to study medicine.

Here, about a third of the way through this 500-page novel, begins what can be called the second part of the work. Now, instead of running away from reality, he vows to attempt to meet it head on. First, his life as a doctor in the working-class suburb of Rancy is chronicled. Caring for the sickest and least educated segment of society, Bardamu descends into the lowest circles of the hell of modern life. Inevitably, he again runs into Robinson, who is living in the neighborhood. When Robinson tells him that he has been hired to assassinate a neighbor, Old Lady Henrouille, who has become a nuisance to her son and daughter-in-law, both of whom want to get rid of her, Bardamu tries to stay out of it. As Robinson is setting the bomb that he hopes will detonate later and kill the old lady, it suddenly goes off in his face, blinding him. At this point, Bardamu gets involved with the Henrouilles and helps them arrange for both the old lady and Robinson to work in the crypt of a church in Toulouse where they serve as guides for tourists interested in seeing the mummies preserved there. Finally, after the trip to Toulouse, Bardamu returns to Paris where he works in a privately run mental institution. Here, he seems to conclude at the end of the novel, he will be safe from man, the most dangerous predator in the universe. Living among the insane, he has finally found his place in the world.

This second part of the novel, which some critics have found slower to read than the first part, is highlighted by the author's strong social protest against poverty and ignorance as well as against some of the tools that, in his view, society uses to maintain the social status quo: alcohol, the press, and modern cinema.

Although this description offers only an overview of the plot of *Voyage*, it should be clear that the overriding concern of the novelist is to depict the conditions of modern life. The words of the great Catholic novelist of the interwar years, Georges Bernanos, still apply to *Voyage:* "Pour nous la question n'est pas de savoir si la peinture de M. Céline est atroce, nous demandons si elle est vraie. Elle l'est" ("For us the question is not to decide if Céline's view of life is horrible, but whether it is true. It is)".[2]

As the first part of the novel is characterized by flight and a search for self and for meaning to existence, the second part is static and shows the hero willing to stay in place, to compromise if necessary, while awaiting death and attempting to find out what meaning he should eventually assign to that event. Living and working among the poor, Bardamu, like Céline himself, comes to the realization that life for most people in our modern consumer societies is humdrum and boring. The major difference between the rich and poor is that the former have the means to buy forgetfulness, while the poor, whom Céline knew all too well, do not have any such opportunity. Much has also been written about the Bardamu/ Robinson relationship, but Merlin Thomas's assessment is probably the most sensible. To him, each of these characters represents a different view of death. Bardamu, who has a role to play in life, is still struggling to go on living. Robinson, however, who has no role to play, is happy to have his life ended. Murdered by Madelon, he "had decided upon his own death: he could have avoided it. . . . it all amounts to a question of ultimate acceptance of the lot of humanity."[3] As the novel ends, Bardamu has clearly decided to go on living. He knows that death is what awaits him at the end of the night, but his time has not yet come.

Céline showed that his knack for inventing catchy titles was no accident when his next book, *Mort à crédit* (*Death on the Installment Plan*), appeared in 1936. Like *Voyage*—and all the novels that would follow—this book is adapted from the author's own experiences. It goes back in time to the period that precedes the action recounted in *Voyage*, to Céline's childhood and adolescence.

Although he enjoyed publicly poking fun at Proust, Céline nonetheless admired his ability to fashion an imposing multivolume novel out of the stuff of memory. As if to mimic Proust, Céline begins *Mort à crédit* by showing us the mature Ferdinand at work as both a doctor and a writer. But when he lapses into a state of delirium brought on by both an attack of malaria contracted in Africa and a recurrence of dizziness caused by war wounds, we cannot help thinking of Proust and of the privileged moments, like the one provoked by the dipping of a butter cookie, the famous *madeleine*, that brought back understanding of past events through the process of involuntary memory. Here though, Céline, who was always proud of his war record and, through the darkest days of exile after World War II would always consider himself to be a true patriot, stresses his difference from Proust. Whereas the latter always wrote in long, highly stylized periodic sentences about upper bourgeois and aristocratic characters, Céline used this fit of delirium to summon up recollections of his working-class past and express them in a slang that is even more daring than the one experimented with in *Voyage*. Furthermore, the style relied more and more on what he later called his "style télégraphique," little bits of sentences, divided and punctuated by three or more dots. The reason for this technique, he claimed, was that in order to achieve the emotional effect that he sought, he had to write the way people talk, adapting oral speech slightly so that the reader, even though reading, would still have the impression of being in the presence of genuine working-class speech. Beginning with his childhood in the fictional Passage des Bérésinas, the transposed Passage Choiseul of his youth, where the family lives and his mother works, the first-person narrator, Ferdinand, paints a bleak picture. His father, a loser stuck in a dead-end job, takes out his frustrations by beating his son. His mother, unfortunately, is not much better, and the family eats only noodles for most of their meals because his mother is afraid that anything else will leave odors in the lacework that she has for sale. The relatives are just as bad, with the exception of his grandmother, Caroline, who dies in due course, and his uncle, Edouard, who understands, helps, and consoles him.

Leaving school in his early teens, long before finishing his *baccalauréat* degree, he works at two different jobs and is fired from each one. His Uncle Edouard luckily intervenes and suggests that the boy be sent to England for language study. Enrolling for a year in Meanwell College in England, Ferdinand eventually has an affair with the headmaster's young wife, Nora, and returns home. Like Molly of *Voyage*, Nora is treated with sensitivity and warmth and stands out in Céline's fiction for this reason. Back home, Uncle Edouard once again comes to the rescue and introduces Ferdinand to an inventor and con man, Courtial des Pereires. Just as Robinson had slowly assumed more and more importance in the earlier work, now Courtial, with his quacky experiments and projects, becomes a major character as the novel progresses. But when he finally commits suicide near the end of the work because his idealistic vision cannot be achieved (just as Robinson had been killed off by his creator because there was no place for him in life), Ferdinand realizes that, like Bardamu in *Voyage*, he will have to go ahead on his own and make sense out of life.

Returning to Paris from the experimental farm that Courtial had organized, he decides that he will have to get away from his family and seek true independence. Ironically, he seizes upon the army as the place to find this fresh start in life, and it is with this intention in mind—joining the army—that we leave him at the end of the novel.

Mort, although a successful novel by any criterion, did not achieve the same overwhelming success as *Voyage*. It did, however, solidify Céline's reputation as a pessimistic writer with a generally negative view of family and social relationships. Despite the warm feelings that the narrator expresses for his Uncle Edouard (and some of the warmest pages that Céline ever wrote concern this character), it is difficult to disagree with this assessment. Like *Voyage*, *Mort* was immediately translated into all the major European languages and kept Céline's name alive as an important author (seemingly, but not really, of the Left) in a world about to go to war.

Céline's royalties from the publication of *Voyage*, in France and around the world, were substantial. He used them to buy a house in Saint-Malo, but he still continued to live in his shabby Paris apartment and never stopped working among the poor and dispossessed. The translation of his work into Russian resulted in the accumulation of a vast sum of money held in his account in the Soviet Union. Since the Soviets would not send him the money, he accepted an invitation in 1936 to visit what the French Left held as an article of faith to be the workers' paradise and to spend his money there. As a result of that trip, Céline published the first of four political pamphlets that appeared during 1936–41. *Mea Culpa*

(Through my fault), the first of them, attacked Russia as a brutal dictatorship organized on the philosophical basis of materialism. Its citizens he announced, live in filth and depravation and are exploited by a new ruling class — the Party. The title of the work is obvious: Céline repented for having allowed people to believe that he was sympathetic to the organized political Left in France.

His next pamphlet, *Bagatelles pour un massacre* (Trifles for a massacre), exploded on the political landscape. In this work, Céline's political consciousness, comparatively subdued in his two novels, where he makes extensive use of understatement, and only beginning to show itself in *Mea Culpa*, now directs itself in a frontal assault on international Jewry. Claiming that the Jews in France, with their brothers in London and New York, are planning another war in which they intend to wipe out the Aryans, he calls for the neutralizing of Jewish power in France. Reaction to the work, which runs on for over 400 pages, was mixed in France, and in fact many intellectuals, including André Gide, the reigning pontiff of French letters, thought that he was kidding, that the anti-Semitic tone was so exaggerated that it could not be sincere and must be ironic. But when, in the following year, 1938, Céline published another pamphlet, entitled *Ecole des cadavres* (School for cadavres), that picked up where the first one left off, going so far as to propose a Franco-German alliance against Russia and the Jews as the only way for Europe's Aryans to survive, there could be no doubt about his intentions. As a result of these pamphlets, Céline found himself politically isolated from both the Left and the Right, and he remained in this state for the rest of his life. The last of the four pamphlets, *Les Beaux Draps* (A nice mess), was published during the Occupation in 1941 and castigates the French army for running away from the Germans. The basic proposition of the work is that France ought to institute what Céline thought would be a true form of communism in which everyone would receive the same salary no matter what form of work he did. In this book he drops the anti-Semitism of the years 1937–38 and presents himself as a true patriot and a decorated hero of the Great War. In fact, after the outbreak of hostilities, Céline served on board a French vessel in the Mediterranean that was shelled by the German Navy. Although he openly called for a Franco-German alliance in 1938 to counter what he took to be Soviet, British, and Jewish attempts to start a new war, he rallied to the defense of his country once the Germans attacked.

Céline's major literary projects during the Occupation were his two-part novel *Guignol's Band*, and the fragments of what may have been a large novel entitled "Casse-Pipe" (Kick the bucket).

The word "guignol" in French usually refers to a kind of marionnette show, the "Grand Guignol," that inspires deep emotion in children because of the extremes of human behavior that it can depict. The word can also be used to refer figuratively to a human being who is comic and ridiculous, and it is this meaning that Céline presumably wanted to give to the novel. The old narrator, who is in fact none other than Ferdinand himself, gazes back over the course of the next 900 pages and reflects on the foolish and laughable youth that he once was and of the "band" of characters that he came to know while residing in London for a year during World War I.

Guignol's Band I, published in Paris in 1944, deals with the underworld characters — pimps, prostitutes, and the like — that Céline knew during his year in London. Various adventures in the first volume culminate in a flight to the French consulate where Ferdinand demands to be reintegrated into the French Army, since he has concluded that service at the front could not be more dangerous than life in the London underworld. It is here, however, that he meets Sosthène de Rodiencourt, a would-be magus who seeks access to the fourth dimension of existence. Ferdinand falls under his spell, much like the earlier Ferdinand of *Mort* had been bemused by Courtial. As part 1 ends, we find them going off together in search of adventure. In the second part of the novel, which was not published until 1964, two years after Céline's secretary had accidentally come upon it, the quack inventor, Colonel J. F. C. O'Calloghan, who is working on a new type of gas mask, and his lovely niece Virginia, become major characters. The same type of unbelievable and far-fetched events take place throughout this second part, which culminates, once again, with Ferdinand's symbolic crossing of London Bridge in order to leave these characters behind and seek more adventures elsewhere. The plot line of the two parts is generally incoherent, and most critics have found that the novel fails for this reason. However, J. H. Matthews contends that this failure of narrative was a deliberate strategy on the part of Céline. In this novel, "plot is downgraded," he claims, "so that readers will not concentrate upon narrative incident so much as on the manner in which Ferdinand gives an account of events."[4] This might well be the case; but it does not make this tedious novel any easier to read.

"Casse-Pipe," preserved in a few fragments that constitute less than 200 pages of text, is centered on barracks life in the cavalry during the period of 1912–14. Chronologically, it fits into Céline's life between *Mort* and *Voyage*, just as the two parts of *Guignol's Band* may be read as an insert in *Voyage* between the episode in Paris after Bardamu is wounded and his trip to West Africa. The sections of the novel that remain are all that survived the plunder of Céline's Paris apartment after his departure in May 1944. Remaining fragments of it may be rediscovered at a future date.

Féerie pour une autre fois (Fairy tale for another time), which appeared in two volumes in 1952–54, is generally considered to be Céline's weakest work of fiction. It must be admitted, however, that in comparison to the critical attention devoted to his other novels it has not yet been closely studied. Ostensibly written during his exile in Denmark, where he fled in 1945 and remained until 1951, when he was granted amnesty and allowed to return to France, this book is best considered as a transitional work that shows Céline moving from the transformation of his lived experiences into the form of a novel, as in *Voyage, Mort* and *Guignol's Band*, to what will become, in his last three books, chronicles that do not seek to fool the reader any more, and where the first-person narrator is Céline himself. In the opening pages of *Féerie*, part 1, we find the embittered narrator in Paris, but throughout most of the book he is in prison in Copenhagen lamenting his fate, pointing out, among other things, that there are many real collaborators freely walking the streets of Paris, while he is in prison and in exile. The action of *Féerie*, part 2, written before the first part but published after it, is set in Paris and revolves around an Allied air raid on the French capital. The word "féerie," which denotes a form of entertainment that includes an element of magic and supernatural, is essentially Céline's ironic fantasy about himself. It fails as a novel, if that is what it is supposed to be, but is perhaps redeemed by the fact that it points the way to Céline's last three works, generally hailed by critics as masterpieces.

Once the Allies had landed in France, Céline realized that it was only a question of time until Paris would be liberated and he would be called to account for his prewar writings. Convinced that he stood virtually no chance of receiving a fair trial from the Communist-dominated Resistance, he decided to flee. In July 1944, he left Paris with his wife Lucette, the former ballet-dancer whom he had married the year before, his friend the actor Le Vigan, and his now-famous cat, Bébert. After a short stay in Baden-Baden, he made a trip to Berlin to visit hospitals and then remained for several months in Kränzlin, in Brandenburg, northwest of Berlin. When the Vichy government, by now in exile, retreated to Sigmaringen, Céline moved there and joined the French colony in November 1944. He stayed on with them as a kind of house physician until March 1945. At that time, and allegedly to recover money he had hidden in a friend's back yard in Copenhagen before the war, he left for Denmark. He arrived there safely three weeks later.

The events of this nine-month period were to become the subject matter of Céline's last three works: *D'un château l'autre* (*Castle to Castle*), published in 1957, *Nord* (*North*), which he brought out in 1960, and *Rigodon* (*Rigadoon*), which he completed the morning of the day he died, 1 July 1961. This last text was not published, however, until 1969.

The events of Céline's life during this period of flight are not recounted in order in the trilogy. Nor does he seek strict verisimilitude, as would a professional historian. The subject matter, while based on the author's personal experience, includes a certain amount of fiction and fantasy. The end result, however, is that we have over a thousand pages that describe life in the closing days of the Third Reich. The Allied bombardments, the reactions of the French puppets to their inevitable fate, and the growing awareness of the general population that their cities will soon be overrun by the enemy are all vividly recounted.

These three books are also remarkable in that they reflect Céline's contempt for the Germans. The same man who had sought a Franco-German alliance in 1938 now scoffs at them and their leaders. Another recurrent theme is that of the corruption of leadership, for the masters in the Third Reich never seem to lack any of the creature comforts so absent from the lives of ordinary citizens. A third continuing theme is that of the collapse of Germany itself, the confusion and disintegration of a whole society. Finally, what is perhaps the most important theme of the three works, and which links up with *Voyage* in this regard, is that of sheer survival. Céline will do anything, flatter any person, do whatever is asked, merely to go on living, to survive until another day when the conditions of normalcy will finally be at hand. Both the fright and desperation that he experienced, and the cunning required to overcome them, are recounted by Céline in his usual self-deprecating way. Convinced of his own political innocence, for which he argues throughout these pages, he also strikes a note for the poor and dispossessed, with whom now more than ever he identifies. These three volumes, properly called chronicles rather than novels, are the last works of Céline's literary career.

In April 1945, a French court issued a warrant for Céline's arrest as a collaborator, but it was only eight months later that French officials in Copenhagen demanded his immediate extradition. The Danes responded by imprisoning both Céline (for fourteen months) and his wife (for two months). In February 1947, Céline's declining health caused him to be hospitalized. After another four months, his health restored, he was allowed to go free on condition that he not leave Denmark. He thus remained in that country until his amnesty in France was declared in April 1951. The last ten years of his life were lived in quiet and seclusion on the outskirts of Paris where he earned his living, as always, by practicing medicine. As mentioned above, his last three books, the chronicles, were composed during this period.

In the United States, the number of writers clearly influenced by Céline is greater than for any other European writer, living or dead. Henry Miller for years was fond of telling anyone who would listen how much he owed to Céline. Jack Kerouac, in the frenzied, breathless flight of *On the Road* (1957) and in the analysis of the effect of drugs on his heroes, took his cue from Céline's famous delirium scenes in which his hero, overcome by the pain of living, escapes from reality into a kind of therapeutic dreamworld. Joseph Heller, in *Catch-22* (1961), took the whole idea for his novel from the first part of Céline's *Journey*.[5] As Bardamu learns in the opening pages of the novel, while serving at the front in the late summer of 1914, there is nothing more insane than war between two civilized nations. Wounded and rehabilitated in Paris, Bardamu decides that the only way to avoid returning to the combat zone is to act crazy. But French doctors know that anyone insane enough not to want to do his patriotic duty is really sane, and this is precisely the "catch" that Heller places at the heart of his own novel. Ken Kesey, in *One Flew Over the Cuckoo's Nest* (1962), expanded on the theme of the man who voluntarily decides to live in a madhouse. In this, too, he follows Céline, for if Bardamu is forcefully interned in an asylum early in *Journey*, by the end of the novel he is a doctor in charge of one. Finally, the most interesting Céliniste to surface in recent years has been Kurt Vonnegut, Jr. Céline's influence in him, however, does not grow out of *Journey*, but rather from the later novels, mentioned above, that chronicle among other things the Allied destruction of a large part of Germany's civilian population in 1944–45.[6] As Céline's prestige grows, more American disciples will no doubt emerge.

Céline's future reputation as one of the two great novelists of twentieth-century France seems secure. Although the linguistic fireworks found in his novels obviously suggest a comparison with James Joyce in English, scholars are only now analyzing his prose to discover the secrets that make it work. As no great novelist or school of fiction has arisen in France in the quarter century that has elapsed since the death of Camus, Céline and his work have to a large extent filled the vacuum.

Notes

1. Léon Trotsky, "Novelist and Politician," *Atlantic Monthly*, no. 156, October 1935, 413.

2. George Bernanos, "Au bout de la nuit," *Le Figaro*, 13 December 1932; *Essais et écrits de combat* (Paris: Pléiade, 1971), 1297.

3. Merlin Thomas, *Louis-Ferdinand Céline* (New York: New Directions, 1979), 61.

4. J. H. Mattheus, *The Inner Dream: Céline as Novelist* (Syracuse: Syracuse University Press, 1978), 128.

5. See the interview with Joseph Heller in *Playboy* 22 (June 1975):68: "Louis-Ferdinand Céline's *Journey to the End of the Night* was the book that touched it [*Catch-22*] off. Céline did things with time and structure and colloquial speech I'd never experienced before, and I found these new experiences pleasurable. . . . I was lying in bed, thinking about Céline, when suddenly the opening lines of Catch-22 came to me . . ." (editor's note).

6. See Vonnegut's introductions to the 1976 Penguin Book editions of *North* and *Castle to Castle*, and his introduction to the Penguin Book edition of *Rigadoon* (1975). In all Vonnegut discusses Céline's influence on him (editor's note).

The Logic of the Reception of Céline's Works in the Thirties

Philippe Roussin*

The first stage of the dialogue between Céline's works and their public, established at the time of publication of the first works, and found at the beginning of the chain of interpretations that constitute the history of successive receptions to this day, is partly preserved but partly lost. I foresee neither a gradual official approval of the initial aesthetic departure that made a classic of a work like *Journey to the End of the Night*, nor a process of updating new meanings until then only potential, nor even a natural process of selecting primary meanings attributed to the works by later reception. But this rupture of relations between the work and the public (the aesthetics of reception has turned up many examples) was brought about by changing times after the war when the anti-Semitic law was thrown out.

As always, such a rupture has created a shift in or at least the conditions for a reorganization of meaning. Some of Céline's works have been favored; others have been neglected. We would like to put aside the preoccupations of postwar reception and go back to the meanings the first readers attached at the beginning of what was later to become a series — I have in mind Céline's second novel and his satirical tracts — in order to determine which of the potential meanings glimpsed by the prewar reception were subsequently verified in later works. Even if the meanings attached to his works were no longer emphasized and integrated into later receptions, they have continued to orient and to constrain the production.

The scandal that Céline's work provoked at publication, the polemics it launched, its rejection by some of the critics, the immediate success it knew with the public, all attest to the distance existing in 1932 between what the Constance School has called the "horizon" of the work's expectation and the reader's experience. This distance takes on specific modalities according to the different categories of the public, and of groups of readers and critics. For example, at the same time that the scandal allows us to measure a gap between the code of the novel and the aesthetic and moral norms on which criteria of reception were based, it also shows how sharp the conflict between interpreters was, and illustrates each group's struggle to impose its own aesthetic norms as legitimate for the evaluation, measure, and meaning of the work. *Journey* undeniably surpasses the public's expectation. But if synchronic description makes the work stand out from other books produced at the time, the novel's noncontemporaneity reveals by contrast other novels' dependence on norms that suddenly seem to have been surpassed by literary evolution.

*This essay was written for this volume and appears here with permission of the author. Translated from the French by Jóhanna Eiríksdóttir Hull for this volume.

This significant originality is far from being equally emphasized in the diachronic dimension.

The way critics analyze it,[1] the words and key concepts in *Journey*'s reception are as follows: scandal, war, naturalism, language—as expression and symbol—pornography, picaresque, lampoon, society, medicine, lived versus artistic experience, fiction versus reality, authenticity. This series of words and concepts gives rise to the following question: Is it suitable to include or to exclude such a book from the literary canon? We could say that the contrast in receptions we just mentioned naturally gives birth to such a problematic at its center, and that such a contrast is never more than a formalization inside the synchronic space of the maximal tension between the system of current norms and the code of the work. The history of literary evolution teaches that the artistic revolutions against the dominating aesthetic norms are regularly conducted in the name of *realism*, taking for their slogan the struggle for the natural and the simplification of the artificial of the preceding period. There would, then, be nothing particularly atypical in the key words of the reception, but rather a confirmation. However, we would like to show that the reception, which is the response to the question *Journey* asks, not only indicates the distance between horizons, but also has something to do with the ethical component in the social function of the work and with the ties between changing style and the turning of history.

The form of the first-person narrative with which slang is often associated, the construction of the story stemming from romanesque times, as well as the fictionalization of historical events, constituted the main grounds for surprise and immediate interrogation regarding *Journey*'s place in the literary system. Critics analyzed Céline's stylistic and semantic choices in the light of reflection on literary genres. *Journey* liberated a not yet realized experience and interpretation of history by providing readers the two historical and semantic universes of war and peace—which critical opinion and the public were, until then, accustomed to placing at opposite extremes—in the temporal unity brought out by narrative continuity. A fictional, temporal experience, born out of the narration's figuration of time, imposed itself immediately as a historical consciousness. This new interpretation was not noticed at first, except from the immediate effects of such a rearrangement on the balance of the established division between war and peace novels that were still considered as belonging to distinct spheres. The main surprise effect comes from *Journey*'s displacement of the frontier between art and nonart, between the literary and the extraliterary. Officially, but also in readers' minds, there had existed for about fifteen years books about war, generally written by witnesses, that were not considered literature—they did not aspire to that sort of quality—but were described as *documents*. There were also novels that had war for their subject matter but explicitly limited their content to that subject. This kind of writing, of which we have, by the way, managed to reconstitute the production cycles, represented an important part of publishing after the war. It is to this publishing that the renewed appetite for reading can be in part ascribed, and from which *Journey to the End of the Night* benefited.

The choice of first-person narrative in *Journey* was received in the same way as that first structural choice that led critics to search for a relation with a genre of writing they knew had to be situated outside the literary system. Of course, it led interpretation in a different direction than a third-person narrative would have, but one very convergent with that of the historical documents and testimonies we just mentioned. Two series of diverging opinions appeared, born from the mixture — according to the logic of literary genres — of this narrative form. They were in confrontation, led by groups of readers who, without the exact hybrid type of the book, would not otherwise have had the chance for a head-on debate.[2] Just as time in the novel spanned the frontier that had until then separated two temporal universes and united two distinct categories of writing, the choice of first-person narrative amounted to working into the novel the preferred mode of enunciation of the documentary literature we just mentioned. The autobiographic form, which reports lived events and which passes itself off right away as nonfiction (cf. K. Hamburger), first-person narrative, could feed the most contradictory receptions and play on the maximum of oppositions between fictitious and nonfictitious, literary and nonliterary, at the center of the system. Thus, in the movement of opinions the work released, we must count the importance it has had among people used to war narratives, not only because the axis of gravity of legitimate reading was displaced in this way, but also because the temporal unity of war and peace opened up by the book had to acquire a specific meaning with this public. In conclusion, we might think that it is for this category of readers that slang, a slightly coded usage in relation to social hierarchies, corresponded most to a linguistic experience.

At the other extreme, one is conscious that questions from literary critics about *Journey*'s genre, and in particular its inclusion in the romanesque genre, resulted indirectly from the question posed by its narrative. Doubtlessly there were plenty of motives other than the narrative form that led to such questions. They arose from the discovery of a network of anomalies and deviations from dominant norms, which, when respected by authors, usually allowed for the description of their works. Thus critics focused on the book's length, and this trait immediately became significant for describing the work in its relation to novels that embodied the norm of genre from a triple point of view: aesthetic, commercial, and rational. Journalists brought up the form of the *saga* that seemed destined to succeed the short novel: "the form after the war in France was the 200-page novel." But this sole criterion seemed equally discriminating as the definition of the book, which, by its excess, left the novel and fell into the *epic*: "there is in the genius of the English or Russian novelist an epic virtue the French rarely has."[3] Following the same idea, people spoke of two, even three to four novels in one: novels of war and peace, or novels of war, of Africa, of America, and finally of the suburbs. Except by the communist critics, already won over to the saga form, the length of which designated by contrast the anemia of the French-style garden of letters, this excess of content was regarded as a flaw in composition. These academic debates among the established judges of good taste fed arguments for a more moral rejection by the "good" bourgeoisie.

More worthy of interest than these remarks on the deviation from the norm of the novel from the point of view of volume, is the response that a part of literary criticism brought to the mode of expression proposed by the book. In other words, what did critics think of the embedding of *lyricism* in the epic, the intrusion into fiction of a feigned autobiographic authenticity? It is the vocation of literary criticism to reveal the form of the enunciation, not its transparency, or its insignificance, as the readers who annexed the book to the sphere of war narratives did, nor its object as the leftist literary critics did. Thus criticism was led to place the novel in the subgenres of *satire* and *picaresque*, a designation which allows consideration of the first-person narrative and the object of the work, and one which seems to criticism to define more than that *naturalist* reference more frequently used to define the typical character of the book. To the extreme left, and from a very different perspective, the word *rebel* defines an identical reality. In any case, it formalizes that unity of perspective proper to first-person narrative, the effect of which is that the characters who appear in it "can not be grasped except in a permanent relationship to the first-person narrator."[4]

First-person narrative, fictitious autobiography, episodic journeys, and the narrator's social status conjure up not only a villainous *Gil Blas* but also the undersides of war, the colonies, and America. Critics also spoke of "disguised autobiography . . . that has nothing of a novel about it"; "this is not a novel, the author talks about himself, speaks alone or almost." There is also question of a "monologue, an indictment, a stream of memories, of inventions, of hallucinations, all inextricably mixed."[5] By putting the accent on the enunciative structure of expression, from the epic to the novel and then to picaresque, criticism touches on the limits that mark the boundary of narrative literary space. Perceiving the ideological function of slang, in emphasizing the "I," criticism relates *Journey* to what the Left calls without further ado "a continuous form of invective," the "popular style, hard and raging, of a man of the people who speaks of the outrage done to him."[6] Thus criticism came to describe the book that flaunts its nonfictional construction, by relating it to a doxological-and-no longer-narrative genre: the *lampoon*. "It is a confession mixed with lampoon, a mixture of picaresque narrative and lyrical reportage, a *Diable boiteux* [*Limping Devil*] written by a Vallès or Mirabeau of 1932";

"It is a lampoon, an indictment of an unprecedented violence"; "the long novel he just had published is primarily a vast lampoon"; "we must not consider the book a novel, but a lampoon of the modern world."[7] By nature closed to the ideology of authenticity and to the pathos of lived experience, this criticism necessarily inscribes the antiartistic tendency of the book in a literary perspective, relative to a history and an evolution of genres.

The generic conception that orients this criticism absolutely constrains its comprehension of the text. The debate about genre guides the attribution of meaning. *Picaresque* and *satirical* refer to values carried by these two fictional forms (carnivalesque narrative, fallen world, world upside-down, chaos, the grotesque) but they express the perception of *Journey*'s distance from the canons of realism that govern ordinary novels. These terms finally relate the book to modes of fiction in the literary system of a bygone era in the evolution of forms. At the same time, a return to the preromanesque, the picaresque-satire-lampoon series, can be read as a displacement of the critical focus toward utterance (*énoncé*), considered as *discursive mechanism*, a shift from narrative toward the discursive. To interpret the book as a lampoon is to go back to thinking, for example, that the status of truth does not fall under the problematic of representation, but under a constitutive preoccupation with the structure of enunciation.

By describing the book as a lampoon, literary criticism gives an answer, from the point of view of genre division, to the question the book puts to it; it also fixes, in anticipating with a degree of astonishing precision, that which will be the subsequent reality of literary evolution. In an altogether different register, no longer aesthetic and generic, but ethical and sociological, this description of the book as a lampoon aids in understanding its immediate effect on the intelligentsia: "the book might end up pleasing both the simple and the refined . . . the refined because they feel themselves in the presence of a savage force, to which they aspire or which they miss as something inaccessible. They experience in this book the same nostalgia as that which seizes a gallant man when he sees a beautiful brute get his way with a desired woman. Mr. Louis-Ferdinand Céline has raped literature; many other writers would like to do as he, but they dare not or cannot."[8] The success of *Journey to the End of the Night* — and also of course *Bagatelles pour un massacre* — must be considered as a French example of this ephemeral and unnatural alliance between the elite and the populace. H. Arendt has shown how much this rests on the pleasure that the postwar elite took in observing the populace destroy respectability.[9] This dimension is explicitly present in the interpretation, outside of France, of Walter Benjamin and Maxim Gorki. Benjamin insisted on the undifferentiated experience of the masses and subproletariat, and opposed the absence of all literary theory among populists such as Dabit, who exalted a "work where the revolt is not born of aesthetic

discourse . . . where there is no longer a question of art, of culture."
Gorki, thinking of that historical itinerary that leads from the knight to
the criminal in the detective novel by way of the picaresque hero, deemed
Céline ripe for fascism. Both Benjamin and Gorki give *Journey* a social
meaning exactly opposite to the one generally recognized in France.[10] This
foreign perspective confers a cultural sense to a dimension of the work that
remains inassimilable, and it eludes the primary perception of the French
public.

Of the four poles among which interpretations of the work are
distributed, literary criticism justifies and supports a set of positions less
determined by conformity with or surpassing of aesthetic norms than by
their solidarity with current *moral norms*, to which, in any case, literature
is bound to yield. To readers for whom the French novels of the twenties
constitute aesthetic references, the form of expression, style, level of
language, social types, and sets of themes of *Journey* represent a provocation. What criticism had localized at the margins of the romanesque
genre, these readers hasten to place outside literature, and that is not
surprising, since the novel epitomizes their literary experience. It is the
ethical dimension of the social function of the work that makes for
scandal. Its rejection is told, naturally, by its exile to the extraliterary hell
of pornography, the sphere of obscenity; the displaced linguistic ban forces
a representation of a world that situates "all men in that which is the most
debased in man"; we call to mind *"a work infected by filth, loathsome
garbage, a novel of abjection, filled with stench, which stinks of hospital
. . . scum."*[11] The transgression it symbolizes and its discontinuity with the
literary system explain the work's character as event.

I do not linger on the meaning attributed by such readers. I will say a
few words later about the literary references associated with the terms
they put in motion. I only want to point out how much this violent
rejection finds as its natural complement those who adopt the book
precisely because it is not "literary." With this third interpretation, we
come to all those who, faced with the classical dichotomy of literature/
reality, regularly valorize lived experience at the expense of artistic
experience. The illusion and the implication of the first-person narrative
produce here their full ideological effect, since the process is received as a
sign, guarantee, and proof of nonliterary authenticity of the text. Against
the fiction of the novelist, and because it recalls the experience of the
narrator of war narrative, the first-person narrator assures that lived
experience is attained and told. *Life, humanity, sincerity, authenticity,
absence of aesthetics* are the terms most frequently used: "Céline is not
made of literature, even less of literary bluff. Because he has felt, loved,
suffered, *truly* hated, he has written *truly*"; and this, which testifies to the
proximity of the authentic narrator and the lampoonist's "I": "Why after
all, all this racket? . . . Because the book is the confession of a man,

because he dares to speak the truth, the whole truth; because he is the lone report against all, the revolt . . . against the sophisms, lies, hypocrisies."[12] As utterance (*énoncé*) of feigned reality (cf. K. Hamburger), the first-person narrative anticipates these readers' expectations, and the success of the book stems from the fact that it seems to prove, in the face of all opposition, notably that of literature, that experience can still be told and taught.

Let us conclude with the last interpretation of the work, which not only prevailed over all the others and very largely fashioned the meaning first readers gave it, but also characterized later reception until it gradually acceded to a linguistic modernity. Perception of the work was biased, as we have seen, by its very strong contrast to the romanesque works that appeared simultaneously. Its tendency toward prosaization, based on the antinomy of the artificial and the genuine, leads, however, to directly allying the work with a current that came alive again at the time the book appeared. *Journey* was so narrowly associated with this current that the work was received as a quasi-official resurrection of the naturalist and realist tradition.

In this reference system, thanks to which the work is perceived as up-to-date, the association with naturalism actually dominates. An important topic of the day was the *return to Zola*, remarkable above all in that it metamorphosed a moment of literary history into a tradition and aesthetic goal, and signaled the French contribution to the elaboration of socialist realism. In its interactions with this return, *Journey* is aesthetic, takes the community of the literary project as self-evident, and anticipates the same kind of rapport with the public as Zola had.[13] Let us first consider this last point. In the division of opinion over the novel, in its success as a result of scandal, in the legitimation earned by its market and public readership — "the public has decided," wrote the press — and in the unfavorable verdict of the legitimate authorities of canonization (critics and the Goncourt Prize jury), the book repeats the history of naturalism: "The adventure of Mr. Céline is that of Émile Zola fifty years ago." What is the aesthetic kinship? The naturalist epithet spontaneously redescribes a nonliterary prose that revels in filth, medical documents, certain images of degeneration, a proximity of the seediest part of town: "Mr. Céline takes on the allure of a second Zola . . . the dissolute evocation, the explorations of a certain cesspool, the bias of Cambronne's words, can allow for a belief in a resurrection of a cesspool naturalism." The term, inversely and positively, also imposes itself as the preceding and last literary school, so that this social novel on the exploited classes could be called "the leprosarium of the Parisian suburb": "the book all the naturalists projected, dreamed and failed to produce," which "has truly condensed in itself the turpitude of the last twenty years," "the naturalist groundswell."[14]

What are we to think of this dominant characteristic of the naturalist reference? It indicates that the changing horizon the work imposes, far from being oriented toward an unknown experience, is perceived, positively and negatively, as a reordering in the form of a return, rather than as a surpassing, sometimes even as the sign of an out-of-date form and of a nontopicality (cf. "not a sign of a new day; the liquidation, the newest purge of naturalism and of realism").[15] Barbusse wrote in 1932 in *Zola*, "This large shadow has to be put not behind us, but in front of us. . . . It has to be turned not toward the nineteenth century but toward the twentieth." It is significant that the antiliterary tradition of the avant-garde of the twenties, of dadaism and surrealism, is recalled only in exceptional cases apropos of this declaratively antiliterary book, while it is true that the return to Zola is directed as much against the romanesque of the twenties as the poetic domination of experimentation: "This book marks the moment when we begin to back-pedal." The man who welcomes the book as a guide to a *twentieth century that has not yet begun* is exceptional. The comparison with naturalism, understood either as a durable aesthetic or a past moment of literary evolution, predetermines the sense given to the topicality of the work: the annulment of the *secret divorce* of literature and moral standards pronounced after the war, the *evolution of the novel* insofar as *the literary hacks understood their epoch*, the return to an aesthetic and to a function of representation, social description. Thus the work exhibits the collection of themes offered to the literature of which Berl dreams, and which follow up Zola's effort: war, colonies, Africa, the Orient, America, factories, gates and suburbs of Paris. Here the novel becomes a vast social fresco and pulls itself up to the rank of the great epic form—a terminology heralding imminent debates.

According to the perspective proper to this interpretation of the work, the narrator-as-physician suppresses all questions about the literary-linguistic status of the "I" as much as it facilitates the connection with Zola (the kinship of the novelist and the medical doctor), allowing old metaphors to come alive ("The doctor Céline in a suburb dispensary running a pitiless scalpel over society's pus and sores"). But above all, medical discourse is perceived as the only possible discourse of reality. Those who understand the work by referring it to naturalism settle the questions of invention and linguistic violence (lyricism, slang, popular turns of phrase) by referring to a necessity to conform to realist norms, and by showing that *Journey* puts new lexical spaces into writing. This understanding keeps them from attaching a social meaning to the work and excludes all creation that would not be coherent with the logic of representation. In particular, that understanding which considers *Journey* an example of naturalism remains necessarily closed to the negative—"The cursed part, the shameful part" that the book exhibits according to Bernanos—and blinds itself to that which Bataille refers to, beyond the *pathetic game of Zola*, as "the degeneration of those whom misery casts out of humanity."[16] A social fresco, not a rogue novel, thus decides this literary proximity.

Essentially these are the responses that early reception offers to the new question the work poses. These readers' interpretations will not only determine, to a large extent, the reception of the works that succeed *Journey* in the course of the decade, but they will also orient the production of the later works. I will give only two examples here.

With *Death on the Installment Plan* the only valorized component associated with naturalism — social representation — had to disappear. This association did, nevertheless, survive, in particular when it was a question of responding to the formal, strictly linguistic undertaking of the new work. Readers accepted the recognized interpretation, the explicit reference to naturalism continuing to guide the perception of the text as pornographic, scatologic and suspected above all of catering to a pursuit of effect. (When the form of the spoken style was perceived as lacking finality, the novel was, in reverse, situated relative to a backward and nontopical posterity of symbolism.) It was good sport to attack Céline from this point of view, focusing on the question of obscenity. It remains no less true that the scandal and the pursuit of effect on the public constricted the structural dimension of Céline's production. Insofar as this scandal and pursuit of effect represented the surest means of maintaining contact with a reading public that had spontaneously designated the success and scandal of the first book, they were means of maintaining its proper artistic readability. We find here a real *homology* with naturalism: Céline's desire to retain the public — and the refraction of such finality on the production, in terms of artistic effects — constituted a fundamental aspect of the social situation of those works in the literary camp, in other words, of their readability in synchronic dimension.

Those who do not characterize the new "spoken style" of *Death on the Installment Plan* as pornography or literary writing, but seek its model in political crises, are rare. Hébert, the editor of the revolutionary Père Duchesne and his verbal sans-culottism, as well as E. Drumont, were mentioned in 1936.[17] But this was because *Journey* had already been approached as a scurrilous lampoon. Once again, the lampooning potential was known by interpreters before they knew of works that, for postwar reception, would symbolize its realization. We focus on this last point because of the value we can attribute to it from the point of view of literary communication, and because it concerns the historical dimension of this exteriority of the 1930s works I have mentioned, and which I think is, in principle, a continuation of the dialogue instituted between these works and the public. The profanitory and nonliterary value, which made *Journey* famous, predisposed readers to reject violently *Death on the Installment Plan*, and, subsequently, to receive *Bagatelles pour un massacre* very favorably in 1938. Of all the works of the decade, the anti-Semitic tract was the one that was the most often classified, at the moment of its publication, as a "masterpiece." This contrast in reception is in effect the result of one and the same perception of the meaning and of the situation of Céline's works. The approval of *Bagatelles* is related to the progress of anti-Semitism in French opinion after 1936, but it also attests that "literarily" this work, more than the preceding novel, responds to the reading public's expectations. Received as a literary work, a book by a known writer, *Death on the Installment Plan* was rejected precisely for that reason. It is inscribed as rupture with regard to prior experience that determines the context where the meaning of later works can inscribe themselves. On the contrary, *Bagatelles pour un massacre*, which coincides with this expectation, can take its place in the series of the works as synchrony constructs and conceives of it.

The articles the *Nouvelle revue française* devoted to each of the works from 1932 to 1938, under the pen of the same editor, permit us to outline the contours of this expectation, and to approach the meaning, both literal and social, that the intelligentsia attributed to them. In 1933, the first recognized merit of *Journey* is that it "disturbs, that it threatens, that it insults." In 1936, it is deplored that the author has become a literary hack: "One does not write *Journey to the End of the Night* twice. . . . There is a danger that his violence will make every new book by Mr. Céline pale in comparison. . . . there are less facts in this book . . . more words and more clever words. . . . The author has gained more self-assurance. He knows his voice. He abandons himself to it." In 1938 there is rejoicing in finding the familiar characteristics of the first work: "*Bagatelles pour un massacre* is Mr. Louis-Ferdinand Céline freed. No more romanesque constraints. . . . It is in the name of independence straightforwardness and lyrical emotion that Céline has now come to speak. . . . The Céline of *Bagatelles* joins and prolongs the Céline of *Journey*. There is no doubt that it is at the moment he is directly moved and reacts as he likes, without worrying about fiction or composition, that Céline gives the best of his works."[18] The enunciator of lampoons shares many traits with the first-person narrator. Here and there the illusion of extraliterary authenticity of the writing is very strong. This fiction of nonfiction, as well as the violence associated with it — secondary attribute or essential component, we do not know — is that which is expected. In any case, the works were well received — while waiting to find their meaning — as with *Death on the Installment Plan* — so far as they conceal an inassimilable dimension. (People amused themselves by speaking of the Céline case: "I am interested in his books not at all as works that are supposed to represent the literary norm, but as quasi-monstrous exceptions."[19] The anomaly is a premature figure for the evolution of forms in modern history.) For the prewar novels to become classics and for the initial aesthetic deviation to blur, the rupture of relationship between the works and the public, the putting beyond the law, has to authorize the disappearance of this inassimilable dimension. The theory of literary communication teaches that the dialogue between the works and the public is an interaction, that the characteristics of the works always contain in a contradictory manner certain characteristics of reception groups.[20]

Notes

1. This study is based on a selection of 700 articles (daily newspapers, weeklies, and literary reviews) in the Bibliothèque L.F. Céline, Université Paris VII.

2. See Käte Hamburger, *Die Logik der Dichtung* (1957). I have used the French translation: *Logique des genres littéraires* (Paris: Collection Poétique, Editions du Seuil, 1986).

3. *Carnet de la semaine*, 26 October 1932; *Oran-Matin*, 19 December 1932.

4. Hamburger, *Logique*, 274–80.

5. *L'Ouest*, 26 December 1932; *L'Ecole Libératrice*, 17 December 1932.

6. *Le Monde*, 26 December 1932.

7. *Nouvelles littéraires*, 10 December 1932; *Marianne*, 7 December 1932; *Le Mois*, December 1932; *Manuel Général de l'Instruction Primaire*, 17 December 1932.

8. *Revue de France*, 15 January 1933.

9. H. Arendt, "L'alliance provisoire entre la populace et l'élite," in *Le Système totalitaire* (Paris: Editions du Seuil, 1972).

10. W. Benjamin, "*Zum gegenwärtigen Gesellschaftlichen Standort des französichen Schriftstellers*": Zeitschrift für Sozialforschung, vol. 1 (1934), in *Gesellschaftlichen Standort*, vol. 2, pt. 2; Gorki "Premier Congrès des Ecrivains Soviétiques," *Nouvelle Revue Française*, November 1934.

11. *Comoedia*, 31 December 1932; *Les Débats*, 18 December 1932.

12. Anon., *Le Cri du Jour*; R. T., "La Revanche," *La Patrie Humaine*, 24 December 1932.

13. On the return to Zola, see J.-P. Morel, *Le Roman insupportable: l'Internationale littéraire et la France (1920–1932)* (Paris: Editions Gallimard, 1985).

14. *La Métropole*, 18 December 1932; *Le Mât de Cocagne*, December 1932.

15. *La Liberté*, 28 November 1932.

16. G. Bataille, "Céline (Louis-Ferdinand): *Voyage au bout de la nuit*," *La Critique sociale*, 7 January 1933, 47.

17. G. Brunet, "Le Cas Céline," *Je Suis Partout*, 6 June 1936; F. Porché, "Le Cas Céline," *L'Echo de Paris*, 11 June 1936.

18. Articles by Marcel Arland in *Nouvelle revue française*, March 1933; 273 (1 June 1936); 293 (1 February 1938).

19. G. Brunet, "Le Cas Céline," *Je Suis Partout* 6, no. 6 (1936).

20. M. Neumann, "Remarques sur la réception littéraire en tant qu'événement littéraire et social," *Actes du Congrès de l'Association internationale de littérature comparée* (Innsbrück, 1979), Vol. II "Communication littéraire et Réception," AMOE (Innsbrück, 1980).

JOURNEY TO THE END OF THE NIGHT

Shut your eyes, that's all that is necessary. There you have life seen from the other side.

— Céline's epigraph to *Journey*

Our dreams too will be imprisoned some day or other. That's another dictatorship we've got coming to us.

— "Homage to Zola"

A story you make up is worthless. Only a story you pay for is any good.

— *Paris Review*, 1960

[Remarks on the Detroit Chapter]   Henry Miller*

The capital of the new planet — the one, I mean, which will kill itself off — is, of course, Detroit. I realized that the moment I arrived. At first I thought I'd go and see Henry Ford, give him my congratulations. But then I thought — what's the use? He wouldn't know what I was talking about. Neither would Mr. Cameron[1] most likely. That lovely Ford evening hour! Every time I hear it announced I think of Céline — Ferdinand, as he so affectionately calls himself. Yes, I think of Céline standing outside the factory gates (pp. 222–225, I think it is: *Journey to the End of the Night*). Will he get the job? Sure he will. He gets it. He goes through the baptism — the baptism of stultification through noise. He sings a wonderful song there for a few pages about the machine, the blessings that it showers upon mankind. Then he meets Molly. Molly is just a whore. You'll find another Molly in *Ulysses*, but Molly the whore of Detroit is much better. Molly has a soul. Molly is the milk of human kindness. Céline pays a tribute to her at the end of the chapter. It's remarkable because all the other characters are paid off in one way or another. Molly is whitewashed. Molly, believe it or not, looms up bigger and holier than Mr. Ford's huge enterprise. Yes, that's the beautiful and surprising thing about Céline's chapter on Detroit — that he makes the body of a whore triumph over the soul of the machine. You wouldn't suspect that there was such a thing as a soul if you went to Detroit. Everything is too new, too slick, too bright, too ruthless. Souls don't grow in factories. Souls are killed in factories — even the niggardly ones. Detroit can do in a week for the white man what the South couldn't do in a hundred years with the Negro. That's why I like the Ford evening hour — it's so soothing, so inspiring.

Notes

1. Perhaps William John Cameron (1878–1955), who served on the editorial staff of the *Detroit News* and was later the editor of the *Dearborn Independent*. He worked at the Ford Motor Company from 1918 to 1946 (editor's note).

*Reprinted with permission of New Directions Publishing Corporation from *Sunday After the War* (New York: New Directions, 1944), 23–24. Copyright 1944 Henry Miller.

Marxist Criticism of Céline's
Voyage au bout de la nuit

Paul A. Fortier*

Voyage au bout de la nuit, from its publication in 1932, created around itself an atmosphere of mystery and controversy. The author, who called himself Céline, was unknown. The grammar used in this text resembles that of factory workers, taxi drivers, and hoodlums — an idiom hardly considered to be a fit vehicle for art. The vocabulary is a curious mixture of neologisms, medical terms, and slang, frequently too coarse for mixed company. Yet the language of this novel bears the stamp of high artistic achievement; it moves swiftly and evokes powerful images with an economy of means rarely found in literature, let alone in the lower-class conversations which it imitates.

The setting of this strange and powerful novel shifts from wartime France — both at the front and in the hospitals behind the lines — to an equatorial African colony, then to an American automobile plant, and finally to various lower class milieux around Paris. Bardamu, the narrator, provides a unifying thread with his virulent criticism which spares nothing, least of all himself.

Immediately after the publication of *Voyage au bout de la nuit* Léon Daudet, a founder of *Action Française*, began a campaign to have this novel awarded the Goncourt prize. Daudet's efforts were seconded by George Altmann's laudatory article in the *Monde*.[1] The Goncourt Jury announced informally that its coveted prize would be awarded to Céline. But a last minute manoeuvre deprived the author of official recognition — a disappointment ironically noted by Jean Fréville in *L'Humanité*[2] and by Georges Bernanos in *Le Figaro*,[3] among others. Céline was not the loser in this affair. The different political orientations of the four newspapers mentioned indicate the wide range of outlook among critics who admired his work.

A novel written in an approximation of working class style, set in the disadvantaged sectors of society, and generally recognized as great art, would certainly appeal to Marxist critics, all the more so because it roundly condemns all aspects of the capitalist society which it depicts. It is not surprising, then, that Louis Aragon and Elsa Triolet translated the novel into Russian. But after the short articles written when the novel appeared such as those by Paul Nizan and Jean Fréville,[4] several years elapsed before the appearance of two more serious Marxist interpretations — both by Russian Marxists.

By 1935, the *Atlantic Monthly* published a study entitled "Novelist and Politician" by Leon Trotsky.[5] Immediately identifying the "novelist" as Céline, Trotsky notes the artistic maturity of *Voyage au bout de la nuit*

*Reprinted with permission from *Modern Fiction Studies* 17, no. 2 (1971):268–72. © 1971 Purdue Research Foundation, West Lafayette, Indiana.

and predicts—quite accurately: "Céline has written a book which will survive, independently of whether he writes other books, and whether they attain to the level of his first" (p. 413). Trotsky notes that the novel is full of black pessimism, and—with obvious relish—he rapidly summarizes Céline's debunking of such sacred cows as military valor, the white man's burden, mechanized efficiency, scholarly altruism, petty bourgeois frugality, patriotism, love, motherhood.

Taking his transition from an allusion to Poincaré in Céline's novel, Trotsky shifts his attention to Poincaré's *Memoirs*, singling out examples of poor taste and hypocrisy. Trotsky suggests that these faults result from the politician's fervent belief in a bourgeois liberalism which has long since ceased to be a liberating force and has hardened into conventionality, or worse. Céline, we are told, rips away such sham to show bourgeois society in all its horror and depravity. Trotsky explains this is part by the novelist's truculent pessimism, but also by the nature of his art: "Céline's style is subordinated to his receptivity of the objective world. In his seemingly careless, ungrammatical, passionately condensed language there lives, beats, and vibrates the genuine wealth of French culture, the entire emotional and mental experience of a great nation, in its living context, and its keenest tints" (p. 414). According to Trotsky, the moving power of *Voyage au bout de la nuit* derives mainly from the fact that the novel is a faithful artistic reexpression of reality. But he points out that "hopelessness ever leads to docility" (p. 420). The novelist's pessimism, which also contributes to his success, is a threat to his originality: "By rejecting not only the present but also what must take its place, the artist gives his support to what is. To that extent Céline, willy-nilly, is the ally of Poincaré" (p. 420).

Trotsky's adroit use of dialectic leads to what seems to be the main point of his article: the difficulty for a non-Marxist to formulate a valid criticism of society. Trotsky uses Céline's novel, and Poincaré's *Memoirs*, merely to build up a highly sophisticated bit of propaganda.

The Russian language edition of *Voyage au bout de la nuit* appeared in 1936 with a critical preface by Ivan Anissimov.[6] The second paragraph of this study suggests the critic's point of view: "Louis Céline a écrit une véritable encyclopédie du capitalisme agonisant" (p. 165).[7] An encyclopedia, in spite of what Anissimov seems to think, does not usually contain the same amount of creative fiction as a novel.

Anissimov finds Céline's point of view somewhat ambivalent: "Céline n'est pas un adversaire conscient du capitalisme, mais seulement un grand artiste qui ne cache pas la vérité" (p. 165).[8] The critic goes on to analyse the "truth" revealed by the author using a double-edged approach. A brief synopsis turns each section of the novel into an encyclopedia article on different aspects of capitalist society—war, African colonies, American industry, Parisian slums; each synopsis is followed by a critique of the author's presentation. After summarizing Céline's vision of wartime Paris, for example, Anissimov comments: "il s'est figé dans l'horreur. L'idée de lutte ne lui vient même pas á l'esprit. L'indignation à laquelle il est en proie, est sans but. Il ne réfléchit pas au méchanisme social qui a engendré la monstruosité qui s'étale à ses yeux" (p. 167).[9] These statements are entirely off the point. Céline was not immobilized by horror or overcome with aimless indignation; he undertook the difficult enterprise of writing a novel. We do not know what Céline thought about fighting capitalism, but obviously a novel is not a weapon to fight an entire social and economic system. The most it can do is satirize, which is precisely what Céline's novel does, as Anissimov himself pointed out (p. 165). Finally, the novelist constructs a work coherent in artistic terms; he cannot shift his aim and comment convincingly on social structure. That is the job of the critic. Anissimov's study suffers from a basic misunderstanding of the difference between art and reality.

Whatever it might be, *Voyage au bout de la nuit* is not a fully developed Marxist analysis of the capitalist system. Yet, because of this, Anissimov condemns the novel for being passive (p. 167), philistine (p. 168), cynical (pp. 169, 171), hypocritical (p. 169), sterile (p. 170), nihilistic (p. 171), and abstract (p. 171). So that the reader may be fully warned, the critic expresses such condemnation sixty-four times in eight pages. At the beginning of his study, Anissimov pointed out that Céline was not a Marxist; the effort involved in going through his novel and condemning it, because this is true down to matters of detail, is pointless. Anissimov's study seems important mainly as an example of the difficulty for a Marxist to interpret foreign literature in Russia during the height of the Stalinist era.

Céline travelled to the Soviet Union in 1936 to spend the royalties on the Russian translation of his novel. A year later in a pamphlet, *Mea Culpa*, he proclaimed his disgust with Russia and with the communist system. In 1938 and 1939 he poured out violently anti-communist opinions in two virulent polemical works. Trotsky's cavalier treatment of Céline and Anissimov's outright condemnation were fortunate in the short run. The Marxist world was spared the embarrassment of singing Céline's praises, only to have him turn anti-communist.

Trotsky had predicted that *Voyage au bout de la nuit* would be an enduring work of literature, and time has borne him out. He and Anissimov agree that this novel — in which Céline, not unlike Balzac, creates a model of an entire society — accurately reflects conditions in the capitalist world. The text of the novel presents, for example, in the war situation a strange division of roles. The ordinary soldiers like Bardamu or Robinson bear the greatest hardships, without believing in the struggle. Officers encourage the soldiers, more or less subtly, to continue their pointless efforts. Above them are the shadowy beings who profit from the war; the press, the organizers of "benefits" for the soldiers, the faceless

Argentinians. In Africa the natives are doubly oppressed by the disease-ridden climate and by the rapacious European soldiers and traders. The whites—from the lowliest clerk, like Bardamu, to the Director General of the trading company himself—inflict suffering on the natives, but are exposed to the rigors of the climate and are exploited by the stockholders of that company, who, safe in Paris, only profit. Bardamu's description of the factory in Detroit fits into the same pattern. There are workers like himself, the foreman, and the doctor who help keep the system going, and Ford, an impersonal entity that somehow controls everything and profits from it. Each one of these situations is characterized by excessive noise and by violence. These two themes highlight the parallel inherent in the tripartite structure of each of the three situations mentioned.

A tentative explanation of these parallels could be found in Marxist theory which has long pointed out that a developed industrial system requires colonies or spheres of influence for markets, raw materials, and investment of surplus capital. Rivalry over colonies or spheres of influence is, in the Marxist approach, seen as a prime cause of war, specifically of the First World War[10]—which Céline describes. Similarly the stratification of war society, colonial society, and industrial society ties in with a statement by Lenin:

> It is characteristic of capitalism in general that the ownership of capital is separated from the application of capital to production, that money capital is separated from industrial or productive capital, and that the rentier, who lives entirely on income obtained from money capital, is separated from the entrepreneur and from all who are directly concerned in the management of capital (p. 59).

The foregoing may suffice to suggest that Céline's novel could be interpretted from a Marxist viewpoint.

Céline, the author of *Voyage au bout de la nuit*, was not, had never been, and was never to become a communist or a Marxist of any kind. But his novel presents a microcosm of early twentieth-century society. It should be possible for a Marxist critic—fully realizing the difference between Céline's ideas and his own—to put aside controversy and analyse this novel in terms of one of the great critical and ideological systems of our age. The model for such a treatment can already be found in George Lukacs' studies of Balzac. Lukacs points out quite clearly that the royalist utopian vision, on which Balzac based his novelistic world, had been singled out for special irony by Marx,[11] then he goes on to illuminate both Balzac's art, and the society from which the author drew his material, by analysing the texts in Marxist terms. A similar study of *Voyage au bout de la nuit* could promote understanding of a novel which, almost forty years after its publication, remains both powerful and mysterious.

Notes

1. October 29, 1932.

2. December 19, 1932.

3. "Au bout de la nuit," December 13, 1932.

4. Paul Nizan, "Au bout de la nuit," *L'Humanité*, December 9, 1932; Jean Frèville, "Il y a des livres . . . ," *L'Humanité*, December 19, 1932.

5. Volume 156, No. 4 (October 1935), 413–420. Subsequent references to this study will be identified by page number in parentheses in the text of this article.

6. A French translation of this preface appears in *Les Cahiers de l'Herne No. 5: Louis-Ferdinand Céline II* (1965), 165–172. We refer to this version, identifying references by page number in parentheses in the text of this article.

7. "Louis Céline wrote a veritable encyclopedia of dying capitalism" (translated by J. E. Hull).

8. "Céline is not a conscious adversary of capitalism, just a great artist who doesn't hide the truth" (translated by J. E. Hull).

9. "He is immobilized by horror. The notion of struggle never even enters his mind. The indignation that overcomes him is aimless. He does not reflect on the social mechanism which has engendered the monstrosity unfolding before his eyes" (translated by J. E. Hull).

10. V. I. Lenin, *Imperialism: The Highest Stage of Capitalism*, revised translation (New York: International Publishers, 1939), p. 11. A subsequent reference to this work will be identified by page number in the text of this article.

11. *Balzac et le réalisme français* (Paris: Maspero, 1967), p. 27.

The View from a Rump: America as Journey and Landscape of Desire in Céline's *Voyage au bout de la nuit*

Philip H. Solomon*

"Je reçus tout près du derrière de Lola le message d'un nouveau monde" (I received in the area of Lola's behind the message of a new world) (p. 55).[1] This message that Bardamu, the protagonist of *Voyage au bout de la nuit* (1932), receives from the body of Lola, his American mistress, is a desire to foresake the terrors and stupidities of World War I, of a French army all too ready to use soldiers like Bardamu for cannon fodder, and come to the United States with its promise of a new and better life. A study of the textualization of that message in the narrative of Bardamu's American adventure will permit us to explore certain thematic images as they structure the landscapes that will serve as the context of Bardamu's desire. In the course of this study we shall also examine certain

*Reprinted with permission from *Yale French Studies* 57 (1979):5–22. © 1979 Philip H. Solomon.

relationships between Bardamu's desire and the shaping of the plot in which it is manifested.

Lola had come to France as a volunteer to aid in the French war effort before America's entry into the conflict. The relationship between Lola and Bardamu will last only so long as Bardamu plays the fearless, patriotic French soldier. He loses his mistress when, in the course of recuperating from a mental breakdown occasioned by his fear of the war, he confesses to her that he is a coward. Bardamu's interest in Lola is, as we might suspect, primarily sexual. His delight with her body is enhanced by his perception of her as a typical American woman. And his easy enjoyment of her convinces him that the means to success in America will be found through the bodies of Lola's female compatriots:

> Je n'en avais jamais assez de parcourir ce corps américain. . . . un pays apte à produire des corps aussi audacieux dans leur grâce et d'une envolée spirituelle aussi tentante devait offrir bien d'autres révélations capitales au sens biologique il s'entend. Je décidai à force de peloter Lola d'entreprendre tôt ou tard le voyage aux Etats-Unis comme un véritable pèlerinage et cela dès que possible. Je n'eus en effet de cesse et de repos . . . avant d'avoir mené à bien cette profonde aventure, mystiquement anatomique. (p. 55)

> I never tired of caressing this American body. . . . a country capable of producing bodies of such startling grace and tempting spiritual elevation was supposed to offer many other essential revelations, biologically speaking to be sure. My petting with Lola led me to decide to undertake, sooner or later, a voyage to the United States as a real pilgrimage, and just as soon as possible. I could find, in fact, no peace or rest . . . before having concluded this profound, mystically anatomical adventure.

Bardamu's project takes shape presumably during the moments he and Lola spend in bed. We can read "parcourir [le décor] américain" for "parcourir ce corps américain," since the exchange between Lola and America is predicated upon Bardamu's assumption that Lola's horizontal, submissive, penetrable body will be the model for the "body" of America. This series of metonymic exchanges — Lola's body for that of the American woman, for America itself and an assumed way of life — reveals more than just a simple project of conquest with comically mystical overtones. The passage from Lola's body to that of America is indeed a *passage* — a text, of course, by the protagonist-turned-narrator but also a voyage and, coextensively, a narrative impulse, an inception of plot. The psychodynamics of desire and narration are indissociable here. Desire is activity within an absence or lack. Thus, as Freud noted, an essential characteristic of desire is its "mobility, the ease with which it passes from one object to another."[2] This displacement in search of cathexis and, ultimately, inertia, is a temporal phenomenon, generating History as well as (his)story. Lacan situates desire along the chain of signifiers — the metonymic movement of the text — with the phallus functioning as the signifier of desire, symbolizing in its presence/absence (the castration complex, detumescence, etc.) the lack that is constitutive of desire and the deferral of a final meaning — signified — that would end the chain.[3]

The satisfaction desire seeks is, as Freud has shown, the repetition of a pleasure previously experienced. The literary equivalent of this sort of repetition would be metaphor. According to Jakobson, metaphor and metonymy constitute the two modes of the development of discourse. The various manifestations of metaphor, as the term is used by Jakobson — repetition, recall, mnemonic devices of various sorts — effect, insofar as the plot of a text is concerned, what Peter Brooks has called a "binding of textual energies." This process is based upon "a system of repetitions which are returns to and returns of, confounding the movement forward to the end with a movement back to origins, reversing meaning within forward moving time . . . offering the possibility (or the illusion) of 'meaning' wrested from 'life.' "[4]

Insofar as Bardamu's plans to travel to America are concerned, he postulates the end of desire as a return to the pleasure he enjoyed with Lola, in the form, ultimately, of a secure and financially comfortable existence in that New World. The attainment of that goal would, according to these premises, eliminate the further need for *passage* — test or voyage. Bardamu's project recalls an earlier moment in the novel. Bardamu had volunteered to join the army in a burst of naive patriotic enthusiasm. But very quickly he discovered the devastation and meaninglessness of the conflict in which he was engaged. He compares his loss of innocence with respect to the war and all that the war connotes to a loss of sexual virginity: "On est puceau de l'Horreur comme on l'est de la volupté" (One is a virgin with respect to Horror as one is with respect to sensual pleasure) (p. 17). This deflowering leads to an arousal — the desire to escape the war at any price, even if it means surrendering to the Germans. If one were to locate the beginning of the plot of *Voyage*, that which will impell the forward movement of the text, one would have to situate it in this revelation — the beginning of Bardamu's discovery — of the true nature of the human condition. Lola's body intensifies the aroused desire and gives it and the novel's plot a new direction by opening up the possibility of finding a better life elsewhere by means of a voyage to another land.

Bardamu's trip to America is delayed by a substitute voyage to Africa. Although a detailed analysis of his African sojourn is beyond the scope of this article, some attention needs to be given to the relationship between it and the eventual pilgrimage to America. Although the voyage to Africa maintains the impulse to seek a better life outside of Europe, the sort of existence that Bardamu discovers in the jungle is revealing of the futility of such amelioristic perspectives. Bardamu's voyage has been paid for by the company that employs him (he does not have enough money to travel to

America), and, in exchange for their "generosity," Bardamu has agreed to run a trading post in a remote part of the country. If Europe is the Old World and America the New World, then Africa is the Archaic or Primitive World. The theme of sexuality which has been associated with his desire for a better life, that has served as a point of departure for the voyage, manifests itself in several ways. Sexuality is taken over by the African landscape as it ebbs away from the Europeans. Vegetable and insect life proliferate in the hothouse atmosphere: mosquitoes reproduce by the "billions," and great swarms of termites devour habitations as soon as they are built (p. 126); the vegetation of the Europeans' gardens grows "deliriously" (p. 162); the forest is "monstrously abundant" (p. 162). Amid this fertility run rampant, the Europeans, unable to adapt to the climate, "melt away" (p. 147), consumed by anemia, tropical diseases, interminable periods in the case of the women. Sexual desire similarly "melts away" in the heat and humidity.

In his trading post Bardamu struggles fitfully to stay healthy and sane, his strength sapped by constant diarrhea. Fire and fever, countervailing forces to the oppressive heat, will constitute Bardamu's means of escape. He burns down the trading post and in the grip of a delirious fever is carried to a port city, where he is placed on a boat—an anachronistic galley ship—that conveys him to the shores of America. Fire, that of the blaze that destroys the trading post and that of the fever, is associated traditionally with purification and regeneration. But it is associated with sexual desire as well. Thus fire as the agent of his escape to America serves to recall Lola as it renews the desire that stimulated Bardamu's project of conquest; it closes the African episode as it opens the American one, impelling the plot forward.

When Bardamu arrives in New York he is both surprised and disconcerted by the architecture of this American city as contrasted with its European counterpart. The difference between the two landscapes is conveyed by sexual metaphors. Whereas the European city is depicted as feminine, the American city, which Bardamu had expected to be equally feminine as an extension of Lola's body, turns out to be masculine in nature:

> Figurez-vous qu'elle était debout leur ville, absolument droite. New York, c'est une ville debout. On en avait déjà vu nous des villes bien sûr, et des belles encore, et des ports et des fameux même. Mais chez nous, n'est-ce pas, elles sont couchées les villes, au bord de la mer ou sur des fleuves, elles s'allongent sur le paysage, elles attendent le voyageur, tandis que celle-là l'Américaine, elle ne se pâmait pas, non, elle se tenait bien raide, là, pas baisante du tout, raide à faire peur. (p. 184)

> Imagine that it was standing up, their city, absolutely erect. New York is a city standing up. Of course, we'd already seen lots of cities, and fine

ones at that, and ports and even famous ones. But at home, cities lie down alongside a coast or a river, they stretch out on the landscape, awaiting the traveler; whereas the American one does not swoon, no, she stands stiff, not at all ready to be laid, stiff enough to scare you.

Bardamu's masculinity appears to have been diminished, transferred in part to the landscape with its phallic verticality. Indeed, the overpowering effect of the landscape on Bardamu suggests that he has become, at least temporarily, impotent, with all that this term connotes insofar as the successful completion of his pilgrimage is concerned. And we may suspect that there will be an attendant transformation of Bardamu's role—from active to passive, from conqueror to victim.

Another aspect of the New York landscape reinforces the disparity between it and Lola's body. Whereas the latter was open to penetration, entry into New York's buildings—a house or building is, of course, a traditional Freudian symbol of the female body—is obstructed for the poor and shabby-looking Bardamu by a "système de contraintes" (system of restraints). Not only is Bardamu frightened by the "system," but he also "caves in with shyness" (m'effondrais de timidité)—this last notation suggesting detumescence:

> Mais à la pensée d'avoir à pénétrer dans une de ces maisons je m'effarais et m'effondrais de timidité. . . . Pour eux c'était la sécurité peut-être tout ce déluge en suspens tandis que pour moi ce n'était rien qu'un abominable système de contraintes . . . en couloirs, en verrous, en guichets, une torture architecturale gigantesque. . . . (p. 205)

> But at the thought of having to penetrate one of these houses, I grew frightened and caved in with shyness. For them this suspended deluge perhaps meant security, whereas for me it was nothing but a system of restraints . . . hallways, bolted doors, entrance gates, a gigantic architectural torture. . . .

Although Bardamu has begun to perceive that there may be no place for him in America, that he has entered a wasteland characterized by the qualities of vertical rigidity, hardness, and closure, it is necessary that his desire continue, for not only is it constitutive of plot but of self, of personality as well.[5] To foresake all desire is to succumb to the entropy that both menaces and tempts the Célinian protagonist, in the form of a dissolution whose final stage would be a return to randomness as a molecular diffusion in space. This entropic force resembles the Freudian death wish in that it is both a desire (usually repressed) to return to the inorganic and the affirmation of individuality:

> Tout notre malheur vient de ce qu'il faut demeurer Jean, Pierre ou Gaston coûte que coûte pendant toutes sortes d'années. Ce corps à nous travesti de molécules agitées et banales, tout le temps se révolte contre cette farce de durer. Elles veulent aller se perdre nos molécules, au plus vite, parmi l'univers. . . . (p. 333)

All our misfortune comes from our having to remain Jean, Pierre, or Gaston, whatever the cost, year in and year out. Our body, a costume of agitated common molecules, is rebelling all the time against that terrible farce of lasting. They want to get themselves lost, our molecules, as quickly as possible, amid the universe. . . .

To endure becomes an "ecstasy" in the Heideggerian sense of a "standing outside," *ex-stasis*, the timeless ground of being.[6] At one point during Bardamu's stay in New York, overcome by depression and solitude, he seems to have lost all desire. And no longer having a reason to exist, he experiences a collapsing within himself that is ambiguously pleasurable and frightening, and which we can interpret as an initial phase of the dissolution of self: ". . . plus rien ne m'empêchait de sombrer dans une sorte d'irrésistible ennui, dans une manière de doucéreuse, d'effroyable catastrophe d'âme (nothing any longer prevented me from sinking into a sort of irresistable ennui, into a kind of cloying, dreadful catastrophe of the soul) (p. 203). If desire as the maintaining of a "firm" structure of the self is antithetical to this kind of collapse, it is at the same time centrifugal in nature, fragmenting, a violence to self and other.[7]

Since Bardamu had predicated the satisfaction of his desire on the repetition of the pleasure he once enjoyed with Lola and has made women the mediators of his conquest of America, he is delighted to see all around him numerous substitutes—or so he thinks—for his ex-mistress: "Souvenir de Lola! Son exemple ne m'avait pas trompé. C'était vrai. Je touchais au vif de mon pèlerinage" (Souvenir of Lola! Her example had not deceived me. It was true. I was getting to the heart of my pilgrimage) (p. 193). Appearances are, however, deceptive. The women are as imposing as the architecture around him. A group of beautiful women seated in the lobby of the Laugh Calvin Hotel (the name seems oxymoronic, given the austerity of Calvinism), where Bardamu is staying, have the same sort of mechanical, rigid symmetry, hardness, and impenetrability as the facades of Manhattan's buildings. They are jewel-like objects to be venerated, as if the lobby were a temple, rather than be made love to. Such a setting excludes the possibility of laughter as it literalizes the term "pilgrimage":

> . . . plongées en de profonds fauteuils, comme dans autant d'écrins. Des hommes attentifs autour, silencieux à passer et repasser à certaine distance d'elles, curieux et craintifs, au large de la rangée des jambes croisées à de magnifiques hauteurs de soie. Elles me semblaient ces merveilleuses attendre là des événements très graves et très coûteux. Evidemment, ce n'était pas à moi qu'elles songeaient. (p. 196)

> . . . sunk in deep armchairs, as in so many jewel-cases. Attentive men all around them, silent, passing back and forth at a certain distance from them, curious and timid, giving a wide berth to the line of crossed legs revealing magnificent heights of silk. It seemed to me that these marvelous creatures were awaiting events of a serious and costly nature. Clearly, they were not thinking of me.

Bardamu joins the other worshippers of these women who resemble, with their cold, statuelike beauty, the movie stars that appear on the posters and in the films of the movie houses he has begun to frequent — "parfaites, pas une négligence, pas une bavure, parfaites . . . mignonnes mais fermes et concises en même temps" (perfect, without a fault, without a blemish, perfect . . . delicate but, at the same time, firm and concise) (p. 201).

The one unknown woman in New York that Bardamu dares approach shares these same attributes of cold, hard perfection, and, ultimately, lifelessness. In this case the woman herself is not described but rather the environment in which she works — a modern cafeteria — and whose material qualities she shares. In the cafeteria Bardamu must perform his "rite alimentaire" (feeding ritual) (pp. 205–206) according to the prescribed rules, which, of course, forbid fraternization between customers and employees. This religious motif recalls the hotel and the movie theatre as temples where women serve as objects of veneration. Having gained entrance to this formica temple, Bardamu will try to "pick up" one of the busgirls. The light that illuminates the cafeteria is harsh and glaring, reducing everything to a blinding play of surface reflections, transforming the food into something resembling the plastic and metal of which the cafeteria is constructed. "Mes fraises sur mon gâteau" (the strawberries on my cake), Bardamu remarks, "étaient accaparées par tant d'étincelants reflets que je ne pouvais pas me résoudre à les avaler" (were caught by so many shimmering reflections that I couldn't bring myself to swallow them) (p. 207).

The sterility of such a decor is reinforced by the imagery of the hospital that appears in the description of the cafeteria. It is compared to an "operating room" and its employees garbed in immaculately white uniforms are depicted as "nurses" (p. 206). Hitherto positively valorized as a refuge from the war or, in the case of Bardamu's stay in Africa, as a shelter from the heat and humidity, the image of the hospital is, in our present context, negatively valorized. Bardamu's approach to the girl in question is less an attempt to seduce her than a despairing effort to extract some sign of life from the landscape of which she is a part: "J'en avais assez d'être seul! Plus de rêve! De la sympathie! Du contact!" (I had enough of being alone! No more dreaming! Some sympathy! Some contact!) (p. 208). But Bardamu receives no response from the girl, and the incident, which David Hayman has compared to a "dumb show reminiscent of the early Chaplin films,"[8] ends with Bardamu's polite ejection from the premises. Having failed to act according to the rules, the "system of restraints," having tried to rebel against the dehumanization that characterizes the environment of the cafeteria, he is shown to the door by the bouncer "comme un chien qui vient de s'oublier" (like a dog that has just forgotten himself) (p. 208).

"C'était peut-être la Grèce qui recommence" (It was perhaps Greece reborn) (p. 193), Bardamu had thought to himself upon first seeing the beautiful women of New York, their perfect forms evoking in his mind the ideal of Classical Greece.[9] But, to recall Nietzsche's *The Birth of Tragedy* — which Céline had probably read — however beautiful these women may be, they are, as Bardamu has discovered, flawed; for they embody the Apollonian extreme, perfection of form, self-control, distance, plasticity, without the Dionysian element of overflowing life. According to Nietzsche it is the synthesis of Apollo and Dionysus that produces great art. For Céline, one manifestation of that synthesis can be found in the dance which, in Erika Ostrovsky's words, "can be considered the movement of life . . . transfigured into art."[11] Bardamu will later meet a woman who approaches the Célinian ideal — Molly, the beautiful prostitute with a heart of gold and the body of a dancer.

Masturbation becomes a means of profaning those temples in which female beauty is worshipped, of breaking the "system of restraints." Exchanging the "sweet" and "warm" (p. 205) space of the movie theatre for the intimate confines of his room at the Laugh Calvin hotel, the movie projector for his mind's flow of images, Bardamu masturbates himself to sleep. By means of fantasy, the metonymy of desire is replaced by metaphor, a repetition of the pleasure enjoyed with Lola and, by extension, a conquest of those untouchable women Bardamu has been forced to admire from afar. No longer excluded from the life around him, he eliminates the distance between himself and external reality by transforming the latter into a world of satisfied desire.

Another form of masturbation concerns the use of money. As we have seen, a principal "restraint" under which Bardamu is obliged to operate is that of poverty. In America, Bardamu had been warned, "c'est tout millionnaire ou tout charogne! Y a pas de milieu" (you're either a millionaire or a stiff! There's no in between) (p. 186). In the heart of the city he discovers the temple of money, a temple more forbidding than the others. Through the use of ecclesiastic motifs, Céline explicitly condemns the commercial orientation of this New World. Manhattan is characterized as a "borough of gold," into which "one enters only on foot" (p. 192). The dollar is a "Saint-Esprit," a "host" not to be eaten but "placed on the heart," as one places a billfold in the interior pocket of a jacket (p. 192). The barred window of a bank teller is compared to the grille of a confessional, with the Dollar becoming the priest receiving the confession (p. 192).

Bardamu's attempt to "pick up" the girl in the cafeteria links that formica temple with the temple of money in a masturbatory fantasy, for his approach to the girl is preceded by a reverie that transforms him into a wealthy man able, by means of his money, to have the girl he desires: "Ça doit faire un drôle d'effet, pensais-je, quand on peut se permettre d'aborder ainsi une de ces demoiselles au nez précis et coquet 'Mademoiselle, lui dirait-on, je suis riche, bien riche . . . dites-moi ce qui vous ferait plaisir d'accepter . . .' " (It must have a strange effect, I thought, when one can take the liberty of approaching one of these girls with their neat, coquettish noses "Miss, one would say to her, I am rich, very rich . . . tell me what you would care to accept") (p. 206). The use of money to make reality conform to one's desires, derived according to Freudian theory from the child's attribution of magical powers to his feces during the anal stage of development, is analogous here to Bardamu's activities in his hotel room. Bardamu's fantasy is completed by the vision of a world that is antithetical to the hostile landscape of New York: "Tout se transforme et le monde formidablement hostile en vient à l'instant rouler à vos pieds en boule sournoise, docile et velouté" (Everything is transformed, and the formidably hostile world comes in a moment to roll at your feet in a clever ball, docile and velvety) (p. 206).

The connection between money, sexuality, and excrement leads us to yet another of the metaphoric temples that dot Bardamu's New York landscape, that mark the route of his "pilgrimage." Unlike the others, this one is located below the surface of the city—in an underground mensroom. Bardamu gains access to it from the street. Penetrating between the "monsters of houses" (p. 193) that border it, houses from which Bardamu and others like him are excluded, the street is a *passage*, not only by virtue of its physical configuration but also by virtue of its opening on to other streets of a similar nature along which Bardamu will walk in *Voyage* as will his incarnations in future novels. There would seem to be no *end* to the misery Bardamu has discovered, for the street points "vers le bout qu'on ne voit jamais de toutes les rues du monde" (toward the end one never sees of all the world's streets) (p. 192). One link between this perspective and the project that originally brought Bardamu to America is established by the image of the street as a "triste plaie" (sad wound) (p. 192), with its connotations of a negatively valorized female orifice. To enter that "wound" is to confront the subterranean aspects of existence, to explore a system that is peristaltic, excremental rather than sexual in nature.[11] Bardamu enters the lavatory through a "hole" in the street, down a staircase of "pink marble" (p. 195).

The activities that take place within this mensroom contrast radically with the sort of existence one finds above ground:

> Ce contraste était bien fait pour déconcerter un étranger. Tout ce débraillage intime, cetter formidable familiarité intestinale et dans la rue cette parfaite contrainte! J'en demeurais étourdi. (p. 196)

> This contrast was just the thing to disconcert a foreigner. All this intimate exposure, this extraordinary intestinal familiarity, and in the street that perfect restraint. I remained overwhelmed by it.

The opposition between "débraillage intime," "familiarité intestinale" and "parfaite contrainte" recalls and anticipates other aspects of Bardamu's voyage. During the trip to Africa on the *Amiral Bragueton*, when

Bardamu had become the *pharmakos* for the ship's passengers, "débraillage" *(la braie* was the trouser worn by the Gauls' both *débraillage* and
braguette [the 'fly' of a pair of pants]—the latter is present in *Bragueton*—
are derived from it) had been negatively valorized as the 'venting' (literally
'unbuttoning') of man's propensity for violence toward others, exacerbated
in this instance by the tropical heat. As for excrement and the sharing of
toilets, both will later be negatively valorized as, for example, in the case
of the overflowing privies that characterize the Parisian *zone*, where
Bardamu will sporadically practice medicine, and which symbolize the
moral and physical corruption of its inhabitants. For Bardamu in New
York, "débraillage" and defecation, associated thematically and syn-
tagmatically, are depicted as forms of liberation, signs of life that become
means to human contact. The men on line waiting their turn to enter the
stalls are no longer the solitary figures they were in the streets above. A
spirit of camaraderie links these total strangers—whose only bond might
be their exclusion from the temple of the dollar—as they anticipate the
pleasure of relieving their needs, "la perspective . . . paraissait les libérer
et les réjouir intimement (the prospect . . . appeared to liberate them and
give them an inner pleasure) (p. 195).

As for the act of defecation itself, we know from Freudian theory that
the child passes though an anal stage during the course of his development, when libido is concentrated in the anal zone. Thus the release of
tension inherent in the act of defecation is erotic. As evidenced by the
joyous attitude of the men on line, the pleasures of defecation serve as a
regressive substitute for genital satisfaction in this constipated, commercial
society. Céline refers to this coming together of men for the purposes of
defecation, men who in the streets above are alienated from themselves
and from one another, as the "communisme joyeux du caca" (the joyous
communism of crap) (p. 196). This expression with its felicitous allitera-
tion sums up, as it were, this entire episode as an attack against a
psychologically repressive—and thus neurotic—society founded upon
privilege and possession, a society which, as we have seen, worships the
dollar. The episode could serve as an illustration of Norman Brown's thesis
that modern capitalistic society is structured by sublimated anality taking
the form of the love and manipulation of material goods and money.[12]

Bardamu's attitude toward this "scatological rite" (p. 196), one that
serves as the underground response to the rites of the other temples
Bardamu has discovered, remains ambiguous. On the one hand, he is
attracted by the communal pleasure of those in the city who, like
Bardamu, are victims of New York's "systems of restraint." On the other
hand, he is disgusted by the odors emanating from that activity. Unaware
at this point that the W. C., like the "sad wound" of the street, will open
on to other scenes of elimination, other underground aspects of existence,
he is not ready to share the fate of those around him, to resign himself to a
limited existence with limited pleasures.

Whatever other interpretations we may give to "débraillage" and defecation, they are unmistakably signs of life in an otherwise sterile, lifeless environment. This function is reinforced by Céline's use of the associated imagery of secretion. When Bardamu decides to visit Lola, having finally found her address in New York, he longs for the presence of a French-style concierge in the building, for she would be able to tell him what sort of existence Lola has been leading since he last saw her. The gossip with which a concierge might enlighten Bardamu—permitting him a penetration of the New York landscape hitherto impossible—is depicted as a kind of ooze emanating from all parts of the building and channeled through her. What would be disgusting in other contexts becomes "tasty" when compared to the "insipid" ambiance in which Bardamu has been struggling: "Détritus, bavures à suinter de l'alcôve, de la cuisine, des mansards, à dégouliner en cascades par chez la concierge, en plein dans la vie, quel savoureux enfer" (Leavings, salivations that drip from the alcove, from the kitchen, from the attic rooms, to spill in cascades through the concierge's place, immersed in life, what a tasty hell) (p. 211).

Bardamu's decision to see Lola again is a tacit admission that his project to conquer America has thus far been a failure. This visit to his former mistress constitutes a return to origins, to the point of departure for the trip to America, a metaphor that reverses the metonymic movement of the plot/voyage and permits the reader to more fully comprehend Bardamu's present situation. That Bardamu will be unable to renew his relationship with his former mistress removes the "danger" of a premature "discharge" or "short-circuit" of the plot's energy.[13] At the same time, this inability to repeat a previously enjoyed pleasure provides the plot with another impulse, sending Bardamu to Detroit as it closes the New York section of the American adventure.

Bardamu, as we have noted, still finds Lola desirable. Musing on being able to once again have sexual relations with her, Bardamu employs the image of burglarizing a building, breaking through a "system of restraints": "Un corps luxueux c'est toujours un viol possible, une effraction précieuse, directe, intime dans le vif de la richesse, du luxe . . ." (A luxurious body always makes for a possible rape, a precious break-in, direct and intimate, into the heart of wealth, of luxury) (p. 212). As for Lola, her opinion of Bardamu remains unchanged. She still considers him a loathsome coward, a thoroughly despicable person, and wishes to rid herself of him as soon as possible. His departure is delayed by the arrival of some of Lola's women friends. Consonant with the passivity Bardamu had acquired upon landing in New York, it is Lola's friends, and not Bardamu the Frenchman, who direct the conversation about France. Not only do they tell Bardamu about Le Chabanais and Les Invalides, they inform him as well about the merits of various Parisian brothels.

Although Bardamu is unable to effect the sexual "break-in" with Lola that he desires, he finds another means of penetrating her defenses. When

Lola relates that her mother is being treated for cancer of the liver by the best and most costly specialists and that a cure is expected, Bardamu, putting to use some of the medical knowledge he has acquired, demolishes her prospects for the future by telling her categorically that her mother's ailment is fatal. "I've got her," Bardamu says to himself, noting Lola's fright upon hearing his words. No longer passive, Bardamu now can dominate his ex-mistress. Now he is prepared to use language to commit the "effraction" he desired. He tells Lola that cancer is hereditary: ". . . . je la voyais devant moi blêmir Lola, faiblir, "mollir" (I saw Lola before me grow pale, weaken, soften) (p. 221). "Faiblir" and mollir" contrast with the rigidity and hardness that Lola previously shared with the New York landscape. Her near collapse recalls as well the submissive Lola of Paris. It is only by means of threatening Bardamu with a gun — with its obviously phallic connotations — that Lola is able to reassert her "firmness" and put an end to Bardamu's verbal assault. Bardamu escapes with some satisfaction and enough money to permit him to leave town.

Having abandoned New York for Detroit and the possibility of employment in the Ford automobile factory, Bardamu discovers that he has foresaken the sterile landscape of New York for an equally sterile factory setting:

> Partout ce qu'on regard, tout ce que la main touche, c'est dur à présent. . . . Il faut abolir la vie du dehors, en faire aussi d'elle de l'acier, quelque chose d'utile. On l'aimait pas assez telle qu'elle était, c'est pour ça. Faut en faire un objet donc, du solide, c'est la Règle. (pp. 225–226)

> Everywhere one looks, everything one's hand touches, is at present hard. . . . Outside life must be abolished, also made into steel, something useful. It was not loved enough as it was, that's the reason. Hence it's got to be made into an object, into something solid, that's the Rule.

Bardamu once again longs for a female body whose qualities would be antithetical to those of his surroundings — "un vrai corps que je voulais toucher, un corps rose en vraie vie . . . molle" (I wanted to touch a real body, a pink body endowed with real life . . . soft) (p. 226). And it is by means of money that Bardamu is able to fulfill his wishes, by purchasing the services of prostitutes in a brothel on the outskirts of the city.

One of those prostitutes is named Molly, a name derived from the Latin *mol*, meaning "soft." Physically, she resembles the ideal Célinian woman, for she is both flesh and perfect form; specifically, she shares the qualities of the dancer by virtue of her splendid legs — "jambes longues et blondes et magnifiquement déliées et musclées, des jambes nobles. La véritable aristocratie humaine, on a beau dire, ce sont les jambes qui la confèrent, pas d'erreur" (long, blond legs, magnificently supple and muscular, noble legs. True human aristocracy, one says it in vain, is conferred by the legs, no mistake about it) (pp. 227–228). The elasticity of Molly's legs "corrects" her softness. That which is elastic yields but returns to its former shape, thus courting but not succumbing to the flaccidity that is a sign of inevitable decomposition—flesh and form exist in harmonious equilibrium.[14] Given Molly's profession, one can take this concept of elasticity one step further: her legs yield to permit her to assume the horizontal, submissive position required by her customers but quickly return her to the erect, noble carriage of the dancer; she is a prostitute, available to anyone who can afford her, but her kindness and generosity are freely given; she can continue to exercise her profession and yet offer Bardamu a sincere love and a genuine interest in his self-betterment, in his making a success of himself in America. Molly thus represents a synthesis of the qualities of the American and European landscapes, hitherto opposed. Bardamu's deepening relationship with Molly appears to arrest the displacement instituted by desire, to conclude the *passage* that brought him to the United States.

But the possibility of Bardamu's successfully realizing his project bears with it the seeds of its destruction. Molly's many virtues transform her into a kind of Circe who enchants her Odysseus with the lure of an idyllic existence—a *soft* life. Their existence together takes on a dream-like quality as symbolized by the landscape that becomes the setting for their afternoon strolls. As opposed to the urban or factory landscape, this new setting is pastoral—the countryside that borders the city: "Des petits tertres pelés, des bosquets de bouleaux autour de lacs minuscules, des gens à lire par ici par là . . ." (Little scalped hills, clumps of birches around tiny lakes, people reading here and there) (p. 231). A threatening note intrudes upon this landscape, an image of the fragility of the relationship between Bardamu and his prostitute with a heart of gold—"le ciel tout lourd de nuages plombés" (the sky heavy with leaden clouds) (p. 231). Bardamu becomes uneasy in the presence of Molly, disturbed by the stirring of another desire, another activity within a lack. He wishes to resume the journey upon which he knows he is embarked, to explore existence in all its manifold aspects. Life itself becomes the ultimate mistress:

> Comme si la vie allait emporter, me cacher ce que je voulais savoir d'elle, de la vie au fond du noir, pendant que je perdais de la ferveur à l'embrasser Molly, et qu'alors j'en aurais plus assez et que j'aurais tout perdu au bout de compte par manque de force, que la vie m'aurait trompé comme tous les autres, la Vie, la vraie maîtresse des véritables hommes. (pp. 231–232)

> As if life were going to triumph, to hide from me what I wished to know of it, of life in the depths of darkness, while I lost my fervor kissing Molly, and then I would not have enough left, and I would have lost everything in the end through lack of strength, and life would have deceived me like all the others, Life, the true mistress of real men.

Bardamu's encounter with Robinson, his alter ego, gives him a further insight into the nature of that all-encompassing "mistress." Whereas Bardamu's walks with Molly take place during the day, his meeting with Robinson occurs, as did their previous meetings, during the night. Robinson had become in Bardamu's eyes the master hustler, someone who would be certain to find success in America. Robinson's namesake, Robinson Crusoe was, we may recall, able to master the hostile environment of his desert island with the aid of the instruments of his civilization and the zeal of a capitalistic entrepreneur. "Il n'était pas un type dans mon genre Robinson. Il devait en connaitre des trucs et des machins sur l'Amérique" (He wasn't a guy of my sort, Robinson. He was supposed to know the ins and outs of America) (p. 205). The news that Robinson has failed to live up to expectations profoundly shocks and disappoints Bardamu. Robinson has become one of the faceless souls that constitute the "Foreign Legion of the night" (p. 233), an after hours cleaning man in Detroit's office buildings. Unlike Bardamu, he can penetrate the American landscape, but only to perform the menial tasks required of him. And since cleaning the bathrooms is part of his job — he remarks that "lavatory" and "exit" are the only English words he has learned — we can link Robinson's failure with the "scatological rite" that Bardamu witnessed but was not ready to perform. Robinson cannot permit himself such fastidiousness or such pride — and nor can Bardamu once he has left Molly. Bardamu has but one alternative — to leave America and return to France. The architecture of the novel reinforces the illusory aspects of Bardamu's attempts to make a new life for himself first in Africa and later in America by framing these "exotic" adventures within the sections dealing with France.

The disillusionment that Bardamu has experienced in America will result in a change in his role as protagonist. He will be less the focus of the action than an observer-witness, particularly with respect to his relationship with Robinson. No longer will Robinson be the guide in whose footsteps Bardamu will attempt to follow. Instead he will become the exemplary victim whose ineffective struggles to rise above the misery and mediocrity of his situation can be recorded but not imitated. Robinson will die — shot by a spurned girl friend — but Bardamu must survive so that what has occurred can be related: "Je dirai tout un jour, si je peux vivre assez longtemps pour tout raconter" (One day I will say everything if I can live long enough to tell everything) (p. 244). It is the narration, not just of the text of *Voyage* but of the *oeuvre* to which it is a *passage*, that will become the space, the locus of desire. Writing is the activity within a lack that will subsume for Céline all other desires, the continuing voyage through the space of language marked by self-fragmentation and self-mutilation. The plot ends with the silence that is death: "On ne sera tranquille que lorsque tout aura été dit, une fois pour toutes, alors enfin on fera silence, et on aura plus peur de se taire" (One will be tranquil only when everything will have been said, once and for all, then, finally, one will fall silent, and one will no longer be afraid to be quiet) (p. 323).[15]

Notes

1. Page numbers within parentheses in my text refer to the Pléiade edition of *Voyage au bout de la nuit* (Paris: Gallimard, 1962). All translations are my own.

2. *An Outline of Psychoanalysis*, trans. James Strachey (New York: Norton, 1949), p. 24.

3. See Jacques Lacan, *Ecrits* (Paris: Seuil, 1961), pp. 685–695.

4. "Freud's Masterplot: Questions of Narrative," in *Literature and Psychoanalysis*, ed. Shoshana Felman, *Yale French Studies*, No. 55/56 (1977), pp. 289, 296.

5. See Leo Bersani, *A Future for Astynax: Character and Desire in Literature* (Boston and Toronto: Little Brown and Company, 1976), pp. 5–6.

6. Heidegger's definition of this term has been simplified here. Cf. *Being and Time*, trans. S. Macquarrie and E. Robinson (New York: Harper and Row, 1962), p. 377.

7. See Bersani, "Persons in Pieces," *A Future for Astynax*, pp. 286–315.

8. *Louis-Ferdinand Céline* (New York and London: Columbia University Press, 1965), p. 22.

9. Marc Hanrez has commented extensively on this passage in *Céline* (Paris: Gallimard, Bibliothèque Idéale, 1961), pp. 70–75.

10. *Céline and His Vision* (New York: New York University Press, 1967), p. 195.

11. I am grateful to Professor David Hayman of the University of Wisconsin who, in his response to my MLA paper, pointed out to me the significance of the street as "wound" as well as several of the links between the various "temples" that Bardamu visits.

12. See the chapters "The Excremental Vision" and "Filthy Lucre" in *Life Against Death* (New York: Vintage Books, 1959), pp. 179–201, 234–304.

13. See Brooks, "Masterplot," p. 292.

14. See Michel Beaujour, "Temps et substances dans *Voyage au bout de la nuit*," *Cahiers de l'Herne*, No. 5 (1965), pp. 173–188.

15. An earlier version of this article was presented as a paper at the special session on Céline, Modern Language Association, Chicago, 1977.

Céline's *Journey to the End of the Night*: From One Asylum to the Next

Allen Thiher*

Asked recently what I thought might be good background reading for a grasp of Céline, I replied Michel Foucault's *Histoire de la folie*. And by this reply I did not have in mind the last chapters of this history of madness in which Foucault argues that modern literature's essential function has been to attempt to give voice to unreason. Céline does not in

*This essay was written for this volume and appears here with permission of the author.

fact figure among those writers—Hölderlin, Nietzsche, Artaud—whom Foucault sees as expressing the truth of madness in a world in which the psychiatric asylum has banned folly's unreason from the realm of truth. Rather I had in mind Foucault's opening chapter in which he discusses how madness and reason, folly and truth, were able to cohabit in the same discourse during the Renaissance, or roughly from the time of Bosch and Rabelais until Cervantes and Shakespeare. In works by these artists madness could coexist with reason because Renaissance Europeans viewed folly as giving access to a realm that mere reason could not open upon. Hence as Foucault succinctly puts it, "La folie fascine parce qu'elle est savoir"—madness fascinates because it is knowledge.

It is no accident that Céline's favored writers and artists—Breughel and Cervantes, Bosch and Rabelais—are precisely those artists who give most pointed formulation to the wisdom of folly and to a vision in which madness can be a form of moral enlightenment in a world totally given over to folly. In this respect I would claim that one aspect of Céline's sensibility represents a return precisely to a Renaissance worldview. According to this view, madness can coexist with reason in a kind of dialectic in which it is folly not to give in to folly—or only reasonable to accept the enlightenment that delirium can offer. In many respects *Journey to the End of the Night* enacts a renewal of the Renaissance belief that truth demands this total dialectic if the "book of the world" is to be read in its totality.

Céline's work, among others, brings us to ask why did we ever lose this sense of the necessity of folly, of the necessity of recognizing the dominion of unreason? The philosophical villain in Foucault's tale of the exclusion of folly from our culture—or of our tragic loss of tragic unreason—is Descartes, the philosopher whom Foucault sees as emblematically excluding madness from reason's search for a first principle on which it might base certain knowledge. By excluding folly from his "cogito," Descartes mapped out the beginning of the end of that coexistence of reason and folly that had allowed the complete comic and tragic visions of the Renaissance. And, as Céline knew, the exclusion of folly from certainty was accompanied by that rationalization of language and its use by seventeenth-century grammarians that once caused Céline to write in anger that Rabelais's work had been in vain.

What interests us, however, in this perspective is that side of Cartesian thought that, in excluding the irrational from thought, also gave birth to the modern dualism of body and mind, with the body becoming the locus for the irrational. This dualism is largely the basis for the medical tradition that we call modern. One should recall in this context that Céline was a doctor before he was a writer; and that the Cartesian dualism that still underwrites our distinction between the organic body and the psychological subject was the basis for the medical education Céline received after World War I. In *Journey to the End of the Night* this dualism furnishes, for example, the medical model that underwrites the kind of treatment that the good doctor Bestombes gives his war-shattered soldier patients so that they might find a bit more "reason" to get themselves killed: "That, Bardamu, is how I mean to treat my patients, electricity for the body, and for the mind massive doses of patriotic ethics, injections as it were of invigorating morality!"[1] Now, as this example clearly shows, for Céline medical reason of a Cartesian sort is in the service of folly: in context the words of reason here are delirious. Or, in other terms, Céline has subverted the Cartesian exclusion of unreason by showing the Cartesian doctor to be a voice of madness. My claim, or my major claim in this essay, is that a kind of dialectic between a Renaissance sense of the omnipresence of folly and a Cartesian attempt to exclude that folly — an attempt that always fails — provides the motor force that keeps the journey going until its end, somewhere on the other side of reason and unreason. Cartesian medicine may attempt to exclude madness from reason by delegating folly to the realm of the body. But in a Renaissance perspective reason is a mere usurper that will always be punished for its hubris.

My claim entails that we are willing to read in its entirety Céline's *Journey to the End of the Night*. Most criticism — and not a few readers — have concentrated on the novel's first half in which Céline is a master satirist, renewing the kind of irrational tragic sense of laughter that runs in Western culture from Archilochus through Nietzsche. The second half of the novel, narrating Bardamu's life in France after he has finished his medical studies, has been judged to have less interest, some readers finding it to be repetitious and presumably somewhat tedious. I think this judgment is based on the a priori assumption that a work of literature should have a unified tonality throughout. This is a modern aesthetic presupposition and would, for example, hardly apply to much great Renaissance literature. Moreover, I would argue that the second half of *Journey* continues to explore the dialectic of reason and folly by pursuing it beyond satire, to the kind of tragic illumination that can only be understood as an ultimate expression of the truth of unreason: reason must finally be blinded by the illumination of unreason that takes us beyond the day and into the night, beyond the "folly of the day" that Céline's contemporary Blanchot describes. The paradoxical illumination of the night is to reveal tragic darkening of ultimate night, the *Umnachtung* of folly that submerges all in unreason.

To see madness's role in the novel means to recognize more than the recurrent theme, metaphor, and image of *délire*, the term Céline uses to designate both all-encompassing madness and the poetic fury that allows access to that madness. It also means seeing that all episodic experience, from the beginning of the novel to the end, is represented metaphorically or literally as folly. *Journey* begins with a collective outburst of madness (the war) and ends with a singular one (Madelon's shooting Robinson). In another perspective the novel is framed by episodes, set at the beginning and at the end, that take place in insane asylums. If one considers Céline's satire of the war at the novel's beginning as something of a prelude to the work, then one can also see it as a prelude to life in the asylum — or simply life itself. The first episode in the asylum occurs when the wounded Bardamu comes back to Paris where he receives what we might call his first medical lesson: "Le délire de mentir et de croire s'attrape comme la gale" (56) ("the delirium of lying and believing is as contagious as the mange"). After visiting a shooting gallery that seems an insane emblem of life itself, Bardamu has his first overt crisis that demonstrates that, as he often puts it, his head is not very solid. He undergoes an outburst of madness — or an acute attack of sanity in the ironic perspective of our dialectic. He is first sent to an observation post, then to the famous psychiatric hospital Bicêtre, this all to decide his fate in terms of Cartesian medical physiology: he will be shot if he is mad for psychological reasons, but spared if his outburst of insanity is due to organic reasons, say, syphilis. The asylum is the place where Cartesian reasoning is applied in all its mad rigor: for the Cartesian self is empowered with an infinite will that is declared guilty if the subject gives into folly, whereas a few spirochetes in the brain are a mere organic disorder for which no one can be blamed. There is even an explanation as to "why" one might show less than enthusiasm for the universal desire to kill that has broken out in Europe.

It is noteworthy that Céline places a similar character in each of his asylums, first the history professor Princhard in the observation center, and later Parapine, the medical researcher who ends up working in Doctor Baryton's institution at the novel's conclusion. These characters are comparable not only in that we may entertain doubts about their mental state, but each is an "intellectual." Between the two they not only represent the two cultures that C. P. Snow once described, but more especially the two aspects of Cartesian science — the history of the mind's development and the science of the body. True to his function as representative of the body, the medical doctor Parapine decides to refuse speech, a function of mind; whereas Princhard seems to thrive upon venting his demented tirade. Princhard has stolen systematically whatever he could lay his hands upon. He rationally expects this folly to lead to a judgment that he is morally unacceptable for universal carnage. Unfortunately, the historian discovers that the madness of history has caught up with him, which is dementedly expressed in his parodistic analysis of the historical development of the patriot-soldier that so astonished Goethe in 1792 at the battle of Valmy:

> pretty soon they were mass-producing heroes, and in the end, the system was so well perfected that they cost practically nothing. Everyone was delighted. Bismarck, the two Napoleons, Barrès, Elsa the Horsewoman. The religion of the flag promptly replaced the cult of heaven,

an old cloud which had already been deflated by the Reformation and reduced to a network of episcopal money boxes. In olden times the fanatical fashion was: "Long live Jesus! Burn the heretics!" . . . But heretics, after all, were few and voluntary. . . . Whereas today vast hordes of men are fired with aim and purpose by cries of: "Hang the limp turnips! The juiceless lemons! The innocent readers! By the millions, eyes right!" If anybody doesn't want to fight or murder, grab 'em, tear 'em to pieces! (57–58)

I quote this rather extraordinary passage to show Céline's sense of the history of folly, which is, in our terms, also the folly of history. The psychiatrist Bestombe's ranting about the history of psychiatric progress and, later, Doctor Baryton's bombast about the demise of "mind" with the most recent progress in medicine, these tirades are all part of the way Céline shows how "reason in history" subverts itself as the unfolding of folly. In each case rational analysis quickly amplifies to delirium.

Princhard is of course a victim of the development of the democratic *Geist*, while Bestombes is an enthusiastic, if mad, psychiatrist attempting to use the war to further his research in the depths of dementia. It is probably no accident that Bardamu encounters Bestombes in Bicêtre, the famous mental institution where the psychiatric reformer Philippe Pinel supposedly put an end in 1793 to barbarous eighteenth-century medical practices when he liberated the insane from their chains. The irony seems quite pointed, since at the same time the French revolution, according to Princhard, liberated the masses for patriotic carnage, Pinel liberated the insane. And, according to Bestombes, it was this same possibility for mass destruction that made possible the first "scientific" knowledge of the inner working of the human psyche. Armed with the knowledge that several generations of psychiatrists have garnered from traumatized subjects, Bestombes can thus hope to restore mental health so that deranged patriots will be willing to be slaughtered once more.

Good ironic Cartesian that he is, Bardamu goes to Bestombes to admit that he has difficulty in being "body and soul" as brave as he would like (76). He is once again a listener to dementia when Bestombes explains how the supposedly rational progress of psychiatry has been furthered by the unfolding history of mass warfare — delirium itself — so that the doctor has a wealth of explanations for Bardamu's troubles:

You see, Bardamu, the war, by providing us with such unprecedented means of trying men's nervous systems, has been a miraculous revealer of the human mind. . . . Recent pathological disclosures have given us matter for centuries of meditation and study. . . . Let's face it. . . . Up until now we hardly suspected the richness of man's emotional and spiritual resources! Today, thanks to the war, all that has changed! By a process of breaking and entering, painful to be sure, but decisive, nay providential for science, we have penetrated his innermost depths! (78)

Freud may have discovered something about the nature of repetition compulsion from shell-shocked veterans, but Bestombes has found that patriotism is the raison d'être of the psyche. No better image of folly in reason can be found in Céline, I should think.

In any case, Bardamu, his head "marked and that forever," is released from the asylum for no given reason. The image of the hospital and medical practices is, however, never far from view throughout the rest of his travels. He sails aboard the *Admiral Bragueton*, a kind of floating insane asylum, to arrive in Africa. Here, in another ironic reversal of the poles of reason and folly, the only place that attracts Bardamu is the hospital at Fort Gono. The hospital suggests a kind of terrestial paradise offering the only armistice within Bardamu's reach. In the midst of the total dissolution that the tropics promote, Bardamu then falls sick with a fever that seems to prove, against Descartes, the organic unity of body and soul. At the end of his African stay Bardamu is delirious with fever when he is supposedly sold as a galley slave and must row his way to New York. An ironic interlude in the journey in sickness and delirium comes only when Bardamu lives with the prostitute Molly; and Céline was far too conscious of disease etiology for there not to be some ironic intent in his vision of the brothel as a health spa.

After Bardamu's idyll in Detroit Céline picks up his narration by giving his hero a medical diploma. Céline's elliptical narration here should not cause one to lose sight of the way the second half of the novel is centered on Bardamu's experience as a doctor and on his experience of disease and insanity, folly, and science. Much as Bardamu's experience of the war is a prelude to his encounter with psychiatry and Bicêtre, so do his experiences as a doctor to the poor in the wretched suburb of Rancy culminate in his visit with the famous medical researcher Parapine and the resultant description of *délire scientifique*. This symmetry hardly seems accidental, though there is a difference of emphasis. In the first half of the novel Bardamu is a young victim of the reign of madness and must efface himself before others, a Princhard or a Bestombes, when he reports their folly. In the second half he is now initiated in the Cartesian rationality of medical reason. As an official practitioner of science he can take us into the sanctuaries of medical reason and show us its workings. Thus Bardamu comes to the Institute Bioduret Joseph — identifiably the Pasteur Institute — in hopes of getting some advice about the type of typhoid fever afflicting his young patient Bébert. To this end he addresses himself to Parapine:

> Parapine was an undisputed eminence in his special field. He knew all there was to know about typhoid in animals as well as human beings. His reputation went back twenty years to the day when certain German authors claimed to have isolated the Eberthella in the vaginal excreta of an eighteen-month-old girl, so creating an enormous stir in the Halls of

Truth. Only too delighted to take up the challenge in the name of the National Institute, Parapine had outdone those Teutonic braggarts by breeding the same microbes, now in its pure form, in the sperm of a seventy-two-year-old invalid. Instantly famous, he managed to hold the limelight for the rest of his life by publishing a few unreadable columns in various medical journals. (242)

Or as Bardamu sums it up in a pithy observation, "A true man of science takes at least twenty years on an average to make the great discovery, that is, to convince himself that one man's lunacy is not necessarily another man's delight" (241); "le délire des uns ne fait pas du tout le bonheur des autres . . ." (278). Science, in this parodistic perspective, is the ongoing struggle to impose folly as reason on others—a will to power that masks itself as a will to truth.

Parapine prefers in any case to look at the legs of teenage girls, and the next time Bardamu meets him, the famous scientist has been obliged to give up his position at the Institute. He has moved into psychotherapy. He takes groups of "cretins" to the Tarapout cinema where, applying Doctor Baryton's recently developed methods for massaging the unconscious, he leaves his charges in front of the silver screen: there his patients sit happily for hours, watching the same movie over and over, incapable of remembering they have just seen it. Movie houses and mental wards do undoubtedly share a number of common traits, though psychotherapy is usually not reckoned among them. Another common trait, in *Journey*, is that Bardamu first works as a walker-on at the Tarapout before he works as a psychiatrist's assistant in Baryton's asylum. A certain symmetry may be noted here, too, since Bardamu's work at the Tarapout comes to an end with a delirious vision of the dead invading the sky. Bardamu's hallucination marks an end to his working at the palace of hallucinations before he goes to work for the asylum where, presumably, he seeks to help the sick get rid of their hallucinations; and, equally crucial, struggles to keep their folly from taking hold of his mind.

The last part of the novel unfolds in the asylum in which, through Parapine's agency, Bardamu has a job. Bardamu remarks that war and disease are the two infinites of nightmare—"deux infinis du cauchmar" (407)—and we can see that Céline has begun *Journey* with one infinite and taken Bardamu on a journey through the other. Mental disease is illuminated from a number of perspectives in the last asylum, though Bardamu's experience there is quite consonant with his experience of delirium in the rest of the novel: there is no essential distinction between so-called normal individuals and their normal madness, and the delirious who have been officially declared insane. Or as Bardamu describes the latter:

They walked as if they had trouble keeping their heads balanced on their shoulders, they seemed in constant fear of stumbling and spilling the contents. All sorts of misshapen things, things they were dreadfully attached to, were bobbing and bumping about in there.

When the patients spoke of their mental treasures, it was always with anguished contortions or airs of protective condescension that made you think of powerful and ultrameticulous executives. Not for an empire would those lunatics have gone outside their minds. A madman's thoughts are just the usual ideas of a human being, except that they're hermetically sealed inside his head. (357)

Yet delirium, like organic maladies, can be contagious, and Bardamu must take care not to let himself be pulled too far afield by the attraction that vertigo exerts on those who are near it. It would be all too easy to enter the world of madness and never return.

The great example of the power of vertigo to overturn reason is given by Baryton himself when he gives up his asylum and flees to parts unknown. Baryton is first presented as a man solidly rooted in reason. Like Freud he dislikes his psychotics and prefers the "normal." He is something of a positivist and, like the German founder of modern psychiatric nosology Emil Kraepelin, he summarily reduces all mental illness to two major types (though not exactly those of Kraepelin): "Il existe des fous simples et puis il existe d'autres fous, ceux que torture la marotte de la civilisation" (409) — which one might translate as "simple nuts" and "nuts who get excited about the state of culture." Baryton gives an example of the latter type of the insane when he cites his own now silent assistant Parapine who, good medical Cartesian that he is, has discovered that between the penis and mathematics there is no intermediate state. Baryton would disdain such terrible truths and hold on, if he could, to common sense.

Baryton, a psychiatric Lear, is clearly in the grip of dementia even when he most wants to demonstrate his reason. Like Princhard earlier, he is also an historian of contemporary debacles of the mind; and his bombastic tirade tracing the decline of reason is as insane as any delirious speech Céline has created:

"I opened my institution," he confided in me one day in an outpouring of sorrow, "just before the Exposition, the big one, Ferdinand . . . we alienists in those days were, or, if you will, constituted a very small group, much less curious, I can assure you, and less depraved than today! . . . None of us in those days tried to be as crazy as his patients. . . . It was not yet the fashion for the healer to go off his rocker on the pretext that it furthered the cure, an obscene fashion, mind you, like almost everything that comes to us from foreign countries. . . ."

After this xenophobic attack on the likes of Freud and Kraepelin, the good doctor continues in the delirious prophetic mode: "You'll all end up in the nuthouse! *Zoom!* Just one more outburst of madness! One too many! And *wham!* off you go to the loony bin! At last! You'll be liberated, as you put it. It has tempted you too much and too long! That will be the act of daring you've been clamoring for! But once you're in the nuthouse, my little friends . . . take it from me, you'll stay there!" (364–65). One could point out here that the content and structure of the doctor's tirade are analogous to what Céline uses in his later anti-Semitic polemic: a pseudohistorical analysis that ends up being a mad form of prophecy. In the context of *Journey*, however, the doctor's madness is a reversal of reason that is pointed up by Bardamu who, like the Renaissance fool listening to the king, underscores the reason in madness — or madness in reason — that he listens to.[2]

Doctor Baryton is also a Cartesian physiologist, which leads him to conclude that man is only "de la pourriture en suspens . . ." (416) ("rottenness in a suspended state"). But Céline shows that Baryton needs the delirious vertigo that he tries to cure. Bardamu introduces him to English and then, more importantly, to the world of historical adventure when they begin to read Macaulay's *History of England*. The poetic delirium of history (as opposed we might say to the history of delirium) loosens his hold on his Cartesian sense of reason, and he soon sets out in quest of something somewhere else, an act of folly that also seems quite reasonable in the context of life in an insane asylum.

Céline never tires of ironic reversals, and, if Baryton must flee the confines of the asylum into the poetry of his disarray, Robinson then shows up, looking for a refuge from delirium for which the insane asylum might be well suited. Robinson is of course a key character in *Journey*. He has in a sense accompanied Bardamu throughout the trip. Most critics have seen in Robinson a kind of double or alter ego for Bardamu. In the perspective of this essay we can also view Robinson as a key figure in Céline's dialectic of reason and madness, and especially in Céline's treatment of the Cartesian dualism that he alternately accepts and parodies.

One recalls that Bardamu first meets Robinson at night, during the war, when Robinson, a figure of minimal reason lost in the midst of universal madness, is trying to survive by getting himself captured. To realize this rational goal Robinson would like to enter the German lines nude, like his horse, so that they would not know whether to shoot him. Survival centers on the body for Robinson, and protecting it is the first command of elementary rationality. Thus, when Bardamu apparently encounters Robinson in the jungle in Africa, it is Robinson who shows him the way to survival by recommending that he get the hell out of there as best he can. In America, however, it is clear that Robinson is not a very successful survival artist, since in Detroit, sought by the police, Robinson must work at a job that is rotting his lungs.

Robinson's body is the locus for his survival, much as Bardamu's head is the source of his concerns; they are like body and mind traveling together, bound to each, but always separate in their ways of being. Céline underscores this contrast in many ways. In the second half of the novel, for example, when Robinson shows up in Rancy, his arrival marks the beginning of Bardamu's renewed trouble with his head, leading to his demented outburst when a baby is sick. The same contrast is found in the episodes involving the old Mother Henrouille. When Bardamu cannot declare her insane and thus take her off the hands of her children, Robinson accepts the job of arranging her murder: if they cannot eliminate her for her mind, they will get her in the body. I am not saying that there is a systematic allegory here between Cartesian dualism and Bardamu and Robinson. I am suggesting, however, that Céline has distributed their functions in such a way as to emphasize the poles of the Cartesian worldview. In Bardamu we see an often delirious mind watching Robinson, a disintegrating body, trying and finally succeeding in getting to the end of the night.

In the second half of the novel Robinson is not only followed by Bardamu. After he temporarily loses his sight in his miserable failure to get rid of the old Henrouille woman, Robinson goes to Toulouse where the young girl Madelon decides to pursue him. For a disintegrating body the illusions of love are impossible, and so Robinson then comes to the asylum where he wants literally to find asylum. From Robinson's point of view he is being pursued by madness in the person of Madelon: "She's in love, I tell you! Haven't you ever known a woman in love? When she's in love, she's crazy. Crazy, I tell you! And it's me she's in love with and crazy about! . . . Do you know what that means? It means that anything crazy is just her meat! Craziness won't stop her! *Au contraire!*" (389–90). "Alors tout ce qui est fou ça l'excite" — madness takes on sexual overtones in Céline's French, for when Robinson earlier tells Madelon he goes crazy now and then, the poor girl is perplexed until she can feel Robinson's bump where, we discover with her, he, like all of Céline's disintegrating bodies, was trepanned. The wounded body seeks asylum from madness, ironically, in a madhouse, though the irony itself points to the impossibility of realizing salvation.

Journey to the End of the Night abounds in symmetries, and one of the most telling is that between Bardamu's first outburst of madness at the shooting gallery during the war and Madelon's outburst after she, Robinson, Bardamu, and his companion Sophie have visited the same gallery during what was to be a reconciliatory excursion. Immediately after this visit Madelon uses Robinson for target practice in the taxi that is taking them back to the (now useless) asylum. At this point Bardamu resumes his role as doctor, describing with knowing concern what would be the best hope for a quick end for Robinson's perforated body. In the taxi Robinson had provoked Madelon with his insulting defense of the body in the face of her demands for illusions, accusing her of wanting to eat "rotten meat" — *viande pourrie* — with her sauce *à la tendresse*. And a final irony is that it is left to Bardamu to describe with real tenderness the passage from demented body to rotten meat that Robinson undertakes when he dies.

Céline's triumph in *Journey to the End of the Night* is to have renewed contact with that traditional Western sense of the dialectic between mind and body, reason and unreason, that neoclassicism had, in the wake of the Cartesian revolution in science and philosophy, undone in favor of the uncontested supremacy of reason and mind. In Céline's novel the universal metaphor of delirium proclaims the necessity of unreason if one is to have access to the full realm of comic and tragic truths that, according to Foucault, have been suppressed in the West since at least the late seventeenth century. And in renewing our sense of the truth of tragic laughter, Céline also found access to the truth of parody and carnival that the Russian critic Bakhtin also found in Rabelais. Through the reversal of the Cartesian dichotomy of mind and body, Céline offers access to the parodistic reversal of the topology of higher and lower that has always characterized carnival's renewal of culture. One might object that Céline is too black, too cynical, too nihilistic to be read in terms of late medieval carnival or the Renaissance praise of folly; to which I would reply, I can imagine nothing more nihilistic than that summit of Renaissance culture, *King Lear*, and that the mixture of comedy and tragedy, of laughter and bitter tears, are all part of the total vision of tragic truth as it was understood in a world for which madness was as much a truth as reason. With his "reason in madness" Céline renews our tragic acceptance of the demented body and the mind made flesh.

Notes

1. Céline, *Journey to the End of the Night*, trans. Ralph Manheim (New York: New Directions, 1983), 79. All quotations are from this translation (though this does not constitute an endorsement of this translation). French quotes are from the Pléiade edition.

2. Let me indicate my debt to Paolo Carile's work on Céline in his *Louis-Ferdinand Céline: Un allucinato di genio* (Bologna: Pàtron, 1969): "ma questo inizio così sconcertante è un pezzo di bravura, Céline si traveste in una moderna versione del 'fool' della commedia rinascimentale, e sotto quelle spoglie, in un susseguirsi ininterrotto di 'gag', lancia recriminaizioni contro veri o presunti nemici . . ." ("But this disconcerting beginning is a piece of bravura; Céline disguises himself as a modern version of the 'fool' of Renaissance comedy; and beneath these effects, in an uninterrupted succession of 'gags,' he hurls recriminations against real or presumed enemies," 67).

DEATH ON THE
INSTALLMENT PLAN

Since Zola, the nightmare surrounding man has not only taken on more precise form — it has become official.

—"Homage to Zola"

The position of man in the midst of his rubbish heap of laws, customs, desires, of instincts tangled and repressed, has become so perilous, so artificial, so arbitrary, so tragic, and so grotesque at the same time, that never was literature easier to produce than today — or harder to tolerate.

—"Homage to Zola"

. . . let me speak more softly to the world . . .

—*Death on the Installment Plan*

[Remarks on *Mort à crédit*]   Robert A. Parker*

Céline's impatiently awaited second novel, *Mort à crédit*, appeared at last in 1936. This bulky volume seemed almost as formidable as James Joyce's *Ulysses*. Here was no cycle after the manner of Marcel Proust or Jules Romains, but a work that, like *Ulysses*, seems to the Belgian critic Charles Bernard to be written in one sustained, uninterrupted creative impulse. Céline had hoped to make this work resemble a Gothic cathedral — a cathedral in all its variety, its mixture of good and evil, in which everything that at first glance seemed to lie in chaos, would in the end show both design and order. If we may trust M. Bernard, this is exactly what he has succeeded in achieving. Here are heaven, hell, the Inferno, the seven deadly sins, the virtues, the seasons, all that pertains to the flesh and to the spirit, as well as flying buttresses, pillars, curiously stained glass. A book, declares M. Bernard, of genius and baseness alloyed . . . a book of misery and rancors, of bitterness and ridiculous irony . . . all written, apparently, in one breath. The writer never tires, never gives signs of fatigue. A book, moreover, of the most trenchant eloquence, vibrant with the racy, earthy eloquence of the masses. "What accent, what color, what strength in his repetitions!" exclaims M. Bernard. "It does not seem as though Céline were creating these characters . . . they create themselves, right under our very eyes. Out of this comes the truth, the life, forever gushing out, the perpetual renewing of interest. Something new, at last, in literature! A regenerated form; newly discovered veins."

According to those in a position to know, this second novel is even more impressive than the first, more profound, more daring, more shocking, and more penetrating in its exploration of life.

It is fortunate, I think, that we are permitted to read Céline's touching and tragic parable of Semmelweis, as well as this blistering *Mea Culpa*, as a preliminary to reading the translation of his second novel, *Mort à crédit*. These essays reveal the fundamental earnestness of the man,

*Reprinted with permission from *Mea Culpa and The Life and Work of Semmelweis*, by Louis-Ferdinand Céline, translated by Robert Allerton Parker. Copyright 1937 Little Brown & Company. © renewed 1964 Robert Allerton Parker.

his lightninglike flashes of revelation, his determination to pursue truth into no matter what depths it may lead him. For this man, words are not pretty toys, nor playthings to soothe and caress and lull to sleep those who are seeking bedtime entertainment. In these days, when so much of American fiction seems to be the triumphant expression of the brightest boy and the cleverest girl in English Composition 1A—so deft, so felicitous, so smooth and slick; and withal so empty, juvenile, meaningless— Céline must come as a shock to readers who seek only to be amused. He attacks our unconscious complacency; he undermines our tacit assumptions; he defies our most cherished taboos; he makes us revise our moral values. It would be dishonest to deny that he is an anarchist—but his whole work is one long, sustained protest against that anarchy, that lawlessness into which the whole world finds itself plunged to-day. Céline rejects the superficial remedies, the noisy external revolutions, the shouting and the tumult. Because all that he writes is rooted in his own tragic experience, because he has lived these things, vitality and integrity pulsate through every word he utters.

Céline

David Hayman*

When *Voyage au bout de la nuit* first appeared in 1932, critics began classing Céline with the naturalists, as a latter-day Zola. And, in fact, the doctor who had grown up in a semi-slum among the small shopkeepers of Paris and experienced war as a soul shattering event, the traveler who never quite left home, the writer who wrote to quiet the buzzing in his ears, was deeply concerned with reality. It frightened him. As he wrote Milton Hindus: "For me, real objective life is impossible, unbearable. It drives me crazy—makes me furious it's so ghastly. So I transpose it as I go along, without breaking my stride." Céline departs from the rather formulaic reality of a Zola to approach the cruel hilarity of a Villon, breathing deeply over the open cesspool of contemporary vice. He has fathered on our century a horde of gleeful and bitter heretics (Henry Miller, Samuel Beckett, Jack Kerouac, Raymond Queneau, William Burroughs, Jean Genet, J. P. Donleavy, etc) and conquered for prose the language of clownish gestures, conveying with ease and gusto the inarticulate frenzy of the little man staggering through the first half of our apocalyptic century.

He always spoke of his vision as a version of the truth, but not till after World War II, prison and exile did he find words to describe his style and his vision. Only then did he characterize himself as a conscious artist. The spoken word, he claimed, does not sound true when written down

*Reprinted with permission from the *Iowa Review* 3, no. 2 (Spring 1972):72–81.

unless it is manipulated. It is like "a stick in water," to use his own metaphor, "if it is to seem straight, you must bend it a little." The effect, whether contrived or natural, is a gutter style. The voice that comes from the lower depths, explodes through lips wet with spittle. His sentences, full of clusters of vocables, sounds, almost, are activated gestures, capable of projecting silent frenzy and audible rage yet pliable enough to fold neatly into a sigh. More significantly, the chaotic effects are shrewdly arranged, shaped, rhythmically coherent and self-reflexive. For all the lapses of taste and proportion, despite the tedium of certain passages, the bathos and self-indulgence of others, we are convinced that Céline was a shaping as well as an imposing presence behind his fictions and "chronicles."

Céline invented two terms, "lacework" and "emotive subway," to describe his technique. He told Robert Poulet that the writer should leave accurate reporting of life to the newspapers and omit "even from his imaginings" the insipid details of what the reader already knows. In his own work this results in lacunae, in missing transitions and explanations. He establishes "the basic outline, the landmarks; and surrounding them, holes . . ." achieves a "lacework" effect. There are two aspects to the "emotive subway" that Céline describes at length in his hilarious mock-interview with Professor Y. Unable to choose between surface reality and subterranean truth, the author has decided to draw the surface down with him helter-skelter into a subway of his own invention, one that makes no stops and that, accommodating all experience, transports it on rails that are not straight. The omissions — "not everything can be transposed" — the inclusions, and the distortions characterize the vision of a man who wishes "to lay back the flesh" of his subject.

The result is a trammeled farce, giving us a view from below, an unbalanced and vertiginous postlapsarian glimpse of the possibly sublime through the certainly grotesque. It is no coincidence that in the most virulent of his hate pamphlets, *Bagatelles pour un massacre*, he includes several of his curiously airy and fragile ballet scenarios or that the slum doctor Bardamu in *Death on the Installment Plan* distracts himself by writing a cruel romance compounded of childhood longings and adult deceptions. This mingling of excessive attitudes (the melodrama conveyed through the posturing of the distraught clown) results in something more than outrageous assaults on human dignity and wish fulfilling comic destruction.

Céline's novelistic universe is multivalent and hence none of the things it seems to be. On the one hand he condemns the mores of his society through the subjective vision of a sort of *illuminé*, an anti-heroic version of that rebellious angel Arthur Rimbaud. With unmatched intensity and integrity he projects an inverted world where the outside constitutes a norm and where even the laughing reader must be considered as not only "mon semblable mon frère" but also a potentially vicious "other." The symbols of horror and hilarity are, however ambiguously, reversed. A carnival symbolizes the dreary false values of the society it distorts; an insane asylum becomes a haven for the balanced and enlightened; the concierge, that bane of the French city-dweller's existence, has a beautiful soul. We are torn between our more or less balanced sense of decorum and the positive appeal of the ugly and outrageous affronting our sensibilities, between the fascination with a complex comic surface and varying degrees of disgust and outrage. We are disarmed by a narrator who insists upon his hallucinated vision, his near madness, his wounds and maladies, his insignificance, his alienation and frenzy in much the same way the clown carries his cap and bells or wears his insane mask as a badge. On the other hand, Céline forces us to acknowledge the truth beneath the distortions, to admit to the serious and disturbing implications which we don't quite purge with our painful laughter. For he conveys directly, sensuously, through an intensely personal and fast paced rhetoric, a Brobdingnagian universe from which we would normally avert our gaze. Whether he locates his naturalistic inferno in the *banlieu* of Paris, the London underworld, the mind of a collaborator, or in a Danish prison, he manages to involve us in his disgust and gusto while distancing us from himself and affirming the privacy of his vision. Thus in the introduction to *Guignol's Band* we read: "Up to you to understand! Get hot! 'There's nothing but brawls in all your chapters!' What an objection! What crap! Watch out! Dopiness! By the yard! Fluttery twittering! Go get God excited! Rub-a-dub-dub! Jump! Wiggle! Bust out of your shell! Use your bean, you little hustlers! Break open! Palpitate, damn it! That's where the fun is! All right! Something! Wake up! Come on, hello! You robot crap! Shit! Transpose or it's death!"

Such tactics so effectively distance the reader that he can seldom feel more than sympathy (or distaste) for any character other than the narrator-persona in his past-present identities. By contrast, on the visceral level of response, Céline obliges us to participate in all manner of comic, perverse and revolting circumstances. Armed with the medical man's catalogue of horrors, but using conventional stimuli, the emotive clichés of the Gothic novelists and ad-men, he unerringly strikes the responsive nerve while invalidating the accustomed response. This is what he calls his "style emotif" or rather his style "rendered emotive." The result is often the literary equivalent of that most outrageous of all theatrical forms, Grand Guignol, where insane gaiety and brutal horror reign blatant, indelicate and unashamed. We, in our turn, are at once guilty and shameless in our quest for unpleasant thrills, grateful for the vomit we more than metaphorically eat, the spittle we lick, and corruption that oozes through our fingers. There is no denying the revolting but comic immediacy of Céline's description of a Channel crossing in *Death on the Installment Plan*:

> A stocky little character, a wise guy, is helping his wife to throw up in a little bucket . . . he's trying to encourage her.

"Go on, Leonie . . . Don't hold back . . . I'm right here . . . I'm holding you." All of a sudden she turns her head back into the wind . . . The whole stew that's been gurgling in her mouth catches me full in the face . . . My teeth are full of it, beans, tomatoes . . . I'd thought I had nothing left to vomit . . . well, it looks like I have . . . I can taste it . . . it's coming up again . . . Hey, down there, get moving! . . . It's coming . . . A whole carload is pushing against my tongue . . . I'll pay her back, I'll spill my guts in her mouth . . . I grope my way over to her . . . The two of us are crawling . . . We clutch each other . . . We embrace . . . We vomit on each other . . . My smart father and her husband try to separate us . . . They tug at us in opposite directions . . . They'll never understand. . . .

Here the emotive force of Céline's imagery, his grotesque eroticism outweighs the human predicament of the actors. We have seen similar moments portrayed in films from the twenties (though hardly in such detail or with such overtones). The point is of course that, like coitus, vomiting is a mindless activity, though, unlike coitus, it is relatively free of moral stigmas. It is no coincidence that this explosive moment follows a series of verbal explosions and precedes and foreshadows two sexual catastrophes: the rape of Ferdinand by the jeweler Gorloge's obese and lecherous wife and his sweet and terrible encounter with prim Nora Merrywin, each of them an ambiguously public, private event.

The second instance shows us how, while relying upon our visceral conditioning, Céline can modulate his perverse farce, turning even the potentially solemn, tender, delicate moment into a feast of fools, rendering the fleeting instant through a series of stop-action frames, translating words into actions, actions into components of a landscape. When the longsuffering wife of the drunken English school master suddenly gives herself to a worshipping but mute adolescent Ferdinand, Céline cleverly reverses our expectations, fulfills the boy's desires not with bliss but with a storm of violent, desperate and unsatisfying caresses that turn love and affection into a grotesquery for the boy, while they elicit in the reader a perverse sympathy for the angel turned bacchante:

She's stopped talking. Christ almighty! I plunge, I slip in like a breeze! I'm petrified with love . . . I'm one with her beauty . . . I'm in ecstasy . . . I wriggle . . . I bite right into her tit . . . She moans, she sighs . . . I suck her all over . . . On her face I go looking for the exact spot next to her nose . . . The one that tortures me, the magic of her smile . . . I'm going to bite her there too . . . especially . . . I stick one hand up her ass, I massage . . . I dig in . . . I wallow in light and flesh . . . I come like a horse . . . I'm full of sauce . . . She gives a wild leap . . . She breaks loose, she's gone, the bitch! . . . She jumps backward . . . Hell! She's on her feet . . . She's in the middle of the room . . . She's making a speech . . . I can see her in the white of the street lamp . . . in her nightgown . . . all pulled up . . . her hair flying loose . . . I'm lying there flummoxed with my cock in the air. . . .

The expectations of romance, the yearning after an instant of static fulfillment, clash with the programmed discontinuities of farce on both the sensual and the emotional planes. Thus we participate more or less willingly in the frustration of two antagonistic impulses. The result is the sort of thing we call black humor, an unstable amalgam of pleasure and pain which evolves from all manner of double refusals. When Nora rushes off to a suicide motivated by mute despair, we are jarred as much by the boy's reflexive insensitivity as by the poignancy of her act, but we are curiously disarmed by the sympathy underlying the mimesis of the moment: "She flits from one lamp to the next . . . Like a butterfly, the stinker! She's still yelling here and there, the wind brings back the echoes . . . And then for a second there's a terrible scream and then another, an awful scream that fills the whole valley . . . 'Hurry up, boy,' I tell the kid. 'Our lady love has jumped in. We'll never make it. We're in for a dip. You'll see, kid. You'll see.' "

The immediate source of this attitudinal tension is obviously Céline's narrator, the semi-autobiographical Bardamu-Destouches. Hallucinated, obsessed, feverish, mad, a self-declared outsider, he is one of the most imposing and oppressive manipulating presences in 20th century fiction. His famous conversational tone appeals to us almost precisely to the degree we are affronted by it. Far more than the conventional satirist with his "pen dipped in bile," Céline's paranoid narrator is invariably the speaker as enemy. One thinks of the tone of Ezra Pound or Wyndham Lewis, but Céline's persona is the self-declared, the loudly proclaimed vulnerable and victimized misanthrope, a masticator of miseries as well as a punisher of vices and a mocker of follies. If he makes repeated claims on our sympathy, he rejects our respect along with our affection, projecting himself onto the page theatrically, a gesticulating presence, turning us into a captive audience and unwilling actors in a claustrophobe's nightmare. Like Rabelais and the carnival clown, Céline's narrator includes us in the act as not-quite spectators and silent adversaries. Like them, he captivates us by the brashness of his appeal, the challenge and the verve. But here there is another difference to note, for he projects as dominant the very terror and distress which underlies comic destruction and which is ordinarily obviated by our laughter at comic outrage. Further, he assumes a familiarity with journalistic naturalism and a social engagement inconceivable prior to the 19th Century. Even in his most outrageous utterance there is a singular indeterminancy which gives us pause where we might otherwise be liberated.

All of this implies a decorum which permits the artful manipulation of highly conventional materials but eschews intellectual and literary play for its own sake. Appropriately, Céline's most elaborate fiction, *Death on the Installment Plan*, is a dark romance spoken by an increasingly frantic clown, a submerged but defiant outsider who remembers better days, which never were, with a cruel nostalgia and disturbing hilarity. Some of the implications of this stance are terribly immediate in the age of protests and revolutions led either by self-proclaimed clowns like Jerry Rubin and Abbie Hoffman or by defiant underdogs, men who make distruption a creed. But Céline, the clown of reaction, even at his wildest, in the inflammatory anti-Semitic "pamphlets" which were to cause him so much trouble after WW II, was always a loner, complete in himself. His words were and still are actions in their own right. They elicit no further disruption. For better or worse, this too distinguishes him from the satirist and social critic he claims to be and identifies him with the clown-in-his-place as artist rather than with the clown-in-society. Thus, through his strident but protean voice, we experience an uneasy truce with reason in a moral landscape where the sign posts have a way of reversing their directions. This much is clear even in the relatively muted prose of the prologue to *Death on the Installment Plan*:

> Here we are, alone again. It's all so slow, so heavy, so sad . . . I'll be old soon. Then at last it will be over. So many people have come into my room. They've talked. They haven't said much. They've gone away. They've grown old, wretched, sluggish, each in some corner of the world.
>
> Yesterday, at eight o'clock, Madame Bérenge, the concierge, died. A great storm blew up during the night. Way up here where we are, the whole house is shaking. She was a good friend, gentle and faithful. Tomorrow they're going to bury her in the cemetery on the rue des Saules. She was really old, at the very end of old age. The first day she coughed I said to her: "Whatever you do, don't stretch out. Sit up in bed." I was worried. Well, now it's happened . . . anyway, it couldn't be helped. . . .[1]
>
> I haven't always been a doctor . . . crummy trade.[2] I'll write the people who've known her, who've known me, and tell them that Madame Bérenge is dead. Where are they?
>
> I wish the storm would make even more of a clatter, I wish the roofs would cave in, that spring would never come again, that the house would blow down.

The staccato rhythm, the short simple sentences of the first paragraph, each a gesture of sorts, each with its free-floating pronouns contributes an aura of mystery and uncertainty to an utterance which has the immediacy of direct address. The reader is brought in by the first word of the French version, "Nous voici encore seuls." Even if we fail to recognize this as a variation on the traditional greeting of the music-hall clown: "Nous voici encore," we are struck by the familiar tone of a speaker willing to share not joy but a *fin de siècle* world weariness ("seuls"). We may also note the assertion and retraction ("Ils ont dit des choses. Ils ne m'ont pas dit grand'chose"), the touch of informality in the punctuation, the direct address, and the affectation in the spelling of "grand'chose." Yet, though it breaks the frame of our daily existence and introduces us into a vaguely disturbing environment, this paragraph elicits neither smile nor laughter, nor does it seem to prepare us for what is to come. Its gentle tone disarms us. Its distanced rhetoric evokes with almost transcendental sadness the friends scattered to the far corners, dragging out their miserable existences, in aborted promise. While controlling our sentiments by virtue of his authority and our ignorance, the speaker is content to impose a mood that remains to be validated, to locate himself and us in a room that expands and contracts with our imaginations.

The friends, aging "chacun dans un coin du monde," are unlike the "fidèle amie" of the next paragraph, a figure whose demise derives symbolic amplitude from the discreet and doubtless ironic (if not irreverent) allusion to the cataclysm that followed the crucifixion. Are we the butts of a sly clown who inspires a muted respect bordering on affection while inculpating us in the death of a figure of fun? The tone of this paragraph shifts repeatedly as the narrator moves from past to present to future, from circumstance to omen to consequence. It is dominated however by a singularly unstable but pervasive sympathy for the concierge. (This quality is diminished in the otherwise strong Manheim translation which fails to conserve the rhythmic devices in "C'était une douce et gentille et fidèle amie," the efficient source of our attitude.) Kindness, gentleness and fidelity are not qualities one readily ascribes to the prying, acerb and querulous breed of concierges. Yet we are seduced to the point of being surprised when an implicit plea for mourners at the funeral to be conducted by "them" is undercut: "Oh well, she was very old." Such simplicity, clouding a tenderness for extreme age, prepares us to be further disoriented by the brief narrative of her illness delivered in the bromidic bedside manner of a concerned but world-weary doctor. Only later are we free to wonder why Bardamu, who has seen many more terrible deaths and so much suffering, should dwell on the least awesome of demises, the most natural. By then the old lady, already more than an object of perverse concern, will have joined the fringe community symbolized by the slums surrounding Paris, the infamous Zone, where Dr. Bardamu has his practice. For a moment we are jarred when the doctor's advice is punctuated by two virtually untranslatable phrases. The inevitable has happened ("Et puis voilá . . ."). Keeping her alive was at best a doubtful project. We must accept it philosophically. That's how things go in a rotten world. So let's dismiss it with a mild but remarkably powerful "Et puis tant pis . . . , a rhyming commonplace which transfers our sympathy from the mourned to the mourner. We may feel mocked for the emotional paces through which we have been put willy-nilly.

Flippant distress becomes bitter irreverence when, in the next paragraph, the renegade doctor proposes to write his acquaintances and "hers," resurrecting in the process his past. This is at once an exercise in clownish futility and a supreme act of reverence at variance with the expression: "cette merde" ("that shit") which breaks the decorum only to enlarge upon a pervasive raffishness. The death of the old lady is a symptom, part of a larger symbolic context, rather than the sole cause of the narrator's distress. The apparently realistic passage oscillates between the conventions of melodramatic romance (and cosmic allegory) and those of chaotic farce (and iconoclastic satire). Its significance is at once individual and universal, realistic and fanciful, ribald and grave. This is surely confirmed by the Villonesque "Ou sont-ils . . . ," referring us back to shadowy friends of an unspecified past.

Isolated in his despair, the still unidentified speaker prays for an apocalypse in which he has little faith, uttering through clenched teeth an appeal for chaos which may also be a lament for order. It is as though the doctor were straining to equal the powers of the witch-crone in order to bring about his own end. We have as yet nothing to justify this Gothic jeremiad, but in relation to the first paragraph, the narrator's wish helps define the transcendental range of the novel or rather the extreme limits of its meaning. Against these limits Céline's style will strain in its ceaseless attempts to convey and enact a lower more seamy sort of dissolution, one inherent in the process of being human, a process which the doctor, who is a wizard only with words, finds infinitely repugnant and depressingly comic, but for which he feels a compulsive sympathy.

In the penultimate paragraph of his brief overture, the speaker explodes into ellipses over the letters which have deposited their load of grief in Mme. Bérenge's lodge. Their dead "sadness" ("*chagrin*") symbolizes for him not only the life of the concierge but all life and the putrefaction which surrounds him. Like the letters he feels obliged to write, they constitute a secondary reality pivoting about the fire that still warms the empty lodge:

> For almost twenty years all the sadness that comes by mail passed through her hands. It lingers on in the smell of her death, in that awful sour taste . . . It has burst out . . . it's here . . . it's skulking through the passageway . . . It knows us and now we know it. It will never go away. Someone will have to put out the fire in the lodge. Whom will I write to? I've nobody left. No one to receive the friendly spirits of the dead . . . and let me speak more softly to the world . . . I'll have to bear it all alone. (I have replaced the ellipses dropped by the Manheim translation.)

It is appropriate that, after the prologue's enactment of isolation, the novel's overture opens with a reference to the doctor's "genre" or rather to the "thousands of unpleasant comments" he has had about the stories he tells at the clinic where he works. Are the stories, fictional narratives, tales relating to his practice, bits drawn from his writing, gossip? Can they really do him harm, as his cousin Gustin seems to suggest? The question is raised and then seemingly dropped when we turn to other concerns, but it *is* to the point, for the words written on this page are a clown's action just as the rhetorical gestures of the doctor at the clinic are a form of operation. Language is one with the unreasonable and unassuagable rage that generates it, one also with the sympathy that tempers rage and orders violence. The doctor is leading a double life which corresponds to the novel's double mode. He functions socially in a positive way while working out his negative urges through his narratives, reenactments of distress which allay his frustration behind a mask of inaction.

Already we note that dual intransigence, quite apart from the more violent style manifested briefly in the paragraphs cited above, constitutes the "meaningful" substratum of the novel if not all of Célinean utterance. This is, however, not the conscious goal of Céline's narrating persona, as distinct from the authorial persona. The former is of course the Doctor Bardamu, whose past will be adduced in order to explain his present mood and condition, verbally *making* him what he *is*. Though, in the overture, he sees himself as a writer, the author not only of *Le Roi Krogold* but possibly of *Journey to the End of the Night*, he does not present himself as the conscious craftsman but rather as the hobbyist writing to escape misery, terror and absurdity over which he has no control. "I'm not a Yid or a foreigner or a Freemason, or a graduate of the École Normale; I don't know how to make friends and influence people, I fuck around too much, my reputation's bad. For fifteen years now they've seen me struggling along out here in the Zone; the dregs of the dregs take liberties with me, show me every sign of contempt. I'm lucky they haven't fired me. Writing picks me up."

For all his apparent innocence of literary method and aesthetic standards, we are willing to believe this speaker is writing the novel we read. I would suggest that he is actually at two removes from the source of the narrative, being the puppet of a puppet. His immediate master is the speaker of the prologue, the distraught magus who has promised in the midst of a nocturnal storm to "tell stories that will make them come back, to kill me, from the ends of the world" so that "it will be over . . . all right with me" (my ellipses). Significantly, Mme. Bérenge's funeral does not take place in a book replete in climaxes which fail to punctuate the action. Neither the first narrative frame, that of the prologue, nor the second one (the overture) is closed except by implication when the youthful Ferdinand whose education comprises the body of the book decides to join the army, opting for an *assumed* order and discipline after the purgative process of his youth. Furthermore, the novel is neither the promised story-letter of the prologue nor an extension of the fever-induced hallucination which terminates the overture:

> Then I was really alone!
> Then I saw the thousands and thousands of little skiffs returning high above the Left Bank . . . Each one had a shriveled little corpse under its sail . . . and his story . . . his little lies to catch the wind with.

It is rather the perfectly shaped artifact produced by a manipulative persona at one more remove from the action, a narrative persona of whom the other two are states of mind or existential projections. The invisible hand of this persona discreetly informs the apparent chaos of the other visions. It also controls the narrative surface as a youthful Ferdinand moves helplessly but predictably through a series of increasingly devastating climaxes, unsettling grave-comic explosions which modulate toward the instants of enlightenment so characteristic of *Bildungsroman* developments. In describing the art of Céline's narrator, therefore, we are really invoking the hidden arranger of the overt speaker's utterance, the engineer who has laid out the tracks of the "emotive subway." If he is virtually indistinguishable from the other voices and the youthful Ferdinand, he still controls and unifies the triune experience of his protagonist and imposes, on all rhetorical levels, tensions, conventions and structural interplay.

I am suggesting that the art of *Death on the Installment Plan* is ultimately the artifice of narration which maintains in delicate and shifting balance a variety of distinct but interrelated attitudes, developments and contexts. This implies a considerably tighter construction than is generally ascribed even to this, the most intricate and coherent of Céline's fictions. Thus the speaker of the prologue plays with and on the reader's sympathies, imposing attitudinal shifts which reveal (in the sense of document) far less than they convey. In quick succession he expresses gentle resignation, distanced bitterness, tender sentiment, sardonically overstated professional commitment, false callousness, belligerence, nostalgia, muted apocalyptic rage, paranoiac misanthrophy, and comic bathos. . . . Each of these moods contains the seeds of its opposite, that is, not only juxtaposition but superimposition informs the mood painting of the prologue. In later passages, with the accretion of levels of narration and the expanding context, such rhetorical effects undergo enlargement, inversion, and transformation. Young Ferdinand's progress is conveyed through discontinuous and irreverent prose as the tale of a helpless, if educable, fool in a mad world; yet beneath the farcical surface lurk heroism and sentiment. By the novel's end modifications in attitude and rhythm have prepared us to accept the failed magus, Courtial des Perieres, as a quasi-tragic figure. The "poor fool" who blew his brains out all over a frozen highway, reducing himself to a mass of meat, or shrunken Z, has become the tutelary deity of an inverted work, an affirmation of impotency, sad, serious, beyond laughter and even outrage. We are prepared, that is, to accept and understand the clown-magus who presides over the prologue, if not to bury the past.

For the narrator, the triune hero who brings us to this point, the novel has been a process of auto-generation or perhaps regeneration: the turning of a life into words and of words into pseudo-actions. This development involves us in a number of paradoxes. For one thing, the further we are from the present of the speaker, the closer we seem to be to the experience, the more impartially we share the sentiments. For another, the emotive power of the prose, its gestural immediacy, increases as we move into an increasingly stylized and often catastrophic universe. Finally, the more immediate the expressive content conveyed through highly articulated conventions, the more meaningful it is to the evolving character of the triune narrator, the more real its impact on the reader. Based in the boy's experience, enriched by the fancy of the sick doctor, magnified by the magus' apocalyptic fury and despair, emotive realism dominates the book. It is tensed however against a steadier vision of the-world-as-it-is, a vision no less subject to the conventions of farce and romance, but lighter in tone. Long passages which collect and store energy and putrifaction serve to make the eventual release of disgust and horror seem almost pleasant, often hilarious, if not genuinely satisfying or cleansing.

Allied to and underlying all of the attitudes generated toward objects is a complex of attitudes toward the medium itself. Céline has faith in the efficacy of language, a faith undermined by his awareness of the futility of the gestures he has already made. Hence the ultimate paradox that even on the level of expression, hope vies with despair—for the utterance has in each case preceded the writing. In this sense, the novel, like the utterance, is self-reflexive and circular: the last yelp will be followed by the first whimper of a Ferdinand released in tears; the final sigh will be: "Here we are, alone again."

Notes

1. In French "Et puis voilá . . . Et puis tant pis. . . ."
2. In French "cette merde."

Mort à crédit   J. H. Matthews*

From his first novel onward, Louis-Ferdinand Céline had something special to offer and was fully aware of this. In *La Vie et l'œuvre de Philippe Ignace Semmelweis* he had declared, "Great works are those that reveal our genius, great men are those that give it form" (I, 603). At the end of his career, in an interview granted Pierre Audinet appearing in *Les Nouvelles littéraires* on July 6, 1961, just five days after his death, he scoffed once more at those who "bring a message," and exclaimed, "Why do I write? I'll tell you: to make the others unreadable."

In view of his opinion of those about him, one cannot suppose Céline

*Reprinted with permission of the publisher from *The Inner Dream: Céline as Novelist* (Syracuse, N.Y.: Syracuse University Press, 1978).

was astonished at finding the critics too obtuse to understand *Voyage au bout de la nuit*. After all, Semmelweis' life history was adequate proof, for him, that incomprehension and hostility present the individual endowed with superior talents an accurate measurement of his gifts. The ambiguous responses he often made to those who questioned him, to say nothing of his half-truths and outright falsehoods, leave us with the feeling that Céline deliberately sowed confusion and encouraged misinterpretation of his work, in order to give more weight to his contention that greatness draws misapprehension and is penalized by ostracism. On November 28, 1947, he wrote in a letter to Milton Hindus, "In truth, Sartre, Camus, Miller, etc. . . . are really furious to know I'm still alive; they aren't gifted those snots — They lack an *Inner Dream*."[1]

Only extreme perversity could make it possible for the work of any artist to find momentum in the firm assurance that he will never be understood or truly appreciated. It is not surprising, therefore, that, viewed in conjunction with his emphasis in *Semmelweis* on great men's obligation to give form to our genius, Céline's pointed reference to an *"Inner Dream"* betrays a need for recognition having deeper sources than the sardonic pleasure he derived from putting journalists off the scent.

Céline's efforts as a novelist were directed at externalizing an inner dream of a delirious nature. It was in relation to this ambition above all that he wished to see *Voyage au bout de la nuit* evaluated. When no one came forward to assess it in the terms he deemed appropriate, the novelist himself passed judgment on the book in a private letter to Eveline Pollet, written September 14, 1933: "But I've never reread it and never will reread it. I find the whole thing tedious and sickeningly flat. It's odd how that barn-storming in the end takes the reader's fancy. I think he feels the urge to do likewise. Everything lies in *that*. Anyway we don't know ourselves very well. We're covered with civilized garbage."[2]

The silence into which Céline lapsed after the appearance of *Voyage* indicates how sincere was his statement to Mme Pollet. Seriously dissatisfied with his first novel, he evidently was determined to experiment no more with fiction until he had found a way to eliminate the faults that had bred both tedium and flatness. And so for several years his readers appeared to have reason to consider Louis-Ferdinand Céline a one-book man from whom nothing more was to be expected.

This conclusion might seem quite natural to any reader of *Voyage* who took time to wonder which way Céline might head, now, as a novelist. He could not change direction, supposedly, without repudiating his first piece of fiction. He appeared to have followed one route obstinately and clear-sightedly to the very end. And he seemed temperamentally unfitted to explore any other, or even to want to try doing so. Would not a return to the themes developed in *Voyage au bout de la nuit*, meanwhile, carry the risk of repetitiveness? And in any case, having drawn so freely (or so it seemed) upon his own experiences when writing his first novel, had he not used up all his narrative resources at one time, leaving himself with nothing more to say? These questions were raised in a review of Céline's second novel, *Mort à crédit* (1936), appearing in *Le Merle blanc* on May 30, 1936. Here Châtelain-Tailhade took the opportunity to quote from a letter written him by the novelist after his public homage to Zola: "I could people a whole asylum with my memories." Meanwhile, reviewing the book in *Paris-Match* on May 13, Noël Sabord reminded his readers of something Céline had said after *Voyage au bout de la nuit*: "These six hundred pages I've taken from more than fifty thousand, and I've more than a hundred thousand others at your service. I'll make you something like a cathedral out of them, all my own; but give me time to put them in order."

Bringing out *Mort à crédit* finally on May 12 of the year 1936, Céline seemed to give a very direct, perfectly simple answer to those who had been wondering what his next novel would be like. At first glance anyway, his new title seemed a frank admission of his intention to treat the very same themes as before, this time by presenting human existence as "death on credit." Writing his new work (even longer than its predecessor), he presumably had turned once again to the same subject matter — his own life history — to concentrate now on reviving memories of childhood and adolescence. In short, the heading Sabord chose for his review in *Paris-Match* relieved all those who had detested *Voyage au bout de la nuit* of any qualm of conscience about declining even to open *Mort à crédit*: "Defying grammar and honesty, L.-F. Céline pursues in *Mort à crédit* his interminable *Voyage au bout de la nuit*." From its very first page, *Mort à crédit* was destined to be misinterpreted. In the long run, it was to occasion numerous fundamental misconceptions about Destouches the man and about Céline the novelist.

Noting that a certain timidity or shyness had led Céline to hide himself partly behind Bardamu in *Voyage*, Ramon Fernandez contended in *Marianne* (May 27, 1936) that everything leads us to believe the author is telling his own story, now, "bequeathing his memories to posterity." Even with the qualifying assertion that these memories were representative ones, Fernandez still unequivocally invited full identification of Ferdinand's character and outlook on life with his creator's. Doing the same thing, in his review of the novel in *Le Figaro* (May 9, 1936), L'Homme qui rit had spoken of "scatological obsession" as apparently a "morbid defect" in its author. As for the reviewer who on June 11 signed his notice in *Candide* with the initials J. F., he showed how dangerously far it is possible to go, when one has started from such a premise: "Obviously we are dealing with a maniac," said this commentator, one of several too squeamish to quote from the text of *Mort à crédit*. "Mr Louis-Ferdinand Céline is perhaps, in private life, a worthy medical man, full of reserve, restraint and formal dignity. Perhaps his books serve as an indispensable outlet for a repressed temperament. But then one regrets that he has not brought his case before his eminent colleague Freud or at least that he has not been content to set down his public-convenience reverie in a notebook reserved for his own delectation."

Like *Voyage au bout de la nuit*, Céline's *Mort à crédit* is a first-person narrative, recounted by a doctor of medicine.[3] He has the same first name as Bardamu and does not divulge his last name, even to the police. Marcel Lapierre, who had reviewed *Voyage* in *Le Progrès de Bordeaux* on November 26, 1932, treated Ferdinand as "no doubt the Bardamu of *Voyage au bout de la nuit*," when reviewing Céline's second novel for *Le Peuple* on June 3, 1936. Louis Laloy confidently asserted in *L'Ere nouvelle* (May 28, 1936) that readers recognize the narrator of *Mort à crédit* as the very same person who narrated *Voyage*. Another reviewer, Eugène Marsan, was more cautious in one respect. In *Comœdia* on May 12, 1936, he spoke only of a resemblance between Ferdinand and Bardamu. He was far less guarded, however, in his remarks about Ferdinand's relationship to his creator: "He resembles Céline like a brother."

Seeking where the truth lies, we can begin with the commonly held assumption that the narrator of *Mort à crédit* is none other than Ferdinand Bardamu, devoting himself in middle age to supplying details of his formative years, passed over in *Voyage au bout de la nuit*. This basic supposition is open to dispute.

Ferdinand's story in *Mort à crédit* ends with his decision to enlist. He reaches this decision for reasons and under circumstances very different indeed from those that brought Bardamu into the army at the beginning of *Voyage*. Presumably, then, chronologically speaking, the sequel to *Mort à crédit* is not the novel Céline published immediately before it, but *Casse-pipe*, an account of life in the prewar French cavalry of which nothing was known publicly until 1948. Furthermore, the main protagonist's character and attitude to life differ noticeably from Bardamu's in *Mort à crédit*.

His profession brought Ferdinand Bardamu into daily contact with human nature. With one or two exceptions only seeming to prove the rule, he found people to be selfish, cruel, and basically sordid. Yet his idealism was never quite consumed by disillusionment. He never came to look upon medicine the way the narrator of *Mort à crédit* does, as "that shit" (II, 5). Supposing it was once present in his nature, humanitarianism has been drained from Ferdinand, who declares categorically, "Philanthropists piss me off" (II, 9). Suspicion, fear, contempt, and hate are the cardinal points of his relationship with his fellow men (and women). He realizes only too well how "terrible" it is to have lost faith, but he sees no real hope of reviving his own confidence in people, in his job, or even in life itself.

After telling of the burn marks ("That's the poker," he sees at once) on the thighs of a woman who has bullied him with her pleading into coming to examine her sick child, Ferdinand hurries away as soon as he can, although quite sure that she and her drunken husband are only waiting to see the back of him before beginning to fight once again. Not merely abiding by Bardamu's policy of nonintervention, Ferdinand displays downright callousness: "Let him shove his poker right up her asshole," he says. "That'll straighten her out, the bitch! That'll teach her to disturb me!" (II, 7). Ferdinand never misses a chance to affirm his detestation of those who come to him for help. He feels resentment more than the mistrust in which Bardamu held those around him, and makes no secret of it. He says he is thinking of sending his patients to the slaughterhouse to drink warm blood. "I really don't know no more what I could do to disgust them" (II, 6). Is this an early sign that—for some particular reason we can expect to hear revealed before long—Ferdinand had been provoked by momentary anger to take refuge in a ridiculously violent fantasy? We soon find it is not. Instead, it is an important clue to Ferdinand's usual behavior and to the tone he will give his reminiscences.

Ferdinand's need to disgust his readers reflects an irresistible impulse to keep the world at a safe distance while paying people back for all the misery they have caused him. His resentment is not the result of momentary pique. It is fostered by inability to hold out against his patients' persistence: although cursing the woman who appeals to him to examine her child when she meets him on the street, Ferdinand still accompanies her to where she lives. His anger at those who cry out for help comes from rage at seeing them look to *him* to change the pattern of life, to improve a situation he regards as beyond hope. "Just as soon as an enterprise begins to get off the ground," he observes, "it finds itself 'ipso facto' on the receiving end of a thousand hostile, sneaky, subtle, tireless plots! . . . You can't deny it! . . . Tragic fatality penetrates its very fibers . . ." (II, 376). To see any plan through to a successful conclusion, we have to rely on some miracle, he is convinced. Meanwhile practice of a profession for which he is spiritually, emotionally, and mentally unsuited casts Ferdinand in the painfully uncomfortable role of helpless witness to human destiny. As he himself stresses, it makes him testify to degradation, by telling stories other people do not like to hear.

In spite of what we know so far, it still might be argued that one can consider Ferdinand to be Bardamu, older and consequently more embittered. So it would seem to matter little, in the end, whether Céline actually took care to differentiate his storyteller in *Mort à crédit* from the one in *Voyage au bout de la nuit*. It is true, of course, that observations made by Ferdinand at the beginning of the second novel do not contribute anything really new to the picture painted by Bardamu in the first. As *Mort à crédit* opens, the tone of the narrative is muted, resigned, as though Ferdinand has no fight left in him. His concierge has just passed away and death is a presence from the first. Nothing he has to say at this point in his life contradicts or departs from the conclusions set forth in *Voyage* or, indeed, in a letter from Louis-Ferdinand Céline to Eveline Pollet, written on June 2, 1939: "Serious man must be an undertaker's mute or simply a corpse."[4] It is clear that Céline was not going to revise his opinion of life in *Mort à crédit*, that he continued to see man the way he later described him to Marc Hanrez, as having to "go to bed in his coffin every night."[5]

What, though, about the title of *Mort à crédit*? Beyond any question, it catches the imagination. A moment's reflection reveals, however, that the thought of buying death on the installment plan, as though we had signed some purchase agreement, is far more emotional than rational in appeal. Do we really enter into a contract, as we would to be sure to have something we cannot afford immediately? This would turn death into some sort of luxury product, or a necessity we feel compelled to acquire, even though it is beyond our means. *Mort à crédit* displays an ambivalent attitude toward death, since Ferdinand intimates that he looks upon it as a release from life. In his very first paragraph, he remarks pointedly, "Soon I'll be old. And it will be over at last" (II, 5).

Why not resort to suicide then? In his *Les Noyers de l'Altenburg* André Malraux, son of a suicide, extolled suicide as a profoundly responsible and therefore admirable act. Céline disagreed, though not for moral reasons. The suicide leaves a distressing mess for other people to clean up (after des Pereires has shot himself, revolting details of the process fill several pages of *Mort à crédit*). More important still, the act of self-elimination is not complete until the last hurdle — dying — is behind us. After telling how he and an acquaintance, Metitpois, have been discussing the best way to die, Ferdinand describes the other man's death as two seconds of stoicism followed by eighteen minutes of "howling like a polecat." Metitpois ends up under the piano in the drawing room: "The small arteries of the mycardium when they burst one by one, that's no ordinary harp . . . It's a pity no one don't get over angina pectoris. There'd be wisdom and genius enough for everyone" (II, 16).

Death is no victory. It is just the final proof of the futility of life. This fact above all resolves the apparent inconsistencies in Céline's title. When anything is bought on credit, interest charges have to be paid. *Mort à crédit* emphasizes that we pay now and die later. The finance charges on death, meanwhile, are levied against the living: Ferdinand pitilessly reports on his father's physical decline and describes the collapse of Courtial des Pereires's ambitions and illusions. No man in his right mind wants to buy death on the installment plan, but everyone has to do so, all the same. Thus Céline's *Mort à crédit* stands in the same relationship to Flaubert's *L'Education sentimentale* as *Semmelweis* does to his *Bouvard et Pécuchet*.

Life is a *farce* — to take the word in the sense that, following the practice of his native Normandy, Guy de Maupassant understood it when writing many of his short stories. That is to say, life is a practical joke, cruelly played at someone's expense, without regard for the suffering it may bring him. In *Mort à crédit*, the joke is on mankind, and played by death. Events may be touched by comedy, of course. But the comic simply highlights, never quite concealing, the underlying misery of man's role as victim in a situation that, try as he may, he cannot fully control or turn to advantage. "I rejoice in the grotesque," Céline explained to Léon Daudet, "only on the confines of death."[6]

Young Ferdinand learns this from harsh experience: the gradual process that inevitably turns a life into a death is illuminated by the malevolence of those about us. We must pay off our installments in suffering and pain, living in a general atmosphere of spitefulness until death is ours. His education in living (while *Voyage* is Céline's answer to Maupassant's *Bel-Ami*, his *Mort à crédit* is *Une Vie*, *Notre Cœur*, and *Fort comme la mort* all in one) has not instilled resignation in Ferdinand. Far from it, he finds himself in complete agreement with Dylan Thomas, who advised, "Do not go gentle into that good night / Old age should burn and rave at close of day." Entrusting the narration of *Mort à crédit* to a man already in his middle years, Céline extends him no hope of any mode of salvation through literature, the transcription of lived experience, such as Jean-Paul Sartre offers Roquentin in *La Nausée*, or Michel Butor gives Léon Delmont in *La Modification*. Viewing his life in retrospect, Ferdinand does not share with the narrators of Gide's ironic tales an aspiration to self-justification. And self-redemption is as far from his mind as self-revelation. Ferdinand's account of what has happened to him is an act of aggression, directed in rage against all who may read it.

Referring to those to whom he might write to report the death of Madame Bérenge, his concierge, Ferdinand comments. "They've changed souls, the better to betray, to forget, to speak always of something else . . ." (II, 5). Very soon he is explaining, "Me I could speak out all my hate. I know. I'll do so later if they don't come back. I prefer to tell stories. I'll tell such tales that they'll come back just to kill me, from the four corners of the earth. Then it'll be all over with and I'll be well satisfied" (II, 6).

In *Voyage au bout de la nuit* Bardamu did not give his readers the opportunity to think the world any different from the way he described it. In contrast, reporting that his cousin Gustin Saboyat (another doctor, as it happens) frequently advises him to change his manner as a storyteller because "It isn't always dirty in life," Ferdinand confesses very willingly in *Mort à crédit*, "My case has a bit of mania about it, some partiality" (II, 8). Nowhere could this partiality show more clearly than in the account he proceeds to give of his early life in the bosom of his family.

. . . *Mort à crédit* may be divided into two unequal parts. Relatively brief, the first is a sort of preamble giving an impression of Ferdinand's life as an adult and of his mature outlook on existence. The second, vastly longer, reanimates the years extending from his earliest recollections up to the moment when, contemplating giving military life a try, he stands on the threshold of manhood. A *zeitroman*, this is an ironic *bildungsroman*:

Céline demonstrates with harsh insistence that the child is father to the man.

Summing up *Mort à crédit*, David Hayman speaks of it as "the reminiscences of a sick and tormented man of his impoverished and harassed childhood and adolescence, reminiscences born of hallucination brought on by fever."[7] Such a résumé is less faithful to the truth than it sounds. Ferdinand does begin to tell of his childhood while fever confines him to his room. He even notes, "When fever stretches about, life becomes soft like a boozer's belly . . . You sink in an eddy of guts" (II, 26). But the important thing is this. The account he offers of growing up at the turn of the century is no less hallucinated and hallucinatory when his bout of fever has subsided. Mention of fever excuses nothing, here, and is not meant to do so. In fact, Ferdinand avows, "It's run behind me, madness has . . . twenty-two years and more. That's a fine thing. It's tried fifteen hundred sounds, an immense hubbub [Ferdinand is alluding to a buzzing in his ears, the same famous buzzing sound that Céline claimed to hear all his life—as a result of having been trepanned, he said], but I've been delirious quicker than it has. I've screwed it, I've had my way with it at the 'finish line' " (II, 23). An attack of fever early in the novel is not to be taken as excusing the way Ferdinand remembers things—even as a schoolboy, he tells us with characteristic vulgarity, he wiped his asshole on memories (II, 188)—it merely pitches his narrative on a certain tone.

Delirium marks Céline's second work of fiction even more than his first. *Mort à crédit* shows how sincere were his criticisms of naturalism in his 1933 talk at Médan. It demonstrates the inadequacy of the naturalist method for treating reality the way he chose to deal with it. "You are only too right," he observed in a letter to Elie Faure, "so far as the essence of man is concerned. One has to place oneself deliberately in a nightmare state to come close to the true tone!"[8] In his second novel the border between true-to-life detail, caricature, and unfettered imaginative flights has no permanence. It appears at best as a tenuous dividing line, with no serious claim on the attention of a writer who doubts its esthetic usefulness.

Recounting his story, Ferdinand consistently violates two fundamental tenets of the naturalist code: impartiality and objectivity. It is easy enough, of course, to identify passages evoking scenes that take their coloration from fever. Some of these remind us of Bardamu's confession that, during an attack of malaria and amoebic dysentery (from which he suffered, just like Destouches), he could not tell the real from the absurd, and lived in a twilight world. It is not difficult to see when and where Ferdinand enters that same world. Making love in the Bois de Boulogne, he and Mireille draw a crowd. An orgy follows, before the mob marches up to the Arc de Triomphe and eventually has to be dispersed on the Place de la Concorde by no less than twenty-five thousand policemen. Isolating such incidents, however—detaching them from the novel as extraneous elements, the way Bardamu allowed his readers to do in *Voyage*—leads to very wrong deductions about *Mort à crédit*.

Making sure the narrator of this novel acknowledges how much his life has been touched by delirium and dementia, Louis-Ferdinand Céline takes his stand at a considerable distance from the naturalists. Measured by the yardstick of nineteenth-century French naturalism, the story told in *Mort à crédit* lacks acceptable proportion. Stepping repeatedly outside prescribed limits, Ferdinand is always going too far in what he has to say and in his manner of narration. Even more than *Voyage au bout de la nuit*, this novel is the product of an imagination that finds expression through visual effects. Gestures, externalizing acutely felt emotions, are exaggerated to the limit of credibility and beyond. Typically, things are not perceived in normal perspective and dimension. During an attack of fever, Ferdinand sees a man's hat as impossibly oversized, its brim "so vast that a velodrome . . ." (II, 25). The interesting thing is that the hat belongs to someone the narrator knows, Léonce Poitrat, employed as an accountant at the clinic where Ferdinand works. Even when describing the man while not in the grip of fever, Ferdinand still affirms that Poitrat has an erection "hard as thirty-six biceps" (II, 25).

True detail is often no more than a stepping-stone to antinaturalist effect in *Mort à crédit*. When fever makes Ferdinand describe his mother's legs, seen when she raises her skirt to run, they are so hairy (reminding him of a spider) that they become entangled in one another and she is rolled along on a bobbin. The ludicrousness of touches like these, defying acceptance as faithful to reality, is a sign to the readers that he is being taken into a domain Céline began to make his own when writing *Mort à crédit*. Letters addressed to Hindus in 1947 illuminate both the creative process itself and the motivation behind its implementation.

On September 2, Céline explained, "What throws me into a rage, you see, is the insensitivity of men—the malady of the world is insensitivity— To get out of that obsession I set about things the best I can—"[9] On July 7 he responded to a query, "The relationship between reality and my writings? My God, real objective life is impossible for me, unbearable—I go mad with it, into a rage, so dreadful does it seem to me, and therefore I transpose it as I dream and go along . . . I suppose it's more or less the general malady of the world called *poetry* . . . In me it must be a bit more lively, stubborn, than in other people."[10] Questioning him, Hindus presumably was feigning incomprehension in the hope of hearing him amplify an aside in a letter dated March 30, where Céline bemoaned his situation in Denmark: "but you know I am much more of a poet than a prose writer and I write only to transpose. . . ."[11] Fortunately, the vagueness of the words "poet" and "poetry" is counterbalanced by stress upon transposition as the key to intention and method. Louis-Ferdinand Céline, whose storyteller introduces into *Mort à crédit* scraps of a legend about a king called Krogold, commented on May 29, "I am a Celt, above all a *bardic dreamer* — I can recount legends like having a piss, with a facility that disgusts me, scenarios, ballets as many as you like [his collection of texts published in 1959 under the title *Ballets sans musique, sans personne, sans rien* testifies to this facility], telling tales is really my gift — I've submitted it to realism in a spirit of hate for the spitefulness of men — in combative spirit — but in reality my music is legend. . . ."[12]

Céline made no secret of the fact that in his fiction transposition of reality followed upon the intervention of imagination, granted total freedom to modify the raw material furnished by the everyday world. He expected, so he declared in a letter to Hindus on May 15, 1947, to be acknowledged one day as having rendered the French language more sensitive, more emotional, and less confined by academicism, "through a knack consisting (less easy than it seems) in a monolog of spoken but TRANSCRIBED intimacy — That immediate spontaneous transposition is the trick — In reality it is a return to the spontaneous poetry of the savage."[13]

Céline's concept of the role of the novelist in transposing the real rested firmly on a clear idea of the fiction writer's function. "I want to be charmed, bewitched," he informed Hindus in a letter dated simply the 12th, " — I don't want to be instructed! 54 years of life and what a life — 27 of daily medical practice have taught me too much raw reality — I want realism to be made to 'sing' for me — anything that doesn't sing for me is shit."[14] This statement casts light on another, made a little later in the same letter: "French literature is scarcely ever delirious — it is lyrical reluctantly — no lyricism between Villon and Chénier! 4 centuries!" Lamenting the absence of delirium in the literature of France, Céline — whose preface to *Guignol's Band* confessed that he could not bring himself to read other books ("I find them rough drafts, not written, still-born . . ." [II, 518]) — commented, "I'm not speaking of surrealism which is a fabrication, intentional, conventional delirium, a simulation without an echo, without a heart — nothing at all — Sartre, Camus, Guilloux and a thousand others fall into that fabrication — Green, etc." In a long postscript, he returned to the same theme: "Ah! I want to be enchanted — Harpagon reasons too much in my opinion, Volpone enchants me. . . . Be delirious if you like, but be delirious JUST RIGHT, watch out. Being delirious just right has to go to the core of man of his soul not his head — All the Sartre, Camus and Green delirium comes from the head and even *Le Grand Meaulnes* . . . So highly spoken of . . . Goat droppings" (p. 81).

The principles summarized here clearly had a greater influence on *Mort à crédit* than on *Voyage au bout de la nuit*. In his new novel, Céline set out to oblige readers to see transposition of reality as something more than a side effect of the fever periodically confining Ferdinand to his bed. Not content with allowing his narrator, whether sick or well, the same kind of exaggeration in descriptive detail, Céline placed him in situations that can only be termed delirious by nature. They are borrowed from the world Ferdinand knew as a child, a world dominated by the frightening presence of his father.

. . . In *Voyage au bout de la nuit* Bardamu was spared the madness that signalled Semmelweis' final collapse beneath the unbearable weight of the world's hostility. But in *Mort à crédit*, Ferdinand has lived under the menace of insanity for as long as he can remember, first at home, in enforced proximity to a father subject to crazy rages, and then, after attaining adulthood, as a victim of recurrent attacks of fever. In addition, "fever or not, I still have such a buzzing in both ears that it can't teach me much more" (II, 23).

The circumstances under which he grew up, and those under which he has lived since, account for the tone Ferdinand gives his narrative, touched everywhere by frenzy. In *Mort à crédit* details are accumulated with far less respect for the sober pattern of external reality than in *Voyage au bout de la nuit*. For it is not only the nature of events related but the impact they have had on the sensibility registering them that brings Ferdinand's story much closer to delirium than Bardamu's. All the same, it seems perfectly appropriate to link *Mort à crédit* and *Voyage*, so long as one goes on attempting to situate Céline's fiction in relation to the naturalist tradition. To be more exact, among the Célinian novels it is *Voyage au bout de la nuit* and *Mort à crédit* that come closest to respecting the traditional view of fiction for which, in France, naturalism has represented the norm since the nineteenth century. In consequence, departures from naturalist criteria—more noticeable and less excusable, apparently, in the second novel than in the first—seem to be merely unfortunate breaches of convention, committed by a writer who therefore must be judged guilty of having lost control, here and there.

Considering *Mort à crédit* by supposedly reliable inherited standards for fictional transposition of reality, traditionalist readers find, or think they find, enough that is reassuringly familiar to compensate for more or less disturbingly innovative features. And so, viewing the novels Céline published in the thirties in the light of the naturalist esthetic, they fail to acknowledge *Mort à crédit*'s originality as an exploratory work of fiction. In this novel, rather than attempting to repeat *Voyage au bout de la nuit* or to prolong it by several hundred pages, Céline was trying to go beyond the earlier work, in an effort to remedy the weaknesses he had detected in his first experiment with narrative form.

Technically speaking, in *Mort à crédit* Céline began to take a road that would lead him to his highly distinctive later novels. Looking at the latter, critics have displayed remarkable unanimity in judging them to be deplorable proof that Céline's talent declined after 1936. All agree that his fictional writings slipped their moorings after *Mort à crédit*, drifting willy nilly on a sea of chaotic emotions, liberated by terror and hate, at the expense, naturally, of narrative unity. So confidently do they condemn Céline's later novelistic effort that they do not appear to have paused to ask themselves whether he might not have set out deliberately — aware of what he was risking — upon oceans he knew as well as anyone else to be uncharted. Certainly, they fail to appreciate that Céline was heading for new waters from the moment he began writing *Mort à crédit*.

If we are to believe Céline himself, Denoël (who had published both *Voyage* and *Mort à crédit*) did not understand the first volume of *Guignol's band*, the next of Céline's novels to appear. Denoël was not to be alone in feeling puzzled. The critics' inability to come to terms with this 1944 novel was less a sign of hostility from all sides, for which Céline himself inclined to take it, than proof that the full significance of *Mort à crédit* had eluded them.

Notes

1. *L'Herne*, No. 5, p. 101. [Full reference: *Cahiers de l'Herne* 3 (1963); 5 (1965). Reprint. *L'Herne: L.-F. Céline*, ed. Dominique de Roux, M. Beaujour, and M. Thélia (Paris: Minard, 1972) (editor's note).]

2. *L'Herne*, No. 3, p. 101.

3. Quotations from *Mort à crédit*, in *Oeuvres*, ed. Jean Ducourneau, vol. 2 (Paris: Balland, 1967) — editor's note.

4. Ibid., 108.

5. "Conversations avec Louis-Ferdinand Céline," in Hanrez, *Céline*, p. 277. Interview dating from 1959.

6. Letter probably written in December 1932. See *L'Herne*. No. 3, p. 92.

7. David Hayman, *Louis-Ferdinand Céline* (New York and London: Columbia University Press, 1965), p. 31.

8. See the undated [1932] letter in *L'Herne*, No. 5, p. 48.

9. *L'Herne*, No. 5, p. 94.

10. Ibid., 84.

11. Ibid., 72.

12. Ibid., 76.

13. Ibid., 75.

14. Ibid., 80.

"I'll Protest If It Kills Me": A
Reading of the Prologue to *Death*
on the *Installment Plan*   Wayne Burns*

The novel of adventures, the tale, the epic are [an] ingenuous manner of
experiencing imaginary and significant things. The realistic novel is [a]
second oblique manner. It requires something of the first: it needs
something of the mirage to make us see it as such. So that it is not only
Don Quixote which was written against the books of chivalry, and as a
result bears the latter within it, but the novel as a literary genre consists
essentially of that absorption.

—José Ortega y Gasset

I'm first of all a Celt—*daydreamer, bard*. I can turn out legends like
taking a leak—with disgusting ease. Scenarios, ballet—anything you
like—just while talking. That's my real talent. I harnessed it to realism
because I hate man's wickedness so much; because I love combat.

—Céline in a letter to Milton Hindus, 29 May 1947

I

The first thing to be said about *Death on the Installment Plan* is that
it is not a prolongation of *Journey to the End of the Night*—not, as it may
initially seem to be, first a prolongation forward (for thirty-two pages)
into the life of the mature Ferdinand who appears in *Journey* and then one
backward (for more than 540 pages) into the childhood of the same
Ferdinand. The mature Ferdinand of *Death* is not the mature Ferdinand of
the end of *Journey*, nor is the eighteen-year-old at the end of *Death* the
same Ferdinand who enlists in the army at the beginning of *Journey*. For
all their fundamental likenesses, the Ferdinand of *Journey* and the
Ferdinand of *Death* are, in both character and function, quite distinct,
and they render the two novels quite distinct.

Why distinctions so primary have not been generally recognized I
have difficulty understanding. Perhaps it is because most readers and
critics read *Journey* first, since it is better known and more widely
discussed and is, in the opinion of most critics, Céline's best novel. Then, if
they go on to read *Death*, they may be inclined, for obvious reasons, to see
it as a backward extension of Ferdinand's adventures in which Céline
draws upon his boyhood to repeat, even more savagely, everything that he
has said in *Journey*. Approached in this way, *Death* may well appear to be
a lesser novel, despite the fact that nearly all critics concede its superiority
in matters of structure and style. But to read *Death* in this way is like

*Originally written for this volume, this essay now appears in *Enfin Céline Vint* (New
York: Peter Lang, 1988).

reading *Great Expectations* as a revision of *David Copperfield*. *Death* is neither a greater nor a lesser *Journey*; it is a distinct and separate novel that makes its own demands in order to express its own intentions. The similarities are always there. They are bound to be there in any two novels of any novelist. But they are there with variations and developments that make *Death* a quite different and, in my judgment, a much greater novel.

II

In the first thirty-two pages of *Death*, which have come to be designated the prologue, Céline introduces Ferdinand Bardamu, the mature "I" who stands behind the boy "I" who then, in the succeeding five hundred forty-one pages, tells the story of his growing up. Or, put another way, the boy "I" is the "I" the mature "I" conjures up from his memories in order to present the fullest possible account of what he was like as a boy and what he went through in growing up. It therefore follows that if we, as readers, are to understand the boy we must first understand the man: whether he is the same Ferdinand who narrated *Journey*, a few years older but otherwise essentially unchanged, or whether he is a Ferdinand who has, in growing older and becoming a writer as well as a doctor, taken on a somewhat different character.[1]

As the novel opens, Ferdinand is mourning the death of "Madame Bérenge, the concierge . . . a good friend, gentle and faithful."[2] Alone again, he has no one left to mourn with him:

> Those people are all so far away . . . They've changed their souls, that's a way to be disloyal, to forget, to keep talking about something else.
>
> Poor old Madame Bérenge; they'll come and take her cross-eyed dog away . . . Someone will have to put out the fire in the lodge. Whom will I write to? I've nobody left. No one to receive the friendly spirits of the dead . . . and let me speak more softly to the world . . . I'll have to bear it all alone. (15–16)

Now these words, I submit, could not have been spoken as Ferdinand here speaks them by the Ferdinand of *Journey*. While there may be lines in *Journey* that approximate these, when Ferdinand is speaking of Molly or Bébert or Alcide or Robinson, the tone is different, the expressions of sentiment more guarded. The Ferdinand of *Journey* could hardly bring in Bérenge's "cross-eyed dog" as unashamedly as Ferdinand does here; nor could he then add, as Ferdinand does here, the line about putting out "the fire in the lodge." And the Ferdinand of *Journey* could never, under any circumstances, acknowledge that he might wish "to speak more softly to the world."

In the paragraph that follows, as Ferdinand speaks of Madame Bérenge's final moments, he does lapse into the kind of bitterness he so often expresses in *Journey*. Yet even here the tone is different. While he knows that he can talk about his hatred, and promises to do that "later on if they don't come back," he would rather "tell stories . . . stories that will make them come back, to kill me" (16). This final phrase, "to kill me," can neither be erased nor denied. It is there, prophetically there. It has to be, since the stories he proposes to tell them (and us) are not stories that anyone wishes to hear, and he must therefore be killed for telling them. "Then," he concludes, in a voice more resigned than defiant, "it will be over and that will be all right with me" (16).

In the passages that follow Ferdinand continues to speak more softly, and seemingly with more self-assurance. In talking with his cousin Gustin, who is also a doctor, he is affectionate, at times even playfully affectionate, and always compassionate. And if he says scathing things about his patients en masse he is kindness itself, for all his ferocious grumbling, when he treats them individually. But then Ferdinand could never, even in his worst moments in *Journey*, be unkind to his patients — not even when, by his own admission, he behaves "in that stupid way" in treating a sick child:

> I had been feeling very strange in mind and body, and the screams of this little innocent made a ghastly impression on me. What screams, my God, what screams! I couldn't bear it another second.
>
> No doubt something else too made me behave in that stupid way. I was so furious I couldn't help expressing, out loud, the rancour and the disgust I had been feeling, too long, inside myself.
>
> "Hey," I said to this little screamer, "don't you be in such a hurry, you little fool! There'll be plenty of time yet for you to yell. There'll be time, don't you worry, you little donkey! Pull yourself together. There'll be unhappiness enough later on to make you cry your eyes out and weep yourself silly, if you don't look out!"[3]

When Ferdinand suffers the same kinds of provocation in a comparable scene in *Death* he reacts altogether differently — not because he suppresses his feelings of rancor and disgust but because he no longer has such feelings to express or suppress. After putting up with the antics and lamentations of a drunken mother and father, he does everything he can for their sick little girl; then, in a gesture "that was better than talking" (18), he tries to cheer her up by making a swing for her doll. Conceivably the Ferdinand of *Journey* might have done something like this, although I can't recall an instance in which he actually does, but — and this is the crucial point — he could never, having done such a thing as making a swing for a child's doll, go on to observe: "I thought I'd cheer her up. I'm always good for a laugh when I put my mind to it" (17). In *Journey* Ferdinand is never good for a laugh — at least not for this kind of a laugh, with no trace of bitterness or satiric bite in it. These are the words of a gentler, more relaxed, more self-assured Ferdinand — a Ferdinand much like the real-life Céline who appears in the reminiscences of his friends of these years.

III

In mentioning the real-life Céline I am not, I hasten to add, trying to validate my interpretation by an appeal to biography. Whether the Ferdinand of *Death* is more like Céline than the Ferdinand of *Journey* is of no real consequence here. What matters is that passages such as this — and they recur throughout the early pages of the novel — tend to modify Ferdinand's character in just those ways that lend credibility to his becoming, like Céline himself, a writer who is at once a "daydreamer, bard" and a relentless "realist."[4] Although Ferdinand has not, like Céline, won fame and fortune with his first novel ("I wasn't making enough money yet to go off and write full time" [34]), he has been writing "big fat books" (31), and he is presumably the author of *Journey*: "a little pimp, Bébert . . . He ended up on snow. He'd been reading the *Journey* . . ." (36). At any rate Gustin's remarks, when Ferdinand first mentions his writing, echo the critical refrain that *Journey* gave rise to: " 'You could talk about something pleasant now and then.' That was Gustin's opinion. 'Life isn't always disgusting.' "

Against this opinion Ferdinand offers no defense. Instead he concedes that Gustin may, in part at least, be right:

> In a way he's right. With me it's kind of a mania, a bias. The fact is that in the days when I had that buzzing in both ears, even worse than now, and attacks of fever all day long, I wasn't half so gloomy . . . I had lovely dreams . . . Madame Vitruve, my secretary, was talking about it only the other day. She knew how I tormented myself. When a man's so generous, he squanders his treasures, loses sight of them. I said to myself: "That damn Vitruve, she's hidden them some place . . ." Real marvels they were . . . bits of Legend, pure delight . . . That's the kind of stuff I'm going to write from now on. . . . (19)

Although Ferdinand's manner is playful — as, for instance, when he is talking about squandering his treasures — he is nevertheless responding seriously to Gustin's criticism. "I might," he remarks a bit later, "have consulted some sensitive soul . . . well versed in fine feelings . . . in all the innumerable shadings of love. . . ." But, he adds, "sensitive souls are often impotent" (27). And so, when he rediscovers the "bits of Legend" that he had written earlier, "the kind of stuff I'm going to write from now on," he again turns to Gustin:

> I wanted to talk to him about my Legend. We'd found the first part under Mireille's bed. I was badly disappointed when I reread it. The passage of time hadn't helped my romance any. After years of oblivion a child of fancy can look pretty tawdry . . . Well, with Gustin I could always count on a frank, sincere opinion. I tried to put him in the right frame of mind.
>
> "Gustin," I said. "You haven't always been the mug you are today,

bogged down by circumstances, work, and thirst, the most disastrous of servitudes . . . Do you think that, just for a moment, you can revive the poetry in you? . . . are your heart and cock still capable of leaping to the words of an epic, sad to be sure, but noble . . . resplendent? You feel up to it?" (26)

Gustin's response to Ferdinand's affectionate banter is wonderfully appropriate: he dozes on without saying a word. But that doesn't stop Ferdinand, who proceeds to read the part of his legend that recounts the death of "Gwendor the Magnificent, Prince of Christiania." And while Gwendor's death is a mixture of gore and sentimentality, the rhetoric with which he expresses it is truly impressive, as Ferdinand himself points out when, at a climactic moment, he interjects, "Get a load of this" (26). Nevertheless Gustin, who may still be dozing, remains unimpressed:

> Gustin's arms dangled between his legs.
> "Well, how do you like it?" I asked him.
> He was on his guard. He wasn't too eager to be rejuvenated. He resisted. He wanted me to explain the whole thing to him, the whys and wherefores. That's not so easy. Such things are as frail as butterflies. A touch and they fall to pieces in your hands and you feel soiled. What's the use? I didn't press the matter. (27)

Yet if Ferdinand does not press the matter he still continues to read—until Gustin, in what may be taken as his ultimate critical statement, falls "sound asleep" (28). And his later expressions of kindly tolerance, when Ferdinand is about to read more of his legend, are equally discouraging: "Go on, Ferdinand, go ahead and read, I'll listen to the damn thing. Not too fast, though. And cut out the gestures. It wears you out and it makes me dizzy" (33).

IV

While there is, by this time, no mistaking Gustin's response to *King Krogold*, Ferdinand's attitude remains ambiguous. From the time when he and Vitruve and Mireille find the first part of the legend "under Mireille's bed," where she not only sleeps but earns her living, there is a tone of mockery in just about everything he says about the legend—a tone which belies his seeming sincerity in defending his "masterpiece," particularly when his defense ("Such things are as frail as butterflies" [27]) seems almost as absurd as the "masterpiece" he is defending. For that matter the legend is riddled with lines totally out of keeping with its overall mood and tone—as, for instance, in the following passages:

> Gwendor's army has just suffered a terrible defeat . . . King Krogold himself caught sight of him in the thick of the fray . . . and clove him in twain . . . *Krogold is no do-nothing king* . . . He metes out his own justice. . . . (26; my italics)

> After the battle King Krogold, his knights, his pages, his brother the archbishop, the clerics of his camp, the whole court, went to the great tent in the middle of the bivouac and dropped with weariness. The heavy gold crescent, a gift from the caliph, was nowhere to be found . . . Ordinarily it surmounted the royal dais. The captain entrusted with its safekeeping *was beaten to a pulp.* The king lies down, tries to sleep . . . He is still suffering from his wounds. He wakes. Sleep refuses to come . . . He reviles the snorers. He rises. He steps over sleepers, *crushing a hand here and there,* leaves the tent. . . . (33–34; my italics)

That the italicized lines are intentional seems beyond question. But are they to be understood as the inadvertent slips of a hopelessly naive Ferdinand? Or of a Ferdinand who cannot quite stomach the rhetoric of his "romance"? Or are they direct authorial intrusions on the part of Céline in which he is playfully undercutting the pretensions of the legend? The truth is, unless I have somehow been remiss in my reading, the novel provides no satisfactory answer to these questions.

Equally puzzling, though in a somewhat different sense, is the passage in which Gwendor meets Death:

> "O Death! Great is my remorse! Endless my shame . . . Behold these poor corpses! . . . An eternity of silence will not soften my lot . . ."
> *"There is no softness or gentleness in this world, Gwendor, but only myth! All kingdoms end in a dream . . ."*
> "O Death, give me a little time . . . a day or two. I must find out who betrayed me . . ."
> "Everything betrays, Gwendor . . . The passions belong to no one, even love is only the flower of life in the garden of youth."
> And very gently Death gathers up the prince . . . He has ceased to resist . . . His weight has left him . . . And then a beautiful dream takes possession of his soul . . . The dream that often came to him when he was little, in his fur cradle, in the Chamber of the Heirs, close to his Moravian nurse in the castle of King René. . . . (27; my italics)

The words of Death that I have italicized express Céline's titular theme so eloquently that they might stand as an epigraph to the entire novel. But why, if this is true, are they tucked away in the middle of the gory legend, then encased in the rhetorical trappings that Gustin, and Ferdinand too at times, find either boring or funny? Are the italicized words another disguised authorial intrusion in which Céline is mocking the pretensions of the legend from a still different angle — by inserting lines more appropriate to the death of his old teacher, Metitpois, than to the poeticized death of Gwendor? Or is the entire passage a virtuoso performance in which Céline, via Ferdinand, is exercising his literary prowess ("I could make alligators dance to Pan's flute")[5] by demonstrating that he can, when he chooses, imbue his high-flown rhetoric with significant meaning? To these and related questions the novel once again provides no clearcut answers.

But—and I know this question will, to many critics, seem danger-ously heretical—does this lack of certainty really matter that much? Do we, as readers, have to know exactly how much Ferdinand the writer knows at any given moment about his own writing—especially when the effects of that writing are not dependent on how much Ferdinand knows? Do we, in reading *Don Quixote*, have to know exactly how much Don Quixote knows at any given moment when the effects of what he is saying and doing are not dependent on how much he knows? Nevertheless, it may be objected, Sancho Panza is always there to let Don Quixote (and the reader) know just how foolish he is being. Where is Ferdinand's Sancho?

The obvious answer is Gustin, who plays a straightforward Panzaic role throughout Ferdinand's readings. Vitruve also functions Panzaically, as does her niece Mireille. But it is Ferdinand himself, in his real or assumed naïveté, who most effectively undercuts his own dreams of what is "noble . . . resplendent." Up to the time of his delirium, Ferdinand is a divided personality: on his Quixotic side, he tries to believe in and defend his romance even as, on his Panzaic side, he can't help revealing how his own life and the lives of all those around him give the lie to all his idealistic fancies—just as Metitpois's death gives the lie to "his classical memories, his resolutions, the example of Caesar . . ." (29). The effect of these Panzaic revelations is therefore to permit us, as readers, to see clearly what Ferdinand has only begun to see dimly, namely, that the gory agonies in his legend are but rhetorical fantasies he has concocted in a vain attempt to escape what he and the people around him are going through; that his legend is to him what drinking is to Gustin, what Mireille's dirty stories are to her, what his mother's memories of his father are to her.

V

Toward the end of the prologue Céline sends Ferdinand into a fever or delirium in which he comes close to madness before he finally resolves his inner conflicts. The delirium is brought on by his trip to the Bois with Mireille, the girl with the "sumptuous ass" (37). "Christ Almighty, what a rear end. That ass of hers was a public scandal" (23). Yet this is not, he explains, what attracts him: "What attracts me is your imagination . . . I'm a voyeur. You tell me dirty stories . . . And I'll tell you a beautiful legend . . . Is it a bargain? . . . fifty-fifty . . . you'll be getting the best of it" (36). Ferdinand then tells her the story, complete with settings and costumes, of "Thibaud the Wicked, a troubadour." "The tone appealed to Mireille; she wanted more" (37). But on the way home they abandon his "beautiful Legend for a furious discussion about whether what women really wanted was to shack up with each other"—a discussion that ends up with Ferdinand talking about dildoes and Mireille, going still further, talking about girls growing phalluses "so they can rip each other's guts out" (37). At this point, apparently feeling that Mireille has not only outdone him but will tell the whole world that he has "behaved like a beast" (38), Ferdinand first resorts to violence and then goes off into a delirium that ends with the words: "It was hell" (39).

When he comes to, after being brought home by an ambulance, he is in bed, and his mother and Vitruve are in the next room waiting for his fever to go down. But fever is not all he is suffering from: "Fever or not, I always have such a buzzing in both ears that it can't get much worse. I've had it since the war. Madness has been hot on my trail . . . no exaggeration . . . for twenty-two years" (39). But he outruns her; he raves faster than she can: "That's how I do it. I shoot the shit. I charm her" (40). Yet it isn't easy: "My thoughts stagger and sprawl . . . I'm not very good to them. I'm working up the opera of the deluge . . . I'm the devil's stationmaster . . . The last gasp is very demanding. It's the last movie and nothing more to come. A lot of people don't know. You've got to knock yourself out. I'll be up to it soon . . ." (39–41). By the time he gets to the last few lines Ferdinand's near madness has been transformed into near sainthood, and he is once more the Ferdinand he was in the opening pages. He is knocking himself out—for us—so that we can know what we don't yet know: the truth about life and death. And he does this knowing full well that we, his readers, will come back to kill him.

In putting Ferdinand back together again as a near saint who is writing (as well as doctoring) in order to save us, Céline comes as close to revealing Ferdinand's deeper motives as he ever comes in the prologue. For his compassion, though always disguised, is always there. It is there when he is mourning Madame Bérenge's death; when he walks blocks out of his way because a stray dog is following him and he has to feed it and try to save it; when he speaks so tenderly to Gustin, as he always does, and excuses his looking "to the bottle for forgetfulness" (31); when he says, "I wouldn't want to be too hard on Vitruve. Maybe she has had more trouble than I have" (21); when he looks at his mother's crippled leg "as skinny as a poker" and says, "I've seen it all my life" (47). Céline cannot, however, permit Ferdinand to remain a near saint—either as doctor or writer. No one would believe in him then. He cannot even permit him to be a near hero. Heroes can only feel and see and know what Gwendor knows, or what Metitpois knows, "with his classical memories, his resolutions, the example of Caesar"; whereas Ferdinand feels and sees and knows what Death knows, what Death tells Gwendor: that "there is no softness or gentleness in this world . . . but only myth! All kingdoms end in a dream" (27).

In bringing Ferdinand to a full understanding of these words Céline renders him forever incapable of being heroic, or for that matter, of acting, or speaking, or writing heroically—except in play or jest. When Ferdinand can no longer believe in dreams and myths he can no longer be a hero. He may perform actions that outwardly correspond to those of a hero; he may even risk his own life to save others; yet so long as he performs these actions without believing that they will somehow make people or the world better, without, in short, believing that they have any meaning beyond their material consequences, his actions cannot possibly be heroic. To be heroic they would have to derive from, or express, beliefs or faiths or dreams or myths that evade or deny the real world. For Céline as for Ortega y Gasset "materiality" contains a "critical power which defeats the claim to self-sufficiency of all idealizations, wishes and fancies of man . . . the insufficiency of all that is noble, clear, lofty."[6] In the novel, Ortega explains, "reality, the actual can be changed into poetic substance" but only "as destruction of the myth, as criticism of the myth. In this form reality, which is of an inert and insignificant nature, quiet and mute, acquires movement, is changed into an active power of aggression against the crystalline orb of the ideal. The enchantment of the latter broken, it falls into fine, iridescent dust which gradually loses its colors until it becomes an earthy brown. We are present at this scene in every novel."[7]

I have quoted Ortega at such length because his critical argument so closely anticipates the dramatic argument with which Céline concludes the prologue — as he brings Ferdinand, still in bed, and still so feverish that he intermittently lapses into delirium, into direct conflict with his mother's idealized account of her life with his dead father:

> She's telling Madame Vitruve the story of her life . . . Over and over again, to make it clear what a time she's had with me. Extravagant . . . irresponsible . . . lazy . . . nothing like his father . . . he so conscientious . . . so hardworking . . . so deserving . . . so unlucky . . . who passed on last winter . . . Sure . . . she doesn't tell her about the dishes he broke on her bean . . . how he used to drag her through the back room by the hair . . . Not one word about all that . . . nothing but poetry . . . Yes, we lived in cramped quarters, but we loved each other so. That's what she was saying. Papa was fond of me, he was so sensitive about every little thing that my behavior . . . so much to worry about . . . . my alarming propensities, the terrible trouble I gave him . . . hastened his death . . . all that grief and anguish affected his heart. Plop! The fairy tales people tell each other . . . they make a certain amount of sense, but they're a pack of filthy stinking lies. . . . (43)

Ferdinand here defines it all, both for himself and for the reader: "Nothing but poetry," or "a pack of filthy lies." Enough to make Ferdinand leave his sick-bed to vomit. And when the lies continue he "can't stand it," and takes refuge in his legend: "If I've got to be delirious, I'd rather wallow in stories of my own" (44). If, in other words, he has to wallow, he would rather wallow in his own "pack of lies" than in his mother's. And that is what he immediately proceeds to do:

> I see Thibaud the Troubadour . . . He's always in need of money . . . He's going to kill Joad's father . . . Well, at least that will be one father less in the world . . . I see splendid tournaments on the ceiling . . . I see lancers impaling each other . . . I see King Krogold himself . . . He has

come from the north . . . He had been invited to Bredonnes with his
whole court . . . I see his daughter Wanda, the Blonde, the Radiant . . .
I wouldn't mind jerking off, but I'm too sticky . . . Joad is horny in love
. . . Oh well, why not. . . . (44)

In his interjected comments, Ferdinand is jerking off to, or trying to jerk
off to, his own stories in much the same way that his mother, as he sees her,
has been jerking off to hers. But his mother's fantasies, as he listens to her
talking to Vitruve, overwhelm his own: "I can't stand the sight of her
anymore, she gives me the creeps. She wants me to share in her fantasies
. . . I'm not in the mood . . . I want to have my own fantasies . . ." (45).

At this point Ferdinand lapses into another delirium in which he sees
himself in his "gallant ship" on "a long tack across the Etoile" (45), only to
come to as his mother says: "Ah, if only your father were here"—words
that so inflame Ferdinand's feelings of hatred that he yells them straight at
his mother: "My father, I say, was a skunk! I yell my lungs out . . . 'There
was no lousier bastard in the whole universe! from the Galeries-Lafayette
to Capricorne. . . .'" At first his mother is "stupefied. Transfixed . . ."
(46). After that she attacks—with words, fits, and finally the umbrella,
which she breaks across his face. But Ferdinand refuses to give way. In a
finale that is at once a prevision of the rest of the novel and a restatement
of the artistic commitment with which he opens the prologue, he declares
that he will not put up with his mother's idealized memories: "I'll protest
if it kills me. I repeat that he was a sneak, brute, hypocrite, and yellow in
every way" (46).

Everything Ferdinand says or does in his battle with his mother
reveals his powerful Oedipal jealousy: "The deader he is the more she loves
him. Like a she-dog that can't get enough . . . But I won't put up with
it . . ." (46). And when she starts up again and is "ready to die for her
Auguste," he threatens to "smash her face," but instead, "in a blind rage,"
he smashes her, as well as himself, with gestures and words that come
straight from the depths of his Oedipal agony: "I bend over and lift up her
skirt. I see her calf as skinny as a poker, without any flesh on it, her
stocking all sagging, it's foul . . . I've seen it all my life . . . I puke on it,
the works . . ." Unnerved finally, his mother backs away and runs for the
stairs, while Ferdinand—and this is the final touch—hears "her limp all
the way down" (46–47).

VI

This is the mature Ferdinand who is, in the guise of the boy
Ferdinand, about to tell the story of his growing up. And he has, through
his words and actions, foreshadowed the nature of the story that he feels he
must tell, the way that he feels he must tell it—or, more accurately, he has
foreshadowed the first 325 pages of the story that he feels he must tell;
namely, the story of his inability to deny his feelings in order to become

like his parents. And because both his father and mother, along with nearly everyone else in their world, are mired in middle-class poverty and ideals that sustain people in that condition, it is to be the story of his struggle to overcome the neglect and even hatred, disguised as love and sacrifice and virtue, to which he is constantly subjected. And because he has come to realize that "there is no softness or gentleness in this world," that the myths in which these ideals are enshrined are like his own legend, or on another level, Mireille's "dirty stories," or the fairy tales his mother tells about his father, his story is to be not a legend or a fairy tale, but a protest against all "the fairy tales people tell each other" (43) — all the fairy tales that people jerk off to.

What Ferdinand's words do not foreshadow, however, is the latter or Courtial half of the novel, which is something of a legend or fairy tale in itself, though of a totally different kind. Courtial, the fatherly Quixote, takes the sixteen-year-old Ferdinand as his Panzaic son, and together they defy the world's lies with hopes and dreams of their own — until the world finally catches up with them and reduces their "crystalline orb" to an "earthy brown." Céline's choosing not to foreshadow or in any direct way acknowledge or anticipate this latter half of the novel raises a number of questions for which once again, I have no very satisfactory answers.[8] Possibly he felt that he could not allow Ferdinand to speak directly about that part of his life in which he was happy without lessening the intensity of the tragic outlook he is trying to establish. Or possibly Céline felt that everything Ferdinand says about his legend and about the stories he is going to tell actually does apply to the second half of the novel, since it too ends on a note of despair. It can even be argued that Courtial is present in spirit if not in name when Ferdinand tries to speak more softly to the world, or when, more specifically, he remembers the pitiful dreams of Auguste, his dead father: "I think of Auguste, he liked boats too . . . He was an artist at heart . . . He had no luck . . . he drew storms now and then on my blackboard" (47).

Yet Ferdinand's softness never impairs his vision. Auguste's dreams, unlike Courtial's, are but impotent fantasies. For him there is nothing in this world but the lies he tries to live by and would have others live by. He, along with almost everyone else, has become like the people Ferdinand described earlier in *Journey*: "they really have got love in reserve . . . Only it's a pity people should still be such sods, with so much love in reserve."[9] The distinction Ferdinand draws here is critical. For if he can pity people for being such sods he cannot pity what they do, as sods, to themselves and one another, in the name of some fairy tale or another. What they do, as sods, he hates; the fairy tales that provide them with both impetus and justification for doing what they do he hates even more. And he is determined to express his hatred so forcefully that he will, as he promises in the very beginning of the prologue, "tell stories that will make them come back, to kill me, from the ends of the world."

Having revealed so much about himself and the stories he will tell, the mature Ferdinand makes his final exit by first asking Emilie, the maid, who is still there beside his bed, to lie down with him in her clothes, so that she can accompany him on a make-believe cruise (presumably a continuation of the cruise he embarked on earlier in his delirium). The significance of the ports of call on this cruise Emilie "doesn't get," although her response indicates that she understands the lying down part: " 'Tomorrow,' she says. 'Tomorrow. . . .' " With only this promise to sustain him, Ferdinand is "really alone," as he was at the opening of the prologue; and he sees, as he returns to his delirious state, "thousands and thousands of little skiffs returning high above the Left Bank . . . Each one had a shriveled little corpse under its sail . . . and his story . . . his little lies to catch the wind with" (47). And these are the same "dead" (now corpses and in skiffs), the same "lies" ("the fairy tales people tell each other . . . a pack of filthy stinking lies") Ferdinand encounters at the beginning of his cruise: "The whole town is on deck. All those dead — I know them all . . . The pianist has caught on . . . He's playing the tune we need: 'Black Joe' . . . for a cruise . . . to catch the wind and weather . . . and the lies . . ." (45).

Notes

1. At this point I should perhaps try to explain more fully what I am and am not trying to suggest about the changes or developments in Ferdinand. To begin with I am acknowledging that Ferdinand is, in both novels, a fictional character, that the only way we can know what he is like is through what he says and does in the fictional circumstances in which he appears. I am not, I must emphasize, trying to read in thoughts and feelings that I think might be there, or should be there in such a character created by such an author as Céline may, correctly or incorrectly, be thought to be. I am trying to see the Ferdinand of *Journey* as the text of the novel presents him, the Ferdinand of *Death* as the text of the novel presents him. Now it may be — and here I am, I realize, getting into deep water indeed — that the Ferdinand of *Journey* really is, at some deep authorial level, indistinguishable from the Ferdinand of *Death*. But this level, though it may be of speculative interest, need be of no concern here. What matters is the character who emerges from the words on the page. And if those words suggest that Ferdinand has changed, then he has changed — regardless of what may lie behind the changes. David Hayman discusses the prologue to *Death* at some length in his "Celine" *(Iowa Review,* Spring, 1972, pp. 76–81). While I have found Hayman's analysis perceptive, his critical approach is so far removed from my own that I am not aware of specific indebtedness. In "The Darkest Journey" *(Wisconsin Studies in Continental Literature,* VIII, Winter, 1967, pp. 99–103) John Fraser also discusses the prologue to *Death* — at some length and with real insight. Once again, however, I do not see that his criticism has any specific relationship to my own.

2. Céline, *Death on the Installment Plan,* translated by Ralph Manheim, New Directions, New York, 1971, p. 15. Further quotations will be followed by page numbers in parentheses.

3. Céline, *Journey to the End of the Night,* translated by John H. P. Marks, New Directions, New York, 1960, p. 271.

4. Milton Hindus, *The Crippled Giant,* University Press of New England, Hanover, 1986, p. 93.

5. Ibid., p. 88

6. José Ortega Y Gasset, "The Nature of the Novel," translated by Evelyn Rugg and Diego Marin, *Hudson Review*, 10, 1957, pp. 30–31.

7. Ibid., p. 40. I have discussed Ortega's theory of the novel at some length in an earlier study: Wayne Burns, *The Panzaic Principle*, Pendejo Press, Vancouver, B.C., 1968 (reprinted in *Recovering Literature*, 5, 1 [Spring 1976], 5–63). See also my *Journey Through the Dark Woods*, Howe Street Press, Seattle, 1982.

8. The omission of the Courtial half suggests another possibility. It is almost as if, when Céline wrote these first thirty-two pages, he was thinking of a novel that would not include much more than Ferdinand's struggles with his parents and the people in their world — a novel that would be little more than an extended version of the first three hundred and twenty-five pages of the novel as it now stands. Perhaps he had not yet thought of such a character as Courtial, much less of using him to give the novel the wholly different turn that it takes following his entrance. And perhaps, when he did get around to adding the Courtial half, he felt no need to revise the first thirty-two pages.

9. Céline, *Journey*, p. 393.

POLITICS, PAMPHLETS, AND *PROFESSOR Y*

Enthusiasm is to let yourself go into delirium. Freud certainly did! But alas, today our delirium is pretty well confined to political fanaticism — even more ridiculous. Oh I know! I got caught up in it too!
— Letter to Milton Hindus, 5 August 1947

It's the Rule of the game! lyricism needs its 'I'. . . .
— *Conversations with Professor Y*

The Jews, Céline, and Maritain
[An Excerpt]

André Gide*

I

Critics in general have been been somewhat unreasonable in talking about *Bagatelles pour un Massacre*. It is astonishing that it could be misunderstood. Because, after all, Céline played for high stakes. He even took the highest possible risk, as he always did. He did not mince his words. But he did his best to warn that none of this was more serious than Don Quixote's charge under the open skies.

Remember the row his first two books caused? The press was dumbfounded and no longer knew which tone to take. Some were indignant. Others were in ecstasy. They shouted genius, scandal. The books were praised to the sky or thrown in the garbage. They were seen everywhere. I remember seeing *Death on the Installment Plan* in the place of honor in the grandest and the lowliest window displays. Even the little stationery shops out in the country, which ordinarily only sold newspapers, had him on display. You bumped up against him. You could not miss him. This we all know, and Céline most of all. So when Céline starts talking about a sort of conspiracy of silence, of a coalition to hinder the sale of his books, it is obvious that he is joking. And when he makes the Jew responsible for his slump in sales, it goes without saying that he is joking. And if he were not joking, he would be completely loony. The same when he mixes Cézanne, Picasso, Maupassant, Racine, Stendhal and Zola in a jumble with the Jews of his massacre. What else do you need? How better to show that you are kidding? Just as when he gives us as a "Chief Rabbi's declaration" a statistic that is plain rubbish, or when he amuses himself by playing the martyr, the plagiarized, etc. He declares with great eloquence that he loathes subtleties, the "complex Goncourt babies," "Prout-Prousts," "Mr. Paul Cemetery Valéry," and he proves it. He tries his best not to be taken seriously. That being the case, if you get indignant it is

*Translated by Jóhanna Eiríksdóttir Hull for this volume from *Nouvelle review française* 26 (1938):630–34. Gide's quotes from *Death on the Installment Plan* are taken here from the Ralph Manheim translation of the novel (New York: New Directions, 1966).

you that has put yourself in the wrong, which is so often the case with critics—to not take the books for what they are.

Céline excels in invective. He hooks it onto anything. Jewishness is only a pretext. He has chosen the densest pretext possible, the most trivial, the most widely known, the one that most readily mocks the nuances, allows the most summary pronouncements, the most enormous exaggerations, the least concern for fairness, the most intemperate indulgence of the pen. And Céline is never better than when he is the most outrageous. He's a creator. He talks about Jews in *Bagatelles* just as he talks about the maggots which his evocative force has just created in *Death on the Installment Plan:*

> By the effect of intensive waves, of malignant "inductions," by the diabolical instrumentality of a thousand wire networks, we had corrupted the earth . . . stirred up the jinni of the grubs . . . in the innocent bosom of nature . . . There in Blême-le Petit, we had given birth to a special race of absolutely vicious, unbelievably corrosive maggots, which attacked every kind of seed, every conceivable plant and root . . . trees! harvests! the peasants' houses! the very structure of the land! even dairy products! sparing absolutely nothing . . . Corrupting, sucking, dissolving . . . encrusting the plowshares! . . . absorbing, digesting stone, flint as well as beans! . . . (515)

In the same book he spasmodically paints the gratuitous excess of his lyrical rage. The passage is a little long, but it is worth quoting all of it:

> For his private delectation I turned Courtial . . . shouting at the top of my lungs . . . into a heap of soft, slimy inconceivably sickening turds . . . how unbelievably loathsome he was! . . . He was in a class by himself! I went at it hammer and tongs! I stamped on the trapdoor right over the cellar, in chorus with the nut . . . I outdid them all in violence . . . thanks to the intensity of my revolt! my sincerity! my destructive enthusiasm! my implacable tetanism! . . . my frenzy! . . . my anathematic writhing! . . . It was unbelievable what a paroxysm I could work myself up into in my total fury . . . I got all that from my dad . . . and the performances I'd been through . . . For temper tantrums I had no equal . . . The worst lunatics, the most delirious interpretive screwballs didn't stand a chance if I decided to take a fling, if I really wanted to bestir myself . . . Young as I was . . . they all left with their asses dragging . . . absolutely bewildered by the intensity of my hatred . . . my indomitable fury, the eternal thirst for vengeance that I harbored in my flanks . . . With tears in their eyes they entrusted me with the task of crushing that turd . . . that execrable Courtial . . . that sink of iniquity . . . of covering him with new and unpredictable kinds of excrement, slimier than the bottom of the shithouse! . . . a mass of unconscionable purulence! . . . of making a cake out of him, the most fetid that could ever be imagined . . . of cutting him up into balls . . . flattening him out into sheets, plastering the whole bottom of the crapper with him, all

the way from the bowl to the sump . . . and wedging him in there once and for all . . . to be shat on for all eternity. . . . (367)

Here I open a parenthesis. Leafing rapidly through the book, I had at first considered *Death on the Installment Plan* very inferior to *Journey to the End of the Night*, which I had read with uneven, but at moments, especially toward the end of the book, considerable amazement. At the insistence of a friend, I looked at the whole book again (I am talking about *Death on the Installment Plan*), this time without skipping a single sentence, and was convinced that it need not yield anything to the former. I even find here and there the accents of a singular sensibility, and I am not talking about the portrayal of the English mistress, his unavowed love, or her suicide which gets a bit on my nerves—but of this figure of an uncle, hardly sketched at first, whom he evokes again toward the end of the book with consummate skill, and which seemed newer than those, though very successful, of the father and the mother, or the somewhat conventional one of the inventor.

It is not reality that Céline paints. It is the hallucination reality provokes. And it is here that he is interesting. Who would think of recognizing in the lines that follow, the innocent Tuileries garden, even on a holiday?

> Only delirium, a chopped-up crater for three miles around, rumbling with disaster and drunks. . . .
>
> At the bottom of the crater, in the red-hot oven of hell, thousands of families were looking around for their pieces . . . Sides of meat, chunks of rump, kidneys gushing and spurting as far as the rue Royale and up into the clouds . . . The stink was merciless, tripe in urine, whiffs of corpse, decomposed liver patty . . . You got a mouthful with every breath . . . You couldn't get away from it . . . The terraces were inaccessible, blocked off by three impregnable bulwarks . . . Baby carriages piled as high as a six story building. . . . (308–9)

It is the same with *Bagatelles pour un Massacre*. As one hopes he will continue to do in his future books, he piles pathetic and unimportant practical jokes six stories high.

In one of the most successful dialogues, toward the end of the book, he has Gutman, his obliging interlocutor, say, "But you're raving, Ferdinand! . . . God you're drunk! . . . You're drunk as a wallowing pig, mark my word." And Ferdinand continues to lose his temper with the most stunning lyricism, parading his grievances and his belligerence to the great amusement of his readers. Of some readers. Others could find improper a literary game that, aided by stupidity, could lead to tragic consequences. As for the question of Sémitisme itself, it is not touched upon. If one wants to see in *Bagatelles pour un Massacre* something other than a game, then Céline, in spite of all his genius, would be without any excuse in stirring up trite passions with this cynicism and offhanded flimsiness.

Cry Havoc

George Steiner*

Lecturing at Oxford in 1870, Ruskin stated what was to him and his audience almost a platitude when he said, "Accuracy in proportion to the rightness of the cause, and purity of the emotion, is the possibility of fine art. You cannot paint or sing yourself into being good men; you must be good men before you can either paint or sing, and then the colour and sound will complete in you all that is best." In 1948, in *What Is Literature?*, Sartre made the point more specific, but again with assumptions old as Plato about the essential morality and humanism of art: "No one could suppose for an instant that it would be possible to write a good novel in praise of anti-semitism." In a footnote, Sartre challenges those who would disagree with him to name such a novel. If you counter that such a book *might* be written, he says, you are merely taking refuge in abstract theorizing.

Matters are, however, not so straightforward. Even if we set aside the fact that a work of art or literature can affect its audience in unforeseeable ways, that a particular play or picture may move one man to compassion and another to hatred, there is now a good deal of evidence that artistic sensibility and the production of art are no bar to active barbarism. It is a fact, though one with which neither our theories of education nor our humanistic, liberal ideals have even begun to come to grips, that a human being can play Bach in the evening, and play him well, or read Pushkin, and read him with insight, and proceed in the morning to do his job at Auschwitz and in the police cellars. The assumption of humane culture so serene in Ruskin, Sartre's confident identification of literature and freedom, no longer hold. Perhaps they were naïve; so much great art, literature, music has flourished under tyranny and under the patronage of violence. For the modern instance, we need think only of the politics of Yeats, T. S. Eliot, and Pound to resist any facile congruence between the creation of major poetry and the kind of radical humanism, of libertarian commitment, that Ruskin and Sartre had in mind. And in one case (though, as I shall point out, there is a second and even more perplexing example), the most extreme form of political barbarism has coincided with a body of work that a number of critics set in the forefront of modern literature.

The facts about Louis-Ferdinand Céline are worth recalling if only because of the falsifications, dramatic half truths, and professions of mystery with which his apologists cloud the air. In 1937, Céline published *Bagatelles pour un Massacre*, in which he cried out for the eradication of all Jews from Europe, in which he described the Jews as ordure, as subhuman garbage to be thoroughly disposed of if civilization was to

*From *Extraterritorial*. Copyright © 1971 George Steiner. Reprinted with the permission of Atheneum Publishers, Inc. Reprinted by permission of Faber and Faber Ltd.

regain its vigor and peace be preserved. If we except certain obscure pamphlets published in eastern Europe at the turn of the century and associated with the forgery of the so-called "Protocols of Zion," Céline's was the first public program for what was to become Hitler's "final solution." A second anti-semitic screed, *L'Ecole des Cadavres*, followed in 1938. *Les Beaux Draps*, published in 1941, set out the author's conviction that the defeat and *misère* of France were the direct result of Jewish intrigue, Jewish foulness, and the well-known pestilence of semitic influence and treason in high places. In 1943, when Jewish men, women, and children were being deported from every corner of western Europe, to be tortured to death and made nameless ash, Louis-Ferdinand Céline republished *Bagatelles pour un Massacre*, with appropriate anti-semitic photographs.

The fact that these texts have not been translated into English and that it is nearly impossible to quote from them without physical revulsion makes it necessary to underline their character. With a scatological crudity comparable only to that of Streicher's *Stürmer*, Céline depicts the Jew as the venomous louse in the body of Western culture. The Jew is shown to be a racial abortion, a nightmarish aggregate of filth and cunning, of sterile intelligence and avarice. He must be castrated or totally isolated from the rest of mankind. His influence is everywhere, but many gentiles are unable to detect the reek of marsh gas. Let the Jew henceforth wear a plainly visible emblem of his subhuman status. In 1937 and 1938, these screaming tracts were like matches set to oil. By 1943, they had become an accompaniment—obscene, mocking, and triumphant—to daily atrocity. After the Allied landings, Céline joined various dignitaries and hooligans of the French pro-Nazi establishment at Siegmaringen, in Germany. In March of 1945, Céline, furnished with a German safe-conduct, succeeded in making his way to Denmark. Imprisoned in Copenhagen between December of 1945 and June of 1947, he benefited by an amnesty and returned to France in June of 1951. He died ten years later, almost alone and generally despised.

Since then, however, critics have gone back to Céline's work and a strong case has been put not only for its intrinsic merit but for the decisive influence it has had on modern fiction. Increasingly, it does look as if the novels of Günter Grass, of William Burroughs, and of Norman Mailer would not have been written without Céline's precedent. Allen Ginsberg expresses a whole trend of opinion when he terms Céline's *Journey to the End of Night* "the first genius international beat XX century picaresque novel written in modern classical personal comedy prose by the funniest & most intelligent of mad Doctors whose least tenderness is an immortal moment." In France, Céline's novels are appearing in the Pléiade edition— an outward consecration of classic status—and they have recently been reissued in, or newly translated into, English. A writer who proclaimed the Jew to be excrement and democracy a foul joke is now the object of a considerable critical and academic cult. In paperback, *Journey to the End of Night* figures prominently on the university-bookstore shelf. Obviously, there is a puzzle here, and one that may have bearing beyond the particular case. What light can the work of Céline throw on the nature of imaginative creation, on the vexed problem of the humaneness or amoralism of art and literature? Does Céline offer a genuine counterexample to Sartre's hopeful claim?

. . . It is to the novels and tracts themselves that we must go back if we hope to see Céline whole—a return complicated, as Dr. Ostrovsky rightly points out, by the fact that Céline's postwar fiction is difficult to obtain and by the more obvious fact that most of his political writings were pulped after the liberation of France. Ralph Manheim's virtuoso translation of *Death on the Installment Plan* is a great help. What is required now is more readily available editions and translations of *D'un Château l'Autre* and *Nord*, which recount Céline's journeying through the vulgar hell of the German collapse.

There are obviously different approaches to the problems posed by Céline's work and great influence. There is a medical reading, whereby the grave head wound suffered by Céline in 1914 gradually affected his reason and engendered the insane hatreds and scatological obsessions of his later writings. One may argue that Céline's vision of the waste and horror of war made his intimations of a second World War a maddening torture. To avoid that catastrophe, to arrive at an understanding with Germany at whatever price, was the supreme duty of an honest man. So far as the Jews were an obstacle to this understanding, so far as their very presence in Europe caused psychological tension and kindled ultra-nationalist sentiments, they must be eliminated. In Céline, a justifiable pacifism went mad. Metaphorically, it can be argued that his loathing of the human animal—his view of the world as "a mixture of asylum and slaughterhouse," in Dr. Ostrovsky's phrase—induced a specific detestation of the Jews. There is in the Jewish presence a kind of flagrant, ostentatious humanity, a resilient at-homeness in the world. When carried to extremes, misanthropy will soon find the Jew in its path.

Undoubtedly, Céline's infernal sociology had deep roots in his sense of the French language. He used that language with both a sweep and an idiomatic intensity equaled perhaps only by Rabelais and Diderot, from both of whom he learned much. The style that made *Journey to the End of Night* an event in the history of modern prose is a deafening, nerverending barrage, a breathless accumulation of invective, scabrous direct address, slang, and colloquial idiom tied together—or, rather, put into a loud, fiercely evocative Morse code—by Céline's famous use of dots and dashes instead of regular punctuation. Céline handled the French language like an earthmover, digging deep into its argotic traditions, into the raw speech of Parisian slums and hospital wards, into the visceral tonalities of patois, and lifting to the light a trove of words, popular elisions, technical exactitudes left out of view in the habitual decorum and shapeliness of the French literary idiom. Céline restored to the novel what it lacked in the hands of Gide and Proust, what it had possessed in Zola — a frank physicality. Fine as it is, Ralph Manheim's rendering of the brawl between father and son in *Death on the Installment Plan* gives only a partial reflection of the sickening power of the original:

> I'm caught up in the dance . . . I stumble, I fall . . . That does it, I've got to finish the stinking bastard! Bzing! He's down again . . . I'm going to smash his kisser! . . . So he can't talk anymore . . . I'm going to smash his whole face . . . I punch him on the ground . . . He bellows . . . He gurgles . . . That'll do. I dig into the fat on his neck . . . I'm on my knees on top of him . . . I'm tangled up in his bandages . . . both my hands are caught. I pull. I squeeze. He's still groaning . . . He's wriggling . . . I weigh down on him . . . He's disgusting . . . He squawks . . . I pound him . . . I massacre him . . . I'm squatting down . . . I dig into the meat . . . It's soft . . . He's drooling . . . I tug . . . I pull off a big chunk of mustache . . . He bites me, the stinker! . . . I gouge into the holes . . . I'm sticky all over . . . my hands skid . . . he heaves . . . he slips out of my grip. He grabs me around the neck. He squeezes my windpipe . . . I squeeze some more. I knock his head against the tiles . . . He goes limp . . . He's soft under my legs . . . He sucks my thumb . . . he stops sucking . . . Phooey! I raise my head for a minute . . . I see my mother's face on a level with mine. . . .

Céline's identification with the historical and local genius of the French tongue was so much the core of his deranged being that he must have hated the unhoused, esperanto trait in the Jewish sensibility. As his tracts make plain, he could not accept the literary mastery of French achieved by such "outsiders" as Proust, Henry Bernstein,[1] and Maurois,[2] wanderers at home in several languages but earthbound in none.

What is absolutely certain is the unity of Céline's world image (he wrote the childishly anti-semitic play *L'Eglise* at the same time as or even earlier than his first novel). To separate the novels from the prophetic and inflammatory pamphlets is not only dishonest; it is to relinquish any chance of coherent insight into this single and singular personage. The frenetic energy, the populist oratory, the Rabelaisian genius for magnification that animate the *Journey* and *Death on the Installment Plan* are equally overwhelming in *Bagatelles* and *L'Ecole des Cadavres*. Whole pages, memorable in their hysterical élan, are interchangeable between the fictions and the libels. Nor did Céline recant. Dr. Ostrovsky's statement that he refuted the charges made against him at the time of his condemnation is at best ingenuous. What he sought to refute were allegations — some true, others false — regarding active collaboration with the occupiers. The man was of a piece, and here again the specific quality of his great gift affords a lead.

One of the ways of thinking responsibly about Céline is to ask whether or in what degree words had become a substitute for reality. Logorrhea is the very condition of Céline's achievement and limitation (his head injury may be pertinent). He was a great master of words but was also mastered by them. Dr. Ostrovsky's study of the manuscripts suggests that close labor lies behind the avalanche of Céline's writings. But it is clear that he had the facility needed to pour out language in fantastic amounts, that each snarl, cry, bout of laughter leads to the next with an inevitable, self-generating rush. If Céline's novels have no natural end, this is not only because of their autobiographical nature — a point in which he clearly resembles Thomas Wolfe — but because the torrent of speech has an autonomous dynamism, a weird inner life stronger, one suspects, than anything else in Céline's bruised, isolated, one might almost say "autistic" consciousness. It is conceivable that Céline, especially after the partial loss of creative confidence that seems to have followed on his return from the Soviet Union in 1936, began taking words for reality, that he no longer related the turbulent geyser of language inside him to any substantive realization. When the facts caught up with his barbarous fancies, when he allowed these fancies to be republished in macabre justification of the facts, Céline was no longer able to tell the one from the other.

It is worth observing that in Céline's true heirs — in Grass, Burroughs, Kerouac — something of the same frantic loquacity prevails. Often their language is animate with energies that exceed the novelty or intelligence of what is being said. The contrasting branch of modernity that leads from Joyce and Proust to Nabokov and Borges is radical in its valuation of time and man but conservative in the formality and tight governance of its expressive means. Céline's letters during the war and after (of which a fair selection appears in the two remarkable Céline issues — 3 and 5 — of the Paris magazine *L'Herne*) belie any easy notion of mental decline or lapse of control. Even casual notes bear the mark of that gross, fierce rhetoric. But some concept of essential abstraction, of a break between word and fulfillment, may help one approach the undeniable unity of Céline's work and may give a clue to the coexistence of a literary talent of the first rank with obvious moral bestiality.

Though Sartre's statement is overconfident, it does remain true that such coexistence is rare, or at least is rare in cases we can document; the career of Gesualdo suggests that musical genius and an exquisite insight into poetry are not necessarily impediments to repeated murder. What is not clear is whether Céline offers a valid exception to Sartre's proposition. Even at their best, in *Journey* and in such parts of *Death on the Installment Plan* as the narrator's hilarious, lyric, lunatic visit to England, Céline's vision and techniques of presentation border on the pathological. Even in these virtuoso flights, as in certain writings of Swift, the excremental and sadistic compulsion seems to go beyond artistic purpose. It may be that Céline is one of those exceedingly rare cases in which an image of life that can scarcely withstand a moment's adult investigation has by sheer force of words been given the stability, the impact of true literature. The works remain a wild artifice, luminous but unnatural — as are flashes of total vision in the epileptic. Far more disturbing, far more subversive of Ruskin's and Sartre's humanism, would be the case of a man in whom explicit barbarism coexisted with the creation of a classical, imaginatively ordered work of art.

There is such a case. One of the young Fascists of the 1930's on whom Céline exercised great influence was Lucien Rebatet. During the Occupation, M. Rebatet collaborated actively with the Nazis. His denunciations of Resistance fighters in the notorious periodical *Je Suis Partout*, the joy he voiced at the death of Jews and hostages, made Rebatet's name one of the most loathed in France. Arrested at the time of the Liberation, he was sentenced to death. In solitary confinement, with chains on his feet and in daily expectation of the end, he managed to write a vast novel and smuggled more than a thousand pages and fragments of manuscript out of prison. *Les Deux Etendards* was published, in two volumes, by Gallimard in 1951 (a decision reportedly taken on the advice of Camus). The book has been published in German but not in English. It is, in my opinion, a greater work than any of Céline's, with the possible exception of *Journey*, and one of the secret masterpieces of modern literature. It narrates the coming of age, deep amity, and final separation of two young men in France between the wars. They are in love with the same young woman, who is a creation comparable in fullness of life, in physical and psychological radiance, to Tolstoy's Natasha. The articulation of this threefold relationship and the great fugue of erotic fulfillment with which the novel draws to its close are major acts of the imagination. Unlike Céline's fiction, Rebatet's novel has the impersonal authority, the sheer formal beauty of classic art. Pardoned by special decree, Rebatet now lives in Paris in semi-clandestinity. His name remains strictly taboo except among a growing number of readers, many of them young people, to whom *Les Deux Etendards* is a revelation.

Thus, Lucien Rebatet, more than Louis-Ferdinand Céline, constitutes what theologians call a "mystery." In him a profoundly generous imagination, a grasp of the sanctity of individual life that has led to the invention of lasting literary characters coexist with Fascist doctrines and aims of murderous action openly avowed (Rebatet looks with scorn on any attempts to divide Céline the novelist from Céline the publicist, and on any effort to relegate Céline's or his own convictions to scholarly obscurity). Here we touch genuinely on the puzzle of the dissociation between poetic humanism on the one hand and political sadism on the other, or, rather, on their association in a single psyche. The ability to play and love Bach can be conjoined in the same human spirit with the will to exterminate a ghetto or napalm a village. No ready solution to this mystery and to the fundamental questions it poses for our civilization lies at hand.

But recent history has thrust it upon us, and those who regard it as "outside their scope" will hardly bring the study of literature back into touch with the darkened fabric of our lives.

Notes

1. Henry Bernstein (1876–1953) was the author of critically acclaimed dramas and of *Judith* (1922) (editor's note).

2. André Maurois (1885–1967), novelist and member of the Académie, wrote on British history and literary figures (editor's note).

Occupation and Exile: 1940–51   Patrick McCarthy[*]

To understand Céline's wartime role one must look at the personalities and politics of the Occupation. A world, as he had said, had collapsed. A new breed of men had replaced the discredited leaders of the Third Republic. What was the new order? One must examine the politicians who praised Céline and the newspapers that published his letters.

Frenchmen had put their trust in Pétain, victor of Verdun. By the terms of the armistice France was divided into two parts: the southern half was to be administered by the Vichy government, the north was to remain under the control of the Germans until the imminent defeat of England. Pétain's government was conservative and authoritarian, but it was not fascist. Its philosophy was one part hero-worship of Pétain, one part subservience to big business and one part Action Française monarchism. It harked back to a France of smiling peasants and benign aristocrats. The men of Vichy did not welcome German hegemony but they accepted it — at least for the time being. Laval, the prime minister, like Céline a pacifist and a defeatist, sought, by juggling, to please the Reich while retaining some independence.

While the cult of Pétain ran high in the Vichy hotels and Charles Maurras became the philosopher of the National Revolution, a different breed of men reigned in Paris. Their doctrine was French-style National Socialism. It called for nothing less than the building of a fascist France. Anti-semitism was the main plank in the platform: an end to the class war and the uniting of all Aryan Frenchmen. As for foreign policy, the Fascists demanded collaboration with the Germans and entry into the war on Hitler's side. Thus would France take her place in the new Europe. This doctrine was very vague. The fascist clans never banded together in a solid organization, although the *parti unique* was a recurrent dream. They

*Reprinted from *Céline* (New York: Penguin Books, 1977), 107–217. © 1975 Patrick McCarthy. Reprinted by permission of Viking Penguin Inc. Reprinted by permission of Georges Borchardt, Inc., and A. P. Watt Ltd.

were united by a deep hatred for the Third Republic and a feeling that the radical right—the Action Française and the Ligues—had not gone far enough. For the rest they squabbled over doctrinal trifles, competed for German patronage and flaunted slogans like socialism and revolution.

The two main leaders were Doriot and Déat, both of whom tried to enlist Céline's support. Jacques Doriot, "the black-haired Danton," began as a worker, joined the Communist Party and rose to become mayor of the red bastion, Saint-Denis. In 1934 it was he who organized the counter-riots of 9 February to demonstrate against the Ligues. Afterwards he called for something like a Popular Front, but the official communist leadership under Maurice Thorez was not yet ready to move: Thorez was still following the doctrine that the socialists were the number one enemy. Doriot was expelled from the party and over the next few years he drifted rapidly to the right, inspired by Hitler's success. He became an ardent anti-Communist and an expert in denouncing his old comrades. In 1936 he founded the Parti Populaire Français, a fascist-type organization with its newspaper *L'Emancipation nationale* and its hired thugs from Marseilles. In 1939 Doriot had been defeatist, now he hoped to reap his reward. His great rival was Marcel Déat, a former socialist and professor of sociology. In the 1933 Socialist congress Déat clashed with Léon Blum, when he proposed that the party abandon its internationalism in an age of resurgent nationalism. He attacked Blum's "byzantinism" and called for a dynamic, authoritarian line. Like Doriot, Déat was attracted to strong action, like Doriot he was drawn to Hitler. In 1939 Déat denounced the Anglo-French guarantees to Poland in a famous article entitled "Die for Dantzig?." After the defeat he founded the Rassemblement National Populaire, where he assembled the former pacifists and syndicalists who had found their way to collaboration.

Doriot led the right wing, Déat the left; but ideological differences counted for little. Personal rivalry kept the two men apart. To their ranks flocked politicians and journalists, some sinister, others merely eccentric, all anxious to grab the spoils of the new order. There was Fernand de Brinon, the Vichy government's "ambassador" to Paris and a long-standing supporter of Franco-German cooperation. He was being rewarded for years of organizing youth congresses and cultural contacts. There was Laval's friend, Jean Luchaire, the golden boy of the Occupation, whose daughter Corinne was a film-star. Luchaire's dinner-parties at the Tour d'Argent drew the celebrities of the collaborationist camp but never Céline. A stranger figure was Eugène Deloncle, at first a supporter of Déat who quarrelled with him and sold his soul many times over. His shadowy career ended in 1943 when he was executed by the Gestapo for plotting with anti-Hitler elements in the Wehrmacht.

The politicians had their battalions of intellectuals. If many leading French writers were in opposition—Malraux, Mauriac, Aragon and younger men like Camus and Sartre—many were not. Montherlant and Giono were prepared to be sympathetic to the new order, Béraud continued his anti-English tirades, Drieu was an avowed fascist and the young team of *Je suis partout* cried hysterically for collaboration. There were great differences among these writers and, in particular, there was a gulf between the most clearly fascist of them and Céline.

Robert Brasillach describes his evolution to fascism in his autobiographical work *Notre avant-guerre* (1941). As a schoolboy at Louis-le-Grand and a student at the École Normale he absorbed Charles Maurras' heady doctrines. Disliking the tepid politics of the cautious Third Republic he turned to the nationalism, the monarchism and, most important perhaps, the strong dose of anarchism in the Action Française. But, as he grew older, he felt that Maurras was out of date and that his anti-German stance was sterile. Brasillach was attracted to the new Nazi Germany. On his visit to Berlin he was impressed: "One cannot judge Hitler like an ordinary head of state," he writes, "he is called to a mission which he believes to be divine."[1] Brasillach became a fascist. He supported Mussolini in Ethiopia and the Nationalists in Spain. In fascism he saw a great new dawn: "the universe was ablaze, the universe sang and mustered itself, the universe toiled."[2] For him the war was a tragedy and the defeat a blessing in disguise. Now that the despised Republic was overthrown, a rebuilt France could stand alongside Nazi Germany. "Only a French fascism can collaborate with the new world," writes the innocent Brasillach.[3]

He greatly admired Céline: "Instinctive anti-semitism found its prophet in Louis-Ferdinand Céline."[4] But the two men have little in common. For Brasillach fascism was a glorious struggle. Not so for Céline who picked up the negative side — anti-semitism — but had no faith in the new fascist dawn. Whereas Brasillach supported the Germans out of idealism, Céline did so out of the starkest realism — because France had no other choice.

The same question of romanticism separates Céline from Rebatet, another fiery young idealist. He too despised the Third Republic and came to Fascism via Maurras' monarchism. Rebatet hated the leftward drift of the 1930s, and *Les Décombres* heaps anathema on Blum, the Popular Front and its intellectuals like André Malraux. Rebatet was drawn to the pageantry of Nazi Germany. He describes the solemnity of Hindenburg's funeral, the torchlight procession across the Prussian plain, the tomb at Tannenburg. Rebatet was wildly emotional. He loved the French army: "I am an admirer of the sabre, I would have welcomed its reign with joy."[5] He hated Jews. The Stavisky scandal and the flood of Jewish refugees from Eastern Europe made him furious. For him, as for Brasillach, collaboration offered the opportunity to create a new world. "We are in the act of living one of the greatest chapters of human history," he writes.[6]

Such romanticism was quite alien to Céline, child of the Passage. Drieu la Rochelle was closer to him in age and he too remembered the battlefields of Flanders. In *Voyage* Drieu saw his own vision of the postwar world—grim and meaningless. Both writers have a deep sense of decadence and see death everywhere around them. But there the resemblance stops. Drieu insists that "the hands of deep despair in probing death soon feel the secrets of new life palpitating within."[7] Certainly decadence reigned in the France of the Popular Front; but then "suddenly there was Fascism. Everything was once more possible, o' my heart."[8] Drieu had the Célinian sense of despair—which Brasillach and Rebatet did not—but he was able to transcend it.

The difference between Céline and his admirers emerges clearly in a conversation he had with Rebatet in the winter of 1940. Rebatet had just returned from Vichy, where he had spent "two stupidly debilitating months" witnessing "bar-room chatter, plots in hotel corridors."[9] Exasperated by this new version of Third Republic parliamentarianism, he left Vichy to look for a stronger line in Paris. He came at once to visit Céline, newly established on the rue Girardon. Like other visitors he was struck by the furnishings: "rustic Breton style, the sort of thing an office clerk would have chosen if he had been left some money." After paying his respects to Lucette, Rebatet was admitted into the little study where Céline sat in his old dressing-gown, surrounded by the heaps of paper that were the first draft of *Les Beaux Draps*. Rebatet was struck by "Céline's blue, Gallic eyes, gay and malicious, with frankness and despair in the background." The two discussed politics. Rebatet talked about the opportunity the defeat offered, the mistakes of Vichy, the hopes of Paris. Céline interrupted: "The only true thing is that the Fritz have lost the war." Rebatet was astounded—even Churchill would not have claimed that. The German armies had swept across Europe. A Nazi victory seemed certain and with it the new Fascist order Rebatet had come to discuss. But Céline would not budge. Rebatet left him and went off to the offices of *Je suis partout*, where he declared that the author of *Bagatelles* had gone mad. That was not the reason. The pessimism that separated Céline from the left in the 1930s, was now to alienate him from collaborators.

It was only a partial alienation. Céline wrote in the Paris press. He attacked Germany's enemies and called for anti-semitism. But he had no time for the supposed triumphs of collaboration. He stood out against the optimism of the editorials.

. . . In the rosy collaborationist world of 1941 there was one black spot—Vichy. In October of the previous year the press had lavish praise for the Montoire meeting, which was in reality inconclusive but which launched the slogan of collaboration. But already the virulent *Au pilori* had warned Pétain that it expected him to take a hard line—on England, on Jews, on anything.[10] Pétain did not seem to want to do this. Criticism mounted, after Laval, who was counted as pro-German, was dismissed in December. *Révolution nationale* complained that Pétain's foreign policy was weak: he was sitting on the fence, perhaps even hoping for an English victory. When he backed the Legion of Volunteers Pétain rose briefly in the press's estimation, but soon there were fresh grumbles. Rebatet's satire of politicians plotting in bars made Vichy seem an effete régime, without the dynamism to build a fascist France. In 1942 came two more disputes, one tiny but symptomatic, the other major. The first was the banning of *Les Beaux Draps*. Fourteen copies were seized in Toulouse in March and the book was banned along with *Les Décombres*. The most plausible reasons are that Céline was known to be anti-Pétain and that his book attributes the defeat not to corrupt parliamentarians but to the cowardice of the French army. Céline, delighted by this new persecution, weighed in against Pétain with incredible violence. The Paris press supported him, and *Au pilori* published a cartoon satirizing the Vichy authorities for seizing *Les Beaux Draps* in the name of the National Revolution.[11] The action was another proof that Vichy was unreliable — why should it ban the prophet Céline? More important were the Riom trials which spluttered and collapsed. The plan had been to convict Blum, Daladier and Reynaud of leading France to defeat. The Paris press was wildly enthusiastic and, on the front page of *L'Appel*, a raving Constantini described his dream of seeing Blum executed in public.[12] But the despised politicians showed great flair in defending themselves. No legal grounds could be found for convicting them and the trials were abandoned. This was another proof of Vichy's folly, perhaps even complicity. There are several reasons for the press's onslaughts against Pétain. The Germans were using it as a threat to keep Vichy in line and Laval was using it to try and regain power. But there was a real difference between hard-line collaboration and Pétain's waiting-game.

The press's style was as important as its content. The virulent writing that had been the pamphleteers' prerogative had been vulgarized. Many of the articles read like third-rate Céline. There was no question of logic: the collaborators did not attempt to analyse the economic situation or to report the war accurately. Instead they went target-hunting as Daudet, Céline and Béraud had taught them. They overwhelmed their readers with tirades of rhetoric. Their language was extravagant: sensational headlines jockeyed with sick cartoons. *Au pilori* gives accounts of Jewish crimes that no sane reader could possibly believe. Its front page is invariably a jumble of slogans about Europeanism, revolutions and purges. Each paper tried to outdo the others in invective. Constantini accused Deloncle of being soft on Jews, Doriot tried to prove he was more anti-communist than Déat.[13]

What was Céline's role in this press? He wrote nothing until February 1941. The collaborators wondered at his silence: eight months had gone by since the defeat.[14] Céline was working on *Les Beaux Draps*, which appeared in March, and he had as little love as ever for journalism. Still, from February 1941 to April 1942 he published about ten short articles, usually in the form of letters to the editor.[15] His aim was to ram home the lessons he had been teaching in the pamphlets: to wean the French away from heroism and to attack the Jews. For a short time he seemed to toy with the peculiar notion that the Nazi new order might work. Such optimism was both alien and fleeting. The pessimistic views he had expressed to Rebatet were closer to the real Céline. In 1942 the banning of *Les Beaux Draps* produced three hate-filled articles, and then Céline withdrew altogether. He published nothing more until April 1944. He was convinced that collaboration was a worthless enterprise and that he had been right when he had prophesied the Reich's defeat.

His moment of optimism shows itself twice in his articles. In December 1941 he took part in a discussion organized by *Au pilori* to promote the *parti unique*. There are two descriptions of conversations with Céline. On 11 December the newspaper reports him lamenting "the lack of liaison among the French who have the formidable mission of enlightening public opinion and directing the political parties."[16] Using Céline's name, *Au pilori* calls for unity. On 25 December it describes a meeting that has taken place in its offices. Among those present were Déat, Deloncle, Constantini, P.-A. Cousteau, the third member of the *Je suis partout* team, and Céline. They agreed on a common programme based on racism: the Jew was to be eliminated from French life, the Catholic Church was to declare itself racist, there was to be a minimum wage of 2,500 francs. This programme was summed up by Céline "in concise, striking phrases."[17] Naturally enough nothing came of it. It is clear that Céline's role was slight. *Au pilori* was using his name to attract support, but he gave little time to the project.

Before encouraging Déat, he had turned a helping hand to Doriot. In November 1941 he gave an interview in *L'Emancipation nationale*.[18] The reporter was Maurice-Ivan Sicard, an old admirer of *Voyage* and a member of the Parti Populaire Française since 1936. The delighted Sicard heard Céline utter the words that would be remembered at the Liberation: "We must work and struggle with Doriot." The statement must be understood in the context of the discussion. The two were talking about the Russian campaign and Céline had a kind word for the Legion—"It's very good, the Legion, it's the best thing around." He was inspired, not by any great confidence in Doriot or the Legion, but by his fear of the Russians. The remark about Doriot stands as possible evidence of collaboration, but it cannot be used to argue that Céline had any lasting faith in the P.P.F.

The moment of optimism did not last. In April 1942 Céline took back his praise for the Legion, dismissing it as "entirely Jewish."[19] In the same month he attacked the inconclusive ending of the Riom trials. He makes two kinds of criticism. He condemns the revelation during the trials of Third Republic behaviour—"the legal demonstration of our complete, utter and unchallengeable rottenness." He goes on to castigate Vichy for suspending the hearings: 'To the true patriot—how suspicious this attitude is."[20] The Riom trials and the banning of *Les Beaux Draps* — as well as the German failure to defeat England — wrote *finis* to any optimism. But Céline had never hoped for much. In February 1941 he published his "act of faith" in *La Gerbe* and called for "two weeks, no more, to start France moving, two weeks if we know what we want."[21] The next month he wrote to a friend that *"La Gerbe* seems to me more Jewish than ever."[22]

Céline picked on the negative side of collaboration: anti-semitism and anti-communism. In December 1941, when the Occupation authorities had begun to deport Jews, he lamented the popular indifference to anti-semitism. He compared it with the German attitude: "At bottom Chancellor Hitler is the only one who is talking about Jews." Céline adds the damning sentence: "It is the side of Hitler that most people like the least . . . it is the side I like the most."[23] Along with other collaborators he affirmed that the Jews were still a mighty force in the land — he too still needed a target. In October 1941 he wrote a satirical piece in *Au pilori* entitled "Long Live the Jews."[24] He puzzled over the strange and incurable love the French felt for Jews. The country needed to be "rebuilt entirely on a racist-communal basis." Not that there was any chance of this happening, he hastens to add.

On the Russian question he was equally predictable. The Nazi-Soviet fighting was the real struggle of the war: "Comrade Stalin's Asiatics are massacring white Soldiers . . . We are not sufficiently aware of the need to protect the white race."[25] To Céline the Russians were not an actual people but a mysterious menace, the contemporary manifestation of the Asian hordes. Like the Jews they had become dehumanized incarnations of evil. Still, he knew that the fighting on the Eastern front was real enough and he was ready to join in. "I would have liked to go off on a boat and settle things with the Russians," he tells Sicard. Once again the prophet of peace was anxious to go to war. Céline explained to Robert Chamfleury, a friend in the opposite camp, that the fear of Russia was the pivot of his political views: "I am resigned to supporting them [the Germans] because they are removing a worse danger."[26] This cannot be accepted at its face value, but it does indicate the terror that filled Céline's mind since his 1936 trip to Moscow.

In his negative opinions Céline was an orthodox hard-line collaborator; differences arose when he discussed the theme of grandeur. In April 1941, during his so-called optimistic period, he engaged in a controversy in *Pays libre*. A woman journalist, Maryse Desneiges, attacked him for portraying the French army in *Les Beaux Draps* as a cowardly rabble."[27] She pointed out the heroism of individual men and took the usual line in blaming the defeat on the politicians. Céline would have none of it. This seemed to him a new phase of his pre-war battle: he had to convince the French that they should never go to war. The defeat should have been proof enough, but here was Maryse Desneiges praising the army and claiming, by implication, that it could conquer. More is at stake than

Céline's attack on a romantic woman journalist. Orthodox collaborators should have been on Maryse Desneiges' side. They wanted the French to fight for Germany — Pierre Clémenti states this explicitly in the same issue of *Pays libre* as Céline's article.[28] Her interpretation of the defeat suits them well and, although they do not realize it, Céline is their enemy.

Faced with a revival of the sickness he had diagnosed in *Bagatelles*, Céline delivers a broadside: "Cornealian hamming never fails to fill the theatre in France."[29] The adjective "Cornelian" is significant, because the collaborators are appealing to precisely this current of French history. To Céline Cornelianism is "a tradition from which we deserve to die, all of us, I hope, and once and for all." Talk of France's military glory, of Napoleon and of the new Europe, amounted to one thing: another cataclysm. "It is with great strokes of bravery that slaughter-houses are replenished," Céline warns.

Céline's place in the pro-German ranks was a lonely one: he was always destructive. Another controversy in *L'Appel* about Péguy reveals this. The collaborators had undertaken to rewrite the whole of French literature. Gide was excommunicated, on the grounds that his subtle moralizing had undermined French youth. Left-wingers like Malraux and Aragon were anathema. Proust was very suspect, although Brasillach tried hard to save him. In place of these writers the collaborators exalted Barrès, the true nationalist, and Péguy. But Péguy presented a problem because he had been a Dreyfusard as well as a nationalist, a friend as well as an enemy of Jaurès. With his son's cooperation, a Péguy suitable to the needs of 1941 was worked out. Then Céline intervened. In a thunderous letter to *L'Appel* he demolished the simple view of Péguy, servant of Joan of Arc and the Virgin Mary. He replaced it with a confused Péguy 'at one and the same time Dreyfusard, monarchist and third-rate ham."[30] In a private letter to Lucien, Combelle, Céline performed the same hatchet-job on Brasillach's Proust. Proust was nothing but a Jew whose novel was constructed like the Talmud. It was 'tortuous, arabesque, a disordered mosaic', quite the reverse of what the collaborators should be looking for.[31]

Céline repeats again and again that the whole enterprise of collaboration is doomed. The Vichy government is beyond contempt and Pétain merely the "man who is at the moment deputizing in Vichy for the Rothschilds."[32] This is a standard collaborationist line, although rarely expressed with such violence. But Céline turns on the Paris leaders too. In a letter to Lucien, Combelle is quite frank: "And then what can one say to the French. Except long live Stalin and long live de Gaulle? . . . Radio London is making all your efforts perfectly and grotesquely useless."[33] In his articles Céline repeated this view. One of his favourite techniques was to demand a course of action, while insisting on its futility: anti-semitism is essential but the French love Jews, the German alliance must be strengthened but Vichy is London's tool. Céline was playing his Cassandra role. Once again he had a grasp of his age. He understood that the mass of the French people ignored the Paris press and that they hated the Occupation forces. He understood as few did — except de Gaulle — that the fall of France did not mean the end of the war, and that the Russian invasion was more of a problem than a victory. Most of all Céline knew that he himself was not made for victory parades. His side had to lose.

The real significance of his writings lies in his determination to alienate all parties. In an amazing passage, that equals Constantini's hysteria, he demands the heads of Pétain's ministers: "Let them all be hanged . . . I will watch them swing."[34] His "act of faith" consists chiefly of onslaughts on the collaborators. He dismisses them as "a bunch of screaming supernationalists" who have jumped on the bandwagon.[35] Under Blum they were Popular Fronters, now they are collaborators. This attitude was not at all unique. The collaborators spent their time quarrelling, as they scrabbled for power. But no one goes as far as Céline when he condemns the whole movement as "chatter" and "hypocrisy."

. . . For the collaborators he remained the prophet of *Bagatelles*. They liked to invoke his name, even if they had to select from his writings what suited them. They could not make much use of him, because his defeatist strain was unacceptable. Saint-Paulien, who is Maurice-Ivan Sicard under a new name, says that Céline was difficult to publish.[36] There was a wild delirium in his writings that could not be channelled along orthodox lines. He would keep crying out that death was everywhere, when the press was talking about building a new France. He was "unusable."[37] He was neither a journalist of day-to-day issues like Cousteau, nor a hopeful dreamer like Drieu. He was a phenomenon that Sicard admired with trepidation.

Small wonder that Céline played little active part in collaborationist politics. He was a member of no organized groups. He met Doriot,[38] he claims, only three times during the Occupation and he knew Déat very slightly. Otto Abetz, the Reich's ambassador, proposed Céline's name for an important post in the anti-semitic campaign, but nothing came of it.[39] Rebatet remembers seeing Céline once in a meeting of the Insitut des Questions Juives. While incompetent speakers droned on about "Jewish-Marxist tyranny," Céline, seated by himself, interrupted with stage whispers about "Aryan stupidity." The audience grew restive — there must be a Jewish spy in the hall. Fighting broke out and the meeting was abandoned. To the disappointed Germans it was another proof of French frivolity.[40]

Such action as Céline did take was on a strictly individual basis. In 1942 he signed a petition to protest against the Allied bombing of Billancourt.[41] He also wrote to the organizers of an anti-semitic exhibition, complaining that "in visiting your exhibition I was surprised and a little hurt to see that in the bookshop neither *Bagatelles* nor *L'École* was on display." Such negligence was another proof of "the frightening lack of . . . Aryan intelligence and solidarity."[42] Céline's name might be used for group projects — *Au pilori* wrote to Xavier Vallat telling him that Céline wanted him to attend the *parti unique* discussions — but he took small part in them.[43] He was still an anarchist.

He had some contact with the wartime authorities, both German and French. Karl Epting, head of the Institut Allemand, set up to encourage cultural contacts, became a friend of Céline's. He remembers that Céline asked for paper — which was very scarce — to publish his books and that he made similar demands for friends.[44] As a doctor Céline dealt with Dr. Knapp, an official in the Reich's public-health programme, who was in charge of Franco-German cooperation. Céline made demands on behalf of his patients: he asked for extra ration cards, special drugs or exemptions from the Service du Travial Obligatoire. On certain matters he had to go to Fernand de Brinon's office and the secretary, Simone Mittre, recalls that he never asked for anything for himself.[45] It was always a patient who needed to go to the South of France or who had to be given a pension. And whenever he was leaving Simone Mittre's office, Céline would tell her: "You know, the Germans are going to lose the war."

These are not the actions of a man anxious to throw his weight behind the Nazi cause. When the Liberation authorities assessed Céline's guilt they found little to criticize in his deeds. He was tainted by association: his trip to Berlin in 1942 to inspect German hospitals was seen as proof of criminal links with the Nazis. In reality it was an isolated event. Epting testifies that Céline's contacts with the Germans were innocent enough. Socially Céline remained within his pre-war circle of friends — Aymé, Gen Paul and the others. Some of them, like Le Vigan and Ralph Soupault, compromised themselves, but this was not a fascist nor even a political group. Céline shunned the fashionable *tout Paris* of the Occupation. He was too much a 1914 patriot to rub shoulders with German officers. . . .

Céline had everything to fear from the liberation that the B.B.C. was promising: "That will really be the start of the troubles," he predicted.[46] He could not forget that he was marked down for execution. He had now given up sending letters to the press — except for the one to *Germinal* — and he was toiling away at *Guignol's Band*. His period as a pamphleteer was over and he was a novelist again, although *Guignol's Band*, seemingly a book about London in 1915, has much to do with the France of 1943. But Céline could not and did not withdraw quietly from politics. He had to reap the whirlwind he had sown. Not surprisingly one old friend found him "much less gay . . . as if he foresaw already the troubles that were to overwhelm him."[47] *L'École des cadavres*, banned since 1939, was republished in 1943 to the fury of the Guallists. Céline was doing nothing to placate his enemies. Geoffroy entertained him along with Lucette and Gen Paul to Christmas dinner in 1943. It was not a festive occasion although Céline, unpredictable as ever, seemed "happy, relaxed, charming."[48] But he spent the day telling Geoffroy that the Russians would soon be in Paris.

Céline was now increasingly nervous. The Resistance showed a flair for assassination. In June 1944, Philippe Henroit, the new Minister of Information, was gunned down in public. More executions had been promised and men like Hérold-Paquis went round with armed bodyguards. There was talk within the Resistance of executing Céline.[49] In the flat above him on the rue Girardon lived Robert Chamfleury and the actress, Simone. Chamfleury's flat was a centre for agents parachuted in from England and for young men fleeing the S.T.O. Six members of his group, led by the novelist Roger Vailland, were outraged at the "collaborationist" gatherings in Céline's flat. They hated to see the cartoonist Ralph Soupault arrive to converse in complete freedom with the monstrous author of Bagatelles. They decided to machine-gun the entire nest of vipers on the avenue Junot. The spot was chosen, the time set, the assassin would disappear down the narrow sidestreets. But Vailland's band contained too many intellectuals. Simone started the debate: Céline was the author of Voyage as well as of Bagatelles. Did they have the right to kill him? Yes, replied Vailland, no said others. The moral theorizing began and action gave way to words. Vailland had to be content with maligning Céline in his post-war Drôle de jeu. But the Resistance had more efficient gunmen.

Robert Chamfleury points out that Céline's relationship with the maquisards was not as simple as Vailland claims. Céline knew perfectly well that his neighbour's flat was a Resistance headquarters and he never betrayed him. Several times young men lost their way and knocked on Céline's door instead of on Chamfleury's. They were redirected without a word. One night Chamfleury brought down a maquisard who had been tortured by the Gestapo. Dr. Destouches looked at them, bandaged the man's hand and sent him away. Céline was not trying to buy insurance. He was not imitating the scores of Frenchmen who helped the Germans with one hand and the Resistance with the other. It was his Jekyll and Hyde character that made him treat the wounded maquisard.

By early 1944 rumours of Allied landings were circulating openly. R.A.F. plans bombed the Paris suburbs. In April, Danoël published Guignol's Band. It received an excellent review from Albert Paraz,[50] but few readers had time for novels. Céline's remark about the "gigantic dishonesty" of the Resistance brought him more publicity. On 6 June the Allies landed in Normandy and the Resistance rose up in the enemy's rear. Railroads were cut, reprisals were severe, France was in a state of civil war. In Paris electricity functioned only a few hours a day, the métro stopped and food prices soared. The atmosphere was unreal: a four-year period was dissolving into chaos.

A short piece that Céline published in 1944 gives a clue to his state of mind: the preface to Albert Serouille's *Bezons à travers les âges*. With his unfailing kindness Céline had encouraged Serouille to write the book and persuaded Denoël to publish it. In the preface he sees the history of Bezons as a legend: he dwells on the medieval marquis, who gave his name to the town, and the bridge over the Seine which kings of France had crossed. Such beauty is "divine relaxation."[51] Céline does not forget that legends are cruel, too, and that Bezons' past is full of crimes — "the web of History is atrocious," he concludes. Contemporary events have brought a new phase of suffering and the bridge, destroyed so many times, was bombed in 1940. Céline, child of nearby Courbevoie, identifies with Bezons' pain: "from all sides death holds us in its grasp — by hunger, bombings, weariness and hatred." He seeks a refuge, however fragile, in the past, because he is terrified of the future: "Our tomorrows are impossible . . . hunted, tortured, cursed." What a contrast with the "tomorrows full of song" that Louis Aragon was promising the Resistance. The Nazis were in retreat and Aragon's hour had come. Céline, the collaborator, was trapped.

Céline had long been thinking about escape. Brittany was too close and the separatists could offer nothing. He kept his eyes fixed on Denmark where he had hidden his pot of gold. In July he fled. Lucette, whom he had married the previous year, went with him and so did Robert le Vigan. Céline set out for Germany, hoping to cross into Scandinavia. The rest of the hard-core collaborators waited until Leclerc's tanks were in the Paris suburbs. Not so Céline. He was "the migratory bird who anticipates a change of scenery by flying away first."[52]

He left the Gare de l'Est wearing a thick overcoat and surrounded by twenty trunks. Terrified of starving to death in the ravished German countryside, he carried cases of farm tools to be exchanged for food.[53] Perched on his shoulder was le Vigan's cat Bébert, destined to become the most famous cat in French literature. The strange cavalcade set out across a country where the Resistance was sabotaging the railways and Allied planes dominated the air. Céline's furniture in the rue Girardon was left to the mercy of all comers. Marie Canavaggia retained the manuscript of *Le Pont de Londres*, which was not to see the light of day for twenty years. Céline's literary interests were entrusted to Denoël who was shot next year near the Invalides.

The trio arrived safely in Baden-Baden which was an oasis of peace. A spa town, it had escaped the waves of Allied bombers. The Brenner Park-Hotel, where Céline stayed, struggled to maintain pre-war standards of luxury and its huge gardens were green and tranquil. Céline could not enjoy them for long. He pressed on further. When he reached Berlin it was being bombed twenty-four hours a day. Karl Epting met him and they had dinner in "some sombre restaurant that the bombs had not yet destroyed." Epting remembers seeing Céline leave with Bébert on his arm "through the ruins of rows of bombed-out houses."[54]

Berlin was intolerable. Céline had to wait while the Reich's authorities considered his request for a visa to go to Denmark, but he wanted to find a quieter spot. A colleague, Dr Hauboldt, found him a place in a little village called Kränzlin. It was teeming with refugees and Céline was billeted in a run-down castle. Kränzlin was hardly pleasant, but it was better than Berlin. He later told Marc Hanrez that he was interned there, because he refused to issue propaganda statements for the Nazis. There is no evidence for this. Hauboldt was doing him a service in finding him a refuge that was not being bombed.[55]

Céline stayed there until November. Then he heard that the main body of the collaborators had fled to Germany and established themselves at Sigmaringen. For the time being he preferred to throw in his lot with Frenchmen. He travelled to meet his old acquaintances Rebatet, Déat and the others. And in Sigmaringen, a little town on the Danube, the last act in the drama of collaboration was played out.

The pro-German faction had waited until August, not knowing what to do nor where to turn. Only now were they forced to realize that the Wehrmacht was not invincible. One night, word was handed down from Doriot that flight had been arranged. Hérold-Paquis describes the confusion of the exodus.[56] Along with Rebatet, whom he cordially hated, and Cousteau, he crowded into a lorry on the rue des Pyramides. First it crashed into a parapet on the Quai du Louvre, then it broke down at the foot of the Champs-Elysées. Passers-by looked at them in mocking silence. Finally they were able to go. Huge traffic-jams had formed on the outskirts of the city. The Parisians, awaiting only the Liberation, continued to ignore them. They set out along the road to the east.

They stopped at Nancy where the P.P.F. supporters were housed in a convent. Intrigues were rampant: de Brinon was denouncing Laval, Déat was losing ground to Doriot. While they were at Nancy the editor of the local pro-German newspaper was killed in what seemed like an accident. It heightened the tension. They went on by train to Baden-Baden. The station in Metz had been destroyed and they had to shelter in tunnels from Allied bombers. Only when they crossed the Rhine did they feel safe. At Baden-Baden they split up. The P.P.F. group went to Bad-Mergentheim, the main body to Sigmaringen.

Sigmaringen was a beautiful town built around a Hohenzollern castle. Untouched by the *Hitlerjugend* and the Nuremburg rallies, it regretted the fallen dynasty and the princes who had walked its streets. The castle, which stood on a steep bank overlooking the Danube, was full of rococo furniture. Its library contained first editions of Racine and Goethe. In this fairy-tale setting the collaborators dreamed of impossible German victories. They saw de Gaulle scurrying back to London, themselves parading down the Champs-Elysées.[57]

Not all of them were like this. Brasillach was not even there. He had decided to stay behind in Paris. He hid in a tiny flat and went out as little as possible. At the Liberation he was discovered and thrown into prison at Fresnes. Drieu had stayed behind too, and he committed suicide after two unsuccessful attempts. But the politicians came to Sigmaringen. Pétain, Laval and the Vichy ministers were brought to Germany, with or without their consent. Déat had arrived, Luchaire, Darnand, Constantini, Chateaubriand and the others. Pétain considered himself a prisoner and no longer head of state and Laval, realistic as ever, knew the game was up. But the Paris collaborators went on spinning webs of intrigue.

Doriot had refused to go with the others. He was living at Mainau in a house where Laforgue had once lived. He spent his time organizing his followers into a Committee for the Liberation of France. It had its own radio-station run by Hérold-Paquis and its own agents, who were sent across the French border never to be seen again. Doriot also sent an ambassador to Sigmaringen; but he was coldly received, because Fernand de Brinon had set up a governmental commission which flourished in spite of Pétain's refusal to recognize it. Each of the leaders had his obsession: Darnand, parading around in an S.S. uniform, was pursuing the deserters from the Charlemagne division, formed out of the remnants of the Légion; Luchaire, who had set up a radio-station, was trying to have the rival Hérold-Paquis station banned; Chateaubriand, who was trying to publish French books in Germany, had plans for a three-hundred-page biography of Doriot. Knowing no life but politics, these men continued to buy and sell one another. They devised fantastic schemes for splitting the Russian-American alliance, and no German believed more passionately than they in the new secret weapons. As they plotted they were able to turn a deaf ear to the bombs falling on nearby Ulm.

Rebatet describes Céline's arrival: "His eyes were still full of the journey across a battered Germany, he was wearing a bluish cloth cap, of the kind engine drivers used to wear around 1905, two or three of his fur-lined jackets with their layers of dirt and their holes, a pair of moth-eaten mitts hanging from his neck, while beneath the mitts, on his stomach, in a rucksack, was the cat Bébert." The rank-and-file collaborators who had never seen Céline were amazed: was this "the great fascist writer, the prophet of genius"?[58] Darnand's militiamen could not believe it. Needless to say Céline scorned the politicians' intrigues, which he would later satirize in his funniest book, *D'un château l'autre*. He began work as doctor to the French community. . . .

. . . The Reich's borders were closed to the flood of people wishing to leave, but an exception was made for Céline. He was granted a visa to go to Denmark.

In March 1945 he set out again. By then the atmosphere in Sigmaringen had worsened. Hope had flickered when Von Runstedt launched his Ardennes offensive in December. Already the collaborators saw themselves back in Paris. But Von Runstedt was halted and the Allied advance continued. In March Déat noted in his diary: "Time presses on and the counter-offensive has not begun."[59] In February Doriot had been killed. He was making his way to Mengen to meet Déat in an attempt at reconciliation, when an American plane sprayed his car with bullets. He died instantly and he was buried on a cold morning, while squadrons of Allied bombers thundered overhead. A few of the P.P.F. followers went on intriguing even as the coffin was being lowered. But for Hérold-Paquis, who had struggled to believe in Doriot's destiny, it was the final blow. An unknown man appeared and threw French soil on the grave. Rebatet turned away to walk back to Sigmaringen: "Everything is finished," he said to Paquis. "I don't believe in anything any more, not in an idea nor a man nor a war."[60]

Next month Rebatet, Bonnard and others stood at Sigmaringen station to see Céline off. The night before he had offered a celebratory round of beer, for which he never paid. Now he stood on the platform with Bébert, whom Le Vigan no longer wished to keep, on his shoulder and his immense passport, stamped with its special *Ausweis*, in his hand. He even had a porter, Chamoin, to help him with his innumerable cases. The train came in slowly. One of the last to function in the Reich, it was burning wood instead of coal. Céline got aboard beaming and waving his passport.[61]

He made his way across a country where the armies of five nations were fighting the most devastating war in history. He saw the ruins of Hamburg bombed into rubble and lit only by the fires of incendiaries. The population lived in air-raid shelters while sirens wailed night and day. It was Armageddon. Miraculously the train went on. According to Céline, there were twenty-seven changes and he had to walk a total of eighteen miles.[62] On 27 March he crossed the Danish border and went on to Copenhagen. He and Lucette made their way, through streets still occupied by Germans, to Karen Jensen's flat. There they hid as Hitler's forces collapsed, the Russians entered Berlin and the war ended.

. . . In April 1945 a warrant had been made out in France for his arrest. In December he was discovered, living in Karen Jensen's flat. The Liberation press was exultant. *Franc-Tireur*, staffed by Céline's former admirer George Altman and by Madeleine Jacob, the Pasionaria of the Liberation, had a huge headline proclaiming that the "French-Nazi writer," the "miserable Hitlerite" who had "sullied and betrayed" France was to be brought to justice.[63] *Samedi-Soir* was delighted that the French ambassador, Guy de Girard de Charbonnière, was trying to have Céline extradited.[64] The Danish authorities, anxious not to displease the French, clapped him into prison to make sure he did not escape.

He remained there from December 1945 until February 1947. Later he described his experiences: "During my seventeen months of solitary confinement [in the section of the jail reserved for prisoners condemned to death] I was taken out each day for twelve minutes in a cage two metres by two metres . . . so that I could take the air. I could see nothing from that cage . . . and God knows it was cold in the winter, you can imagine. Exposed to the Baltic cold."[65] Even allowing for Céline's exaggeration, his year in prison was hard. Lucette, who was held in custody for a short time, was allowed to visit him on condition they spoke English, so that the guards could understand. As she knew little English, this was an added burden. Céline's health grew worse and he suffered from pellagra and mycosis. He did not know when, if ever, he would be released or whether he would be extradited. He did know that Girard de Charbonnière — whom he castigated as an "ex-Vichyite"[66] trying to cover up his past — was working to have him sent back to France.

He had received two other blows. In September 1944 his name was put on the black-list drawn up by the National Committee of Writers. The list, which included Drieu, Montherlant, Brasillach and many others, was composed of the writers who had compromised themselves under the Occupation. The National Committee, dominated by communists and fellow-travellers, demanded that their works should not appear in magazine or book form. The second blow fell in December 1945, when Sartre published his *Portrait d'un anti-sémite* which contains the sentence: "If Céline could support the Nazis' socialist theses the reason is that he was paid."[67] This groundless accusation could have helped to establish Céline in people's minds as the blackest of traitors. It is thrown as an aside into a brilliant study, but it is surprising that Sartre should have made such a remark without checking his facts.

But then France was in no mood to extend tolerance to collaborators. The purge was in full swing throughout 1945 and 1946. There had been some four and a half thousand summary executions in the months after the Liberation; horizontal collaboration was punished by the shaving of heads, and the prison camp of Drancy, which the Nazis had used for Jews, was opened to Vichyites and fascists. The country was eagerly awaiting the trials of the pro-German faction, not just out of a desire for revenge, but because they were a "part of the great task of renewal."[68] The Liberation was a period of exalted optimism. "From Resistance to Revolution" was the communist cry. "The people are under arms tonight because they hope for justice tomorrow," Camus had written on 24 August 1944 as the barricades went up around him.[69] Having defeated the Nazis, the Resistance hoped to create a new and pure republic. The first stage was the trials, where the country would solemnly renounce the past. They were to be a public cleansing, where the guilt incurred during the Occupation would be washed away.

. . . Céline's months in solitary confinement, however unpleasant, were a light price to pay for avoiding Liberation justice. In February 1947 he was released from prison and interned at the Rhyshospitalet. In June he was freed and allowed to go and live in an attic on the Kronprinsessegade.

From his window he could look out over Rosenborg park and the palace where the crown jewels were kept. But Céline was not interested in crown jewels. He was now an old man, "crippled with rheumatism from head to toe,"[70] broken in spirit and kept alive by his hatred. He was under the surveillance of the Danish authorities and he could not return to France. He was terrified of being sent back to prison or extradited and his trial was pending in Paris. He had hired a Danish lawyer, Mikkelsen, and two French lawyers, Naud and the star of the far-right, Tixier-Vignancourt. Céline had other troubles. Denoël's death had left the publishing house in a state of confusion. As it had published books like *Les Beaux Draps* and *Les Décombres*, it was under investigation. In any case Céline's books were banned. "I no longer have any way of earning a living—neither medicine nor writing," he says.[71] He could not practise as a doctor in Denmark and it was useless for Lucette to try and start a dance school. . . .

. . . One day Mikkelsen took them on a drive to Elsinore. Céline ignored the history museums at which they stopped on the way, but at Elsinore he got out of the car and went on to the terrace overlooking the sea. The mists, the outline of the Swedish coast, the lonely cries of the gulls created a desolate atmosphere. Céline looked at the ocean: "It's a sea to fish for souls," he said.[72]

The remark shows a brooding Céline who puzzled over his suffering and was not content with cries of hatred. François Löchen, the pastor of the French reformed church at Copenhagen, saw this hidden side of his character. Céline visited the church in the autumn of 1947 to hear a "sermon in French."[73] Löchen, who had been minister at Bezons, became friendly with him and introduced him to Denise Thomassen who ran a French bookshop. Céline and Lucette had Christmas dinner with Löchen and his family and Céline explained, in the course of conversation, "how there was no suffering to which he was indifferent." He rejected utterly the Christian notion that suffering could be redemptive; but he was aware of pain as a mysterious entity which shaped the human condition and could not be solved by terrestrial remedies. Löchen felt that Céline was a man "of deep sensibility, curious, in a discreet, anxious way, about the Beyond." Unlike Christians, Céline felt that the force controlling the world was "painful and incomprehensible."[74] But his sense of life as an agonizing riddle and his sympathy for human misery were the marks of a man who was still, in his own way, searching. . . .

From the time he left prison Céline had been pouring out letters to friends. He wrote to influential supporters like Raoul Nordling, Swedish Consul in Paris, and the Danish critic Ernst Bendz. In particular he wrote to Milton Hindus and to his most devoted supporter Albert Paraz.[75] Paraz, who had met Céline in 1934 in a café on the rue Lepic, was a novelist and pamphleteer. He had been gassed in 1940 and spent years in and out of hospitals, before going to live at Vence near the Mediterranean. His ill-health did not affect his fighting spirit. Influenced by Céline to the point of imitating his slangy vocabulary and virulent rhetoric, Paraz was an excellent polemist. In 1947 he became convinced that a great writer was being persecuted. He began to correspond with Céline and to look for ways of helping him.

In his letters Céline talks about books, politics, his friends, the past and especially the present. His correspondence is a good guide to his state of mind but there is sometimes a distortion. In particular the letters to Paraz seem to be written with one eye on publication. Céline is harsher than in the letters to Hindus. There is more of the pamphleteer and less of the man, more bitterness and less humour.

. . . Throughout 1949 Céline was preparing for this long-delayed trial. His letters, printed in *Valsez saucisses*, repeat the themes of his *Réponse aux accusations* and of the statement he would make to his judges. His view was simple: "I did not collaborate, however strange it may appear. My enemies will have to resign themselves to that fact."[76] Unfortunately the matter is not so easy. An ordinance of 27 June 1944 defined collaboration as any action or writing that aided the Nazi war effort, supported anti-semitism and harmed the Resistance.[77] Céline could not be tried for his pre-war pamphlets, only for his behaviour from 1940 to 1944. Maurice Vanino, a Resistance historian, has analysed the case and he concludes, not surprisingly, that Céline was guilty.

Evidence of collaborationist actions is slight. Vanino is unable to show that the *parti unique* discussions amounted to anything or that Céline's contacts with the German authorities were much greater than his position as doctor and writer demanded. On the question of his writings, Vanino has more to work with. Céline could find no way of explaining *Les Beaux Draps*, except to forget that he ever wrote it.[78] He could explain the re-publishing of *L'École des cadavres* only by blaming it on Denoël.[79] He wanted to forget about his letters to the press on the grounds that they were not really articles. Vanino will not accept this. He singles out the remark about Doriot and the criticism of the Resistance. He demolishes Céline's claim: "From the time the Germans arrived I took no interest in the Jewish question."[80] This conflicts with the admiring remark about Hitler and the letter to the organizers of the anti-semitic exhibition. Vanino also digs up the Rouquès matter. In the 1943 preface to *L'École*, Céline attacked Rouquès for the 1939 lawsuit and called him "the doctor of the international brigades." This, claimed Céline's accusers, was tanta-mount to denouncing him to the Gestapo as an anti-fascist. Céline could only reply that Rouquès was known to one and all as a communist sympathizer, so that the preface made no difference. Vanino does not agree.

It is impossible to see how Céline could be found not guilty. One may argue endlessly about the vagaries of Liberation justice. Why was the house of Denoël acquitted on the charge of publishing collaborationist books? If Denoël was innocent how was Céline guilty? There is no obvious answer. But, as the law stood, Céline had committed punishable offences. His claim that he was hated by the Germans, the Vichyites and the collaborators was irrelevant. His writings were sufficient proof of collaboration. The question of to what degree he was guilty is more complex. Vanino considers him a hard-line collaborator, but this is surely exaggerated. Céline had made his main contribution to the Nazi cause before the war. *Bagatelles* and *L' École* were his major works, the wartime writings were slighter. This should have entitled him to a milder punishment than Rebatet or Cousteau. But the arbitrariness of the purge — Hérold-Paquis's typist received twenty years hard labour while Albertini, a leader in the Rassemblement National Populaire, was sentenced to five years in prison — makes such comparisons difficult. If he had been tried in 1945, Céline's fame would probably have brought him a long jail sentence.

As it was, his trial on 21 February 1950 was an anti-climax. *Combat* and *Le Libertaire* had polled their readers.[81] They found that, although most people thought Céline guilty, tempers had cooled since 1944. Among the writers interviewed André Breton and Roger Vailland were anti-Céline, Paulhan, Mac Orlan, Aymé and the inevitable Paraz were for him. Camus declared that, while he loathed the views expressed in the pamphlets, he had lost faith in the trials — "political justice is repugnant to me."[82] Other newspapers showed interest. *Radar*, a glossy and sensation-loving magazine, sent a reporter to Denmark. She paints a vivid picture of Céline living in total poverty, a sick man stretched out on a pallet: "Céline, the swashbuckler, 'big mouth' Céline is no more than a poor, broken devil." *Radar*'s conclusion is that, in spite of his crimes, Céline should be pitied.[83] It is clear that he has become a news item, more bizarre than reprehensible. His picture is in the magazine near photographs of Ingrid Bergman and the boxer Ray Faméchon.

The hearings aroused much interest and little passion. Céline stated, with scant regard for the truth, that he would have liked to attend, but that his doctor had forbidden it.[84] The prosecution read out extracts from *Les Beaux Draps* — sometimes provoking outbursts of laughter from the audience. Naud and Tixier-Vignancourt produced Céline's letter of defence and statements from his friends. Arletty sent a letter which declared that, as Céline had been born, like her, in Courbevoie, he could not have betrayed France.[85] The decision was swiftly reached: Céline was declared guilty and condemned to one year in prison, national unworthiness and the confiscation of half his property. The *Combat* reporter considered this an extremely lenient sentence and Paraz writes gleefully that Madeleine Jacob was blue with anger.[86] Even Céline was pleased. "I was condemned for *reasons of state*, if they had not knocked me at all they would have disavowed the Resistance,"[87] he said with some accuracy.

But he still had to remain in Denmark or else go to prison. By the next month he had fallen into deep depression. The nervous excitement of the trial had left him exhausted. He was no longer pleased. "They only half cut my head off," he writes to Raoul Nordling.[88] Paraz kept up his campaign, urging admirers to plead and petition on Céline's behalf. He began work on a third book, *Le Menuet du haricot*, which renews his attacks on the Resistance—"made up of very low scoundrels, fortunately few in number"—on Sartre, Madeleine Jacob and, a new enemy, Maurice Merleau-Ponty.[89]

Céline's lawyers were hard at work. In August 1947 an amnesty had been extended to men who fought in the First World War. It might be applicable to their client. Céline was suspicious: "This so-called Amnesty is only a Resistance trick."[90] He was sure that, if he returned, he would be clapped into prison. The example of the Commune continued to haunt him: "They were judging the *communards* in 1880 and harshly."[91] In December Naud was optimistic, Céline not so. But on 26 April 1951 he discovered that he was pardoned. He could scarcely believe it. Paraz writes that Jules Moch, the socialist Minister of the Interior, granted the amnesty without knowing that Louis-Ferdinand Destouches was Céline; when Moch realized it he was "mad with rage."[92] Céline did not delay. In June he took an aeroplane to Nice, leaving behind him a country he had never ceased to castigate. The days of exile were over. He could return to the Paris suburbs he knew so well.

Notes

1. Robert Brasillach, *Notre avant-guerre*, Paris, 1941, p. 276.

2. Ibid., p. 236.

3. Robert Brasillach, *Journal d'un homme occupé*, Les Sept Couleurs, Paris, 1945, p. 183.

4. Brasillach, *Notre avant-guerre*, p. 189.

5. Lucien Rebatet, *Les Décombres*, Denoël, Paris, 1942, p. 573.

6. Ibid., p. 539.

7. Drieu la Rochelle, *Nouvelle revue française*, May 1941, p. 183.

8. Ibid., p. 185.

9. Rebatet, "D'un Céline l'autre," *L'Herne*, 3, pp. 45–6.

10. "Lettre ouverte à Pétain," *Au pilori*, 12.7.1940.

11. Ibid., 8.1.1942.

12. Constantini had anticipated the Riom trials by a year. His article appeared in the first number of *L'Appel*, 6.3.1941.

13. One thing the press did not learn from Céline was humour. Despite their follies these newspapers show no trace of the comic spirit.

14. See *La Gerbe*, 13.2.1941.

15. A not quite accurate list of Céline's articles is given in *Essai de bibliographie complète* in *L'Herne*, 3, pp. 15–39. One might wonder why Céline, who loathed journalists, wrote anything at all for the press. The answer is that he was playing out his role as pamphleteer. His style and themes are the same as in *Bagatelles*. The difference, noted in

Chapter Four, between his writings and his life, persists throughout the war. But, although that is stressed again in this chapter, the journalist and the man are considered together. Céline was a public figure, whose words and actions were watched by collaborators and Gaullists alike. In any case, as pointed out in the Introduction and in Chapter Five, all his roles overlap. During the war, the pamphleteer and the private citizen, Dr Destouches, were completely interwoven.

16. "Prologue du parti unique," 11.12.1941.

17. "Vers le parti unique," 25.12.1941.

18. "Entretien avec Céline," *L'Émancipation nationale*, 21.9.1941. pp. 1–3. Sicard had been writing for *Le Petit Crapouillot* when Galtier-Boissière attacked the Rosny brothers.

19. Céline, "Qui détient le Pouvoir?," *L'Appel*, 9.4.1942.

20. "Céline nous écrit," *Révolution nationale*, 5.4.1942.

21. "Acte de Foi de Louis-Ferdinand Céline," *La Gerbe*, 13.2.1941.

22. Céline to Lucien Combelle, 20.4.1941, *L'Herne*, 5, p. 65.

23. "L.-F. Céline nous écrit," *L'Appel*, 4.9.1941.

24. Céline, "Vivent les Juifs," *Au pilori*, 2.10.1941.

25. *L'Émancipation nationale*, 21.9.1941.

26. Robert Chamfleury, "Céline ne nous a pas trahis," *L'Herne*, 3, p. 66.

27. Maryse Desneiges, "D'une Française . . . à L.-F. Céline," *Pays libre*, 22.3.1941.

28. Another headline in this issue runs "Mourir en Combattant."

29. "Louis-Ferdinand Céline répond au *Pays libre*," 5.4.1941.

30. "L.-F. Céline nous écrit," *L'Appel*, 4.12.1941.

31. Céline to Combelle, 12.2.1943, op. cit., p. 65.

32. Céline, *Vivent les Juifs*, op. cit.

33. Céline to Combelle, 20.4.1941, op. cit.

34. "Céline s'explique," *Au pilori*, 8.1.1942.

35. "Acte de Foi' de Louis-Ferdinand Céline, *La Gerbe*, 13.2.1941, p. 1.

36. Saint-Paulien, *Histoire de la collaboration*, Paris, 1964, p. 257 ff. A fugitive from French justice, Sicard lived in Spain for many years after the war. He published this book under a pseudonym but reveals his identity in the introduction.

37. Interview with Robert Poulet.

38. "Réponse aux accusations," op. cit., p. 332.

39. Maurice Vanino, *L'École d'un cadavre*, p. 32.

40. Rebatet, "D'un Céline l'autre," *L'Herne*, 3, p. 48.

41. Saint-Paulien, op, cit., p. 276.

42. Maurice Vanino, op, cit., p. 28. He is quoting a letter from Céline to Capitaine Sezille.

43. Ibid., p. 32.

44. Karl Epting, "Il ne nous aimait pas," *L'Herne*, 3, p. 57.

45. Simone Mittre, *L'Herne*, 5, p. 283.

46. Céline to Mahé, Mahé, *La Brinquebale avec Céline, La Table ronde*, Paris, p. 237.

47. Morin.

48. Geoffroy, op. cit., p. 12.

49. Robert Chamfleury, op. cit., pp. 60–66.

50. *L'Appel*, 20.4.1944.

51. Céline, *Oeuvres complètes*, vol. 3, p. 511 ff.

52. Robert Aron, *The Vichy Régime*, Putnam, New York, 1958, p. 513.

53. Rebatet, "D'un Céline l'autre," *L'Herne*, 3, p. 50.

54. Epting, op, cit., p. 59.

55. Céline told the same story to Paraz (Paraz, *Le Gala des vaches*, p. 237). But Rebatet refutes this version (Rebatet, op. cit., pp. 49–50).

56. Jean Hérold-Paquis, op. cit. This is a graphic, eye-witness account of the exodus. It was written in Fresnes where Paquis was waiting to be executed.

57. Paquis, Saint-Paulien and others have described these fantasies in colourful detail. Aron gives a more sober account of Sigmaringen.

58. Rebatet, op. cit., p. 51.

59. Marcel Déat, *Journal*, 16.3.1945, in *L'Herne*, 5, p. 143.

60. Paquis, op. cit., p. 114.

61. Rebatet, op. cit., p. 54.

62. Céline to Dr Camus 30.6.1947. "Lettres d'Exil" in *Écrits de Paris*, October

63. *Franc-Tireur*, 19.12.1945.

64. *Samedi-Soir*, 16.2.1946.

65. Céline to Eveline Pollet, August 1947, op. cit., p. 111.

66. Céline to Paraz, 19.8.1947, Paraz, *Le Gala des vaches*, p. 111.

67. Sartre, *Portrait d'un anti-sémite*, Les Temps modernes, December 1945, p. 462.

68. Peter Novick, *The Resistance versus Vichy*, Columbia University Press, New York, 1968, p. 38.

69. Reprinted in Albert Camus, *Resistance, Rebellion and Death*, Modern Library Books, New York, 1963, p. 28.

70. Céline to Hindus, 31.4.1947, op. cit., p. 74.

71. Céline to Eveline Pollet, 23.7.1947, op. cit., p. 111.

72. Héron de Villefosse, op. cit., p. 34.

73. Céline to Pasteur Löchen, *L'Herne*, 3, p. 132.

74. Note by Pasteur Löchen to Céline's letters, op. cit., p. 131.

75. These letters are another monument to Céline's will to survive. They may be read as a systematic campaign to win over supporters. Letter-writing was the only form of action left open to him. He made good use of it. His correspondence reveals too his old flair for game-playing. Letters written to different people on the same day show complete switches of style and mood. The letters to Paraz are obviously political. They portray the great patriot and artist Céline, exiled in the snowy northern wastes. With Hindus, Céline is trying to woo a potentially useful supporter. He is patient with Hindus' questions about his writing. He gives the appearance of baring his soul, he even cajoles. With Perrot he allows himself to dwell on happier days in Montmartre; with Eveline Pollet he is occasionally flirtatious. Raoul Nordling was the Swedish Consul in Paris in 1944. It was he who helped arrange the cease-fire between the German garrison and the Gaullists, thus avoiding a battle which would have destroyed much of central Paris. He was now willing to try and arrange a cease-fire between Céline and his enemies. Ernst Bendz was well known in Scandinavia as a critic of French literature. Benjamin Perrot was an old neighbour from the rue Girardon in Montmartre. Milton Hindus was an American academic who tried, rather pompously, to be nice to the pariah Céline. He met with the same fate as the Russians. For his account of the relationship and particularly of his visit to Denmark, see Milton Hindus: *The Crippled Giant*, New York, 1950. For the viewpoint of Céline and his supporters, see Paraz's letter to Marcot, 21.12.1951, *L'Herne*, 5, p. 296.

76. *Valsez saucisses*, p. 238. In these pages Céline and Paraz discuss Céline's defence.

77. The legal basis of the purge is discussed by Peter Novick, op. cit., p. 79 ff. He concludes that Liberation justice was not very just.

78. The "Réponse" makes no mention of *Les Beaux Draps*.

79. Letter to the court quoted in *Combat*, 22.2.1950. Céline's statement runs: "I am not proud of republishing it in 1943. Denoël wanted to compromise me.

80. "Réponse," op. cit., p. 319.

81. *Combat*, 21.2.1950; *Le Libertaire*, 13. 1.1950. Both newspapers had their roots in the Resistance.

82. *Le Libertaire*, 20.1.1950.

83. *Radar*, 5.3.1950.

84. Letter to the court, op. cit.

85. *Combat*, 22.2.1950.

86. Paraz to Marcot, 1.3.1950, op. cit., p. 291.

87. Céline to Paraz, 23.2.1950, *Valsez saucisses*, p. 358.

88. Céline to Nordling, 10.3.1950, *L'Herne*, 3, p. 139.

89. *Le Menuet du haricot* was not published until after Paraz's death in 1957.

90. Céline to Bendz (undated), op. cit., p. 127.

91. Céline to Paraz, 8.11.1950, *L'Herne*, 5, p. 145.

92. Paraz to Marcot, 1.5.1951, op. cit., p. 294.

[Remarks on *Bagatelles pour un massacre*]

Merlin Thomas*

In 1937 — rather before many of his contemporaries — he had become convinced that another European war was on the way. Whatever else we can say about Céline's views, it is certainly clear that he always believed that war was the greatest possible evil and stupidity. All he wrote, from *Voyage* to *Rigodon*, bears this out. At the same time, his pacifism was mixed with patriotism and with . . . xenophobia. . . . He was genuinely proud to have been awarded the Médaille Militaire for bravery in 1914, and he volunteered for active service at the outbreak of war in 1939 (at the age of forty-five). What a curious — yet not unduly contradictory — set of views he seems to have held at the time of writing *Bagatelles!*

There is a minimal structure to *Bagatelles*, in that most of it is allegedly framed in conversations between Ferdinand (sometimes in this work referred to as Céline directly) and three friends, two of them doctors — his cousin, Gustin Sabayote, and Léo Gutman (a Jew) — and the third a painter, Popol. The opening conversation (with Gutman) is largely about ballet, and includes the transcription of two scenarii (*La Naissance d'une fée* and *Voyou Paul, brave Virginie*) which were later to be

*Reprinted from *Louis-Ferdinand Céline* (New York: New Directions, 1979), 136–56. © 1979 Merlin Thomas. Reprinted by permission of New Directions Publishing Corp. and Faber and Faber, Ltd.

published again in *Ballets sans musique, sans personne, sans rien* (Gallimard 1959). The refusal of these two works, first by the Opéra, and then by the organizing committee of the 1937 Exhibition, is the pretext for the full open declaration of anti-semitism:

> J'en aurai jamais des danseuses alors? . . . J'en aurai jamais! Tu l'avoues!
> C'est tout pour les youtres . . . Ah! tu vas voir l'antisémitisme! . . . Ah!
> tu vas voir la révolte! . . . Ah! le réveil des indigènes! . . . (p. 31)

> What no ballerinas for me, ever? . . . I'll never have any! You admit it!
> They're only for the Yids! . . . Just you wait for the antisemitism! . . .
> Just you wait for the revolt . . . the awakening of the natives! . . .

And the work ends with yet another ballet scenario (*Van Bagaden*, also republished in the 1959 volume), ostensibly prepared for the Leningrad ballet, but never performed. But the body of the work is an almost uninterrupted monologue from Céline, during which a number of main themes are developed, but which does not have a close knit argumentative pattern.

There are three principal themes in the work. First an assault on communism along the lines already sketched in *Mea Culpa*, directed against its materialism and lack of true brotherhood and egalitarianism, with now the added nuances that the USSR is Jewish-controlled, and that communism and fascism are equally useless. Secondly, a generalized attack on the present state of France, both bourgeoisie and proletariat, again for selfish materialism fostered by the Jews who have infiltrated French society and who control the media. Thirdly—and of course the justification of the whole work in Céline's view—the warning that international Jewry is planning another war in order to bring about the self-destruction of the Aryan masses of Western Europe, who are too stupid to realize what is in store for them: in order to prevent this catastrophe it is no use thinking of either Russia or England as allies since they are Jewish controlled and part of the plot—the only solution is an understanding with Germany. All this needs now to be illustrated by quotation in order to give also an impression of the polemical virtuosity as well as of the monumental naivety in places.

After being exposed to Ferdinand's first outburst, Gustin protests, and receives an answer worth noting:

> Mais t'es antisémite ma vache! C'est vilain! C'est un préjugé! . . .
>
> Je n'ai rien de spécial contre les Juifs en tant que juifs, je veux dire simplement truands comme tout le monde, bipèdes à la quête de leur soupe . . . Ils me gênent pas du tout. Un Juif ça vaut peut-être un Breton, sur le tas, à l'égalité, un Auvergnat, un franc-canaque, un "enfant de Marie" . . . C'est possible . . . Mais c'est contre le racisme juif que je me révolte, que je suis méchant, que je bouille, ça jusqu'au tréfonds de mon benouze! . . . (p. 49)

But you bastard, you're an antisemite! That's nasty! It's a prejudice!
     I've nothing particular against the Jews as jews, I mean just as poor
sods like the rest of us, bipeds looking for food . . . They don't worry me
at all. A Jew, he's probably as good as a Breton, on the whole, all things
being equal, as an Auvergnat, a free-mason, a good little Catholic . . .
Maybe . . . But it's Jewish racialism that I won't take, where I became
nasty, where I boil with rage right down to the seat of my pants! . . .)

This is both explosive and insidious stuff. It seeks to provide a slight
alibi in the opening section and then to provide a justification. One can
certainly turn the racialist argument back on him as can be seen in many
passages in *Bagatelles*: "Le Juif est un nègre, la race sémite n'existe pas,
c'est une invention de franc-maçon, le Juif n'est que le produit d'un
croisement de nègres et de barbares asiates" (p. 121) ("The Jew is a negro,
the semitic race doesn't exist, it's a masonic invention, the Jew is no more
than the product of a cross between negroes and Asian barbarians"); or
again: "Ce qui nous gêne le plus dans les Juifs, quand on examine la
situation, c'est leur arrogance, leur perpetuelle martyrologo-dervicherie,
leur sale tam-tam" (p. 127) ("What exasperates most about the Jews, when
one looks at the situation, is their arrogance, their perpetual dervish-
martyr complex, their obscene noisy publicity"). There is also a kind of
incantation (pp. 181–2) which contains his essential view (expressed, of
course, many years before the foundation of the State of Israel):

> . . . Si l'on refoulait tous les Juifs, qu'on les renvoie
> En Palestine avec leurs caïds franc-maçons — puisqu'ils s'adorent —
> Nous cesserions d'être "Intouchables."
> Au pays des Emirs négrites . . .
> Nous n'aurions ni guerre, ni faillite . . .
> Avant longtemps . . . longtemps . . . longtemps . . .
> Et nous aurions beaucoup de places vides . . . immédiatement
> Tout de suite . . . les meilleurs en vérité. . . .
>
> . . . If one threw out all the Jews, sent them back
> To Palestine with their masonic bosses — since they love each other —
> We'd cease to be the "Untouchables."
> In the land of negroid Emirs . . .
> We'd have neither war nor bankruptcy . . .
> For a long . . . long . . . long . . . time
> And there'd be lots of jobs going . . . immediately
> At once . . . the best if you want to know. . . .

Examination of the text surrounding the above passages justifies a summary of his viewpoint along the following lines. He is saying "I've nothing
against Jews as such,[1] but I am against their arrogant pretensions which do
of course explain why they have been persecuted down the ages as they are
so fond of reminding us. And in their own surroundings they are, no
doubt, very nice people, but they have no business here in France holding

down all the best jobs." Céline's "mistake" as a polemist was to imagine
that such arguments would appeal to any but a tiny minority of literate
persons. And *Bagatelles* was far too sophisticated and difficult to be read
by the semiliterates who would have agreed with him, and who have their
counterparts in England now on the extreme right.[2]

I have already described some of Céline's attitude to communism in
connection with *Mea Culpa*. One further set of illustrations is useful,
because it provides a link forward to the third pamphlet, *Les Beaux Draps*,
as will be seen later. He is all for a *genuine* communism of an egalitarian
kind: he knows from experience what social inequality means. The
following passages are all extracted from a torrential section of text which
is very representative of the overall tone of the book.

> . . . je suis pas réactionnaire! pas pour un poil! une minute! pas fasciste!
> . . . Mais pas du tout! mais moi je veux bien qu'on partage! Mais moi je
> n'ai jamais demandé mieux! Là! mes quatre sous sur la table! . . . Je
> veux bien tout remettre sur la table. Si l'on partage 'absolument'. . . . Je
> me sens communiste de toutes fibres! de tous les os! de toute barbarque!
> et ce n'est pas le cas pour bezef! (pp. 54–5)

> . . . I'm not a reactionary! In no way! not for a moment! not a fascist!
> . . . Not at all! I'm all in favour, me, of sharing! I've never wanted
> anything else! There! My four halfpennies on the table! . . . I'll put all I
> have on the table. If there's a *total* share-out. . . . I feel myself
> communist in every fibre, in all my bones! in my flesh! and that's not
> true of the majority!

That is the kind of communism he gladly adopts, but what passes for
communism is very different, and is, according to him, a Jewish invention.

> Ce qu'on appelle communisme dans les milieux bien avancés, c'est la
> grande assurance nougat, le parasitisme le plus perfectionné des âges
> garanti admirablement par le servage absolu du prolétariat mondial
> . . . l'Universelle des Esclaves . . . par le système bolchévique, farci
> superfasciste, boulonnage international, le plus grand coffre-fort blindé
> qu'on aura jamais conçu rivé compartimenté, soudé au brasier de nos
> tripes pour la plus grande gloire d'Israel, la défense suprême des éternels
> youtres pillages, l'apothéose tyrannique des délires sémites! . . . (p. 55)

> What's called communism in intellectual circles is merely a syrupy kind
> of insurance policy, the most impeccable parasitism ever down the ages,
> solidly guaranteed by the total servitude of the worldwide proletariat
> . . . the Slaves Commercial Union . . . devised by the Bolchevik system,
> stuffed, hyper-fascist, international riveting, the greatest armour-plated
> strong-box ever imagined, bolted, compartmentalized, soldered in the
> brazier of our guts for the greater glory of Israel, the supreme defence of
> sempiternal yiddish robberies, the tyrannical apotheosis of semitic
> delirium! . . .

He also feels it necessary to underline his own situation with respect to all this:

> Rappelons un peu les événements: Monsieur Gide en était encore à se demander tout éperdu de réticences, de sinueux scrupules, de fragilités syntaxiques, s'il fallait ou ne fallait pas enculer le petit Bédouin, que déjà depuis belle lurette le *Voyage* avait fait des siennes . . . J'ai pas attendu mes 80 ans pour la découvrir l'inégalité sociale. A 14 ans, j'étais fixé une bonne fois pour toutes. J'avais dégusté la chose. (p. 55)[3]

> Let's get the chronology right. Monsieur Gide was still at the stage of asking himself, all reverent with hesitations, with sinuous scruples, with syntactical delicacy, whether or not it was a good idea to bugger his young Bedouin, when *Voyage* had already long ago had its effects . . . I haven't waited till I was 80 to discover social inequality. At 14 I was fully aware for good and all. I'd tasted it.

There is an interesting passage near the end of the book which denotes his non-engagement with political parties, his contempt for right and left alike. He seeks to emphasize here that if the new war comes, the sufferer will be, of course, as usual, the ordinary man:

> Quand ça deviendra trop compliqué, Thorez s'en ira au Caucase [he was roughly right], Blum à Washington [here he was very wrong] (s'ils ne sont pas butés) chargés de missions très complexes, toi t'iras voir dans les Ardennes, te rendre compte un petit peu, de l'imitation des oiseaux par les balles si furtives . . . si bien piaulantes au vent . . . des vrais rossignols, je t'assure . . . qui viendront picorer ta tête! . . .
>   Ferdinand, quand c'est la bataille, le fascisme vaut le communisme, . . . Dans la prochaine Walkyrie, tu peux le croire très fermement, que ça soye Hitler qui remporte ou son cousin Staline . . . ça sera pareil au même . . . la façon qu'on sera têtards, nous. (p. 191)

> When it becomes too difficult, Thorez will go off to the Caucasus, Blum to Washington (if they are not bumped off) entrusted with highly complex missions, and you, you'll go off to the Ardennes to find out a little bit about how furtive bullets can imitate birds . . . chirping away so nicely in the wind . . . real nightingales, honestly . . . which will come and peck your head!
>   Ferdinand, when it comes down to battle, fascism is the same as communism . . . In the next version of the *Walkyrie* you can be dead sure of one thing, whether it's Hitler who wins or his cousin Stalin . . . it will amount to the same thing . . . we'll be the twits just the same. . . .

Of course a communist would tend to say that anyone who could equate Hitler and Stalin in 1937 was nothing more than a fascist. Maybe. But the point is here that Céline has already — at length and with great bitterness — made known his views on Stalin and the USSR, and regards Hitler as no better. Hardly the words of a pro-Nazi, one may reasonably feel.

There is little difficulty in finding passages in *Bagatelles* on other topics — such as the consumer society and corruption by the media — which can command acceptance nowadays. It is in fact astonishing that anyone could have written with such acumen and foresight in 1937 — if we disregard the *explanation* of the phenomena given by Céline, which is, of course, that of Jewish influence and policy. Here he is describing — with the aid of a typically coarse opening gambit[4] — the process of subjection of the public to the forces of 'standardization':

> On encule un millimètre, le premier centimètre c'est le plus dur, le plus coûteux . . . pour les suivants ça va tout seul! Tous les pédérastes nous l'affirment. N'importe quel trou du cul peut devenir, bien enculé de publicité, un immense n'importe quoi. . . . La publicité, pour bien donner tout son effet magique, ne doit être gênée, retenue, divertie par rien. Elle doit pouvoir affirmer, sacrer, vociférer, mégaphoniser les pircs sottises, n'importe quelle himalayesque, décervelante, tonitruante fantasmagorie . . . à propos d'automobiles, de stars, de brosses à dents, d'écrivains, de chanteuses légères, de ceintures herniaires, sans que personne ne tique . . . ne s'élève au parterre, la plus minuscule naïve objection. Il faut que le parterre demeure en tout temps parfaitement hypnotisé de connerie. (pp. 123–4)

> You get your prick in one millimetre, the first centimetre is the hardest, the most costly . . . thereafter there's no problem! Every pederast will tell us this. Absolutely any arse hole can become, well buggered by advertising, an immense whatever you like. . . . Advertising, in order to render its full magical effect, must not be troubled, hindered, diverted by anything. It must be allowed to assert, consecrate, vociferate, trumpet abroad the worst stupidities, no matter what Himalayan, brainless, thundering phantasmagoria on the subject of cars, stars, tooth-brushes, writers, female pop singers, rupture trusses, without anyone batting an eyelid, or making from the theatre pit the tiniest simplest protest. The pit must remain permanently and totally hypnotized by stupid rubbish.

Not only is this an attitude that applies with even greater force to our situation today — we have the added joy of television commercials — but it is an attitude that separates him absolutely from fascist techniques which depend so greatly on slogans and brain-washing propaganda.

More effective as far as the masses are concerned than this enslavement by propaganda (which has its principal effect on the bourgeoisie), is alcohol. The consumption of alcohol in France is higher than in any other country in the world — he produces statistics to show this — and the political power of the alcohol lobby is immense. All this of course he attributes to the "Jewish" plan for "standardization" in mediocrity:

> C'est très simple, aucun nordique, aucun nègre, aucun sauvage, aucun civilisé non plus n'approche et de très loin, le Français, pour la rapidité, la capacité de pompage vinassier. Seule le France pourrait battre ses

propres records de vinasse, ses descentes de picton. Ce sont d'ailleurs à peu près les seuls records qu'elle puisse battre . . . Le Roi Bistrot, possède, lui aussi, tous les droits, par accord politique absolument intangible, à l'immunité complète, au silence total, à tous les encouragements, pour l'exercice de son formidable trafic d'empoisonneur et d'assassin. (pp. 92–3)

It's quite simple, no northerner, no negro, no savage, nor no civilized being either, can get anywhere near at all to the Frenchmen in the matter of speed and capacity of knocking back wine. Only France could break its own records for wine-bibbing, for putting down plonk. They are, moreover, about the only records they can break. The Café is king, and he possesses, he too, full powers, by quite untouchable political agreement, complete immunity, in total silence, and with every encouragement to carry on his terrific trade of poisoner and assassin.

France still leads the field in this respect, and indeed has a mighty alcoholism problem. And it is not so long ago—*pace* Céline—that a French Prime Minister, Pierre Mendès-France, was overthrown partly because he was Jewish and partly because he dared to make the mildest of modifications to the licensing laws. . . .

One of the key causes of the decadence of the arts in France and of the absence of *emotional* response from the public (this for Céline is of paramount importance) is the system of secondary education—part of the Jewish drive for standardization of course. Listen to him on the effect of a *lycée* education on children:

Ils entrent dans l'enseignement secondaire, comme les petites chinoises dans les brodequins rétrécis, ils en sortent émotivement monstrueux, amputés, sadiques, frigides, frivoles et retors . . . Ils resteront affublés, ravis, pénétrés, solennels enculstrés de toutes leurs membrures, convaincus, exaltés de supériorité, babilleux de latino-bobarderie, soufflés de vide gréco-romain, de cette "humanité" bouffonne, cette fausse humilité, cette fantastique friperie gratuite prétentieux roucoulis de formules, abrutissant tambourin d'axiomes maniée, brandie d'âge, en âge, pour l'abrutissement des jeunes, par la pire clique parasiteuse, phrasuleuse, sournoise, retranchée, politicarde, théorique vermoulue, profiteuse, inextirpable, retorse, incompétante énucoïde, désastrogène, de l'Univers: le Corps stupide enseignant. . . . (p. 106)

They go into secondary education like little Chinese girls into shortened shoes; and then come out emotionally monstrous, amputated, sadistic, frigid, frivolous and twisted . . . They will remain dressed up, delighted, absorbed, pedantically solemn to the marrow, convinced, supremely self-satisfied, bubbling over with latino-pedantry, inflated with Greco-Roman vacuousness, with this risible "humanist" pose, this bogus humility, this gratuitous fantastic frippery, pretentious warbling of formulae, deadening battery of axioms—handled, brandished down the ages for the dulling of the young, by the worst possible, parasitical, phrase-making, sly, constricted, politico-intriguing, theorizingly worm-eaten, self-interested, unremovable, crafty, incompetent, eunuchoid, disaster-producing clique in the whole Universe, the teaching stupid profession.

Céline would no doubt have been surprised at the kind of ally that statement would have brought him in May 1968.

This kind of non-education — and for him the rot started in the Renaissance — has produced in the twentieth century a non-literature written in what he calls (at various times) "le style du Bachot," "le style de Voltaire," "le style d'Anatole France": a style full of ingenious finesse but drained of all emotional force. However, it is all that Jewish artists are capable of:

> Il faut qu'ils suppléent, qu'ils trichent, qu'ils pillent sans cesse, qu'ils sucent les voisins, les autochtones pour se soutenir . . . les Juifs manquent désastreusement d'émotion directe, spontanée . . . Ils parlent au lieu d'éprouver . . . Ils raisonnent avant de sentir . . . Au strict, ils n'éprouvent rien . . . Ils se vantent. (p. 47)

> They have to deputize, fiddle, pillage all the time, suck their neighbours, the native inhabitants in order to maintain themselves . . . The Jews are disastrously lacking in direct, spontaneous emotion . . . They talk instead of experiencing . . . They reason before feeling . . . In truth, they don't feel anything . . . They boast about themselves.

This line of thought brings with it a whole series of resounding condemnations of French authors down the ages from the Renaissance onwards: "Depuis la Renaissance l'on tend à travailler de plus en plus passionnément pour l'avènement du Royaume des Sciences et du Robot social" (p. 108) ("Since the Renaissance there's been a tendency to work more and more passionately for the coming of the Kingdom of the Sciences and of the Social Robot"). Amongst "Jewish" writers condemned are Montaigne, Racine, Stendhal, Zola and "Proust-Proust" (p. 81). Racine indeed comes in for special treatment — "Racine? Quel emberlificoté tremblotant exhibitionniste! Quel obscène, farfouilleux pâmoisant chiot! Au demi-quart juif d'ailleurs! . . ." (p. 136) ("Racine? What a complicated quivering exhibitionist! Obscene, rummaging, swooning puppy! And one-eighth Jewish too! . . .") — and for a special reason, which he has given often enough, namely the *obscenity* of the literature of love. He makes this point with particular insistence on the same page:

> Ecrire pourtant de cul, de bite, de merde, en soi n'est rien d'obscène, ni vulgaire. La vulgarité commence, Messieurs, Mesdames, au sentiment, toute la vulgarité, toute l'obscénité! Les écrivains, comme les écrivaines, pareillement enfiotés de nos jours, enjuivés domestiques jusqu'aux ventricules depuis la Renaissance (. . .) en ont plein les babines ces croulants dégénérés maniéreux cochons de leur "Amour"! . . . (p. 136)

> Writing of arse, prick, shit is in no way obscene in itself nor vulgar either. Vulgarity begins, ladies and gentlemen, with sentiment, full vulgarity, full obscenity. Writers (male and female) all equally sodomized nowadays, hebraised, domesticated to the core, ever since the Renaissance . . . these degenerate, affected, dirty-minded wrecks have their chaps slavering with their "Love"! . . .

It should, perhaps, be added that he does not spare contemporary English and American writers either—Virginia Woolf, Faulkner, Dos Passos, Sinclair Lewis and D. H. Lawrence are among those dismissed.

A particularly eloquent attack is launched against Hollywood. On the subject of the Jewish-dominated pre-war film industry he is quite tireless, and I suppose some people would be willing to concede his point on this in part. For him Hollywood has replaced Buenos Aires in the white slave trade: European starlets—"des plus belles, des plus désirables petites Aryennes bien suceuses" (p. 138) ("the prettiest, most desirable little Aryan girls expert at sucking you off") — are shown rushing to the casting couches of Jewish film magnates. Hollywood has triumphed too: there is no lack of "standardized" disciples. I am going to use the next quotation in an unorthodox way. The reader of *Bagatelles* is frequently struck by the extent to which Céline's ferocity is defensible, *except* with regard to the anti-Jewish obsession. I omit certain words in this passage, and replace them by the letters x and y, giving the key in footnote. Without the omitted words there is an attack on the media, violent indeed, but certainly arguable: read it again, though, with the words inserted. . . .[5]

> . . . la foule (x) rapplique frémissante, elle déleste de tout son pognon, pour mieux sauter, elle engage tout pour mieux jouir (y), se vautrer (y), se pourrir (y), sa tête, sa viande, son âme et toute sa connerie. Elle se donne. Elle se damne. La foule (x) ne croit plus que les affiches des politiciens et des cinémas (y), les journaux et comptes rendus de films, et les critiques d'art, tous (y). (p. 118)
> . . . the mob arrives all agog, unloads all its money so as to be able to jump better, it pledges the lot so as to have more pleasure, to wallow in it, to rot, head, flesh, soul and all its stupidity. It gives itself, it damns itself. The mob only believes politicians' proclamations and cinema posters, newspapers and film reviews, and the art critics, all of them.

His contemptuous conclusion to this section—devoid of racialist epithets—shows him to be in the grand tradition of polemical writings:

> Jamais domestiques, jamais esclaves ne furent en vérité si totalement, intimement asservis, invertis corps et âmes, d'une façon si dévotieuse, si suppliante.
>   Rome? En comparaison? . . . Mais un empire du petit bonheur! une Thélème philosophique! Le Moyen Age? . . . L'Inquisition? . . . Berquinades! Epoques libres! d'intense débraillé! d'effréné libre arbitre! Le duc d'Albe? Pizarro? Cromwell? Des artistes! (p. 118)

Never were servants, never were slaves in truth so totally, so intimately subjugated, perverted body and soul, in so devout and imploring a manner.

Rome? In comparison? A happy-go-lucky empire! a philosophical Thélème! The Middle Ages? . . . The Inquisition? . . . Children's tales! Epochs of liberty! of extreme relaxation! of unbridled free will! The Duke of Alba? Pizarro? Cromwell? Artists all of them!

The final main theme running through *Bagatelles* is the threat of oncoming war. It probably caused the book to be written, and was also given by Céline after the war as the reason for his anti-semitic writings.[6]

It is as clear as daylight that his analysis of affairs was wrong—even leaving aside his obsessions about a plot by international Jewry to destroy the "Aryans" of Western Europe. No alliance with Germany could have averted war from the moment Hitler came to power in 1933. (The Russians when they signed their pact with Nazi Germany in 1939 were under no illusions about this.) But it must be emphasized that at least up to the German invasion of Czechoslovakia in March 1939, a very large section of public opinion in both France and England supported a policy of trying to reach an understanding with the Axis powers of Germany and Italy. This policy of "appeasement" led to the Munich agreement, and was only abandoned in March 1939. It was supported in both countries by people of differing views: the largest number were probably those who thought that there *must* be a way of peaceful co-existence with Nazi Germany. They were wrong. There were also those—quite numerous on the right—who thought of Hitler as a bulwark against Stalinist communism. He was, indeed, but he brought a terror infinitely more sinister and infinitely more barbarous. And then there were the few—and they *were* very few—who were genuinely pro-Nazi and pro-fascist. My contention is that Céline, despite anti-semitism, was most certainly not amongst these few—though they of course promptly hailed him as a recruit—and that he did have as his principal motive pacifism, which is not one of the fascist virtues. There are, as will be seen, dangerous and even incriminating statements on this whole issue in *Bagatelles* and even more in *L'Ecole des cadavres* in the following year (1938), but they are much more an indication of his political ignorance than of informed adherence to Nazism. (He admitted this ignorance in later years.)[7] Politically uncommitted and isolated as he was in the years before the war, and contemptuously suspicious of the French press, he had no access to real political information. One may reasonably say that in that case he was excessively foolish to write as he did, and indeed guilty. What needs to be established on the evidence is the extent and nature of his guilt. Much depends on what can be established about his conduct during the German occupation of France, but there is some material in *Bagatelles* to be looked at first.

According to Céline, the left in France—or at least its political leaders of the Front Populaire, especially Léon Blum—naturally want an alliance with the Jewish-dominated Soviet Union. The Jewish City of London and the equally Jewish bankers of the USA are anxious for the destruction of Germany, which under Hitler is threatening their control. But of course, a war between Germany and other European states will suit them nicely. Céline rejects any thought of an alliance with Stalin's Russia: his illusions about Russia (if ever he had any) had been as completely shattered as those of Gide. As for England as an ally:

> L'Angleterre alliée? mes burnes! . . . Un an pour mobiliser . . . encore un an pour instruire . . . Nous serons déjà tous asticots quand débarqueront dans les Flandres les premiers invertis d'Oxford . . . la jolie Home Fleet du Whisky se répandra sur l'Atlantique expectante . . . Les Juifs sont rois dans la Cité n'oublions jamais . . . l'une de leurs suprêmes citadelles avec Wall Street et Moscou . . . (p. 60).

> England as an ally? Balls! . . . One year to mobilize . . . another for training . . . We'll all be already maggots when the first Oxford inverts will be landing in Flanders . . . the beautiful whisky Home Fleet will spread itself about the expectant Atlantic . . . We must never forget that the Jews reign in the City . . . one of their supreme citadels along with Wall Street and Moscow!

He was not quite right about all this (even taking "Oxford" to stand as a symbol for the English privileged classes . . .) but this kind of line had often been taken about British *land* participation in the 1914–18 war. And, despite the introduction of conscription in Britain (after Munich) for the first time ever in peacetime, the British contingent in France in 1939–40 was but a fraction of the size of the French army. This was helpful to the Vichy government later.

The war that Céline sees coming is desired by Jewry:

> La guerre pour la bourgeoisie c'était deja bien fumier, mais la guerre maintenant pour les Juifs! Je peux pas trouver d'adjectifs qui soient vraiment assez glaireux, assez myriakilogrammiques en chiasse, en carie de charogne verdoyeuse pour vous représenter ce que cela signifie. (p. 58)

> War for the bourgeoisie was already revolting enough, but war for the Jews now! I can't find any adjectives that are really sufficiently phlegm-covered, sufficiently myriakilogrammically full of shit, of green decay of corpses to describe to you what that means.

The traitor class is the bourgeoisie, ignobly pro-Jewish or Jewish dominated:

> Je me demande toujours ce qui est le plus dégueulasse, une merde de Juif bien aplatie, ou un bourgeois français tout debout . . . lequel qu'est plus infect davantage? Je peux vraiment pas décider. (p. 60)

I always ask myself which is the most disgusting, a shit of a Jew cringing away, or a French bourgeois on his feet . . . which is really more foul? I can't honestly make up my mind.

It is always going to be possible to appeal to the war-like instincts of the ordinary Frenchmen, especially as their women are only too glad to see them off at the Gare de l'Est:

Vous pouvez partir tranquilles . . . vous serez remplacés dans vos boulots promptement, dans vos maisons et dans vos lits . . . la femme, surtout la Française, raffole des crépus, des Abyssins, ils vous ont des bites surprenantes! . . . Cocus des tranchées, pauvre viande "kachère"! vous ne serez pas oubliés vous serez pompés, happés, déglutis, fondus dans la Victoire juive . . . On vous arrangera en pensions pour les veuves bien consentantes! . . . (p. 60)

You can go off without worry . . . you'll be promptly replaced in your jobs, your homes and in your beds . . . Women, especially Frenchwomen, admire men with fuzzy hair, Abyssinians, my dear, they have surprising cocks! . . . Trench cuckolds, poor Kosher meat, you won't be forgotten! You'll be sucked up, snatched up, swallowed up, absorbed into the Jewish Victory . . . There'll be pension arrangements for the willing widows! . . .

If Céline were dictator he would pass a law consisting of three simple clauses: (1) All male Jews from seventeen to sixty to be attached at the outbreak of war to front-line infantry units. None of these conscripts to rise above the rank of captain. (2) No other employment than first-line infantryman to be permitted to any Jew in wartime. (3) Any breach of these enactments punishable by death. He goes on to explain all this by saying:

Mon petit décret, voyez-vous, de mobilisation du juif, de son affectation très stricte, n'est pas une petite rigolade . . . Bien compris, bien admis, bien assimilé par nos youtres, il peut donner des résultats dont vous serez grandement surpris, tout à fait précieux, providentiels, nous évitant, quel miracle, de participer, à toute viande, au plus grandiose charnier des âges . . . qui ne demande qu'à fonctionner . . . qui hurle déjà devant nos portes. (p. 63)

My little law, mind you, about mobilization of the Jew, his strict posting, it's not at all a joke . . . Well understood, well accepted, well assimilated by our jewboys, it can give results (which would surprise you a lot) of a most valuable providential kind, preventing us, what a miracle, from taking part, with all our flesh, in the vastest slaughter of all time . . . which is only too ready to get going . . . which is screaming already at our doors.

This is, of course, an old, charming and Utopian notion—here applied to the Jews—but more usually directed at politicians: would heads of state and their civil service and diplomatic advisers be so willing to engage their countries in war if the immediate consequences for the whole lot of them was front-line infantry service in the ranks? The "if" is too big for there to be any reasonable answer, but the question retains its propaganda value. And Céline gives his version of the idea — predictably — in effective slogan form " 'Un Juif par créneau' . . . telle est ma devise pour la guerre prochaine" (p. 63) (" 'One Jew per battlement' . . . that's my slogan for the next war").

But as Céline is not dictator, and since his law will never be passed the conclusion is:

> En définitive, Français "Cocoricos,"[8] vous partirez à la guerre, à l'heure choisie par M. le Baron de Rothschild, votre seigneur et maître absolu . . . à l'heure fixée, en plein accord, avec ses cousins souverains de Londres, de New-York et Moscou. C'est lui, M. de Rothschild, qui signera votre Decret de Mobilisation Générale, par la personne interposée, par la plume tremblotante de son pantin-larbin-ministre. (p. 177)

> In fact, "cock-a-doodle-doo" Frenchmen, you'll go off to war at the moment chosen by M. le baron de Rothschild, your lord and absolute master . . . at the hour fixed, in full accord with his sovereign cousins in London, New York and Moscow. It's M. de Rothschild, he, who will sign your decree of General Mobilization, via the intermediary, via the quivering pen of his puppet-lackey-minister.

Now we are very conscious in this day and age of the feeling that we have little or no control over our destinies in this area — even under a beautiful system of parliamentary democracy — that the really important decisions are probably not even taken by the politicians, so why bother to elect them? . . . How skilfully does Céline exploit this regrettable feeling!

He only needs to add one further notion — that which came out in 1938 in the form of "Why die for Czechoslovakia?" or in 1939 as "Why die for Danzig?" Near the end of the volume he expounds this in very succinct form, and at the same time ties it in with his anti-semitism and his reasons for wanting an alliance with Germany. This section of *Bagatelles* (pp. 192–3) contains by far the most compromising material in the book: the summary which follows gives a run-down of the "ideas" therein together with the most damaging remarks. He would not mind at all if Hitler attacked Russia. The number of Russian victims would not be greater than those liquidated by Stalin in peacetime. So let him take the Ukraine, Czechoslovakia and Romania too if he wants, so long as he leaves us in peace.

> Moi je voudrais bien faire une alliance avec Hitler. Pourquoi pas? Il a rein dit contre les Bretons, contre les Flamands . . . Rien du tout . . . Il a dit seulement sur les Juifs . . . il les aime pas les Juifs . . . Moi non plus . . . J'aime pas les nègres hors de chez eux . . . C'est tout. . . . Je veux

pas faire la guerre pour Hitler, moi je le dis, mais je ne veux pas la faire contre lui, pour les Juifs. . . .

I'd very much like to make an alliance with Hitler. Why not? He's said nothing against the Bretons, against the Flemish . . . Nothing at all . . . He's only said things about the Jews . . . He doesn't like the Jews . . . Nor do I . . . I don't like negroes away from their own country . . . that's all. . . . I don't want to go to war for Hitler, no, I don't, but I don't want to go to war against him, for the Jews. . . .

To the objection that an alliance with Hitler would be dangerous because of the superior strength of Germany he replies that Hitler would be fully occupied for years in coping with his conquests in Eastern Europe. Moreover even if that were not so "Deux millions de boches campés sur nos territoires pourront jamais etre pires, plus ravageurs, plus infamants que tous ces Juifs dont nous crevons" ("Two million Boches camped in our territory will never possibly be worse, more predatory, more shameful than all these Jews who are destroying us"). He would prefer twelve Hitlers to one Blum — "Hitler encore je pourrais le comprendre, tandis que Blum c'est inutile" ("Hitler I could still understand, whereas with Blum it's not worth trying").

At this point his interlocutor — here Gustin — asks him if he wants to kill all the Jews. The answer is no, but that if there is a war they should be among the victims. Expanding on this, he is led to make what is perhaps the most crude statement of the whole work:

. . . un seul ongle de pied pourri, de n'importe quel vinasseux ahuri truand d'Aryen, vautré dans son dégueulage, vaut encore cent mille fois plus, et cent mille fois davantage et de n'importe quelle façon à n'importe quel moment, que cent vingt-cinq mille Einsteins, debout, tout dérétinisants d'effarante gloire rayonnante. . . .[9]

. . . a single nail off the stinking foot of no matter what wine-sodden, dazed Aryan tramp, wallowing in his vomit, is worth a hundred thousand times more, and one hundred thousand times more again in any way you like and at any moment, than one hundred and twenty-five thousand Einsteins upright, all dazzling with startling radiant glory.

No wonder certain contemporaries wondered whether Céline was not trying to ridicule anti-semitism! Gide in his NRF article in April 1938 already referred to . . . came very close to the truth when he said:

Céline excelle dans l'invective. Il l'accroche à n'importe quoi. La juiverie n'est ici qu'un prétexte qu'il a choisi le plus épais possible, le plus trivial, le plus reconnu, celui qui se moque le plus volontiers des nuances, qui permet les jugements les plus sommaires, les exagérations les plus énormes, le moindre souci de l'équité, le plus intempérant laisser-aller de la plume. Et Céline n'est jamais meilleur que lorsqu'il est le moins mesuré. C'est un créateur. Il parle des Juifs, dans *Bagatelles*, tout comme il parlait, dans *Mort à crédit*, des asticots que sa force évocatrice venait de créer.[10]

Céline excels at invective. He hangs it on to anything. Jewry is here no more than a pretext, chosen by him as the most stupid possible, the most vulgar, the best known, that which most willingly derides subtleties, which allows the most summary judgements, the most enormous exaggerations, the least concern for equity, the most intemperate insouciance of the pen. And Céline is never better than when he is the least measured. He is a creator. He talks about the Jews in *Bagatelles*, just in the way he talked in *Mort à crédit* about the maggots that his evocative power had created.

I think Gide is quite right about the deliberate and provocative exaggerations of Céline's invective: they should not be taken too literally. But, I fear, he is wrong when he takes anti-semitism to be merely a kind of pretext for Céline—it was more than that. Indeed, long after Céline had dropped his anti-semitism, he holds on to certain "scientific" notions about race, still for polemical reasons, in order to demonstrate that the supremacy of the white man is over and that the future lies with the Chinese. . . .[11]

This point of view is beginning to emerge in *Bagatelles*—though here only used against the French—and it is with some remarks about this that I conclude on the subject of this book. What Céline probably wished to leave as the major impression at the end of the work was neither the desirability of anti-semitism, nor the fear of coming war, nor the need for an alliance with Germany to prevent that war, but rather his demonstration of the decadence and hypocrisy of the France of the period. The final sequences of *Bagatelles* are a kind of pendant to the opening section, where there is what he calls a "Baedeker" evocation of his stay in Leningrad, and also a final ballet scenario (pp. 200–226). The author takes formal leave of his public on p. 200—". . . Grande révérence . . . Grand féerie . . . Je vous salue! Votre serviteur! . . ." (". . . Big bow! . . . Big enchantment! . . . Greetings! Your humble servant! . . .")— immediately after a last conversation with his Jewish friend Gutman (Gide in the article just quoted considers this dialogue to be "des mieux réussis"). Gutman suggests to Ferdinand that he is on a very dangerous tack, that he will only make enemies for himself—and that he has gone about things in quite the wrong way. Instead of attacking and insulting his fellow countrymen, he should handle them as the Jews do, much more tactfully. "Regarde un peu les indigènes, les Juifs ne les contrarient jamais eux . . ." ("Look at the natives a bit, the Jews never upset them at all . . .") It is not necessary to do so because the natural French instinct down the ages has been to adore their conquerors, to present their arses for willing penetration—beginning with the Romans: "Ils s'en congratulent encore à 18 siècles de distance! . . . Toute la Sorbonne en jubile! . . . Ils en font tout leur bachot de cette merveilleuse enculade! . . ." (p. 197) ("They are still congratulating themselves about it 18 centuries later! . . . The entire Sorbonne exults over it! They construct their entire *bachot* examination out of this wonderful sodomization! . . .").

This being so, they can surely make do for now with a Jewish prick instead:

> Le paf de youtre c'est bas, j'admets! dans la série animale, mais enfin quand même, ça bouge . . . Ça vaut bien une bite d'Empereur mort? . . . Puisque c'est le destin des Français de se faire miser dans le cours des âges . . . puisqu'ils passent d'un siècle à l'autre . . . d'une bite d'étrusque sur une bite maure . . . sur un polard de ritain . . . Une youtre gaule ou une saxonne? . . . Ça fait pas beaucoup de différence! (p. 197)

> A Yiddish cock is pretty low I admit! in the animal kingdom, but at least it moves . . . It's better than the prick of a dead emperor? . . . Since it's the destiny of the French down the ages to have it up themselves . . . since they pass from one century to the next . . . from an Etruscan prick onto a Moorish prick . . . onto an Italian tool . . . a Jewish rod or a Saxon? Doesn't make much difference!

With this Ferdinand agrees. More than that, he underlines the same point, and gives — for the first time — his view of the future for the French:

> A présent, en pleine décadence, faut se faire étreindre par des larvaires . . . se contenter de ce qui reste . . . Mais plus on se fait foutre . . . plus on demande . . . Et puis voilà qu'on leur promet aux Français, des bourreaux tartares! . . . Des tortureurs impitoyables! . . . Et puis des Mongols! . . . encore plus haineux! . . . plus bridés! . . . Qui croquent la terre et les vermines . . . Ah! comme ils vont nous traverser! . . . Et puis d'autres, plus chinois encore! plus jaunes! . . . plus verts . . . C'est la vie des anges par le pot! . . . Ils nous tuent . . . Voilà comme ils disent les Français! (pp. 198–9)

> At present, in full period of decadence, the only thing to do is to be screwed by a few grubs . . . make do with what's available . . . But the more you get fucked . . . the more you want . . . Well, here's what is promised for the French. Tartar executioners! . . . pitiless torturers! . . . And then some Mongols . . . even more full of hatred . . . more constricted! . . . Who eat soil and vermin . . . Ah! How hard they're going to ram it up us! . . . And then others, still more Chinese looking! yellower! . . . tougher! . . . Paradise via the arse! . . . They're killing us . . . That's what the French are saying.

The whole of this uproarious passage is well sustained . . . Céline was not homosexual, and the choice here of the image of sodomy is part of the triumphant sarcasm of his final address to his compatriots in 1937, an image of the humiliation which he thought they deserved. Being cruel to be kind? A kind of political suicide? Ultimate washing of hands? Elements of all three. There is at present no proposal to reprint *Bagatelles* (or the other two pamphlets). It is easy to see why. But it is totally wrong. No one can fully understand Céline without some knowledge of these works.

I have dealt with *Bagatelles* at some length because it is out of print and virtually inaccessible to most readers, because it is an essential text for the understanding of Céline, and because, despite the disagreeable and sometimes even disgraceful material to be found in it, it is for the most part magnificently written and deserves the description given by Charles Plisnier in a review of it in 1938: "Eh bien! vu ainsi—purement et simplement sous l'angle littéraire—*Bagatelles pour un massacre* est un chef d'oeuvre de la plus haute classe. Un chef d'oeuvre et un tour de force.[12] ("Well, seen thus—from a purely and simply literary stand point—*Bagatelles pour un massacre* is a masterpiece of the highest order. A masterpiece and a virtuoso turn").

Notes

1. He does not, however, indulge in the ultimate hypocrisy of saying "Some of my best friends are Jews." [Page references are to *Bagatelles pour un massacre* (Paris: Denoël & Steele, 1937)—editor's note.]

2. Though we might have to admit that the combined efforts of Arab propaganda and Israeli policies *might* find him an audience again nowadays in some quarters.

3. Gide bore him no grudge, and indeed was one of the few critics to see the literary qualities of *Bagatelles*. In his article about it *(La Nouvelle Revue Française,* April, 1938, reproduced in *Cahiers de l'Herne* pp. 468–70), he says, for instance, "Et Ferdinand de s'emporter jusqu'au plus étourdissant lyrisme; ses griefs s'étalent et sa hargne, pour le plus grand amusement de lecteur" ("And Ferdinand proceeds to indulge in the most astonishing lyricism; his grudges emerge and his bitterness, to the greatest amusement of the reader"). Perhaps a pedantic note is reasonable here. The "hesitations" of Gide alluded to here date back to the 1890s (see *Si le grain ne meurt,* pub. 1926), and when Gide began his communist flirtation—c. 1930—he was sixty-one and not eighty. . . . Céline is behaving like a journalist here in fact!

4. It is noticeable that Céline uses—flippantly and derisively—references to sodomy very frequently in *Bagatelles*. There's no real suggestion anywhere that he was homosexual, though he certainly found the subject of homosexuality of some physiological interest. In *Bagatelles* he finds it convenient to provoke laughter on the subject.

5. For *x* read "aryenne": for *y* "juif" or "juifs."

6. See Zbinden interview (Radio Lausanne); reproduced Pléïade, vol. II, pp. 936–45. [Thomas refers to the Pléïade critical editions of Céline's work—editor's note.]

7. See again Zbinden interview (Radio Lausanne); reproduced Pléïade, vol. II, pp. 936–45; see also above, p. 24, note 4 (quotation from this interview). [The following is note 4 on p. 24 from Thomas's book—editor's note.]

He said of this period in a radio interview in 1957 (see Pléïade, vol. II. p. 939): "Alors voilà, n'est-ce pas: je me suis pris pour Louis xv ou pour Louis xiv, c'est évidemment une erreur profonde. Alors que je n'avais qu'à rester ce que je suis et tout simplement me taire. *Là j'ai péché par orgueil, je l'avoue, par vanité, par bêtise. Je n'avais qu'à me taire . . . ce sont des problèmes qui dépassaient de beaucoup.* Je suis né à l'époque ou l'on parlait encore de l'affaire Dreyfus. Tout ça c'est une vraie bêtise dont je fais les frais" (author's italics) "Well you see, I suppose I took myself for Louis xv or Louis xiv and clearly I was deeply wrong. Because all I had to do was to remain what I am and keep my trap shut. *Guilty of the sin of pride is what I was, I admit, through vanity and stupidity.* I only had to keep my trap shut . . . *they were problems that were far beyond me.* I was born at a time when people were still talking about the Dreyfus affair. The whole thing was crass stupidity and I'm paying for it now").

8.   = chauvinist

9. This because of Einstein's openly professed Zionism.

10. Gide goes on to quote part of the passage in *Mort à crédit* — p. 1009 — about the *asticots* at Blême-le-Petit.

11. See, for example, *Rigodon.*

12. In *L'Indépendance Belge* (19 March 1938).

Why Professor Y?   Stanford Luce*

Despite the seeming nonsense of my title — one might as well ask "Who is Doctor Who?" — it does present a legitimate question. The reference is to Céline's fictional interview with Professor Y in a Paris park where he explains what literature, in his view, is all about.

Originally created in 1955, the professor was the inept end man for Céline's ridicule of professional writers. He is called upon to record the attack on academic formalists. The latter were pompous and pale; they described human emotion from their observation of it in other books. If they had experienced emotion in their own lives they failed to admit it, and thus avoided the challenge of converting raw emotions into literature. Reality was not for them; they copied. As for Céline, he had sought out many ways to experience life: he followed his passions from Moscow to California, Denmark to the Cameroons; he survived the anguish of war, the subtle ways of diplomacy — so discrete from his own nature — at the League of Nations; he had exulted in the study and practice of medicine, and acquired an intimate familiarity with the poor. Unlike most others, he had earned what he wrote about from all these personal encounters with life. Perhaps this brought him to know people too well; he came to recognize their ignorance and insensitivity, the sham, violence, and illusions that misled mankind and that turned the author toward an angry cynicism on the one hand and an appreciation of how authentic emotions could lay bare the stuff of life on the other.

When World War II broke out and Céline's deep anti-Semitism had been exposed to the reading public, he felt obliged to seek safety in Copenhagen and to accept there what was to become nearly seven years of exile. By 1951 his earlier public was decimated yet still hostile; a new generation had gone through school never having heard of the writer; his

*This essay was written for this volume and appears here with permission of the author.

royalties virtually dried up. When he at last returned to Paris, his publisher Gallimard suggested that he play the "publicity game" in order to attract attention to his return to the world of literature. This provocative interview with Professor Y is how he interpreted that suggestion to "play the game." Here he assembled all his thoughts on what literature should be. Since its recent republication in a bilingual English/French format entitled *Conversations with Professor Y*, Céline has at last been able to explain to English readers — albeit posthumously — just where he stands on the art of writing. In *Conversations* we can see both why he wrote in his highly idiosyncratic style and witness an actual demonstration of how he created turbulent emotions out of objects and actions as he transposed them from life onto the printed page. The parodic interview in the park with this so-called academic ends up with a wild spree where, thwarted and sloshed, the professor runs amok through the streets of Paris and is finally deposited in the courtyard of the Gallimard publishing house, beaten and battered, to sleep off his binge and await payment for his interview. Such a heady example of Célinism cannot blithely be set aside. But the basic question of this article still remains: why is the Professor simply called "Y"?

According to the text, Céline had great difficulty finding anyone who would interview him. There still lingered about him a bitter taste of the anti-Semitism that had poured out of his prewar pamphlets. In them Céline had deliberately set out to alienate everyone from him: all classes of society, all men of power; his epigraph to the first pamphlet, *Mea Culpa* (1936), seemed to be a statement of intent: "I am still missing the hatred of a few others. They must exist." Now, since no one wished to become contaminated by association with this persona non grata, every potential interviewer insisted on anonymity. Professor X might have been more expected as a name under the circumstances. But it was Professor Y. Why?

An easy assumption was that Professor X would have sounded too much like a cliché; the unknown is always identified as *x*. Perhaps the solution to such a minor dilemma would have been to substitute a different letter, but if any self-respecting writer were to do so he would certainly have been able to justify its selection. One obvious reason for the letter Y, at least to the English reader, is the sound of the word "why." Céline was quite competent in our language and occasionally borrowed some terms for use in his novels, but the question does not reflect the professor's nature. He was not an inquisitive sort and certainly had no insatiable thirst for knowledge. That sort of an interpretation would contradict what we are led to expect of the man, or even of the book's title. Suppose we were to move from meaning to a pictorial representation of the Y? Taking the shape of the letter as a stick drawing, for instance, it might represent a holdup, a tree, a fork, a wineglass, or even more fanciful suggestions, but none seems helpful in this context. True the professor does overindulge at the bar, but that hardly justifies the wineglass, for instance, and certainly does not illuminate the general thrust of Céline's literary apology.

Another tack might be to consider the letter as an abbreviation or initial. If it were a commonly used letter the identity of the whole word or name would be impossible to establish with any degree of probability. An uncommon letter, however, would be relatively simple to identify, and in French the letter Y is rarely found at the beginning of a word. Some half-dozen of the best known include foreign words such as *yacht*, *yankee*, *yoga*, *yoghourt*, *yo-yo*, or *yucca*, none of which seems particularly significant for our purposes. There are also an equal number of words, all offensive, which indicate the Jew: *yite*, *youde*, *youdi*, *youpin*, *youtre*, *youtron*. Given Céline's record, this group merits further attention. He had been badly burned by the scandal surrounding his pamphlets, and he was in no position to gratuitously insult the Jew once more by portraying him in this quite thankless role of a narrow-minded, unimaginative scapegoat. On the other hand, the letter Y by itself could not become grounds for further prosecution.

It seems fair to assume that his anti-Semitic sentiments would scarcely have calmed down during seven years of cheerless exile which were due almost entirely, as a matter of fact, to his own passionate racism. The Y, without compromising the author—the letter was simply one beyond X—must have helped to assuage his smolder; one can imagine the smug satisfaction he felt at poking mildly at the Jew again, yet this time from a position of relative security. The violent ending where Céline literally pummels the professor into unconsciousness—if he in fact represents the Jew—seems a final catharsis of racist urges released in fictional form. One can imagine as well the pleasure Céline might derive from having a Jew unwittingly help to reestablish him in the literary field where his greatest strength lay. Professor Y was lured on like Jason to sow the dragon's teeth.

The hypothesis of Y referring to the Jew, perhaps even one particular Jew, is not all that farfetched. As a matter of fact, many of the seeds of *Conversations* can be found in the short but revealing exchange of letters that took place between Céline and an American Jew who befriended him during his years of exile in Denmark. The man was Milton Hindus, a young scholar and teacher of English literature at the University of Chicago and Brandeis University. He was fascinated by Céline's early novels, both for their content and for their form. Choosing to overcome the disappointment he felt when the author revealed his anti-Semitism, Hindus initiated the correspondence that was ultimately to include some ninety letters from each. In the course of this relationship the Frenchman clarified his feelings about literature in general and specifically spelled out the goals that he sought to achieve: an original style, a clear-sightedness that left no room for self-deception, and the transposition of reality with all its emotions from spoken language to its written form.

Each man had something to offer the other: Hindus was interested in developing a relationship with one of the most controversial writers of the thirties. And for the first time in his life, Céline himself felt compelled to cry out for help; his situation was perilous, his resources were declining, the French boycott of his works prevented him from continuing his career as a publishing writer.

The warmth and mutual flattery that were present in their early letters were most effective. Céline seemed pleased to have attracted the admiration and assistance of this American scholar. "I want you to know how much I appreciate your kindness to us in our need," he wrote. "And with such flair! Everything you do has been conceived, noted, judged so masterfully that nothing is left in doubt."[1] Even after their catastrophic meeting in 1948 Céline responds sincerely to Hindus's reporting his visit to Mme Destouches's grave in Paris: "Nothing could have touched me more deeply than your affectionate attention. No one has visited my mother's grave since I left Paris."[2] With that one exception, however, their parting had been cold; subsequent letters were infrequent and unexciting. When Céline heard a few months later that Hindus had written up a report of his experience in *The Crippled Giant*, he was furious and determined to do all in his power—he wrote a letter of protest to the president of Brandeis and even threatened suit—to block its publication. Hindus decided to proceed with the publication nonetheless, and happily for him no suit materialized. The rankling memory of that affair seems to have lingered unabated in Céline's mind, however, for some seven years later the title of Hindus's work reappears though in slightly altered form in *Conversations with Professor Y*. The American was probably the intended target, it was his turn to become the "crippled monster" with its reference to the phony emotionalism of maudlin writers. Apparently Céline felt more willing to bestow the quality of a "monster" than the stature of a giant.

Unable to publish his work while in exile, Céline wrote letters, often as many as ten a day. But nowhere else did he elaborate so extensively the rules that shaped his literary work as in the Céline–Hindus correspondence. Not only are the basic premises of his craft to be found there, but also the imagery, examples, sometimes even the phrasing that appear later on in *Conversations with Professor Y*. The letters and the book are so intimately related that to call one to mind inevitably leads to the thought of the other; the parallels are real and frequent.

Only the first letter was lost to the formalities of introduction. The two men very shortly got to the business at hand, discussion of things literary. Céline writes of style, the rendering of emotion through the immediacy of spoken language, the avoidance of pretty phrasing, academic forms. "I seize emotion raw, or better yet poetically, for Man is really, deep down inside, nothing but poetry. . . . And then a special gimmick to convert spoken language to the written form. One must deform the sentences just the least bit so when you read them it seems as though someone were speaking right into your ear";[3] "In a word I hate prose . . . I am a poet and would-be musician . . . getting the message straight through to the nervous system is what counts . . . prattle bores me to death!"[4] He goes on to say that the adjustment from oral to written language is like correcting for the refraction of a stick plunged into water simply by bending it, ever so precisely, so that once in the water it will appear straight. He links this to literature by saying: "To pin down on a page the effect of spontaneous life as it is narrated, you must twist language in its rhythms, cadence, and words, a sort of poetry produces the finest enchantment—the impression, the charm, the dynamism—and then, too, the choice of subject becomes critical. Not everything can be transposed. You have to pluck the raw edge of a nerve."[5] Céline claims this is also the secret of Impressionism, spontaneous, dynamic, touching the quick, the song of colors.[6]

He returns to this theme later on, insisting on the difficulty of the act of transposing, and rightly so. In a letter of 17 October 1947 he further elaborated his meaning with the statement: "It is the 'quick' of the nervous system, the spontaneous harmony, the music of the soul that I am trying to pick up in spoken language and convert to written form. Actually there are few *flashes* in spoken language. I try to seize them and to recreate artificially in writing an ideal spoken language. This is what man tries to do—by the very poetry of his nature—when he speaks." Here he returns to his literary gimmick "to probe the soul of spoken language, by refraction as it were, and steal its secret." Although he was to rework these themes in *Conversations*, he never succeeded in explaining the subtle maneuver more clearly, more meaningfully.

We find discussions in these letters that range from humor and slang to education, movies, and the dance. It would be hard to imagine Céline writing his "poetics" without recalling his correspondence with Milton Hindus. So much of the content of his letters has been repeated in *Conversations* as witness the following snippets: "What gimmick I've invented? Its rediscovering the emotion of spoken language through its written form."[7] He finds it enormously demanding to write the "emotive-yield novel," nor does the cinema manage to pull it off any more readily, for a film has only "canned feelings, it is not sensitive to the wavelength of emotion . . . makes it come out crippled! . . . a crippled monster."[8] When he repeats how in transposing real emotion from spoken language to the written page, he uses the same image as in the letters to explain how the phrases must be ever so gently twisted: "You plunge a stick into the water." But he warns that in order to correct for refraction, "You must break it first. A neat trick! the whole secret of Impressionism!"[9]

His task as he continued to explain it to Hindus was to transpose, resensitize the written form, dredge language back out of the slough of academics, making it pulse rather than reason: "I am a writer of style, a colorist with words, but unlike Mallarmé and his exotic rarities, I use only everyday words. Neither vulgarity nor sexuality play a role here, they are but props."[10] When discussing contemporary literary figures or issues, many appear first in the correspondence to reappear in the *Conversations*. Céline linked together François Mauriac and Paul Claudel — "that super-hypocrite"[11] — as two weathervanes turning in the political winds of the day. He claims both were "coddled by the Nazis,"[12] yet with no adverse repercussions on their postwar reputations. They had adroitly, with excellent timing, altered their public image to that of anticommunists. Mauriac "was to pick up Claudel . . . they were both going to head east! . . . where they would set up a resistance! . . . together! with swords! the works! 'We didn't make it in '14! We'll be there in '74!' . . . to head east, got to go down the Champs-Elysées! . . . if people were around! . . . they recruited! . . . passed out weathervanes for free! and the Théâtre Français crowd bore them along in triumph! . . . for the sake of their wealth, their piety and their goddam resourcefulness!"[13] In the letters to Hindus, Claudel was also compared to Proust, although for the latter's syntax, not his piety. "Proust irritates me with his finicking — that overelaborated way of his — Latinate, Germanized, Judaic — (à la Claudel) — those sentences nipping at their own tails after endless twistings and turns. It all reeks of impotence."[14] It is "archeology, proustiana, work with neither head nor tail."[15]

When discussing realism, Céline lays claims to an intimate knowledge of the subject: "Twenty-seven years of daily medical practice have taught me more than I care to know about raw realism." He goes on to say that unless it is skillfully transposed onto the page it becomes dull, lifeless. "Realism must be made to sing."[16] And: "Truth is no longer enough for me. I need to transpose *everything* . . . if it doesn't sing it doesn't exist for the soul — shit on reality. I want to die with music, not reason or prose."[17] "In short, to be acceptable realism must be lyrical, poignant."[18] Except for poets like Villon, lyricism has few French writers to represent it: "All the Sartre, Camus and Green deliriums are products of the mind."[19] Céline himself steers clear of reason: "I don't broadcast messages to the world . . . not me, no sir! I don't clutter up the air with my thoughts."[20]

In *Conversations* there are numerous references, all pejorative, to the rational perception of realism that allows no room for emotion as it is felt, only as it can be logically structured to fit a logically structured world. As for surrealism, Céline demonstrates absolutely no sympathy: "Surrealism . . . is a fabricated delirium, intentionally created with agreed upon rules, but it is a simulation without echo, without heart — nothing whatsoever."[21] Only Impressionism wins his approval, even though not originally a literary movement, for it developed goals like those we have shown the author to have. Quotations in support of that position can be found in both works.[22] As a further item, note how his fear of ultimate punishment never seems to leave him: "France has always treated its authors very badly (as did the Greeks), at some time or other executioners threatened their life."[23] And: "The true life of the true artist is a long or short game of hide-and-seek with prison . . . the scaffold, however awesome it might seem, will fix him up but good . . . the scaffold, so to speak, awaits the artist!"[24]

In *Conversations* can be found additional comments on topics that are first mentioned in the letters to Hindus. The later version develops in finer detail the failings of modern education, the duplicity of idea-mongers, the tawdry taste of the public, the penchant for maudlin sentiments. With a Rousseau-like fillip, he writes to Hindus that education snips the student's poetic thread.[25] He adds that all one learns in the school room is to play with oneself and to copy others. Céline had already developed the metro metaphor in mid-May of 1947 when he writes that there are several ways to move about in Paris. One "consists in taking the subway, going straight to your destination *by the very intimacy of things* but that doesn't happen without impressing on a person's thought pattern a certain melodious lilt, a melodic rail . . . *and never drifting away, never derailing at whatever cost.* You must plunge into the nervous system, into emotion, until arriving at your station. Transposing spoken language into written language is no easy task." *Conversations* shows this theme in a more highly developed form yet with the same basic concept: "the emotive subway, my way! without all the inconvenience, traffic jams! in a dream! . . . never the slightest pause, anywhere! . . . just straight on, right through, non-stop! in emotion! . . . through emotion! heading for the goal: full emotion . . . start to finish."[26]

This comparison of quotations is sufficient to show how greatly the two productions by Céline resemble each other. The abrupt end of their warm, admiring relationship during Hindus's visit to Korsor in 1948 seems to have continued as open hostility, at least from Céline's point of view. The thoughtful "respects" Hindus had paid to Céline's mother did not offer more than a brief moment of thaw, despite the American's continuing to arrange for monthly packages of coffee and nylons to be sent to Denmark through an intermediary. At length Hindus's hesitation brought him to confront the intransigent antagonism of his former friend, and he determined to treat him accordingly, saying what he honestly felt, calling a spade a spade, when it came to assessing the French writer in *The Crippled Giant.* Even so, of course, compared to Céline's fury and threats of lawsuit to prevent publication of the work, Hindus's "outrage" was of a very gentle sort, couched in tones of anxious civility. The following year it was translated and republished in France under the title of *Céline tel que je l'ai vu.* As mentioned, the suit was never filed, but Céline's anger was no doubt stiffened, his plan for at least muted revenge must have seemed sweet.

The character known at first as Professor Y managed to reveal during the course of the interviews that he was in fact a retired army colonel by the name of Reseda. The word *reseda* assumes an interesting quality when we take into consideration the fact that Céline, after Hindus had sent a photograph of himself, expressed a certain curiosity about the family name "Hindus" and even inquired whether in fact he was of Hindu ancestry—the answer was negative. Be that as it may, the reseda is a flowering plant that grows, according to *La Grande Encyclopédie*, around the Mediterranean basin, spreading through the dry regions of North Africa and specifically as far east as Hindustan. Céline would not normally be expected to know this were it not for the fact that the plant had been used as a sedative—hence its name—and also in the reduction of tumors. It is likely enough that as Dr. Destouches he would have come across this information during his medical studies and might well have inserted into his interview both the Y for a Jew, and the Reseda with its Hindu association to complete the veiled but plausible reference to Milton Hindus.

When *Conversations* appeared, although obviously nothing can be proved in black and white, it is quite reasonable to assume that the creation and naming of Professor Y grew out of the unhappy history of their relationship. It is certain that Céline was capable of such a prank. Professor Y/Colonel Reseda continues to be a bumbling, abject, prostate-ridden military man and is scarcely a person with whom Hindus would gratefully accept identification, even if the "honor" would immortalize him throughout literary history as one of Céline's foils. At all events, as far-reaching as the honor might be, it seems too dubious for Hindus who, to date, has graciously declined all claim to such a posterity.

Notes

1. *L'Herne* (Paris: Minard, 1972), 109.
2. Ibid., 135.
3. Ibid., 111.
4. Ibid., 114.
5. Ibid., 111.
6. Ibid., 111–12.
7. *Conversations with Professor Y*, trans. Stanford Luce (Hanover: University Press of New England, 1986), 16.
8. Ibid., 20.
9. Ibid., 114.
10. *L'Herne*, 113.
11. Ibid., 127.
12. Ibid., 111.
13. *Conversations*, 74.
14. *L'Herne*, 115.
15. *Conversations*, 10.
16. *L'Herne*, 115.
17. Ibid., 118.
18. *Conversations*, 60.

19. *L'Herne*, 116.
20. *Conversations*, 14.
21. *L'Herne*, 116.
22. Ibid., 111–12; *Conversations*, 113.
23. *L'Herne*, 114.
24. *Conversations*, 4.
25. *L'Herne*, 115.
26. *Conversations*, 92.

THE TRILOGY AND
FÉERIE

"So you call yourself a chronicler?"
"Exactly!"
"Without a qualm?"
"Don't exasperate me!"

—*North*

. . . . in those moments when the page turns, when History brings all the nuts together and opens its Epic Dance Halls! . . .

—*Castle To Castle*

Céline's Last Journey: An Essay after the Publication of *Rigodon* in 1969

Jean-Guy Rens and
Bill Tierney*

1969 was again Céline's year in French Literature. His final unedited novel, *Rigodon* (finished in 1961, the year of his death) was published by Gallimard, and once again re-established Céline's reputation as one of the great French novelists. It was a reminder of the explosion of *Voyage au bout de la nuit* into the literary world of 1932. Céline's last voyage is finished.

What does *Rigodon* mean? The Larousse dictionary gives the following definition: "Rigodon: a lively air or dance in double-time, originating in Provence, popular in the seventeenth and eighteenth centuries." It adds another meaning. In the jargon of the veteran fighters of the 1st World War, *Rigodon* means a direct hit, a bomb on target. It has the two meanings, bombs on target and dance. The title of the book captures its contents in the ambiguity of its title. In fact, *Rigodon* is a description of Germany in 1944, and, in the middle of this chaos, a jerky account of a long and complicated journey made by Céline himself, Céline *the chronicler of the Great Puppets*. The novel is the last part of a trilogy describing the oscillations of the year 1944–5. *D'un château l'autre* (1957), the first part, presented the life of the French exiles at Sigmaringen.[1] *Nord* (1960), the middle section of the trilogy, takes place in Eastern Prussia among uncontrollable hordes of Poles, Ukranians, conscientious objectors, gypsies and random vagabonds. *Rigodon* (1969), is, by contrast, not rooted in any one place. It relates a train journey from Mursburg to Warnemünde to Sigmaringen, passing through Berlin; from Sigmaringen to Oddort, to Hamburg, and finally to Copenhagen. With detours and mishaps, Céline relates his flight towards Denmark through the dying agonies of the Third Reich. This novel is centered on a train, or rather a succession of wretched ancient trains which never seem to be making any progress. They drag themselves through ruined stations in ravaged country, through bombardment, and through starving mobs who all want to escape . . . But where

*Reprinted with permission from the *Antigonish Review* 2, no. 1 (Spring 1971):39–59. Translated by Sylvia Díez and Annie Déjardin.

to? To the West, to the South? Céline leaves every man to his own whim. For himself it is the North. In particular Denmark. He is going to recover the savings he had hidden there before the war. He is accompanied by his wife, Lili, by Bébert the cat, and La Vigue, the film star who later betrays his companions to head for Rome and the South. With these fellow travellers Céline rediscovers his old passion for *journeying*.

The journey idea may be a key to the success of the novel. For Céline, travel is a meaningful adventure with a philosophical dimension. It is also strongly associated with a man in full flight and with man being hounded. For him, to move forward in the argument, Man is forced to flee by the evil he finds in the world; and his prose is at its best in descriptions of *flight*. His stuttering syntax mirrors the movements of unreasoned precipitate travel. From *Le voyage au bout de la nuit* to *Rigodon* the circle of journeying in Céline's work is drawn into geometric unity. The last novel brings Céline back to his point of departure. Furthermore, along the circumference of the circle his style has been completely remoulded.

The Style between the Two Journeys — *Voyage* (1932) to *Rigodon*

Céline's style evolved dramatically from his first to his last novels. In Céline's first novel the structure is composed of highly organised sentences with several clauses and many adjectives. In *Mort à Crédit* (1936), the clear logical syntax is done away with, and in its place Céline employs slang and a wide range of vulgar words and expressions. Céline's innovations aim at rejuvenating a judicious French language which had been enervated by nearly four centuries of Classical restraint. For example, the renowned three pause dots . . . replace conjunctions and other linkage devices. Again, after *Bagatelles pour un massacre* (1937) neologisms like *tragedic, agonic and djiboukerie* and startling gigantic exaggerations become an important element in Céline's style. In *Guignol's Band* (1944), the first real Célinean tortures appear, with whole pages of words seeming to recall one another without any apodictic care. Furthermore, each novel remedies the clumsiness of the preceding one. For example, slang is much less used in *D'un château l'autre* than in *Mort à Crédit*. Similarly, the resonant gargling of words in *Le Pont de Londres* disappears in the war trilogy. In terms of linguistic adventure, Céline finally discovered a language which is new but, at the same time, free of all the imperfections and exaggerations which were present during its evolution.

There is, however, one difficulty in this renewal of vitality in his language. It is an extremely powerful vehicle of expression, and too strong for a slight theme. So, in *Guignol's Band*, for example, the drama and energy of the language is out of proportion with its subject. The petty problems of the folk of London cannot equal the fresh sap of the style. Similarly, in the three books which labelled Céline as an anti-semite,[2] we could ask how much of the wildness is due to syntactical necessity . . . The extreme passions of anti-semitism seem to be ideal material for Céline's language. As for many other writers, political themes were a means of dramatising language and filling the sentences with provocative power. Céline could have considered the tragedy of his time as an opportunity for *breaking in* his style. Or he may have been so outraged at his impotence in the holocaust that his only answer was the frenzy of passages like this: "I won't entertain any petty confederates or frightened scraps of humanity . . . fleeing beings, scapegoats . . . melting thickheads . . . But look! Not at all! . . . I reject these puffs of air! I want something solid! . . . Realities! . . . I've got a tooth! . . . A huge tooth! . . . A real totalitarian tooth! . . . A world tooth! . . . A revolutionary tooth! . . . A burning cosmic tooth! . . . To mobilize all the bone-houses of the universe! A real divine appetite! Biblical! . . ." (*Bagatelles pour un massacre*). This is a piece of style for style's sake, and the provocation for it is clear. If it hurts: so what? Céline will be the first to be hurt and he knows it. His violent style seems to aim at provoking the event. His story, as he says early in *Mort à Crédit*, seems to call out for retribution. Céline has developed a stylistic instrument which has large possibilities but little chance of fulfillment until themes emerge which measure up to its intensity.

The Embodiment of the Themes

The Second World War revitalised Céline's old themes. This international cataclysm shattered the fragile dreamworld of *Le Voyage au bout de la nuit*, but, strangely, reinforced the old themes by realising them.

In the first place, consider the hero of *Voyage*, Bardamu, a shadow fleeing from his own dreams. Irresistibly, in the course of time, this will o' the wisp character finds himself being outstripped in flesh and blood by Céline himself, who was pursued and persecuted for very real reasons. Any *persecution complex* in Bardamu was well-justified in Céline by the time of *Rigodon*. In his own life, Céline replaced the Romanesque image which he had created in the Thirties, the image of an individual overpowered by a hostile society which he could not understand or master. In 1944, the myth behind *Voyage au bout de la nuit* — the individual a victim of the overpowering instinct to leave everything at regular intervals — became an oppressive reality. The dream metamorphoses into the waking world. For example, the *Infanta Combitta* (a fantastic phantom galley in *Voyage au bout de la nuit*) sheds its ghostly appearance and becomes the train of *Rigodon* passing through the collapse of Germany. "Five . . . six wagons . . . all prickled out you could say with what sticks out . . . hundred arms, hundred legs . . . and heads! and guns! . . ." (*Rigodon*). "The train was crossing the gruel of the Reich," comments Dominique de Roux.[3] Above all, the violence of war, and particularly the collapse of Germany, brought Céline back into the material world. The suffering consciousness of Bardamu gives way to the living actual misery felt in the flesh and in the nerves. The German defeat and the hunt for the conquered are very remote from the surrealistic galleys of Bardamu.

The setting, the backcloth of this new journey, also undergoes a most profound change. The Flemish fields of the First World War, the scenes of colonial life, the U.S.A. and the description of the Parisian Red suburbs are replaced by the Wagnerian Apocalypse of Hitler's Germany. The Millenium of the Reich is a "a sea of flames!" Each stop of the train in *Rigodon* corresponds to one town destroyed: ". . . heaps of wreckage and bits of shops . . . and full of piles of pavings, in sort of mounds . . . trams on top, one in another . . ." (*Rigodon*). The unprecedented fresco of the fall of a Modern Empire is made even more haunting: ". . . on every collapsed house, every mound of wreckage, the flames were dancing green pink in circles! To the heavens!" (*Rigodon*).

The virtues of napalm bombing and the beauty of burning phosphorous were already discovered in the destruction of Germany. Long before Jean-Luc Godard, the protest singers, and the publicity campaigns displaying to politely distressed minds the misfortunes of the Vietnamese peoples bombed with napalm day after day in the name of U.S. freedom, Louis-Ferdinand Céline had focussed his camera on these visions of the end of the world: "broum! vrang! what they let go! the banks and high ramparts of the canal are lit up in bursts . . . red . . . green . . . and these waterfalls of magnesium! oh for a clear vision of a dazzle . . . the two banks! . . . the rise of banks, in ramparts! what's pretty above all are the explosions, the mines which come to shoot up there in giant green flowers . . . red and blue . . ." (*Rigodon*). The towns that suffered then were Hamburg, Hanover, and Kiel, and the poet was in the thick of the bombing, not safely viewing by proxy from New York or Paris. For Céline, it was a far from commercial proposition!

From *Voyage au bout de la nuit* to *Rigodon*, the narrative has realised itself. It has become an *historical reality*. Bardamu is no longer the martyr of humanity held at arm's length by the author. Céline himself has now become his own comic-strip hero, promoted by history, and he tries to exorcise himself through his adventure by making it an enormous caricature. He decides to be Joinville, the old chronicler, telling the story of St. Louis, Punch and Judy style, but he is simultaneously St. Louis the chronicled. He avoids the implications of this change by creating a division between his literary creation and himself. He digs a ditch between the character struggling in the debris of Berlin and the anonymous doctor from Meudon whom he pretends to be. At regular intervals, every two or three chapters, Rigodon's train vanishes and gives way to the sarcastic man from Meudon. This character expounds the end of the world to all who wish to listen: "the Chinese in Brest, the whites in rickshaws, not pulled! in the harness! . . ." (*Rigodon*). This type of digression has, since *D'un château l'autre*, put many critics on the wrong track. It is the product of

Céline's refusal to completely identify himself as the personage he became in his writing.

Nevertheless, this elusiveness and unwillingness to identify himself with his reality did not affect his ability to describe the death of Germany. And it is ironic that the final apocalyptic apotheosis of the Pan-Germanic dream should find *only* a French writer to capture its last flashes.

Céline's Ghosts

Rigodon is continually enriched by the recognition of the author's old phantasms. First of all, the one that stimulates the Célinean myth of *journeying* — the persecution complex. Let's recall that spectacular scene at the beginning of *Voyage au bout de la nuit*. Bardamu is in the deserted touring fairground with his American girlfriend, Lola. They are in front of the shooting gallery. Bardamu suddenly imagines himself to be a target: "They're shooting at me too, Lola! I couldn't stop shouting it out" (*Voyage au bout de la nuit*). Then at the restaurant, at the hotel, and at the window of his room, in fact everywhere the idea of being the target of humanity haunts him. From the first novel, Céline's hero imaginatively poses as a persecuted man and defines himself as a fugitive. These are both characteristic symptoms of persecution mania; and this same obsession can be seen in the frantic race through Hanover behind a coach carrying a paralysed Englishman next to an Italian looking for *hise bosse*, with his wife Lili and several others on board. All this group are being pursued by a howling mob dragging other coaches behind them. Céline jerks to the rhythm of his crutches, and comments in his chopped style: "in short the alarm . . . they're not racing us for caresses! . . . five . . . six coaches . . . no dream! . . ." (*Rigodon*).

The earlier works also contain scenes of riot where rebelling mobs hurled themselves headlong on the solitary individual. In *Mort à crédit*, the inventors rebelled against the bewildering Courtial des Pereires. In *Le pont de Londres*, the prostitutes rioted. In *D'un château l'autre*, Laval[4] affronts the deceit of the Germans. Descriptions of unrestrained crowds abound in Céline's work, and each new mob is more violent, inhuman, and savage than the last. The revolt of the poor people in Hugo's *Notre-Dame de Paris* resembles a formal stylistic exercise next to Céline's vulgar explosions which are as irrational as they are violent. And where Victor Hugo's mobs are halted on the steps of the Cathedral, Céline's crowds break down the door each time, make the words waltz, and scatter the sentences in crumbs.

The particular interest, therefore, of the coach race in *Rigodon* is its pursuing movement and then its conclusion — a collapsed balcony blocking the street. The fugitives are trapped. They are on the verge of being caught by the chasing horde. The flight has ended with a sudden paralysis and the fugitives are caught in an unforeseen impasse. This is a typical image of persecution, and general rather than local in *Rigodon*. It relates to the idea of the hounded man mentioned in the discussion of Céline's style.

Another phantasm in Céline's world is the cracked head. In *Voyage au bout de la nuit*, the nature of Bardamu's war wound is never revealed. After several scenes from the early stages of the First War, he is suddenly convalescing in a hospital. From what kind of wound does he suffer? We are not told. However, two sentences at the end of the military interlude in Paris give a glimpse of what became later a background motif for Céline: "Joking apart, I certainly must admit that I'd never been very strong in the head. But now I had a fit of dizziness at the slightest thing. As easily as anything I might have been under the wheels of a bus" (*Voyage au bout de la nuit*). From the first World War, the references to a wound in the head increased. For example: in 1944 this dialogue appeared in *Guignol's Band*:

> And your head? Did you get a bullet?
> Oh! a very small one! . . .

Even more insistent is this quotation from *Rigodon* where Céline talks "about this biff between the cranium and the neck . . . also higher up to the left ear . . . not make-believe troubles, established very medically, with two . . . three counter-checks . . . since 1916." Céline's biographers almost go to the point of attributing part of Céline's genius to this "biff between the cranium and the neck." Lucien Rebatet describes Céline in these terms: "a good guy, but disabled in the war, in the head (the flaw in his books). . . ."[5] Some critics go further and describe the three pause points as a literary sequel of that wound in the head. In refutation of all these judgements, it has been clearly established that Céline was never wounded in the head. He was wounded, but in the shoulder, and this left him with a slight paralysis in his hand for the remainder of his life.[6]

However, in *Rigodon* the wound in the head recurs. This time it is received during an aerial bombardment of Hanover, and this time the blow is used, by Céline himself, to excuse all his weaknesses, his slips of memory, and his hallucinations. The *biff* acts as an alibi and a cover. In page after page the blow is recalled: "it's the brick that caught me between the head and neck . . . before the brick hit me, shook me, I had no worries . . . let's resume: this blow with the brick didn't suit me . . ." and so on to the end of the book.

In fact, the second blow on the head is followed by a third at Hamburg. There, a whole shop showers onto his head: ". . . and all the trash! my noggan! you'll say: it's rigged . . . No! like the brick . . . no! what a fate for my head! . . . I've got a big block but even so. . . ." This succession of headwounds is imaginary, but that's no discredit to Céline. After all, what is the great value of objective reality? Is it the only reality? Or does the irrational world have its own reality? Céline's work is not limited to the photographic representations of what he sees. For example, this image of the fractured skull is present behind all his work, but it is not a true objective fact. Céline uses it as a device in different ways in his various novels. He consciously directs our attention towards the handicap that limited him in his life and towards the difficulty he had in writing. He spotlights his bad memory when he begs: "pity the poor chronicler."

He pretends to invent nothing when he writes. He tries to convince us by blaming the syncopated rhythm and convulsed impression in his writing on a fractured mind. Céline withdrew from his work, and established his separation from it in the same way that Mohammed refused to give an account of the Koran. Céline posed as a mediator, an intermediary, a medium, a wounded chronicler, a grotesque dotard, crippled by the Apocalypse.

For example, there is the finality of the end of the world in this passage. It is 1945, the end of one world, with U.S.A. and the U.S.S.R. giants of a new world in Europe. A new era has begun: "Europe died at Stalingrad, I don't want to revive anything of it . . ." (*Rigodon*). It makes the same impression as this quotation from Nietzsche's *Thus Spoke Zarathustra*, in his speech on the higher man: "for today the little people lord it, . . . , such absolute ones! they have heavy feet and sultry hearts; they don't know how to dance." In *Rigodon*, in hiccups, a laughable present gushes through each break in the rhythm of the book. Between the two different dance times of the Rigodon, Gulliver abandons the great European night lit up with phosphorous, and turns his sarcastic eyes on the actual world of de Gaulle, the Chinese, and Algeria. Lilliput, it appears, is everywhere.

Clearly, an imaginary fractured skull was an asset for Céline and it could be argued that it was necessary for the time in which he wrote. Perhaps Europe, shattered by bombing, could not have been described by a simple observer. Céline's physical involvement in and reproduction of the catastrophe was, perhaps, a necessary part of his work as a writer. With the dents his head receives, Céline bodily participated in the blows that pounded the heart of Europe, "Then I put my skin on the table . . . ," Céline explained to Louis Pauwels and André Brissaud in an interview. His skin and Europe's life are inextricably knitted into one cause.

Perhaps also the cracked skull has an aesthetic raison d'être. Céline insisted that he was not photographing reality: "the thatched cottages seemed to become artists enough . . . on both sides of the landscape . . . I should say they became pictures, they leaned and rolled . . . especially the chimneys . . . it's a vision, it's a style . . . oh my head is surely responsible for something! . . ." (*Rigodon*). The head wound aesthetically justifies the giddy syntax and the subject. This passage also draws out a reminder of Van Gogh, whose painting style could be a visual impression of Céline's prose. Gide's famous judgement seems to be appropriate: "This is not reality described by Céline; it is the hallucination provoked by reality."[7]

The head wound acts as the objective and neutral cause of the hallucinatory qualities of the narrative. Thus, Céline has avoided moral inconsistency by finding a continuous cause for his style and subject matter.

The fractured skull has multiple and even contradictory significance in Céline's work. It plays an important functional rôle in every department. The witness of the dying world was appropriately figured as severely handicapped, perhaps a state worse than imminent death. His disablement attached him to the fading world. By this trick, Céline transformed himself from being a simple witness into a miserable co-sufferer with the collapsing fabric of civilisation.

Another important phantasm in Céline's work is his obsession with cross-breeding or even simply with racial confusion. His attitudes, it is well known, have thrown him into disrepute, and they need to be analysed and questioned. Before the war, Céline was claiming that he was not against the Jewish race, but against *Jewish Racism*. He describes the fine distinction: "I've nothing special against the Jews as jewish, I only want to say they're hooligans like all the rest of us, bipeds in search of their fodder. . . ." But the remainder of the pamphlet goes on to contradict the compatriot sympathy of this passage. It has been suggested earlier that this exaggeration was the result of the violence of Céline's style; but it is difficult to decide how much of the frenzy of the attack was a corollary of Céline's technique and a syntactical necessity. This difficulty has made Céline's work impossible to discuss without mentioning anti-Semitism and Fascism, both of which draw hard and fast lines in our sympathies. Yet beyond the extravagance of the language, Céline really feared the foreign element that the Jewish people represented. What worried him was the overlapping and confusion of different people in the same land, perhaps even simply the presence of foreigners. Even when the anti-semitic delirium disappeared from Céline's writing after World War II, an adolescent distrust of the Jews persisted. This feeling endured the vanishing of the grand effects of the pamphlets' style. An irrational fear of the foreigner: that was the only genuine part of this seething anti-semitism.

Of course, if the Jews are foreigners, the negroes, the yellow people, and the Arabs are even more so. From the end of the war, these people were the primary catalyst for Céline's worries: ". . . The yellow army in Brest, the black army at Montparnasse." This is the continual warning, over and over to the last page of *Rigodon*, in all tones including the farcical one.

Of itself, this does not merit critical attention. However, it seems that this sentiment, mostly irrational, issues from a troubled subconscious and can be used to clarify certain interesting characteristics of Céline's world.

Guignol's Band and *Le Pont de Londres* both present a spectacle of England during the First World War, and it is already obvious that Céline is fascinated by the heterogeneous, motley population he has set himself to describe. But it is not until the German disaster that he will instinctively link the idea of war and mixed populations in his view of the world. This relationship between the idea of racial confusion and the idea of war — or more precisely of catastrophe — becomes clear and detached particularly in *Nord* and *Rigodon*. This probably pushed Céline to slightly deform reality. For example, throughout his German experiences, hardly any Germans appear on the stage of Céline's adventures — except maybe for a few soldiers or clerks. And, by contrast, there is an abundance of descriptions of Russian, Polonesian, Gypsy, French, Baltic, Finnish, and Hungarian hordes. On this occasion, Céline even adds: "moldavians, subpomeranians, laplanders, and even higher. . . ." By reiteration of this "Mongrel Theme" and insistence on the racial disorder of the end of the IIIrd Reich Céline shows its importance for him. Céline just cannot hide his personal mythology and prejudices. He doesn't ever try to.

Laughter in Céline

Céline exploded into the history of literature in 1932, when *Voyage au bout de la nuit* was published. His *first* work, written under his real name, Dr. Louis-Ferdinand Destouches, was his medical thesis, passed in 1924. Contrary to expectation, this work was a true literary work, not at all limited by its specialised purpose. The subject of the work was the life and work of a Hungarian doctor, Semmelweis, the promoter of aseptic gynaecology, who died in the greatest distress, half mad and a prey to a passionate persecution complex. The influence on Céline of "the dreadful story of Philippe-Ignace Semmelweis" can be imagined. It affects the Céline of the Underworld already examined, but it also influences a positive feature of Céline's beliefs. It helped to form his idea of *Health*, a value that can be traced in all his work.

Céline can be ranked with Proust as one of the major modern French writers. He owes his success not only to his release from a savage and instinctive world, but for his fund of amazing, vigorous good humour in descriptions of the most painful, hidden wounds of humanity. In his study of Céline, Marc Hanrez speaks of a "pitiless fresco of a decomposing world by a healthy man."[8]

In Céline, the wretched suburbs parade up in the Champs-Elysées under the lights of projectors, and the belly of Paris sweeps over into the *good* quarters. The interplay between the two types of life acts as guarantee for the laughter and serious vigour in his work. There is characteristic irony in many passages in *Voyage au bout de la nuit*. Parapine, the scientist, augured the Courtial des Pereires of *Mort à Crédit*. But Céline's rabelaisian qualities are most evident in and after *Bagatelles pour un massacre* and *Guignol's Band*. His sense of laughter mixes good humour, caustic comments, and imaginative debauchery. Very character-istic are the pages in *Guignol's Band* where the hero hurries to the French Consulate in London to attempt to get back to the front: "I want to enlist,

you pigs! . . . I want to get back to war! To save the Fatherland! . . .
Wooden balls! . . ." This burlesque scene is capped by a spectacular
ejaculation out of the Consulate. The hero is a magnificent glider on top of
a group of refugees who are beseiging the building to escape the European
war.

Céline's interest in a cinematic (i.e. visual) manner of presenting a
comic situation is encountered in more than one scene. The role of the
crowd already noted is one example. Céline could be compared with
Eisenstein in the way they both utilize great masses of people. The term
revolution, moreover, suits *Mort à Crédit* since *the people* only play an
important rôle after this pivotal book of 1936. *Mort à Crédit* showed
Céline the virtues of excess, of mad exaggeration, of the gigantic—and, in
consequence, of the comic.

But Céline's attraction for the cinema is more accountable in terms of
a comparison with Charlie Chaplin (whom he detested). From the
beginning of World War II, Céline used Chaplin's techniques—the sad
comic, self-inflicted irony, and misery exaggerated to the point of snatch-
ing a smile. The image (a key word in discussing Céline) of the doctor of
Bas-Meudon in the Fifties laboriously going back to his home, furiously
being insulted by his neighbours in wall-daubing style: "traitor, quack,
pro-Stalin, pornographic, drunkard . . ," and then to the bitter reflexion:
"but maybe moreover what hurts me most is: 'you know, he's got no car!'
. . . I'm making a big mistake carrying my own garbage . . . the proof,
they don't call me 'Doctor' any more . . . only 'Mister' . . . soon they'll call
me old idiot! I'm waiting . . . a doctor without a housekeeper, without a
maid, without a car, and who carries his own garbage . . . and who writes
books on top of that! . . . and who's been in prison. . . ." This sort of
pathetic Chaplinesque humour fills a hundred pages of *D'un château
l'autre*. Each incident turns back on the author, enlarging the number of
his misfortunes, and causing a new avalanche of catastrophes.

This comical degradation in Céline is accentuated even more in
Rigodon. For example, the famous blow on the head with the brick causes,
among other things, a mad irresistible laugh in Céline, a nervous,
wounded, and uncontrollable laughter. This rises from the ruins and the
corpses of Germany in flames like Bacchic madness and cruelty. Céline
introduced laughter in a leap of strength and health. It culminates in the
sick grin of *Rigodon* where the world vacillates under the repeated blows
of exhaustion, age and bombing.

Affection in Céline

Voyage au bout de la nuit only really begins with this brief reflexion
of Bardamu's on the First World War: "It's men and men only one should
be scared of, always." The novel exhibits a procession of blood-crazy
soldiers, slave-trading priests, lusting and brutal colonialists, parents

flogging their children, and numerous other cruelties. In its extremes of inhumane behaviour, it endorses Céline's thesis. *Voyage au bout de la nuit* is the cry of anguish of a man before the power of hatred. He discovers the spring of this malice in humanity which can never be too ignoble or unhealthy. Céline has set himself a problem. His literary exploration tries to find the way of survival in the face of the ill-will and spite generated by the collective groups in which we live. His hero is an individual, not superior to the norm, but no worse. Can he survive without flight?

The answer in *Voyage au bout de la nuit* is timid and uncertain; but it is there. It appears in two places which serve as high points in the progress of the story. The first incident takes place in Africa, deep in the bush, where Bardamu meets Sergeant Alcide. He is the obscure colonial sub-officer who sends all his money back to France to bring up a small orphaned niece. He sends his pay to a private boarding school for his relative's *good* education. The anecdote takes up two pages, no more, but it is enough to let some light into Bardamu's world. He is surprised by his discovery. He gets up in the middle of the night to scrutinize the face of this sleeping man, to study his difference from all the others, the bastards of the world: "He slept like anyone would. He looked quite ordinary. It wouldn't be a bad idea if there was something to distinguish good men from bad" (*Voyage au bout de la nuit*).

The second episode to let sunlight into Céline's *Night* is the scene with Molly, the Detroit prostitute. She is the only woman who attaches herself to Bardamu for what he is. She is the only woman to escape the dilemma of sex and money which besets and soils all Céline's other female characters. Henry Miller, one of the first people who knew how Céline should be read, wrote very rightly in *The Air-Conditioned Nightmare*: "Molly, she's the milk of human kindness." And Bardamu himself seems to perceive the significance of this second sign of his density: "One's ashamed of not being more generous in heart and everything else or having after all judged humanity lower than it really is." However, the infernal patrol still pursues him, and he returns to hell by quitting Molly and the U.S.A. for France.

Without doubt it is their brevity which brings these two incidents into sharp relief. They are rapid excursions into the realm of affection. Céline is extremely shy of *feeling*. This emphasises the appearance when it occurs. It is sufficient to show what can save a world like Céline's — ordinary selfless affection between two human beings. Affection given without the intricate demonstrations and professional innuendoes of the humanitarianism of Sartre and Camus who both won Nobel Prizes for their fine sentences translated into all languages, but never lived or dreamed.

Mort à Credit seems to mark a halt in Céline's attempt to reinstate affection outside the professional abstractions of other contemporary French writers. But from *Bagatelles pour un massacre*, feeling reasserted itself; and in the post-war trilogy it becomes omnipresent. It is all-pervading and yet, at the same time, more discrete, more contained, controlled and masked by theatrical poses which become more and more violent. They culminate in the burlesque and thundering pronouncements of the Apocalypse's prophet. However, affection is more subtle in *Rigodon*. For example, there is the way Céline *accepts* the presence of his wife Lili as a source of strength, and her presence is felt even in the extremities of the worst catastrophes. Lili appears as the comforting person who provides the only certainty in a world destroying itself. She is the symbol of the solidarity of real affection and attachment. Some words chosen at random illustrate Céline's feeling: "Lili, generous like no one else . . . completely generous! like a fairy! . . . she would give everything! . . ."

These intimacies are always allusive, never substantial. From World War II, Céline even more determinedly refused to indulge himself. But the more he concealed his intentions the more affection and warm feeling assumed an outstanding and purified meaning. From each line oozes the reassurance of human goodness.

Rigodon definitely represents a progression in all respects within Céline's work; and it witnesses a new solidarity even if the confidence is meanly described. Besides being an Odyssey of an epic flight towards the Northern Promised Land, *Rigodon* is also a story of the rescue of a group of abandoned children encountered by surprise at one halt. In presenting them, Céline cannot find words sufficiently grotesque: "all the little cretins . . . limping, slobbering, faces crooked . . . complete imbeciles from a madhouse. . . ." Despite the uncharitable introduction, the children were saved at the cost of a thousand efforts and detours, and finally sent safely as far as possible from the war into Sweden. Céline describes this exploit reluctantly, without the least complacency, as if it were only a diversion from the true road of fate. It was, however, the sort of heroism that would naturally spring from the passion for childhood first revealed in *Voyage au bout de la nuit*: "One never minds much if an adult kicks it, that's always one less sod in the world, you can think, while for a child, the thing's not quite so sure. There's always the future for them, there's some chance." In passing, it may be worth noting that the famous cat of *Rigodon*, Bébert, revives the name of the little sick boy of *Voyage au bout de la nuit* whom Bardamu, only recently qualified as a doctor, was too late to save from dying.

This privileged place granted to childhood gives Céline's vision of Man a new dimension. According to his new vision, man at birth is a hopeful being who has every chance offered to him. The prime offering is the chance to be good. And it is only in the course of years that life destroys this promise of goodness. Therefore, from one angle, Céline's work becomes an impressive illustration or enactment of Rousseau's theory of the corrupting influence of society on Man who is naturally good.

Affection in Céline opens out into a profound and silent unity of ideas and feelings, and it may be a key to his often discredited work. At the end of the *Night*, Céline had a presentiment of light—natural affection. From this spark proceeds the show of generosity between individuals in *Voyage au bout de la nuit*, then, extending itself to the whole part of humanity protected from Evil by their childhood. Affection is Céline's answer to the hatred, malice, shame, and the slackness of the world. But if affection is possible, the modern world has no excuse for its viciousness and selfish aggression. After *Rigodon*, it would be unfair to judge Céline's work without considering his search for and attempts to define a real lasting value. This quest was pursued through the most gruesome abjection and most complete suffering.

The End of the Journey

It was noon on July 1st, 1961, when Céline announced the end of *Rigodon* to his wife. It was time to inform Gallimard. At six o'clock on the same day, Céline died from a blood-vessel bursting in his head. "The albatross answers no more."[9] The head . . . strange that Céline should have died from an injury in his brain. *Rigodon* was no longer quite as fictitious as *Voyage*. But this change from fictional to exaggerated reality was a necessary consequence of the immensity of the disaster, of the *phosphorous furnaces*. To lead Bardamu, a fictional hero like Don Quixote, through the middle of Europe's dying agony would have been artistic obscenity. All that was needed in blazing Hamburg and Frankfurt was a reporter, a mere witness: "the poor chronicler," but with the inspiration of a prophet. Céline laid his head under the hammers of history with a pagan sense of sacrifice; and, to his last breath, he remained intact in his violent and excessive outbursts. He died mocking the gnomes of our times. He died demonstrating that the choice is between humanism or individualism, since humanity is not reducible to the sum of the individuals that compose it.

Like Molière, Céline died on the stage. In one instant, fiction became truth, the perfect consummation of life and art, with life losing as ever!

With Céline's demise and the publication of *Rigodon*, it is of interest to trace the fate of his work with the French public. Like the spectators of decadent Rome, cruel rather than violent, it is always ready to lower the thumb in a moment of unconsciousness. However, *Rigodon* is a cohesive work that is a grand finale to Céline's artistic life. Its action is simple, held tightly in check by the Northern plan for escape. It is full of the ghoulish and mocking counterplay of Céline's world. It has the rich variety of a nightmare. Its rhythm alternates like extreme jazz. The sentences tremble from the tumult of the forces being described. *Rigodon* calls out for a performance, a full viva voce reading. The consciousness of the dead writer gushes out of the hammering of image after image which jostle and concentrate each other as they crowd into the line.

Céline left the world with the sentence broken as ever. The Rigodon has ended. The dancing writer suspended his last effort with three small dots . . .

Notes

1. When the Germans quitted France, they took with them the whole of Pétain's government. All the ministers were kept in close custody in a castle at Sigmaringen. *D'un château l'autre* is Céline's account of the last ridiculous show of authority by the Pétain ministry in exile. Céline jovially referred to Pétain as "Philip the Last."

2. Céline published three pamphlets: *Bagatelles pour un massacre*, Denoel, Paris, 1937; *L'Ecole des Cadavres*, Denoel, Paris, 1938; *Les Beaux Draps*, Denoel, Paris, 1941.

3. *La Mort de L.F. Céline*, Dominique de Roux, Christian Bourgeous, Paris, 1966.

4. Minister of Foreign Policy before the war and *Président du Conseil* under Pétain.

5. *Les Cahiers de L'Herne* (*Céline*, no. 1), Paris, 1962.

6. In his book on Céline, the American critic, Milton Hindus, even speaks of the rion plate Céline carried on his cranium over the place where he had undergone surgery on his skull!

7. *N.R.F.* (No. 295, April '38), Gide: *Les Juifs, Céline, et Maritain.*

8. In *Céline*, by Marc Hanrez, Gallimard, Paris, 1961.

9. An expression used by Dominique de Roux in *La Mort de Louis-Ferdinand Céline.*

Historical Vision in Céline's Last Novels
Colin W. Nettelbeck*

". . . should I, the historian, be forbidden to tack it together bassackward?"

Céline's four postwar novels have received considerable critical attention over the past ten years or so, but they remain less well-known than *Journey to the End of the Night* and *Death on the Installment Plan.* One of the reasons for this is that their narrative structure and their style are more demanding than those of the earlier works, and their cohesion less evident. Perhaps, too, some readers, aware of the degree to which Céline was politically and ideologically compromised as a collaborator and an anti-Semite, intuitively shy away from the material that deals directly with World War II. Another difficulty is that although the two volumes of *Féerie pour une autre fois, Castle to Castle, North,* and *Rigadoon* form a coherent novel cycle—so that an understanding of the whole is illuminating for the reading of any of the separate parts—they have never been published as such. The prestigious—and finely edited—French Pléiade edition of the late novels does not include *Féerie*, and a similar lacuna exists for English readers of Céline, in that *Féerie* has not been translated.

*This essay was written for this volume and appears here with permission of the author.

There is a persuasive argument for better knowledge of these works in the masterly study of Céline's poetics by the French critic Henri Godard,[1] who stresses the continuities between the pre- and postwar novels. Godard underlines the autobiographical principle at work in an oeuvre that ends up embracing a whole existence: from the author's birth at Courbevoie, through his childhood and adolescence in turn-of-century Paris, his experiences in the army, World War I, London, the African colonies, the United States, the Soviet Union, sordid suburban Paris medical clinics, Montmartre under the Occupation, the apocalyptic Germany of 1944–45, to, finally, approaching death in the postwar Meudon villa, overlooking the Seine. Godard believes that even though the external form of the oeuvre was shaped by circumstances of financial need or reader response as much as by artistic or ideological commitment, it never deviates from the rigorous principle that the narrative must be rooted in direct personal experience — leading, thus, to the creation of the new fusion of novel and autobiography that is Céline's mark, that is his response to the twentieth-century crisis of fiction. In this context, to ignore or underestimate the importance of the postwar output can only offer a truncated view of Céline.

Another telling argument for taking greater notice of these works emerges if one focuses more narrowly on their specifically historical dimension, on their portrayal of events of collective significance, and on the ways in which the narrative is shaped to convey a highly pertinent vision of a passion-filled and still controversial period of European history, as well as of the nature of historical time. Between his recording of the details of personal experience on the one hand, and the more universal aspects of his views of art and life on the other, Céline the storyteller is also something of a historian. Although it is undoubtedly right to treat with circumspection, as Godard does, Céline's claim to be a "chronicler," and his almost mystical projection of himself as some sort of historical seer, his constant insistence,[2] in his last period, on the representative and exemplary nature of his personal experience, makes it hard to ignore this ambition of his writing. His claims to have been victimized by history can be dismissed, as they often enough have been, as no more than a manifestation of his well-documented persecution complex. The fact remains that he was directly involved in major historical events, and whether this was by chance or design, he makes of it something rather more than symbolic — a principle of fate, or necessity, similar to the role of Slothrop in Pynchon's *Gravity's Rainbow*. More mundanely, and more bluntly, when Céline decided to abandon the almost-completed *Guignol's Band* in order to write *Féerie*, he was signaling his awareness that his survival as a writer required recognition of the profound historical change that World War II had brought upon the world. Among other things, his last works are also an account of that change.

It has often been pointed out that the order of the events recounted in the last novels is not that of Céline's real-life experience of the period covered, which was as follows: (1) the R.A.F. bombardment of Montmartre, April 1944; (2) beginning of flight to Denmark via Germany: Baden Baden, June–July 1944; (3) internment in the village of Kränzlin northwest of Berlin, August–October 1944; (4) journey to Sigmaringen, November 1944; (5) stay in Sigmaringen with the French collaborationist rump, November 1944–March 1945; (6) journey to Denmark, March 1945; (7) Copenhagen, April–December 1945; (8) Danish prison and hospital, December 1945–June 1947; (9) house arrest in Denmark, 1947–51; (10) return to Paris, 1951. In the novels, the order is: (a) 8 and 1 *(Féerie)*; 5 *(Castle to Castle)*; 2–3 *(North)*; 4 and 6-7 *(Rigadoon)*. The stay in Copenhagen before his arrest as an illegal immigrant and his postprison life in Denmark are mentioned only in passing, and the return to Paris is presented not as part of the series of *events*, but as a constant, if intermittently explicit, narrative *perspective*, from *Castle to Castle* onward.

Céline's general intention—of using his own geographical movement as the basis of a historical narrative—was clear from the beginning, and in *Féerie* he both announces his personal itinerary and lays the foundation of the wider historical context. Simultaneously, of course, he also establishes the burlesque tone and operatic setting that will dominate the late novels.[3] It furthermore seems likely that *Féerie pour un autre fois* was the title projected for the ensemble—in a way similar to Balzac's *Comédie humaine* and Proust's *A la Recherche du temps perdu*. Godard very plausibly suggests that the immediate cause for changing the order of events was the commercial failure of *Féerie* and the concomitant desire to find an interest-catcher: the recognizable collaborationist villains of Sigmaringen being more obviously suited to that purpose than Céline and his companions Lili, Le Vigan, and Bébert the cat wandering from Baden Baden to northern Germany. Certainly such a calculated strategy to win back some of his prewar audience was not beyond Céline. On another level, however, this enforced temporal displacement of his experience appears retrospectively as a brilliant intuitive confirmation of the same compositional instinct that led him to place the Danish prison episode at the beginning of *Féerie*, immediately after the Clémence Arlon prelude. We shall see how these transpositions of individual experience work to create a reflection of the collective and historical experience.

Access to this vision is not straightforward. Near the start of *Féerie* there is a warning of the difficulty of the genre that the author is undertaking: "I'm writing it for you from everywhere in fact! From Montmartre my place! from the depths of my baltavian prison! and at the same time from the seaside, from our shanty! Confusion of places, of times! Shit! It's the fairy-play you see . . . That's what a fairy-play is . . . the future! Past! False! True! Fatigue!"[4] At first sight, the texts of these last novels do seem to be quite haphazard assemblies of times and spaces, an effect intensified by the syntactic and typographic fragmentation of the sentences on the page. Thus, for example, Clémence Arlon and her son in the prologue of *Féerie:*

> I was saying that Clémence had been really pretty . . . in her day . . . our youth! . . . The kid, I look at him again . . . he reeks of falsity . . . it's the same instincts as his mother. He refused to sit down he's leaning against the wall he's embarrassed to be here . . . He's gawky . . . one hand in his pocket . . . They have talked about me at home, at table, to friends, to neighbours . . . Once again, it's all the same thing, the same filth, stupidities at the same time, all together . . . It's been months now that they've been chewing over everywhere why and how it will be good to assassinate me, a laugh! patriotic! . . . it's only about whether they'll put out my eyes, quarter me, bury me alive that they can't reach an agreement . . . That's the talking-point for families, concierges, and in the corridors of the metro (air-raid warnings) . . . So naturally the Arlons who have known me for more than thirty years, they've got a thing or two to say about my weaknesses, my wonts, my disgusting ways![5]

For the hasty or uninitiated reader, the narrative might appear a chaos from which, at best, certain episodes emerge, in a cloudily delineated fashion, and whose only coherence is in a certain rhythmic dynamism, product of a delirious energy, a visionary but formless mix of hilarity and horror.

In fact, however, the text is organized in such a way as to induce the reader into the novels' perspective on time, and more specifically, into their historical dimension. The most obvious sign of that organization is the two-tiered narrative strategy. On the one level, we have the telling of the past—"history"—story: the Paris bombing, life at Sigmaringen, the trek across Germany, etc. and on the other, notations of all sorts on the "present" of the narrator–author, from the painful skin disease that afflicts him in his Danish prison to his battles with his greedy Paris publisher. There is no regular pattern in the shifts between these time-layers, but they happen often enough for it to be clear that they are deliberate. Too many sections of the text are set in the present, too, for the reader to take them as mere interruptions of the real story, though the bulk of the narrative is devoted to the past, indicating the latter's intended predominance.

One might take the point of view that the two levels function mainly to show the links between the storyteller (present) and his story (past), and to translate structurally the novelist's determination to occupy the central position in the narrative. It is certainly true that Céline has little in common with the Flaubertian dictum about the desirable invisibility of a godlike author: the Céline of the last novels is not only omnipresent, but he never lets us forget that he is there, narrator and actor, cajoling and bullying the reader along as he tells his stories about himself. Nonetheless, if this presence is a sine qua non of the narrative, it is not, by itself, an adequate basis for describing the narrative's structure, or for interpreting the novels' meaning. If one takes Céline at his word and assumes a historically referential function for the narrative, then explanation of the two-tiered time scheme requires a further dimension.

In the sections set in the present—that is, at the time of the narration process—the material is presented in a ranting commentary, full of scorn and cynicism, that moves along at breakneck speed, sometimes alluding to the news of the day, but more often registering complaints about Céline's situation, launching attacks on such *bêtes noires* as his publisher or Sartre, or harping on his pet themes of Western decadence and the degeneration of the white race. A couple of typical examples:

> agreement is rare among men, especially Frenchmen . . . you'll never find them agreeing about anybody's merits, virtues, or crimes . . . even dead drunk, vomiting, rolling on the floor . . . anybody, Landru, Petiot, Clemenceau, Poincaré, Pétain, William II, Mistinguett, de Gaulle, Dreyfus, Déroulède, or Bougrat . . . will throw them into dialectical controversies, interminable blahblah! . . . the little triumph of my existence, my tour de force, is getting them all . . . right, left, centre, sacristies and lodges, cells and charnel houses, Comte de Paris, Joséphine, my Aunt Odile, Kroukroubezef and Abbé Piggybank . . . to agree that I'm the foremost living stinker![6]

And again: "only biology exists, the rest is hot air! . . . all the rest! . . . in the world dance marathon . . . the 'Gametes Ball' . . . the blacks and yellows always win! . . . the whites are always the losers, 'make-up base,' painted over, effaced! . . . politics, speeches, bullshit! . . . only one truth! biology! . . . in half a century, maybe sooner, France will be yellow, black around the edges. . . ."[7]

Whatever the reader's opinions about the content of such utterances, their cumulative effect is to produce a sense of directionless uncertainty and anxiety, which, as well as reflecting the personal and singular dimensions of the writer in the present, also corresponds to a more metaphysical discomfort with time. In the recently published primitive version of *Féerie*, Céline uses a metaphor to render his sense of time: "It's not a scythe Time's got, it's a sort of ladle and a monstrous pot, he stuffs everything into it, he gives it a swirl, he has fun stirring it about like an obscene stew, so that everything gets mixed up, confused, smeared everywhere, sticky. . . ."[8] What the novelist is doing in the sequences set in the present is working to transmit an impression of this experience of time—a raw experience, undifferentiated and untransposed. This is what one might call *prestory*, on the individual level, and on the collective level *prehistory*. It is also, from the point of view of generative fiction, pretext. Although it has a contextual function in respect to the rest of the narrative, it is quite distinct from it, and its disorder — deliberate, if not always sustained in a controlled fashion — is in contrast to the narrative of the past, which develops in a carefully constructed cohesion of metaphor and symbol. The storyteller/historian/novelist — interlocking images of a process of structuring time — is not to be confused with the imaging of the narrator in difficulty. The latter, in fact, while provoking the reader's disgust and derision, or pity and indignation, is essentially a device to drive the reader toward the more composed dimensions of the text. In short, the woe-stricken and wrathful vociferations of the narrator in the present serve above all to draw our attention to the story in the past, in very much the way that sharply discordant sounds make one more aware of harmony and more grateful for it.

This is not to suggest that the narration of the past is in any sense a natural harmony. On the contrary, it is an artifice, a construct, and presented as such, with readers being constantly reminded of their dependency on the narrator's good offices. On a page to page basis, there is not always an obvious difference between the time-layers in the way the text looks. There is a similarly elliptical presentation of the material:

> Now I know . . . we have at least two friends! . . . Cillie von Leiden and the hunchback . . . not bad in our situation . . . or, come right down to it, no matter where and when, peace, dead calm, wars, convulsions . . . so many vaginas, stomachs, cocks, snouts, and flies you don't know what to do with them . . . shovelsful! . . . but hearts? . . . very rare! in the last five hundred million years too many cocks and gastric tubes to count . . . but hearts? . . . on your fingers! . . .[9]

There is, however, a substantial difference, in that the cumulative effect of the sequences from the past is that they add up to something: however frequently the narrator–chronicler appears to lose the thread of his story, linearity and continuity are always maintained. This is most clearly perceivable if one considers the four last novels as a single work: the protagonists' intinerary from Paris to Denmark, for all its zigs and zags, is a movement whose direction and purpose are constantly recalled; thematically, too, there is a development that emerges from the apparent confusion as the threat of death is progressively displaced by the realities of survival.

In order to raise the autobiographical perspective into a broader historical one, Céline has recourse to a number of different devices that, together, work to structure the major narrative blocks into a symbolic portrayal of the collective French experience of the war period. The first of these involves the narrative frame and focus. Whereas in the "present" sequences the narrator is consistently alone against the world, the narrative of the past bonds him into a little community, with Lili and Bébert, and sometimes one or two others, such as le Vigan in *North* or Felipe in *Rigadoon*. On the one hand, this group offers the image of a constellation of Céline's principle aesthetic values: the importance of the instinctive

(Bébert the cat), of direct experience (the narrator himself), and of spiritual vitality and formal beauty (Lili the dancer). But more immediately, the group works to widen the frame of the experience narrated. Lili and Bébert are not passive extensions of the narrator, they act independently. They open the way to places and people not otherwise accessible to the narrator—the castle in *Castle to Castle*, for example, or the kindly little hunchback girl in *North*. They directly influence the action, as is dramatically demonstrated in the episode in *North* where Lili sets off the entire Berlin antiaircraft defense—and finds it enormously funny. If the narrative voice is unique, the narrative viewpoint is not simply that of the narrator as character; rather, it is constantly informed by this thrust toward the multiple and the collective. The nexus of aesthetic constellation and an emphasis on collective experience points strongly, once again, toward an intentionally historical dimension in Céline's conception of his art.

The second device he uses to render this aspect of his vision is the creation of a series of symbolic microcosms, spatial structures that, in themselves, transmit a certain vision of history, and that, over the four novels, act as coordinates that allow the reader to plot the graph of historical change mentioned earlier. The suddenness and extent of the change is treated in *Féerie* through the account of the R.A.F. bombing of Montmartre. Although based on the real-life bombing, in April 1944, of the shunting yards of La Chapelle, the material as Céline presents it is not limited to the specific time and place—it is not so much history as recorded facts that interests him (although he does insist on the value of the eyewitness document), as what can be induced from such experience about the direction and meaning of the events. His Montmartre, built on a gruyère cheese of plaster-of-Paris quarries, is a mock-heroic symbol of a France hollowed out by history, references to which are shredded through the text as oblique, polyvalent allusions, tantalizing rather than illuminating, to everything from Greco-Roman and biblical times, through all the periods of French civilization, to World War I and the current catastrophes of World War II. It is a France whose destiny is no longer in its own hands, and whose population, represented by the unhinged and murderous cross-section that scrambles around the concierge's lodge in the beleaguered apartment building, has no cohesion, social or moral. With the R.A.F. planes elevated to the power of apocalyptic angels, instruments of a supremely powerful fate, the image of France and its inhabitants is reduced to a crazed and fractured mosaic, symbol of the disintegration of a 2,000-year-old identity.

In *Castle to Castle*, the depiction of the disarray of the colony of Vichy politicians and other French collaborators in Sigmaringen—or *Sieg*maringen, in Céline's ironic spelling—has its own value; and indeed, the grotesque satire, which won Céline back some of his prewar popularity, undoubtedly acted to allow French readers to look with cathartic humor on the sorry end of one of the more disastrous periods of national history. In the wider historical sense, each of the novel's geographical centers—the castle, the hotel, and the railway station—functions as a symbolic representation of a different aspect of time. The castle contains a whole history of modern Europe, from medieval times on, but it is a history as petrified as the castle itself and detached from the world of the present, which Céline encapsulates in the mad and threatening world of the Hôtel Löwen, where, in crowded corridors with overflowing toilets, a bloodthirsty surgeon, a brain-damaged bishop, a couple of bewildered moviemakers, along with the narrator and Lili, make up a deranged society that lives in danger of being annihilated by a jack-booted Nazi woman and her two great hounds. Down the road is the railway station, equally decadent with its orgies and drunken singing, but more of a symbolic cross-roads. Céline transforms it into a more hopeful reality in the episode where the narrator takes a return train journey, which begins as a trip to attend the funeral of a ex-Vichy official, but which turns around on itself, bringing the narrator back to Sigmaringen in a train full of pregnant women, promise of new birth.

Historical perspective in *Féerie* was limited to France itself. In *Castle to Castle*, it opens into a European dimension—onto the failure of Hitler's "New Europe" and of Vichy's collaborationist "National Revolution" within it, but also onto the potential of something new to emerge from the chaos. In *North* and *Rigadoon*, this European perspective is brought more clearly into focus by the exploration of its frontiers and the emphasis the texts place on the proximity of Poland and the Russian army. An East–West opposition is intimated, and the seismic crisis of Western identity and history reaches here its widest expression, as the little group of protagonists work their rickety way across from Baden Baden to Berlin, up to Zornhof and Rostock, back down to Sigmaringen, and finally north to the safety of Denmark.

The relatively grand spatial sweep so evident in the last two novels reveals the third of the main devices that Céline uses to amplify the significance of the action portrayed—since in retrospect one can perceive similar circular movements in the previous works, but restricted, in *Castle to Castle*, to the single train journey and to the movement around Sigmaringen, and in *Féerie*, to Montmartre. In retrospect, too, the escape north into Denmark appears as a liberation from a history represented as a series of expanding imprisoning spaces—an ambiguous liberation, since we have seen, from the beginning of *Féerie*, that Denmark will itself become a place of imprisonment; but a liberation nonetheless from the more dire threats of disintegration encountered along the way.

It is perhaps not absolutely certain that Céline's image of liberation is intended as a commentary on the liberation of France, although given the lengths to which the author goes to establish himself as historically representative, it is tempting to speculate on that being the case. If so, it is an expectedly unglorious image, far from the proud and noble triumphalism of the official Resistance. Rather, we see a passive and decadent population, utterly dependent on others for its continuing existence. A pessimistic view, once again not unexpected from the author of *Journey to the End of the Night* and *Death on the Installment Plan*, but tempered by the knowledge that survival has in fact taken place. Even when he makes statements like the following from *Rigadoon* — "To the shithouse, I tell you! the whole shebang! the country doesn't exist any more, nothing but bureaucrats! . . . and funerals . . . a hundred languages stronger than ours have gone out of existence!"[10] — he gives himself the lie, to some extent, both by the vitality of his own linguistic invention, and by a narrative full of life-affirming symbols. That he should affirm the demise of the traditional French identity can neither shock nor surprise: he had said much the same thing in the opening pages of *Journey:* "What you call the race is only that great heap of worm-eaten sods like me, bleary, shivering and lousy, who, coming defeated from the four corners of the earth, have ended up here, escaping from hunger, illness, pestilence and cold. They couldn't go further because of the sea. That's your France and those are your Frenchmen."[11]

Many would find such a view less controversial in the post–World War II context than when it was first expressed, although it could also be argued that Céline underestimated the nation's power of recovery. It is, certainly, somewhat paradoxical that he did not believe that France as a whole possessed the strength with which he managed to regenerate his own vision and style.

Allen Thiher contends that history, in Céline's last novels, is a "delirious farce."[12] If one thinks of the description of historical events that the novelist uses as background to his narrative of the past, with the pantomime or carnival atmosphere that he achieves through his clownish characters, Thiher's assessment is accurate. As it is, too, on the level of Céline's general vision of human history, especially in western Europe. The disintegration brought about by World War II under the impact of the Hitlerian dream is neither seen nor presented tragically, but as a vast, tumbling time-wave, inevitable and entropic, that dumps in ruins the work of centuries of civilization and turns to ridicule the pomposity of the power mongers who lay claim to having some control over it all.

In treating it all as a fairy-play, Céline is affirming the power of art, not as a real antidote to time as catastrophe, but as a way of making the experience of it less unbearable. By structuring his plot in the direction of transcendence, his story offers an aesthetic liberation where history seems to offer only survival and continuing decline.

Between backdrop and Weltanschauung, there is an intermediate level, where Céline, without creating a one-to-one allegory, offers a version of the war as it was experienced by the French population as a whole, from sudden collapse and the confinement of an Occupation to which most submitted sheepishly, if not enthusiastically, to the ambiguities of a Liberation that, while marking the genuine heroism of some, and the undisputed treachery of some others, tended to ignore the experience of the majority of the population. If the real-life Céline was too much of an active collaborator to be identified with mainstream behavior and reaction, as novelist he is wily enough to "marginalize" the extreme deeds and attitudes of his autobiography, so that readers are left with a historical vision that is both plausible in itself and subversive of the synthetic history constructed by the alliance of Gaullian and communist politicians, who posited the rebirth of France on the notion of widespread Resistance. By couching that vision in a self-deprecatory and comic mode, he renders his vision disarmingly powerful: in laughing, we allow ourselves to think that perhaps, indeed, things happened more in the way he describes than as recounted in the more official histories.

In coming to terms with the less salubrious aspects of French behavior under the Occupation, Céline participates in the same tradition as contemporaries like Nimier, Laurent, or Dutourd, forcing into the open what the dominant political trends were trying to repress. But the scope of his work is grander, in part because his physical removal to places outside of France provided him with not only his narrative material, but a broad spatiotemporal perspective denied to those whose experience of the war was confined to France itself. Whereas the works of a Nimier or a Dutourd are anecdotal, showing for example how easy it was to make wrong choices, or satirizing the a posteriori clear consciences of ruthless opportunists, Céline's stories build up an etiology of historical change, not ignoring the psychology of individuals caught in particular circumstances, but subordinating it to his images of wider and more abstract cause-and-effect relationships.

Céline's vision of history and his story of it are in many ways in contradiction with those one reads in de Gaulle, who was responsible for molding so much of the political shape of postwar France, but the visions are of a similarly mythical order, and in many ways can be considered as complementary. De Gaulle expounds national hope and transformation in a rhetoric that pounds as stiffly as the nineteenth-century heart in which it was formed. Céline bellows apocalyptic despair in a language that shatters the syntactic shackles that bound it, creating a French whose vitality and flexibility are more suited to the postwar climate of rapid change and uncertainty. His lasting contributions to history are thus at least two-fold: imaginative and linguistic. It is perhaps the latter that will prove more durable, but the pattern of experience that the novelist has woven into his narratives will also remain as a valuable reference for those wishing to explore the more complex aspects of the period.

Notes

1. Henri Godard, *Poétique de Céline* (Paris, 1985). By far the most thorough work on Céline's aesthetics. Nobody has worked more closely than Godard with Céline's manuscripts, which makes questioning his interpretations of authorial intention somewhat perilous. Nonetheless, in my view Godard generally underplays the specifically historical value of Céline's work.

2. See the interviews with M. Chapsal and A. Zbinden, *Cahiers Céline* (Paris: Gallimard, 1976), 2, and Godard's discussion in *Poétique*, 416–18. See also *North*, trans. R. Manheim (New York: Delacorte, 1972), 238: "I can say without boasting that the thread of History passes straight through me from top to bottom, from the clouds to my head to my asshole. . . ."

3. *Féerie*, (Paris: Gallimard, 1952), 30 (all translations from this book are my own) I was going to tell you our exodus! . . . I mean our flight . . . It took . . . three months before all the others! . . . that dragging about! . . . Winfling-Oder . . . Blaringhem . . . Neuruppin . . . Rostock. . . . He dares to complain! the shameless rascal! He swindled the whole of Europe! . . . (What will *you* do the day the tanks come? . . . Ivan at the Tuileries?) I was expected at Stake Square . . . I mean Place Blanche . . . also Pigalle . . . and Monceau! . . . the stalls full of experts! panting! . . . the animal that flees the bullring, what does that warrant? dodges the picks, tridents, voyeurs, Carmens, Josés, alcades all gathered? It doesn't even warrant the sawdust, being dragged around the ring, guts everywhere!

4. *Féerie*, 30.

5. Ibid., 12–13.

6. *North*, 344.

7. *Rigadoon*, trans. R. Manheim (New York: Delacorte, 1974), 107.

8. *Maudits Soupirs pour une autre fois* (Paris, 1985), 119 (my translation).

9. *North*, 155.

10. *Rigadoon*, 4.

11. *Journey to the End of the Night*, trans. John Marks (New York, New Directions, 1960), 4.

12. Allen Thiher, *Céline: The Novel as Delirium* (New Brunswick, NJ: Rutgers University Press, 1972), 170.

Sacer esto: Reading Céline through Georges Bataille
Yves de la Quérière*

From the very first pages of *Journey to the End of the Night* to the end of *Rigodon*, Ferdinand, subject of enunciation of Céline's various books, denounces current sets of social values. He begins before World War I with spirited attacks on French patriotism and religion and ends after World War II on a similar note of skepticism. But shortly after the beginning of *Journey*, his rationalist stance weakens when he suddenly joins the army. At this point, he might have added that all the reasoning in the world would not have prevented him from following his heart. Indeed,

*This essay was written for this volume and appears here with permission of the author.

emotion plays a major and well-known role in the genesis of Célinian texts.

Céline's books mainly pursue emotion around what many call today the *Sacred*. In other terms, Ferdinand first becomes Bardamu, then becomes Céline (character and author in one), by trying to drink from one after the other of those ambiguous sources of transcendence that succeed the much-heralded death of God. They are the dangerous product of man's eternal yearning for something above his down-to-earth, rather vacant and lonely life. Perhaps, he felt, if these sacralized entities helped establish an authentic social bond, society and individuals could redeem each other. This is, in any case, the ever-receding goal of Ferdinand's quest. But if his quest proves fruitless, it is not without peril. He who seeks the sacred will sooner or later stumble into sacrifice.

Thus begins for Ferdinand, at the military barracks in that summer of 1914, a modern pilgrim's progress that inexorably takes him to the end of the night. For if writers are, in a way, wishful thinkers, they often manage nonetheless to give their fancy some bearing on reality. Céline's intervention in the course of the world—via his writing—achieves exactly this, albeit in unexpected ways. The sacred turned loose is ambivalent: attractive, yet at the same time frightening. Victim of a *machine infernale* of his own making, the apprentice high-priest succeeds indeed in becoming sacred, but as a sacrificial victim. Primitive religions need scapegoats. The close emotional bond Céline had sought to secure among his fellow Frenchmen was destined to be formed at his own expense. In his eyes, it is finally against him that an ad hoc form of *union sacrée* occurs.

For these reasons, the trilogy's author–protagonist has become, properly speaking, an authentic *écrivain maudit*. I must emphasize that I am not using this term as a figure of speech. Anathematized as a writer, Céline is facing two extreme choices after the war: to continue writing and defying society, or to give up. Although he chooses writing, he feels ambivalent toward his choice, and this makes him verbally waver in the texts. The trilogy is an ambiguous message, partly sacrilegious, partly prophetic. Out of one side of his mouth Céline praises seventeenth-century skeptics and a Second Empire positivistic frame of mind, while out of the other side he calls with religious fervor for the destruction of a French society that worships nothing but comfort and entertainment. In other words, Prévert's famous "Pater noster"—"Our Father in Heaven, would you please stay there!"—alternates with *Apocalypse now!* But the sarcastic tone that now prevails makes it difficult to decide which message is the "real" Céline, and whether or not all of this is serious. Or perhaps, as Marshall McLuhan's hackneyed quote says, "the medium is [now] the message." Language would then be the last of the writer's idols.

Since Bardamu's fateful enlistment is undeniably at the beginning of Céline's quest, a good part of my argument focuses on the character's military experience. I start with Georges Bataille's famous essay on the army, "Structure et fonction de l'Armée" (1938)[2]; then after confronting Céline and Bataille on that ground, I skip the other books and move directly to additional experiences with the Sacred; finally, I examine — in a purely conjectural way — the very ambiguous assumption of language in the trilogy.

Before I question Céline in Bataille's perspective, let us first remember that *Journey to the End of the Night* was published in 1932, far before Bataille's aforementioned essay. Second, Céline has actively participated in both world wars, unlike Bataille, who never served. Away from action, the latter holds about the outside world that essentially bookish perspective preferred by most French intellectuals, who seldom get involved in anything other than reading and writing. On the contrary, the former seeks emotion through direct participation and throws himself into the middle of things. So, precisely because Bataille sees the army from an outsider's point of view, his perspective may help read through Ferdinand Bardamu's immediate experience.

Before the story begins, this prototype of Céline is a docile carrier of set ideas and proper behaviors that he does not dare to challenge: in other terms, a *Barda-mule* and at the same time *Barda-muet* — or "mute" — the one who never says anything. This is what suggests to me the first two lines of the book: "It all began just like that. I hadn't said a word. It was Arthur Ganate who started me off." The once *mute* young man makes up for his years of silence and starts a mutation *(Barda mue)*, which is about to make him open up, say it all, and become a *bard*. For the time being, "to show that I knew what I was talking about," he plays the skeptic and attempts to demystify patriotism. At least this is what he believes:

> . . . we *are* all in the same boat, we are galley slaves together, rowing like the devil — you certainly can't deny that. . . . You're stuck down in the hold, puffing and panting, all of a muck-sweat and stinking like polecats. . . . And up on the bridge, not giving a damn, the masters of the ship are enjoying God's fresh air with lovely pink ladies drenched in perfume sitting on their knees. They have you up on deck. Then they put on their top-hats and let fly at you as follows:
> "See you, you set of sods!" they say. "War's declared. You're going to board the bastards on *Country Number* 2 yonder and you're going to smash them to bits! Now get on with it. There's all the stuff you'll need aboard. All together now. Let's have it — as loud as you can make it: 'God saves *Country Number* 1!' "[3]

During his little harangue, however, an electrifying scene makes him suddenly speechless: "Whereupon, damn me if a regiment of soldiers didn't come marching past the café where we were sitting, with the colonel in front on his horse and all, looking simply fine and as smart as you make them. I gave just one great leap of enthusiasm. 'I'll go and find out if that's what it's like!' I cried to Arthur, and off I went to join up, as fast as my legs would carry me" (6).

Why, leaving everything behind, does Bardamu answer the call of arms in the way the disciples followed Christ? Most certainly he hopes (without fully realizing it) to transcend ordinary life and gain access to a world of values unknown to contemporary civilians. The society in which he has lived up to this moment is not based on lofty ideas, but on the law of individual profit (everyone for himself), like the homogeneous society described, among others, by Bataille. So, when Bardamu enlists at the most disenchanted time of his youth, his apparent palinody means that he is looking for something that could finally stir his soul.

Indeed, homogeneous society is precisely what he leaves behind, along with Arthur Ganate, in the café of the Place Clichy in Paris where they had been sitting. This type of society gives its members "neither a task to fullfil nor a reason for being. It abandons them to their individual destinies, whether good or bad."[4] Significantly, before Bardamu's apparent change of mind, both young men are doing nothing worthwhile. They kill time chatting about the tiny piece of news that President Poincaré "was going [that morning] to open a show of lapdogs" (3). In a Bataillian perspective, a head of state involved in such unworthy matters is emblematic of a destitute political system. Empty official rites replace the quasi-mystical bond that is supposed to unite people into a nation. What kind of fervor, Bardamu–Céline will ask himself again and again, could ever restore a sense of belonging?

As for Ganate on the other hand, however vacuous his life and environment, they suit him fine. For Bardamu's friend is the epitome of the middle-of-the-road, homogeneous character. Ignoring sacred values for which he feels no need, he remains insensitive to strong repulsions as well as powerful, hard-to-explain attractions. That is why, contrary to Bardamu, Ganate abstains from questioning the usual order of things and shuns heroism in a symmetric way: "Don't be such a bloody fool!" he cries to Ferdinand when the latter runs after the troops like a moth flying toward a candle.

Indeed, when common sense returns to Bardamu a couple hours later, he realizes the immediate consequence of his flight of fancy: "The music stopped. Then I said to myself, as I saw how things were going. 'It's not such fun, after all. I doubt if it's worth it.' And I was going to go back. But it was too late! They'd shut the gates behind us, quietly; the civilians had. We were caught, like rats in a trap" (6). The trap simile, however, still originates in that former way of life Bardamu so enthusiastically renounced. But perhaps his incorporation and, soon enough, the festival of the war will nevertheless help him achieve what his civilian upbringing and environment could not.

This is where Bataille's speculation about the army will help us follow the newly enlisted soldier. As I said before, Bataille never experienced army life and does not want to refer to the armies of a particular time or society. His strictly theoretical approach remains unsubstantiated by any direct observation. And he does not even care about the technical function of most national armed forces today — which is to pursue politics by other means. What he projects instead is the powerfully ambivalent image of a human organization irreducible to any other. Bataille calls it "a state within the state," and for him the nature of this "state within" is, by and large, *religious*. Hence its powerful appeal to many souls.

According to his theory, the army teaches soldiers — not to reduce or annihilate the enemy's fighting potential, as Clausewitz would say — but how to live and die in pursuit of glory. This is, as we see, a finality foreign to personal interest or immediate collective pursuits and unlike any in homogeneous society. It aims at nothing less than changing human nature, and so — for Bataille — it does. First of all, it makes men aware of the tragic character of their destiny: no true heroism without this. Such an awareness distinguishes them as much from homogeneous civilians as from animals of prey. Second, uniting men in a quasi-religious way, the army fuses them into a single body and a single soul, albeit aggressive. But it is not so much the aggressiveness that makes an army differ from a religious order as it is the type of relationship established between its leaders and their troops. At the bottom, murderous *brutes* (as Bataille calls professional, lower rank soldiers) derive a measure of gallantry and moral ascendance from their close association with the leaders. At the top, originally noble leaders who become contaminated by the social and moral baseness of their followers. The result is ambiguous and confers to the whole army the troubling prestige — both attractive and repulsive, of total Otherness.

So glory is supposed to play for soldiers the same role salvation plays for monks. Mainly by means of consented sacrifice, a strict set of rules helps men in both groups to be, so to speak, "born again." At the beginning is initiation: through it the novice sheds the old man and comes to belong fully to the community he chose to join. In the military this metamorphosis comes on the battlefield. The French call it *baptême du feu* — "baptism by fire." Like holy water, fire is indeed supposed to purify. Significantly, however, Céline puts this quasi-religious initiation in the semantic field of sexuality: "One is as innocent of Horror as one is of sex" (9) and "I had suddenly discovered, all at once . . . the whole war. I'd lost my innocence" (10). Let's add here that the French original substitutes more openly sexual pollution for purifying fire: "j'étais dépucelé." This transfer puts upside down our reassuring, watered-down concept of the sacred. For complete Otherness is ambivalent: whoever seeks higher forms of life may find lower forms, his quest for the sublime becoming an endless and frustrating play of opposites.

Thus, as green soldiers quickly realize, fire also maims and kills, and sooner or later their turn may come to die. But, as Bataille writes, there is no heroism without accepting this tragic fate in the most conscious way. Fortunately, however, in a manner reminiscent of Christian reversibility, merit extends from each individual soldier or the entire group to the person of its chief, and each member partakes of the leader's glory. What guarantees this fusion of individuals into a single body and a single soul is the chief's *mana*. Only his mysterious prestige and ascendance over others makes possible for soldiers to confuse their own will with the leader's. Only by this consented selflessness can they hope to become better than their own individual selves.

Bataille, however, never lost sight of the ambiguous relationship between the above-described process of elevation and the horrible vocation of the military. If soldiers accept to die, they also train to kill. Smart-looking uniforms, beautiful parades, and martial music are the face of a coin whose reverse is stained by blood, guts, and the like. These men partake of both the saint and the butcher. Here, as Bataille calls it, *hagiology* goes hand in hand with *scatology*. Not surprisingly, this last word brings us back to the mousetrap.

Bardamu's view of the army — from inside the trap and at the bottom of hierarchy — could hardly be as clear-minded and balanced as Bataille's, who — I dare say — probably thought about it in the peaceful surroundings of a library or a book-lined study. But it is also ambivalent. His military experience does affect Ferdinand in two major and apparently irreconcilable ways. On on the one hand, soul-lifting aspects (hagiology) are for him out of sight, while the infamous (scatology) is overwhelmingly everywhere. On the other hand, while seeing at work those devastating forces others call the Sacred, the young soldier seems unwilling to acknowledge them as such. Perhaps he thinks, like Sartre's Orestes in *The Flies*, that otherworldly entities derive all their power from those humans weak enough to believe in gods. But at certain times the faithful or pseudo-faithful cover the surface of the earth like locusts and, seeking to sacralize society, try to sacrifice everyone. Hence Bardamu's cry of anguish when he discovers war's madness: "It is of men, and of them only, that one should always be frightened" (11). The very same message is echoed throughout Céline's work, from *Journey* to the trilogy. However, a nuance of doubt lingers on: "never had I felt the way of men *and things* to be implacable" (9; my italics). This seems to imply that nonhuman (or inhuman) elements are also at play.

This is not necessarily a contradiction on Bardamu's part. He is simply taking the opposite perspective to Bataille's. Instead of first stating principles and presenting their effects by way of deduction, the recent convert and soon-to-be apostate starts by reporting on what he sees and experiences in the most concrete, immediate manner. As Bardamu sees it, the catastrophe in which he has so irrationally involved himself was brought about by *people*, and seemingly high-minded *people* see to it that it continues and worsens. Whether they actually initiated it or were the mere instruments of some kind of fate has little relevance for Bardamu at this point. He does not want to consider war a disaster beyond man's responsibility. While he does call war an *apocalypse*, he shows unequivo-cally that it is man-made. If, however reluctantly, he continues to take part in the massacre after the first five minutes, he blames first of all his enthusiasm. Had he not listened to the gods, jumping thoughtlessly to the pursuit of glory, he would not have become what they wanted him to be — worse than "cattle marked down for slaughter" as Marks's translation reads (94), but "viande à sacrifice" — meat offered to empty entities elevated to the rank of gods. But it is now time to confront the veteran's experience with Bataille's four main points.

1. According to Bataille, the army teaches how to live, suffer, and die in pursuit of glory. In so doing, it is supposed to change human nature.
. For Bardamu, individual and collective glory is nowhere to be found at war. What he sees again and again is only posturing. Behind the lines, all kinds of shirkers play war heroes in a stage production involving the whole country twenty-four hours a day. Concerned about losing the best parts of the play to civilians and noncombatants, front-line soldiers, on what is properly called *theaters* of operations, give up on real heroism and start acting like everyone else. Glory becomes nothing but a product of propaganda. And since everybody fakes everything, the giant, live su-pershow of war brings individuals and society no sense of communion.
This is not to say that the military do not suffer and die. But staying alive is for them just a reprieve before death and is completely estranged from glory. The rule of life the army is supposed to give them for their own betterment merely consists in "[being] tortured and duped to death by a horde of vicious madmen, who had suddenly become incapable of doing anything else as long as they lived, but kill and be slit in half without knowing the reason why" (30). Suffering inspires nothing but bitterness and disgust. The soldier's "métier d'être tué" (31) — incompletely trans-lated into "suicide business," which misses an oxymoron similar to "profes-sional murder victim" — has nothing to do with heroism. It just brings a sure, brutal death strictly devoid of any redeeming value.
In this perspective, it would be tempting to say that, according to Céline, the army "changes human nature," albeit for the worse. But in fact, he does not even go that far. For Céline, man is immutably ambiguous and worrisome. Environment and circumstances emphasize such and such trait, darken this character and lighten that one, but such changes are merely cosmetic. *Hominian* stock cannot be modified and never will. War, however, uncovers new depths, a mix of positive and negative potential more disquieting than ever, upon which the Sacred feeds: "Who could have foreseen, before getting really into the war, what was inside the foul and idle, heroic soul of man? There I was, caught up into a general rush towards murder for all, towards fire. It was a thing that had come up from the depths and here it was on top of us" (9–10).

2. Tragic awareness distinguishes soldiers from fighting animals. It is a necessary condition of heroism.

First of all, no one around Bardamu is really conscious of his own destiny. This reduces acts of courage to little more than military stunts: "There's not much to choose between being brave and being cowardly. The same man will be a rabbit on one occasion and a hero on the next, and equally unconscious of what he's doing on both. . . . What life and death really are does not enter his mind. Even his own death he envisages unclearly and all wrong. Money and footlights are all he understands" (79).

At the top of the military hierarchy the handsome colonel shows "amazing coolness." In antebellum Paris his performance would have outstaged the best artists of the Alhambra music hall: "He walked about, right in the middle of the road, up and down in the thick of these bullets, just as carelessly as if he were waiting for a friend on a station platform; a little impatiently, that's all." But his example completely fails to emulate Bardamu, who exclaims: "What a monster that colonel must be, though. I was sure that, like a dog, *he had no idea of death*" (8–9; my italics). Moreover, he says in French "*pire* qu'un chien." In fact, "worse than a dog," the colonel is a *monster*. This denies Bardamu's commanding officer any claim to heroism.

As for the bottom of the hierarchy, the troop lacks imagination, and they cannot reach the tragic level either: "The guns meant nothing to them but noise. That's why wars can go on. Even those who fight in them, while they're fighting in them, can't realize what war is. With a bullet in their bellies, they would still have gone on picking up old soles on the road, which might still 'come in handy' " (32).

Second, what Bardamu has to say about his own experience is markedly different. One sentence further in the same text he talks about himself and the other unhappy few: "Most people don't die till the very last moment: but some start to die twenty years before their time, and sometimes earlier. They are the unhappy ones of this world" (32). And much further in the text:

> . . . for me there was no choice: my course was settled. I was up to the neck in reality and could see my own death following me, so to speak, step for step. I found it very difficult to think of anything except a fate of slow assassination which the world seemed to consider the natural thing for me.
>
> During this sort of protracted death agony, in which your brain is lucid and your body sound, it is impossible to comprehend anything but the absolute truths. (48)

What then is absolute truth?

Bataille implied that soldiers accept freely and lucidly to sacrifice their own lives. Bardamu sees himself as a sacrificial *victim* of society, and moreover a recalcitrant one. Forgetting that he did, after all, enlist, he now pretends to have neither chosen nor accepted his fate. There is, in other terms, a tragic awareness, but as we will see later it takes him away from heroism, in the opposite direction.

3. The army is supposed to unite men into a single aggressive body and a single soul. What would be the emblem of this common soul?

Beyond any doubt, Céline's French Army unites fighting men into a single aggressive and perishable body whose immortal soul is supposed to be France. But what actually makes soldiers fight, according to Bardamu, is neither this voluntary absorption of individuals into something larger nor the leader's mana. It is purely and simply coercion, and court-martialization in case of insubordination.

As for mana, at least in *Journey*, military leaders lack it thoroughly, and its alleged necessity does not really show. For those officers holding the most power on Bardamu are the chief of staff and the master sergeant of the regiment, who, far from being charismatic leaders, run the regiment like a kind of business. They never risk death, or injury, but coldly expose to danger the lives of their men — whose enthusiasm they do not even need. The M.P.s take care of those who do not want to fight: "Those who still had a little courage left lost even that. It was from that month on that they began to shoot troopers by squads, so as to improve their morale, and the M.P. began to be mentioned in despatches for the way in which he was waging his own little war, the really genuine war . . ." (26).

The Medical Corps collaborates with the M.P.s. In French, Major Bestombes's name is (in a funny way) ominous: it combines Eros and Tanatos into something not unlike "screw you dead!" plus "screw you, dead soldiers!" His functions consist indeed in repairing the soldiers' war-damaged morale in order to send back to the front lines as many men as possible. Those he finds insufficiently motivated Bestombes cures "by electrical treatment of the body and strenuous doses of the ethics of patriotism for the soul, by absolute injections of revitalizing morale" (91). In case the patient proves reluctant to absorb the treatment, he is quickly court-martialed and executed. As for "cured" soldiers, according to Bestombes they

> shed all secondary concepts and false notions, particularly the sentiment of self-preservation. Instinctively and unhesitatingly they merge with the cause of their country, that real justification of all our existences. . . . Like all essential truths, the truth of our duty to our country is comprehended in the heart — your man in the street makes no mistake about that! (91)

Here mana, this mystical bond between a leader and his men, is being caricatured along with the hypothetical absorption of the individual into the army's body and the nation's soul. Expanding a little more on

Bestombes's all-too-expressive name, the system gives soldiers—if I can say—the finger. For Bardamu, the army's absorption in a "common soul" is nothing but a hoax.

4. Finally, do we see in *Journey* a real interdependence between the brutes and the brilliant, noble part of the army? Is the army a state within the state?

First, the model for Bataille's army comes deliberately from earlier periods of history: it could be, for instance, Frederick the Great's mercenaries. But Bardamu serves in a regiment of dragoons, and the French Cavalry, strongly traditional, is still called today *l'Arme noble*. Consequently, one would expect Bataille's ideas to apply. However, Céline does not make the same sharp and general distinction between the noble and the brute. There are noblemen among Bardamu's superiors, but their nobility is by birth—more formal than substantial. On the other side, if there are lowly characters among the noncommissioned officers—especially the master sergeant, this is nothing but a commonplace of military literature, and their group is given little space in *Journey*. As for simple soldiers, they can generally be called *brutes*, but in a sense closer to uneducated country bumpkins than bloodthirsty hoodlums:

> My riders weren't much good at expressing themselves. They hardly talked at all, as a matter of fact. . . . I tried to talk a bit about this village of Barbagny with the one who was next to me, whose name was Kersuzon.
> "Listen, Kersuzon," I said to him. . . . "Can you see anything ahead of us? I can't see anything at all."
> "It's as black as your bottom," Kersuzon told me. Nothing more. (24)

In fact, in war as in peacetime, little people are society's victims before anything else:

> The poor man has two fine ways of dying in this world, either through the complete indifference of his fellow men in time of peace or by the homicidal fury of these same fellow men when war comes. If people start to think about you at all, then it's how to torture you they think of at once; and nothing else but that. You're of no interest to them, the swine, except when you're bleeding. (78)

So Bardamu's fellow soldiers behave more like sheep than wolves. But let's talk about the dogs and the shepherds of the flock before coming back to ritual slaughter.

All that cavalry officers seem to see in war is a more exciting variety of horseshow. For instance, after Lieutenant de Sainte-Engence has killed two German lancers, his company leader congratulates him publicly as if they were on a racetrack: "He was great. I wish you could have seen him! . . . I missed none of it. I was right behind him. Lunge forward and right!

Zip! Over goes the first of them! Then the point into the other's chest — on the left this time. Cross and thrust! . . . Well done again, Sainte-Engence!" (27). It should be added here that the French word *engeance* (with an *a*) refers to a whole category of nefarious animals or persons. Hyphenated with the signifier of sainthood, this name infers that virtue and malignity are in the army two inseparable forms of something nevertheless sacred. Bataille's view of the military as total Otherness finds support in *Journey* at the lieutenant-captain level, even though it is in passing and in a satiric mode.

Literally at the top of the pyramid, Bataille's theory finds a better application with General des Entrayes, chief purveyor of death for the division he commands. This officer bears an even more ominous name. It is pronounced in French like *des entrailles* — "entrails." His patronym is loosely connected with bloody sacrifices, since in ancient times haruspices were used to split open animals and consult their viscera in order to forecast the future. And the future looks sinister, as is shown by Bardamu's portrait of his chief:

> The Aztecs, so I've heard, used to disembowel eight thousand believers a week in their Temples of the Sun, as a sacrifice to the God of the Clouds so that he would send them rain. It's one of those things that must be hard to believe until you've gone to a war. But once you're there, everything is understandable and the Aztecs' unconcern for other men's bodies is the same as the said General Céladon des Entrayes must have felt for my humble insides; for he had risen in rank until he himself had become a sort of exact god, a kind of horrible, merciless little sun. (33)

As we see, the religious element, essential to Bataille's thinking, becomes a dark joke. At first glance, des Entrayes's appearance shows nothing awesome or even impressive. For example, this little divinity likes Good and Beauty, though under the guise of gourmet dinners and rose gardens. This should be reassuring, like so many representations of a benevolent Almighty — *le bon Dieu*, as the French say. But, like *Deus absconditus* — "the hidden God" — the old, physically impaired general is also hard to approach and "silent." Perhaps his love for roses symbolizes the fact that higher echelons of military authority, far from being outwardly impressive, are on the contrary exerted *sub rosa*. But it does not make the lackluster general any less cruel. No less than a pre-Columbian god, bloodthirsty des Entrayes demands human flesh. Since his lack of majesty makes impossible personal emulation, only sacrifice can confer on his soldiers their leader's *nobility*. This is why the soldier's elevation is achieved, so to speak, post mortem. What sacralizes the victim is mechanized evisceration; only after Bardamu's "humble insides" will have been offered in this way to the Sun God whom he is forced to obey will they deserve the far nobler name of *entrailles*. In these conditions, Bataille's interpersonal bond is absolutely irrelevant, it would serve no more purpose than in the slaughterhouse. According to Céline, the army's awesome

Otherness is achieved impersonally, by an administrative system that produces ridicule and gore instead of glory. In short, it is closer to Kafka's *Strafkolonie* than Bataille's "state within the state."

It should be recalled here that in yet another twist, when brilliant models of military demeanor are offered to the *brutes* at the bottom, this happens far from the front lines. Paris is full of smart-looking officers and auxiliary women dressed in beautiful uniforms, acting more martial than the privates, worn to a frazzle on short R&R leaves. There everyone performs as on a stage. Ironically, this is what front-line soldiers try to emulate.

In conclusion, without invalidating all of Bataille's speculations about the nature of the army, Bardamu–Céline strips them of their positive aspects and turns them upside down. While homogeneous peace-time society shows no concern whatever for its members, in time of war the very same society resacralizes values that had become harmlessly official. But this is done in an oblique way, in such a manner that everyone is not equally involved. The sacrificial frenzy simply sets apart millions of young male victims destined to be killed, and a heartless, mindless officers' corps is entrusted with the job. Whether and how Bardamu, being one of the designated victims, could turn his back to the sacred and escape being butchered becomes for him the central issue.

Glory, he reasons, was the poisonous bait that attracted him and is now threatening his life. A possible antidote could then be cowardice. Instead of standing tall and dying a *hero* like his ill-fated colonel, he would rather crawl away and save his skin. But it is easier thought than done: the M.P.s are watching. Only through deception will he have any chance. He will ape the faithful and pretend to accept *martyrdom*, as Iranian government clerics call it in the 1980s in similar circumstances. This the testament of a fellow soldier, who says to him before disappearing, "ah camarade, ce monde n'est je vous l'assure qu'une immense entreprise à se foutre du monde," rather poorly translated by Marks as: "Ah, my friend, this world is nothing but a vast attempt to catch you with your trousers down . . ." (64). Now, learning from those in power becomes the only way to survive. And what he learns is how to "screw everyone" (a cultural, more than linguistic, approximation of *se foutre du monde*) while pretending to fulfill his duties. In the long run, as we know, Bardamu's plot seems to succeed. Although, fooled by his coolness, his officers entrust him with dangerous missions, during which he manages not to get killed, he is eventually wounded. From one hospital to the other, cunningly working his way to freedom, he finally obtains an honorable discharge. We find him next aboard an Africa-bound ship, where he finds out that tinkering with one's fate is not that simple.

Aboard the S.S. *Admiral Bragueton*, the newly discharged soldier quickly feels like an alien in the midst of his fellow passengers. They first look down at him as an "insignificant dreamer" (114). But when the ship approaches Africa, their erstwhile disdain turns into slander. Later, since he will not talk, rumors spread freely about his alleged perversity. The general consensus is that some hideous crime forced him to run from France. Groping for an explanation, while their malevolence keeps growing and comes more and more into the open, he reviews and rejects rational hypotheses. For instance, as a passenger paying his own fare, is he not a living reproach to this community of colonial civil servants and military officers, all traveling free of charge at taxpayers' expense? They might consider this intolerable provocation. Or, shellshocked as he had been in war, would he be ostracized because they believe him dangerously insane? At the beginning of the trip, he found a dark pleasure in becoming, for the first time in his life, the center of everyone's attention. Now, however, talks he overhears about throwing him overboard seem to threaten his very safety. Staying at all times in his cabin, which he leaves only to eat and answer other calls of nature, he still tries to understand what brought him that low. With a mix of pride and fright, he finally realizes his total Otherness in the eyes of his fellow passengers:

> Without wishing it, I had begun to take the part of the "infamous unworthy wretch," the scorn of humanity, pointed at through the centuries, familiar to every one, like God and the Devil, but assuming always a different shape, so fugitive on earth and in life as to be actually indefinable. To pick out this wretch, to seize on him and identify him, exceptional conditions had been needed, such as only existed on our restricted hulk. (112)

This could be — and has been — attributed to paranoia on the part of Bardamu: he would disproportionately enlarge a few isolated incidents, link them together and imagine a plot against him involving everyone on board. Or, in a manner which is not exclusive of their victim's alleged paranoia, the passengers themselves, overwhelmed by boredom and tropical heat, would substitute for Bardamu a collective phantasm. One could also read through the grotesque name of the ship, formed after the French word *braguette*, which refers to the trouser flies left carelessly unbuttoned by all the uniformed drunks aboard. The title "admiral" associates the navy with this image and, I dare say, lays bare the military's obscene side. And, since the ever-increasing heat uncovers lower instincts, it is not by chance that people *unbutton* more and more. Finally, in this environment of imaginary war heroes, *Bragueton* associates with the English *bragg*. But, as convincing as this could be, it is not the main level of interpretation suggested by the very letter of the text. Not only in the quotation above, but throughout these pages from *Journey*, religious terms — not always properly translated in Marks's version — point toward an intimate, live experience of the Sacred. Indeed, something foreign to secular modes of explanation is taking place here: "The colonial officers at the captain's table, primed with apértifs, the tax collectors, and the governesses from the Congo . . . had endowed me with *an infernal importance* . . ." (114; my italics). The next sentence of the French text refers to Bardamu's newly acquired "troublant prestige" — this mixture of attractiveness and repulsiveness currently associated with the sacred. As for the passengers themselves, Bardamu calls them "devilish" (111). In other words, the hell of war is again claiming the damned. In fact, when captain Frémizon and his escort finally corner him, Bardamu realizes it: "The man seemed to me *like a further fragment of the war confronting me again*, purposeful, murderous, inescapable.

At the same time, drawn up behind him, very much on the alert, four junior officers blocked the companionway, *forming an escort to Fate*" (116; my italics).

A *sacrifice*, "general moral rejoicing [is] imminent aboard the *Admiral Bragueton*" (112). Gathering every day in a *morning concile* (112), "those about to *perform the sacrifice*" (115) plan to *purify the boat of* [the] *putrid presence* (120) of the *beast*. This time *the evil-eyed one* wasn't going to get away with it. And that meant me" (112). Obviously all these signifiers refer to a ritual execution, minutely organized to achieve maximum solemnity. It aims at purifying the community of its bestiality in order to regenerate it. In one word, what we see here in the making is an expiatory sacrifice. As for the victim, his sacralization is guaranteed not only by absolute seclusion from ordinary humanity, but by extraordinary precautions. Since no one can touch sacred beings in all impunity, Bardamu's awesome new status makes it now impossible to throw him overboard in a discreet, expeditious manner. For fear of sacrilege, strict rules must be observed to immolate such a victim. When time will come, a "full, dramatic ceremonial" (116) will indeed be observed.

It is hard to believe in Bardamu's sincerity when he still asks himself, at this crucial time, "what [he] had done for things to come to such a pitch" (113). Although he is understandably reluctant to face it, it is starkly simple and ominous. In joining the army on that fateful day at the Place Clichy where everything began, he has absent-mindedly entered the sphere of the Sacred and — in so doing — become untouchable. He is *branded* (118). The French original — *marqué à la tête* (literally branded "on his head") is a sign of supernatural election, like the little horn-shaped flames on the head of Michaelangelo's Moses. He should never have badmouthed the gods, who are now exacting their revenge. If he once believed he had fooled them and severed for good his ties with the sacred realm, he must now realize they had simply slackened the line, but that the hook is still holding fast to his mouth.

I am not borrowing this fishing metaphor from Céline himself, but from Paul Claudel's play *Le Soulier De Satin*, because it goes to the heart of the matter. Had Bardamu kept his mouth shut, he would not have attracted attention and set himself apart from the flock. Early at the beginning of the war he had already figured himself "swallowing a full mouthful of Flanders mud, more than a mouthful, [his] face split from ear to ear in one flash" (15). In other words, he imagined his mouth "washed out with battlefield mud" like a child's with soap. Worse, not only his mouth but his whole face would be "split open" in the "flash" that would kill him. But punishment symbolically begins with the mouth, the source of evil. Bardamu will come back to the danger of speaking his mind toward the end of the novel, just before the closing words: "let's [talk] no more of all this." These echo the opening line, already quoted here: "I hadn't said anything. I hadn't said a word." And here is the lesson Bardamu learns at last, far later than the *Bragueton* episode:

> One can never be sufficiently defiant with words; words don't seem to be saying anything much; they don't seem dangerous certainly, just little puffs of air, little clicks in the mouth, neither one thing nor the other, and as soon as they reach the ear easily apprehended by one's great soft grey lump of a brain. One's unsuspicious about words . . . and some misfortune ensues.
>
> Among them, there are some hidden away under all the others, like pebbles. You don't particularly notice them and then suddenly they've made all the life there is in you tremble, all of it entirely, both in its weakness and in its strength. . . . And you're terrified. . . . The thing's an avalanche. . . .
>
> . . . So one's never distrustful enough of words, that's the conclusion I've come to. (490–91)

As for Céline, it will take him far more time to apply this to himself. The preface to the Pléiade reedition of *Journey* in 1957 reads: "If I weren't in such a bind, if I didn't need to earn a living, I am telling you as it is, I would destroy everything, I wouldn't save a single line. Everything was misunderstood. All I spurred is malevolence."[5]

Let's go back to Bardamu. It is as if the free spirit who takes the stage to demystify social life finds himself in turn captured and mystified by something much bigger and stronger than him. He gets burned in trying to steal fire from those dark forces buried inside themselves that men sometimes call their gods. Emotion overwhelms him and he feels again the dangerous compulsion to express his feelings. This is why he utters this nostalgic cry in the same preface just quoted: "Ah, we'd better be blind and deaf!" This means, among other things, that once dangerous words have been pronounced, the point of no return has been reached. For were he able to keep quiet, he would still after that *see* and *hear* evil everywhere. It follows that the choice of speaking or not speaking is rigged from that time on. On the one hand, whether he succumbs to the urge to say it all or keeps an expressive silence loaded with meaning (the French call it for this reason *eloquent* silence), he designates himself to the dangerous attention of the sacrifiers. On the other hand, if he successfully hides everything and talks like most people instead of vaticinating, he feels cowardly and becomes the accomplice of an evil that he does not dare anymore to denounce. Significantly, this is foreshadowed as early as the end of the *Bragueton* episode.

The four military officers who prevent Bardamu from reaching the safety of his cabin make the tactical blunder of interrogating him. Their victim jumps on the opportunity to delay his execution and starts talking to confuse and ultimately disarm them. Exploiting their obtusiveness, he flings at them flatteries, commonplaces, and patriotic clichés that put them mentally to sleep and make them forget the sacrifice they were about to perform:

> When not actually busy killing, your soldier's a child. He's easily amused. Unaccustomed to thought, as soon as you talk to him he has to make terrific efforts in order to understand what you're saying. Captain Frémizon wasn't engaged in murdering me, he wasn't drinking either, he wasn't doing anything with his hands, or with his feet: he was merely endeavouring to think. It was vastly too much for him. Actually I had him mentally overcome. (118)

If this means that the pen (or the word) is mightier than the sword, the proof is at best ambiguous, for Bardamu's victory is based on self-denial. Far from exposing his persecutors, his words court them and pay tribute to what nearly had him killed: " 'Among soldiers and gentlemen, should any misunderstanding be allowed to exist? Long live France, then, in God's name! Vive la France!' . . . That was the only time my country saved my life; till then, it had been quite the reverse" (119). Bardamu has no vocation for being a martyr. While disguising his alterity, he could feel ashamed of himself like Peter denying Christ. But on the contrary, he boasts about it: "One is never fearful enough. As it was, thanks to a certain skillfulness on my part, I lost nothing but what was left of my self-respect" (110–11). After a long apprenticeship, lying low and acting cowardly is at last his chosen way of life. This is the wisdom his military experience finally brought him instead of glory. He has become an antihero. As soon as his persecutors slumber in a drunken sleep, he flees them by jumping ship in the middle of the night. Freedom greets him ashore in comforting silence and darkness, and hope rushes back. From now on, willing as he is to shed his useless pride at the first occasion, he might eventually escape the attention of all potential sacrificers.

Precisely, the trilogy in one way may be viewed as representative of the difficulties and pitfalls of writing for a writer who has been deserted by his readers. This emphasis on the making of the book may also be a convenient way to dilute and to an extent neutralize the touchy subject matter of Céline's flight to Germany at the end of the war. Here the French language plays for him a role by and large similar to France's role for Bardamu in the *Bragueton* episode of *Journey*.

Both the relative failure of *Normance–Féerie* and the public ostracism of Céline long after 1945 must for him have raised the question of whether or not to pursue writing. With *Death on the Installment Plan* and *Guignol's Band I & II*, the Ferdinand saga had come to a conclusion, and new pamphlets were politically unthinkable — unless confined to style, such as *Professor Y*. The Céline who has succeeded Bardamu and Ferdinand as subject of enunciation took a sluggish start with *Féerie II*, partly because the writer's style had not evolved enough to support his new narrative mode (the text is too compact and univocal), and partly because, in my opinion, he was skirting those burning questions raised by the cohabitation of the French with their Nazi occupants. Even with a grain of salt, *féerie* and *merveilleux* — categories that translate so inadequately into English by such words as "fairy" and "wonder" — poorly apply to the tragedy of World War II. In any case, for better or worse, Céline had become a legend and was expected to continue walking on a tightrope, tackling issues everyone else would avoid. Failing to do so, he would lose his public. But in doing so, he could lose himself. For he is now, writing the trilogy, far more real in *écrivain maudit* than just fashionable like Sade and Lautréamont — who, if they could scare away anyone, would repel only the most obtuse, uncultured bourgeois. Behind and ahead of Céline, who cannot at this point escape his own image, the Sacred is lurking more than ever. *Bragueton*'s Roman circus has now grown to the size of France, and in fact the circus has become a leitmotiv of the trilogy.

If the Meudon recluse stops writing and becomes silent, as he claims he would have liked, his rediscovered mutism may be interpreted as an admission of guilt concerning the dark years. But if he writes, how could he recapture his audience? As improbable as it sounds, he will attempt to act humble, at least by his standards. In the numerous nonnarrative pages of the trilogy, the writer presents himself as burned-out, as well as burned. On the burned-out side, Céline shows himself ailing and made prematurely old by his imprisonment. He pretends to yearn for retirement: "If I wasn't bugged by debts, I'd be taking it easy. . . . I'm old enough to retire . . . and so I will . . . all I want . . . is short walks, very short, with canes and smoked glasses . . . so nobody'll notice me . . . *enough we have suffered* . . . hell! that settles it!"[6] In any case, he allegedly lost contact with the public's tastes, does not have the patience and humility to listen to his friends' advice, and sulks. On the burned side, his cowardly compatriots made him a pariah in his own country, a convenient scapegoat who will help them dispose of their own war-related guilt. In more openly religious terms, as an untimely and unsolicited prophet, he is perceived by the national community as sacrilegious — and for this reason untouchable. Here we recognize the form of sacralization conferred in ancient times to criminals, as well as the scrupulous isolation of the "infamous, unworthy wretch" aboard *Bragueton*.

In sum, Céline feels he is the victim of a curse. Hence his nostalgic dreams about backtracking, becoming again the lackluster young Bardamu from before *Journey*'s first words, the private lad who had never "talked." Hence his bitter scorn for anything that would confer upon the writer some kind of sacerdotal function and priestly status: unlike a romantic poet, contemporary writers cannot pretend any more to be ahead of the crowd, carrying the torch of progress, nor expect any reverence. For Western history is finished, the future's sole promise is an apocalypse, and prophets of doom meet only with hostility. There is no other important message he would like to deliver. "Reason died in 1914," and with it died all that made France creative and respected: work ethics, selfless education, and pride in a job well done. That his own shrill trumpet contributed to tearing down Jericho's walls does not enter into the picture—though it certainly stays very much on his mind.

This is why Céline's outbursts take in the trilogy two opposite directions: on the one hand he calls—like Rimbaud in his *Illuminations*—for a quick end to Western civilization. Playing biblical prophet, the irrational Céline announces to his contemporaries the fire and brimstone their mindlessness will very soon bring. On the other hand, what is left of the rationalist nostalgically looks back at the turn of the century, praising above all its still unabashed confidence in common sense. Going still further back in time, he claims the free-thinker's heritage of French seventeenth-century Epicureans and defiantly professes at the very beginning of *Rigadoon*: "I say the same as Ninon de Lenclos! God was invented by the priests! absolutely antireligious! . . . That's my faith once and for all!" (1).

In any case, along with yesteryear's traditions and culture, literary genres such as the novel are dying, and academic French has become a fossil, like the Forty Academicians themselves and all current literary celebrities. In such inauspicious conditions, how would Céline make himself heard again—while avoiding the pilori?

He will try by tapping an old rhetorical resource—the *captatio benevolentiae*, albeit in rather unexpected ways. In so doing, incidentally, he breaks with his more customary *captatio malevolentiae*—if I can coin the phrase—that worked so well that it nearly cost him his life. Now Céline appeals to his readers' goodwill by acting mainly as a court jester. In other words, he makes a public display of his downfall. Prophecy mascarades in vaticination, and the prophet turns into a buffoon. However unpalatable his message might be, it is delivered under the guise of black humor. He pretends not to have serious intents, and self-derision guarantees what has been recently called by the American government "plausible deniability."

Court jesters could afford to express, tongue-in-cheek, certain things no one else would ever dare say. Indeed, at the core of the trilogy there is a blanket accusation leveled at postwar French society, as well as a plea of innocence entered by Céline concerning his activities before and during the war. But, as in the *Bragueton* episode, the defendant–prosecutor counts more on his verbal cunning than on an earnest defense based on facts.

As mentioned earlier, romantic dreamers talked and acted as high priests. At least for this writer, fallen as he has from grace, no sacerdotal prestige could ever compensate for the alleged indignities of his trade. Céline would have liked us to believe that he was writing only to scrounge a living—and would have given it all up if he could find another way to purchase noodles and carrots and pay his utility bills. Making a book, he pretended, had become to him nothing but a chore—and one harder and harder to dispatch. His trilogy would be nothing but a commercial endeavor—an undignified compromise between the book market's demands (entertaining the public to promote the sale of his books) and a residual, narrower interest for literature, which focuses—away from ideas—on the problematic of writing.

Indeed, the trilogy is loaded with comments on style and composition like that heavy slab of a volume that closes *Remembrance of Things Past*. Not unlike Marcel Proust (who ironically writes in that very same work that books laden with theories are as distasteful as personal possessions one would leave with their pricetags on), Céline weaves and stretches his narrative in such a way that events are given less importance than authorial interventions. However, he seems to take the opposite point of view to *Le Temps retrouvé*'s on its own generative principle: while the latter unequivocally states that style (broadly defined) is not a matter of technique but a matter of vision, the trilogy appears to give precedence to linguistic invention at the expense of most everything else. In fact, contrary to the famous cathedral-like structure of Proust's entire novel, in Céline's "chronicle" all historical and biographic materials seem to receive, to say the least, a cavalier treatment: chronological interpolations, memory lapses, and pseudo-geriatric harping combine to produce a deliberately broken and confusing narrative. Even the following striking image, which quite properly explains the trilogy's constantly shifting point of view, is presented in a tongue-in-cheek, facetious manner, as if unworthy of serious consideration:

> Bergson tells us! you fill a wooden box, a big one, with fine iron filings, and you plunk your fist in it, a good hard punch . . . what do you see? you've made a crater . . . the exact same shape as your fist! . . . To understand what's happened, this phenomenon, two kinds of intelligence, two explanations . . . the intelligence of the befuddled ant, who wonders by what miracle another insect, an ant itself, has been able to keep all these filings in a state of equilibrium, in the shape of a crater . . . and the other intelligence, genius, yours, mine, explains it by saying that a simple blow of the fist has sufficed . . . as a chronicler I have to choose . . . with the ant explanation I could amuse you . . . scurrying around in the filings . . . with the fist explanation I could entertain you too, but much less . . . the Chinese in Brest . . . all churches in the same boat . . . Demolition and Co . . . Hebraic, Rome, Protestant, tutti

frutti! . . . in the short time I've left to live, I'd better not annoy you too much. . . . (29)

It is a fact that the chronicle continually shifts from the point of view of the *ant* to that of the *genius*. Broadly speaking, the ant takes care of the strictly narrative parts, while the genius — who here and there gives himself the playful name "Nostradamus" — raves, prophesies, and more often than not indulges in histrionics. No more high priest, more trickster than magician (for magic supposes the supernatural), the author-in-the-text plays clown to entertain his public and debases his work as pseudo-comics aimed at a practically illiterate consumer society. The ant experiences everything at ground level with a severely limited, constantly moving outlook. Nostradamus acts as a visionary, madcap genius. Nothing remains in between, where one would expect to find the classic detached observer — with his moderation and sense of perspective. Consequently, the reader is left with an unreliable narrator echoed — and at times contradicted — by a sort of chorus made of one man only, but whose several voices do not sing in unison. In addition, the writer carves out traditional narrative forms and multiplies ellipses. This conveniently dilutes the real author's extraliterary responsibility. But it also lightens his text, varies tones and rhythms — a decisive progress over *Féerie*.

In fact, it is a tremendous progress: all narrative passages in the trilogy belie Céline's posturing as a has-been writer. Lacking the space actually to demonstrate how the gruffy Scheherazade manages to captivate his readers, I will limit myself to an impressionist metaphor: as soon as Céline is finished playing Cassandra, all of a sudden his text stops dragging and takes off like a kite in the wind. Freed at once from rancor and sarcasm, it soars lightly and happily in spite of the tribulations it is about to narrate. Most probably it owes part of its life to the "simultaneous" narrative mode chosen by Céline — which pretends to share with us the events unfolding, not unlike the play-by-play broadcast of a ballgame. But this is not the sole reason. The writer takes hold of the past by reshaping it, and pure storytelling power compensates for his impotence in the face of current or future events. He is now the one to cast spells on others. As paradoxic as it sounds, these parts of the trilogy have a lot in common with the Krogold stories in *Death on the Installment Plan*. They too crash sooner or later on what Henri Michaux called, in a strikingly Icarian poem,[7] "the hard ground of my destiny" — in other words, reality.

I suggest that "reality" is all the more merciless in the trilogy because of Céline's unwillingness to soar above it at any length on the wings of artistic illusion. Perhaps Céline's narrative flights of half-fancy come back to earth so often because he feared being changed into a statue of salt (i.e., reified, forever categorized) if he looked too long toward the past, which no one wants to hear about. For his relevance would have thus ended in 1945. Or he feared being reduced to what the French call a *potiche* — a senescent, useless public character strictly confined to decorative functions, like those pretentious vases that cluttered bourgeois chimney mantels and grand pianos decades ago. He often refers to such *potiches* as the Forty Academicians and, foremost among them, the Catholic François Mauriac and, again, this belies whatever Céline writes about reaching the threshold of senility.

Céline was far from senile. Like the young new novelists of his time whom he professed to ignore, he questions in the trilogy the aims and means of the novelist and takes his distances from his first, still relatively traditional novels. In so doing he attempts to demystify art, to expose the imaginary compensations that give a writer the illusion of power. Writing, he realized, will not change the world. It just changes the language, and most of the time only within the confines of a specific work. Instead of acting on the world, writers would merely act on words. This explains Céline's stubborn rejection of anything sacred, beyond mere artistic values. But can he really desacralize art? I am not sure that trying to impede — mainly through ridicule — the assumption of writing (in a religious sense) could ever remove Céline from the roster of the "most sacred" and bring him back into social acceptance.

The trilogy's artistic success owes a lot to stylistic innovation. But style too, if we are to believe Céline, is nothing but a bag of tricks — a harmless hobby as skilled, yet as out-of-fashion, as lacemaking. However, Céline's professional pride does not completely give way to self-debasement. Not unlike the precious Jean Giraudoux, albeit with a completely different array of linguistic devices, the trilogy's author emphasizes and celebrates style as another way to keep at bay the sacred — or in any case what he feels uncontrollably threatening. In a perspective similar to Boris Vian's, who once wrote that humor is a form of politeness born out of despair, Céline's *petit truc* — his special way with words and syntax — looks to me not only like an elegant challenge to adversity, but also like a *garde-fou* (literally, a protective rail or device against one's potential folly). On the one hand, by focusing the reader's attention on forms, he deflects it — not without shrewdness — from bare facts. On the other, like Candide's garden, language is worth cultivating in the place of metaphysics. Finally, however bitter and rejected he feels, Céline still feels a need for social communion. If, in order to find it again, he must worship something in common with his compatriots, the French language must have looked to him a sure way.

This is in a way the trilogy's wager. However, the aging writer's worshiping the medium in lieu of the work makes one wonder whom he is deceiving — the reader or himself. As far as he is concerned, it may not make sense to change the assumption of writing into that of French. It is a fact that most people in France still value their language as something akin to the sacred — like most Americans their Constitution. But the trilogy acknowledges that French too will share the decline of the whole nation, and ultimately become extinct like so many idioms before it. Moreover, although his writing technique was supposed to give an old tongue a new lease on life, Céline's transposition of spoken French in the written form already confuses his younger compatriots, who today can hardly read him without glossaries.

As Raymond Queneau once observed in an unrelated article published long after Céline's death,[8] the linguistic impact of the mass media may have prevented for a long time the evolution of literary French in the direction of more spontaneous spoken forms. (Radio and television, Queneau observed, impose on the whole nation the same codified standard language and in a way teach it.) But *neo-French* — as Queneau optimistically called "street French" before realizing that it would not become the new standard — keeps changing. So no one but die-hard Célinists will deny that the famous *métro émotif* — patterned after an essentially unstable kind of French spoken on the street during the first third of our century — is today beginning to jump track.

Céline considered expressing emotion the key to writing. Literally like the subway, his *métro émotif* was meant to be an underground system of mass transportation. But more specifically, like the Paris *métro*, these masses his covered tracks were meant to "transport" were strictly Parisian. If Céline aimed at rendering in a written form ordinary Parisian speech (he insists again and again on being an authentic, native Parisian — presumably the epitome of Frenchness), it was in the belief that sharing an authentically common idiom means sharing emotions. In other words, it would conduce French people to feeling really *French*, and in the most ethnic, parochial manner, exclusive of all those strangers — immigrants, foreigners — who were in his eyes threatening the nation's sense of community. No wonder then that, after the war, Céline treats his language as the last social bond. Claiming again and again in the trilogy that he sacrificed himself in all possible ways to his ungrateful country, he nevertheless comes back to the altar, pretending to save his country from the American melting pot into which all of Europe was being thrown. Behind apparently innocuous aesthetic concerns, one can still hear, although somewhat muted, the same nationalist predication as before the war. This time, however, not only is the altar nearly deserted, but the preacher's language has grown apart from his flock's during his years of linguistic and cultural reclusion. Speaking neither the commoner's up-to-date language nor the then fashionable intellectual lingo, the writer ironically owes his mitigated success on his being ostracized; that is, on the very sacralization he sought so hard to escape.

But, in fact, did he *really* try? I suspect his mourning the death of reason to be nothing but posture. It is not, in any case, the current (and curiously ambivalent) fascination — on the part of some scholars — for fascism and other social forms of the heterogeneous, which will soon desacralize Céline. His very ambivalence, the mix of attraction and repulsion he continues to inspire, points in my opinion toward the contrary. Céline *is* sacred. Eventually, one could fear, the unrepentant racist and nationalist will not have, after all, "crusaded for nothing," as he complains he did. Perhaps another type of society, lean and mean like the Meudon solitary—who claimed all over the trilogy to eat very little and drink nothing but water—will bury what has been called *la société obèse*. The question is, then, do we really want to set about toward that kind of holy land, that mystical Orient, and restore a real social bond at the price of the contractual and legal systems on which our much despised homogeneous societies are still based? What is good for literature is not necessarily good for the country.

Notes

1. Victor Hugo. "Sacer esto," in *Les Châtiments*, vol. 4, *Oeuvres poétiques II* (Paris: Gallimard, 1967), 94–95. This poem has been little commented upon and deals with the sacred status of the criminal. It shows Victor Hugo's perfect awareness of the sacred's ambivalence.

2. George Bataille, "Structure et fonction de l'Armée," in *Le Collège de Sociologie*, ed. Denis Hollier (Paris: Gallimard, 1980), 225–65.

3. Louis-Ferdinand Céline, *Journey to the End of the Night*, trans. John H. P. Marks. (Boston: Little, Brown & Co., 1934), 5; hereafter cited in the text.

4. George Bataille, "La Structure psychologique du fascisme," in *Oeuvres Completes*, vol. 1 (Paris: Gallimard, 1970), 339 & ff.

5. Louis-Ferdinand Céline, *Voyage au bout de la nuit* (Paris: Gallimard, 1962), 9.

6. Louis-Ferdinand Céline, *Rigadoon*, trans. Ralph Manheim (New York: Dell Publishing Co., 1974), 15; hereafter cited in the text.

7. Henri Michaux, "Chant de mort," in *Un Certain Plume* (1938). Another of Michaux's poems, "Clown" (*Peintures*, 1938), seems to prefigure Céline's clowning in the trilogy.

8. In *L'Express*, special issue, "Comment va la France?" no. 985 (bis), 1970.

ON CÉLINE

"I've inherited a kind of modesty from my mother, a total insignificance, and I mean total. What interests me is to be completely ignored. I have a propensity . . . an animal propensity, for crawling away . . ."
                                                           —*Paris Review*, 1960

". . . experience is a muffled lantern that throws light only on the bearer . . . it's incommunicable . . . better keep these things to myself . . ."
                                                           —*Paris Review*, 1960

Louis-Ferdinand Céline: Excerpts from His Letters to Milton Hindus

Milton Hindus*

Louis-Ferdinand Céline (the pen name of Dr. Louis Destouches, a French physician) died in Meudon, a suburb of Paris, early in July 1961. He had been born in Courbevoie, another suburb of Paris, sixty-seven years before. In the United States, his death occasioned a two-column obituary in the *New York Times* on July 5, and a mention in the columns of *Time*; in its July–August 1961 issue, the avant-garde *Evergreen Review* carried one of the last interviews with Céline, given shortly before his death to a Mr. Robert Stromberg. In France, notice of the event was understandably much greater. The popular picture magazine *Paris-Match* devoted an article to it, taking as its timely peg the coincidence of Céline's death and Ernest Hemingway's and making an extended comparison and contrast between the literary styles and the politics of the two authors. The newspaper *Arts* featured a discussion of Céline's literary significance by three French authors (who concluded, as one of them put it, that he was "the Rabelais of the Atomic Era") and printed also an interview Céline had granted to André Parinaud a few weeks before he died. The literary *Nouvelle Revue Française*, organ of Céline's latest publisher, Gallimard, carried an article in its August issue commemorating his death.

Who was Céline, whose name is hardly remembered by the American public, to merit such attention? For one thing, he was the author of more than a dozen books (several of them diatribes against the Jews, the Bolsheviks, and the so-called "pluto-democracies," an aspect of his work I have treated in my book *The Crippled Giant*). But what is sure to remain of permanent interest to the world is his major literary accomplishment, the forthright account of his own life. For almost thirty years now, readers have been intrigued and outraged by his two early autobiographical romances, *Journey to the End of the Night* and *Death on the Installment Plan* (*Voyage au bout de la nuit* and *Mort à crédit* in the original French) which are really the two halves of one work—*Death on the Installment Plan* dealing with the childhood and youth of the fictional narrator

*Reprinted with permission of Milton Hindus and the Humanities Research Center, University of Texas at Austin, from *Texas Quarterly*, no. 4 (Winter 1962): 22–38.

Ferdinand Bardamu up to the time of his military service, and *Journey to the End of the Night* dealing with his experiences in the first world war and his travels to Africa and the United States afterwards. *Journey* was a best seller in this country as it was in so many other countries and — what is a surprising coincidence — an intellectual *succès d'estime* as well. The latest literary movement to claim the writer of these works as one of its own spiritual progenitors is that of the Beatniks, but interest in him will probably outlive this association as it has already outlived its association with the earlier existentialism. (Jean-Paul Sartre took an epigraph from Céline for one of his initial imaginative works, and Henry Miller has listed *Journey to the End of the Night* among the books that have influenced him the most.)

These two works gained the suffrage of some of the outstanding literary men of the time: André Gide, Thomas Mann, Henry de Montherlant (who compares Céline's distinction as a stylist to that of the great memoir writer, Saint-Simon), Leon Trotsky, Léon Daudet, Georges Bernanos, Elie Faure, and, as might be expected on ideological grounds, Ezra Pound. The admiration of such men, though not necessarily a decisive consideration, inclines me to believe that Céline's work will continue to excite interest and exert influence in the future. For, as Felix Adler once remarked to Walt Whitman, readers must not only be counted, they must be *weighed*. The weight of some of Céline's readers and the weight of the words they have pronounced in his favor seem to me impressive indeed.

The interest of the following excerpts of my letters from Céline, written over a period of a little more than a year (1947–1948), is self-evident, I think. The letters possess an intrinsic interest in themselves but they also reflect the fact that they come from the writer of *Journey to the End of the Night* and *Death on the Installment Plan* and occasionally relate directly to the composition and characters of these books. In no other of his writings to my knowledge has Céline been so explicit about his literary aims or so analytical about what he takes to be the value of his own accomplishments.

These letters are lively, direct, uninhibited — so uninhibited at times that I have felt compelled to draw a veil of decency over a few of the expressions with the insertion of a series of discreet dots. . . . (Even in France, where publishing standards are not so puritanical as in our country, Céline's works were often published in a bowdlerized version.) The "masculine" language is not incompatible with a generally high, nonpartisan, and, to use Matthew Arnold's word, disinterested standard of taste that is maintained throughout.

Céline's literary heroes are not all unconventional. His three leading exemplars appear to be Shakespeare, Cervantes, and Villon. He also shows humility before the accomplishments of La Rochefoucauld, Molière, Bossuet, Chénier, and Flaubert. He grants the merits of Dostoevsky, Whitman, and Dreiser, while remaining critical of them in important respects. His reaction to Joyce is unfavorable, and his opinion is mixed with regard to both Proust and Gide. He does not admire very much writers like Henry Miller and Sartre, whose names have often been linked with his own by critics, but he does show great admiration for Henri Barbusse (at the time he wrote Le Feu) and for Paul Morand, who was the first to "jazz up" the French language according to Céline. The fact that Barbusse was a Communist and Morand an ambassador of Pétain's Vichy regime seems not to influence Céline's purely literary estimate of their value. He himself, of course, benefited from a similar tolerance among his own enthusiastic critics — Bolshevik Trotsky and Royalist Léon Daudet must have had few ideas in common other than their admiration for Voyage au bout de la nuit. His preference for Barbusse and Morand as against Proust and Gide makes me think of Byron's avowed preference for the poetry of Samuel Rogers, Scott, and Moore as against that of Wordsworth and Coleridge. Contemporaries seem to be hidden by a mist from each other's view, and this is especially true in the case of those writers who, like Céline and Byron, have a polemical bent.

As might be expected, the letters reveal that Céline's aesthetic perceptions become surer the farther back in time they go. The general tenor of his comments on literature reminds me of a parenthetical remark made in an article by Proust on Ruskin: "The public is romantic, but the masters — even the so-called romantic masters preferred by the romantic public — are classical in their tastes."

These letters were all addressed to me from the town of Korsör where Céline spent the greater part of his exile in Denmark. He was at that time under indictment for treason by the French government for the role of a Nazi fellow traveller he had played before World War II and under the German Occupation of Paris from 1940 to 1944. For seventeen months he had been held in protective custody by the Danish government which saved him from extradition at a time when animosities against him in his own country were at their highest. Several years after these letters were written, Céline was tried in absentia in France on charges of treason. He was sentenced to one year in prison, but the sentence was later suspended and the writer was allowed to return to France where he lived in suburban retirement for the last ten years of his life.

I have concentrated my excerpts of letters almost entirely on literary subjects because they seemed to me most likely to be of interest at the present time. Publication of the more personal and other portions of the correspondence must wait. The excerpts here amount to somewhat more than a fifth of the bulk of the whole correspondence, which consists of between eighty and ninety letters from Céline, all now deposited in the Library of The University of Texas, which acquired them some years before Céline's death.

I should like finally to express my indebtedness to Professor Roger Shattuck of the Department of Romance Languages of The University of Texas for the advice and assistance he generously has given me in preparing these excerpts for the press.

Excerpts from the letters of Louis-Ferdinand Céline to Milton Hindus. Translated by Milton Hindus and Mitchell Smith.

March 19, 1947: I've been torn away from several manuscripts on the way to *Guignol's Band.* Did you read the first volume? — Of *Guignol's?* On the same subject, I'm thinking of trying for French publication in Switzerland, Canada, or Belgium — why not the USA? I'm told there's a French publishing house there now. France is boycotting me, and I have to get myself published s.where. I can't go on like this, dying of starvation beside my stack of books: *Voyage au bout de la nuit, Mort á crédit, Guignol's Band.* Easy to sell — classics. Not just to please a quadroon of has-been communizers and obey their ukases — Aragon, Triolet, Cassou, etc . . . That would really be a farce — and insanity has its limits. Until 1944, my novels used to bring me one million francs a year; and my publisher, poor old Donoël,[1] twice that amount! You can see, I've fallen from the top. I was the most expensive writer in France! Always having been a doctor for free, I swore I'd be the most demanding author on the market — and I was!

But these are small pickings beside your American publishing lions — chicken-feed! Alas! Now it's not even a question of chickenfeed. . . . I'm haunted, morally, about getting out of my "untouchable" condition — this being a rotten pariah. That's why I was thinking about medicine in Greenland. But for me to really pull myself out of this, to come back to the surface, the Danes have to take me completely out of prison, one way or another. I'm still (as you Americans say) "on parole." A group of my French friends have devoted themselves to my sad cause. . . .

I snatch at every straw like a drowning man! Yet I'll still have to be in good condition to fight. . . . For 17 months at the bottom of this dungeon I've left the field wide open to my worst enemies!

March 30, 1947: I have to finish vols. II and III of *Guignol's Band,* and then *Féerie pour une autre fois.* I've had to leave so many manuscripts behind. Uprooted, hunted, thrown into bombings, into jail. . . . I can't take it any longer! I don't want any more of it! If the Danes give me that pardon I need so badly, I'll have the time (I think) to finish everything off before I get finished off. . . . But you know I'm much more poet than prosewriter, and that I only write to *transpose*. What follows is extreme fatigue that becomes unbearable in my sickness—anguish. . . . People think I can produce like a journalist—in a stream of inspiration. But I'm a mere man, not a demi-god. . . . I live with insomnia and headache, and I'm 54 years old. I work very rapidly, but not quickly enough for the pace of the world. . . . What's crucial right now is that Danish judge's decision. Then, once I have some freedom — once my condition becomes bearable — enter my last battle, start all over again with an infinitely more hostile public. But that's not serious—I know the music at the bottom of things. . . . If needed, I could make alligators dance to Pan's flute. But then again, it takes time to make a flute and strength to blow; and often the flute feels so light, it seems to slip out of my fingers. . . .

April 16, 1947: I'm pleased you think I'm a stylist. I'm that above all—*not* a thinker, for God's sake, or a great writer. But a stylist, yes. My grandfather was a teacher of rhetoric in Le Havre—I probably get my stylistic skill from him. Also my "rendering of emotions"[2]—a word-apprentice, my enemies call me. I follow emotion close behind with words—don't give it a chance to dress itself up in sentences—take hold of it raw—in its poetic state—for in spite of everything, the deepest layer in Man is poetry. he *learns* to reason and he *learns* to talk—the baby *sings*. . . . The colt gallops—he learns to trot.

Still, to put spoken language into writing is a mere *trick*.[3] And *I* found it—nobody else. Making spoken words *go* in literature isn't stenography: you have to change the sentences and rhythms somehow, to distort them—to use an artifice, so that when you read a book, it's as though someone is actually speaking to you. That's brought about by transposing each word, which never seems to be exactly the one you're expecting—but a little surprise. . . . The same thing happens as with a stick plunged into water. If you want it to *look* straight you have to break it slightly—or *bend* it, you might say. When you put one end in, a normally straight stick looks bent—and the same with language. On the page, the liveliest dialogue taken down word for word seems flat, complicated, heavy. . . .

To reproduce the effect of spontaneous spoken life on the page, you have to bend language in every way—in its rhythm and cadence, in its words. A kind of poetry weaves the best spell: the impression, the fascination, the dynamism. Then too, you must choose your subject—not everything can be transposed. You have to lay back the flesh of your subjects—and this means terrible risks. But now you have all my secrets. . . .

May 15, 1947: I think my contribution to French literature (as people will realize later on) has been this: to make written French more sensitive, more emotionally expressive, and less academic. And this is done (less easily than it seems) by the *trick* of composing a monologue with the intimacy of speech—but speech *transposed*. The *trick* is in that immediate, spontaneous transposition. It's really going back to the spontaneous poetry of the savage: the savage never speaks without using poetry—he *can't*. The civilized, academicized man expresses himself as an engineer, an architect, a technician—and no longer through his feelings.

What you really have is a small-scale revolution along the lines of impressionism. Before Manet, people painted in studios. After Manet, in broad daylight—out of doors. What a tremendous surprise! People rediscovered the melody of colors; I wanted them to discover the melody of the soul—in words. I remember before launching into *Voyage au bout de la nuit*[4] an idea struck me. I told myself there were two ways to cross Paris. First on the surface—by car, bicycle, or on foot—where you bump against people everywhere, stop everywhere, and are subjected to every impression, description, etc., from—say Montmartre to Montparnasse. But then there's the other way—going by métro: going directly to your goal via the very intimacy[5] of things. But you can't do that without imposing a certain melodious, melodic turn on your thoughts—giving them a track to follow—being determined not to vary from the route, not to slip off the track at all costs! You have to plunge deep into the nervous system—into the emotions—and stay there until you reach your goal. Transposing the spoken word into writing isn't easy.

I wonder how some French critics can compare me to the Henry Miller they read in translation—when everything is in the very intimacy of the language—in the way the style "renders" emotion. It doesn't come through in translation! The *trick* is to force a *distortion* into spoken language, so that once it's written down and being read, the reader feels as though someone's actually speaking to him. But real spoken language taken down word for word doesn't give that impression. This *distortion* is really a little harmonic tour de force. Thus the stick you plunge into water won't look straight unless you break it before you plunge it in: *but not too much—just the right amount*. As you see, we're a far cry from Miller and any so-called "verbal audacities." Those who compare the two of us don't understand anything.

Actually, there has been only one unfortunate French critic, Gaucher, who understood the *trick*—in an obscure newspaper article (horror of horrors, in a very stupidly antisemitic newspaper, *Le Pilori*). Gaucher is dead or in prison—he was a great enemy of Léon Daudet.[6] No one read the article, but then there were a thousand other articles at the time which had nothing at all to say.

Re-sensitize the language so that it pulses more than it reasons—that was my goal. I'm a stylist, a colorist with words; but not like Mallarmé, searching out words for exotic sensations. *Common* words; *everyday* words. Vulgarity and sexuality have no part in all this—they're just accessories.

May 29, 1947: I knew nothing about the wonderful eulogy by Trotsky—thanks![7] I knew only about an earlier interview he gave Pierre Seize of *Paris-Soir* where he said more or less: When all European civilization splinters and crumbles, only one book will remain—*Voyage au bout de la nuit.* Your quote confirms this.

May 29, 1947: I'm first of all a Celt—*daydreamer, bard.* I can turn out legends like taking a leak—with disgusting ease. Scenarios, ballets—anything you like—while I'm talking alone. That's my real talent. I harnessed it to realism because I hate man's wickedness so much; because I love combat. But actually, legends are my music. And I don't get them from libraries or from Chinese folklore like all our neo-bards—but entirely from my own making, from my own head. I feel comfortable only in the presence of nothing at all, of emptiness. I've got twenty novels itching me that I'll never finish—novels made from my real music. Then again, the plain agony of living *chokes* me. So to get a little relief from so many sorry trials-by-fire, injustices—so much misery—I turn around and strangle a kind of present actuality. Transpose it. . . .

June 11, 1947: France is weak right now as you know—drunk with political hate. These crises are a familiar pattern in her history. What's more, France has always treated her writers badly (just as the Greeks did!). Almost all of them have had to flee the executioner at one time or the other. France and the French people *don't deserve* the writers who give them so much glory—or vainglory! The history of French literature is a history of constant persecution. There are countless excuses for it.

I'm not familiar with Camus—I've never read him, but I do know Sartre's plays. They're both simply naturalists brought up to date; Freudianized—why not?—more intelligent Zolas—and all this well within French tradition. I really don't know what they could have gotten from me—Miller either. I think I'm a stylist above all—and I repeat: what interests me most is rendering emotions through words. All those "great" writers don't get close enough to the nerve in my opinion. . . . In short, I *hate* prose. . . . I'm a poet and a would-be musician. What interests me is a direct message to the nervous system. . . . I can't stand idle chattering. Look at Aristide Bruant,[8] Villon, Schackspeare [*sic*], du Bellay, Barbusse (in his *Feu*)[9]—all horrified of explanations—Proust explains too much for my taste. 300 pages to tell us Tutu makes Tatade is more than I can take! I'm in as much of a hurry as the Americans think they are. And it's the same story for Gide. But Schackspeare's whole work in 300 pages! Moliére's *Misanthrope* hardly 30 pages long! Economy! But in Gide, I don't see one atom of literary creation. He has taste, perception, is an excellent critic—nothing else. For example he discovered Eugène Dabit (now dead), famous for his *Hôtel du Nord* but whose little-known *La Villa Oasis* I recommend—the French soul in its purest state. Of course I don't reject Sarte, or Camus, or Miller. But for all their good will toward me, I must confess I find Paul Morand[10] (of the post-World War I generation) more to my taste, sturdier, and a lot more highly charged. The difference between sparkling Burgundy and champagne. . . . Don't forget that Paul Morand is the first of our writers to jazz French up. He doesn't have my concern for expressing emotions, but he's a real magician—a jeweler with words. He's a master like Barbusse in *Le Feu*. Proust annoys me with his finicky Latinate, Germanic, Hebraic ways (Claudel too on this last score)—all those sentences snapping at each other's tails after endless wriggling around. It all stinks of impotence. Of course, the public has to be educated—and Sartre does that well enough. But he didn't *earn* his plays—didn't *pay* enough for them. He'd need a couple of years in prison—and three in the trenches—to teach him real existentialism; maybe sentenced to be paralyzed from butt to toe, to be incapacitated an old-fashioned 75%.[11] *Then* he wouldn't go around in circles—*then* he wouldn't create irresponsible monsters (a vice of American writers too—Passos, Steinbeck, etc.)

They're even afraid of themselves—they cheat. They stink of cheating like Baudelaire, who plied himself with poison to be sure he was "damned" . . . Opium, etc. People are still trying to find out why Rimbaud left for Africa so soon. I know why—he was fed up with cheating. Cervantes didn't cheat. He had *really* been in the galleys. The war *really* put Barbusse on the rack. All that's not enough, of course, but the poet is always haunted by a desire *not to cheat any more*.[12] Proust's lungs were falling apart—and he ended up by talking rather nicely about his grandmother. And that part comes off—it's the best in his whole work. Gide gets a sensual kick out of everything, evades all issues—and what does he have to tell us?

Did you know that the best French sea novel was written by a German Jew—Kellerman—living in Ouessant (Brittany)—about 1890? It's called *La Mer*. Hardly ever referred to now.

My scenario in the collection *Dix et une*—the one I mentioned in an earlier letter—is called *Secrets dans l'île*. Oh it's not on a par with Kellerman. Far from it! *La mer* is really marvelous.

I'm still here in the hospital, in a nightmare of threats from all sides—threats of God knows what. Your letters seem to come from the world of the living. . . . Everything in this place is torture—but one keeps on existing—though your spirits have to be given a boost pretty often. The nights are especially ghastly—and they aren't monsters to be laughed off . . . murder, prison, hunger never leave our sight. I've just gotton through with the first chapter of my new book, *Féerie pour une autre fois*. I think this chapter is rather successful—and curious, even for America. It deals with the Bombardment of Montmartre by the RAF in 1945—with various accompanying incidents. All in a fantastic vein. I'll send it to you as soon as it's ready.

June 12, 1947: To get back to the subject I galloped through yesterday, I should point out that after the other war too, we had a surge of existentialism — a certain verbal and visual cynicism you're familiar with in *Tobacco Road*, etc., *Postman Rings Twice* . . . "tough" . . . "rough" . . . a bunch of tripe forgotten and past! One play — *Têtes de Rechange*[13] — is worth rereading. All this is directly related to Restif de la Bretonne,[14] the first man in the field with his *Monsieur Nicholas.* This book — even my father had read it — is really nothing new. What's always new, irresistible, is the human heart — charm. I want to be charmed, bewitched! I *don't* want to be taught. 54 years of life — and what a life — 27 years of practicing medicine every day taught me just a little too much raw realism. I want them to make realism sing! For me, anything that doesn't sing is a pile of crap. "A man who doesn't dance confesses some disgraceful weakness," says an old French proverb. I put dancing into everything! The dancing girl casts a spell on me; the playwright — 999 times in 1000 — bores me stiff. The public certainly needs it educators, its vocational guidance counselors, its "living museums" to help each new generation discover the moon. But when it comes to naturalism, *The Tempest* has all I need. Suppose I'm reading *Of Mice and Men:* first I find *Don Quixote*, then the Russians, then our old naturalism — a hodge-podge of every cliché. More telephones, radios, planes, etc., — modernized — but not one new heartbeat! There are still millions of people left to discover the moon each night. A new kind of music. *Jazz* was something new.

You know, what's really bothering me is that I think Man's a natural poet, like the savage. Education snips his poetic connections. Then he starts to reason and becomes a pain in the ass. Same thing for the horse whose natural gait is a gallop — we teach him to trot. . . . Man naturally *sings* — and we teach him to talk. The baby in the cradle doesn't talk — he sings! Opera is natural, comedy artificial. As for naturalist comedy, it's filth, trash! The so-called *Théâtre Libre*[15] isn't really *"libre"* at all. It's the complete opposite — an expression of constraint — monolithic. The Chinese theatre is infinitely more real than our "realistic" theatre. What we call *ballet* is more natural than what we call *danse libre* — which reeks of mechanization.

As I go along, I want to point out that in my opinion, Jules Vallès'[16] best work is surely his *Le Bachelier* — and you never hear it called his best. At the end of this novel you'll find one of those scenes of delirium[17] so rare in French literature — a duel between "people made too miserable from hating misery." I don't think it's ever been equalled in Russia or America. French literature almost never gets delirious . . . lyricizes reluctantly. No lyric poet between Villon and Chénier! Four centuries! But this scene from *Le Bachelier* is really remarkable. Only very slightly beefed-up. Schackspeare, Cervantes are at ease in poetic delirium. I don't mean surrealism — a fabricated, calculated, prearranged delirium — a fake without echoes, heart — anything! Sartre, Camus, Guillén[18] riddled with it — Julien Green, etc. . . . Birdcrap. . . . "The talent a man wants spoils the talent he has," says Boileau. That's the *snare*, pride does the rest — God! — Mallarmé never gets delirious — he puts pressure on his words — good! — striving toward music. . . . Alas Villon gets there easily. . . . You know Ruysbroek's[19] writing — airy with asceticism, he took his soul in his hand and gave it to whomever he wished . . . that's Bach's beauty too. Also the beauty of Chateaubriand's René — in him, *ennui* took the place of asceticism. That richness, detachment — that free-flowing quality like an open tap — like Chopin, like Louise Labé, like Liszt. But I'm writing in skips and jumps — not thinking too much. I'm not very smart. For proof, just look where I am! In good shape to be playing judge!

P.S. I want to be charmed! Harpagon[20] reasons too much for me. When Molière dances — *Le Bourgeois, Le Sicilien* — I go out of my mind. Still a child. If you like delirium, fine — but look out! — do it *right!* To do it right, it has to come from a man's core — from his soul. Not from his head. With Sartre, Camus, and Green, delirium comes from the head. Even in the highly-touted *Grand Meaulnes*[21] — Horsecrap! Does Greco do it? Yes! Does Picasso! Hm-m-m. But that doesn't tell us very much about the music that underlies everything. . . . We don't *dance* any more — everything's in *Dancing*. Nietzche (so overblown usually) wasn't wrong when he wrote, "I'll believe in a God only if he dances." And if he reasons, the old stick-in-the-mud, send him back to school! Hieronymus Bosch, the painter, far surpasses Breughel in my opinion. He's more daring. For the same reason, Villon's better than Bruant — who has lots of talent and writes along the same lines, in the same vein.

June 14, 1947: Just a detail. I was born May 27, 1894. You can give that year back to the Fates! Your preface[22] flashes with talent and — I repeat — with courage, as they're going to have a hard time forgiving you for raking American neoliterature over the coals so rigorously and with so much force. And you're right — although, of course, there's a certain cynical mirth, a certain manner of burlesque incisiveness in the artistic and emotional depths of American literature with which I am much taken. To my delight I find it in *Dinner at Eight* — that kind of juggling with time, characters — very skillful — very natural — and very profound at the same time. Very specifically American, and really charming — I've always loved it. It's a kind of humorous acrobatic you never find in Europe — even in Noel Coward.

June 30, 1947: Since Medan,[23] I think I've hardly changed my literary opinions at all. Yet, I've become more daring, I think. The truth isn't enough for me. I have to transpose everything. If a thing doesn't sing, the soul doesn't know it exists. To hell with reality! I want to die in music, not in reason or in prose. People don't deserve the restraint we show by not going into delirium in front of them. To hell with *them!* Piles of manure, unjust, sadistic, evil idiots mostly. I've done everything to put myself on their level. Now I'm there. The animal in man (or in woman) gives more enjoyment than this so-called reason — and more truth — and I think more progress too. There's a fantastic lot of drivel in intellectuals. Just look at any library! What a pile of crap! What a sorry mess of chatter!

You said something about translations. The Germans accomplished only one thing during their occupation of Paris: translating German poetry into French. Really marvellous! It was done in *La Receuil* under the supervision of Dr. Epting, director of the German Institute during the war. It's the best proof I know of to show that even the most delicately shaded poetry can be translated. As for prose, *The Nigger of the "Narcissus"* has been beautifully reproduced in French by Gide — an inspired translator, I must admit.

July 7, 1947: The relation between my writing and reality? *Mon dieu,* that's easy. For me, real objective life is impossible, *unbearable.* It drives me crazy — makes me furious it's so ghastly. So I transpose it as I go along, without breaking my stride. I suppose it's more or less the world's pervasive illness we call poetry. But in me it must have become a little more localized, more violent in its attacks than in others. I'm terribly sensitive to certain physical beauties — dancing girls, etc., and out of them I shape a sort of artificial paradise on earth. I've got to be close to Dancing to live. As I think Nietzche wrote, "I'll have faith in a God only if he dances." Likewise Louise XIV had faith in ambassadors only if they were perfect dancers.

But you really have to come over for a visit. I've got a thousand stories to tell you. And I've got the peculiar talent of being able to point them in any direction: tragic, half comic, pathetic — customer's choice. You'll go back to America with a book all done, and one no sillier than any other.

Rendering emotions comes easy for me — just like taking a leak; but even that takes a little more concentration to pull off in writing. As to outward events, 24 years in medicine, two wars, and all the rest have given me things to think about.

July 18, 1947: Admiral Bragueton[24] is pure fabrication. . . . But here I sit in my bewildered "productive" state. That sort of "second state" — so-called "joy of creation" — what crap! — working *Féerie* into shape. It's coming along, but slowly. Prison wears me out too. And now I'm working too hard. That pellagra finished me off — then my age, too. You'll see, my friend Hindus — 54 years are hard on a man — they're a heavy load. . . .

July 28, 1947: As for *Voyage,* I submitted the manuscript to Donoël and to the NRF at the same time. Both accepted it the same day, but Donoël two hours before the NRF. Crémieux was the NRF reader, threw some cogs into the works — so Donoël won out. It's the only one of mine he ever got beforehand—he printed the others in complete confidence without ever reading them first. I don't give a damn what the publisher happens to think about my books. I wouldn't even think of asking him. His taste has to be bad or he wouldn't keep his job of half-grocer, half-pimp. What do you expect from that little jerk? Donoël never understood anything—he published me *by chance*. Afterwards he tried to locate—search out—discover 20 Célines. . . . Braibant,[25] etc. —I agree with poor old Elie Faure[26] (Jewish). . . . When you ask a museum keeper to show you his best Rembrandt, he'll invariably choose the worst—the one that fits his taste, the taste of an old horse's ass. Who gives a damn about publishers, critics, and their lot? Maybe their advice is useful to crappy writers of their own kind—writers whose books they'd almost have written themselves if they weren't so useless. But the publisher's competence ends right there—in the depths of mediocrity—for the simple reason that a human being can't go beyond his own psychic level. He understands everything that falls in his little slot—and hates everything that goes beyond it. Like the monkey who tries to squash things he doesn't understand—just as quickly as he can! The same with critics, the same with publishers: that explains movies and best-selling novels.

How are you going to understand something that's beyond you? Impossible! So, I bring on the bla-bla-bla. There are not as many crazy people around as we think, wrote Vauvenargues,[27] mostly just people who don't understand each other. Of course! As for the publishers—on top of it all he's dazed by everything that he reads, that he feels forced to read.

August 5, 1947: Still, Freud's a great clinical doctor. One of the last I guess of the great clinical school—Charcot, Dieulafoy, Addison, etc. . . . Now the technical sciences take in everything. The mind gets smaller and smaller in the world of mathematics. I'm not sure it won't come out of it completely degenerate and stupefied. There's a touch of the novelist in Freud—a lot even. But then, life itself is a novel. . . . Where are all those grand old aristocrats of the mind like Taine, Michelet, Emerson, Renan. . . . They all ran at the mouth of course—but there were diamonds in the torrent. That explains the price of precious things: lots of waste along with them. . . . But today no one dares to run off at the mouth—we backtrack a hundred times before we come up with one precious thought. No more floods, no more rivers—and scarcely any nuggets either. . . . No more enthusiasm: and I don't mean in the Greek sense of "the God in us." Enthusiasm is to let yourself go into delirium. Freud certainly did! But alas, today our delirium is pretty well confined to political fanaticism—even more ridiculous. Oh I know! I got caught up in it too!

August 20, 1947: I'm a Gandhist too, hopelessly so. He's the one great man of our time—but completely misunderstood. . . .

August 23, 1947: Poor old Ramon Fernandez[28] who traveled around a lot told me just before he died: In any country, ask to see the engineers, the businessmen, the architects, farmers—you'll see "respectable," sharp, sensible people. If you want to see the most confused ones, ask to see the writers—crazy, absurd, irresponsible, idiotic. And that's about the truth. I'm hardly an exception! As a Breton I'm mystical, messianic, fanatic— quite naturally, no effort. Absurd—

Naturally, I was brought up a Catholic—baptism, first communion, church marriage, etc. (just like 38 million other Frenchmen)—Faith? Huh! that's a different matter. Like Renan, alas, like Chateaubriand—in despair. . . . And worse, I'm a doctor—a pagan for my complete worship of physical beauty, health. I hate sickness, penitence, anything morbid. Completely Greek in that respect. I admire the wholesomeness of childhood.

I've never read Joyce—goes too slowly for me. Plays with fly specks. Hemingway—don't know him.

Dostoevsky—too sinister, too Russian—loved prisons in a way that turns my stomach. Redemption, penitence—so much crap. A genius, sure—but then, I like Flaubert.

Poor old Dostoevsky himself, it seems, doted on Paul de Koch alone.

August 29, 1947: Please send me at least ten copies of your printed "post-face."[29] They'll create quite a stir, both here and in France. Besides, it's excellent and deserves lasting notice.

So on to my next book, *Féerie!* Hope another war won't come along too fast—and more vandals. . . . No nothing's troubling my work—no tragedy. Anyway, you know how blasé my generation (two wars) is about all that. Even in prison, I just kept on getting my rough drafts into shape. But I won't go as far as Chénier and turn out immortal poetry under the guillotine! But every man does what he can, doesn't he? You know the Roman slaves' epitaph: *"Fui, non sum, non ero."* But you'd have to come to Europe for the experience of your life—right now! Now's the time, I swear! What hypocrisy: Double-dealing—a sewer! It's the limit! *Everything's for sale!* Hardly anyone's shot or imprisoned unless he's poor. Poverty has never been so damning as it is today! Justice? Diplomacy? One big bazaar! *You can buy anything!* They hunt down writers, journalists, etc., not for their crimes, but because they're poor! *I'm* poor! And that's all that's necessary—it condemns me on every count.

September 2, 1947: I'm for Couperin, Rameau, Jacquin (know him?), Ronsard. —Rabelais? Sure, but he's rotten with academicism, humanism, etc. Dreiser is obviously your number one author. In any case, *cher Hindus,* in your American burlesque, in *Dinner at Eight,* in the feline quality of your women—a life philter completely original heavenly—that

I don't find in Dreiser. Dreiser doesn't teach us a thing. *Dinner at Eight*, *42nd Street* — teach us a lot. The USA isn't Carthage — not completely. Wish I were 30 years younger to get all that straight.

There's an altogether different "American Tragedy" — a sort of Hamletism — made up of too much beauty, optimism, lucidity — and too much humor and common sense (Anglo-Saxon heritage) — Dreiser didn't notice any of it. *Postman Rings Twice* a little off center — that nihilist hamming, etc. . . . But there's a certain marvelous, spiritual American *beauty*, too. Only — your artists' souls are too lazy; not mystic enough, not secluded enough or actively attentive enough at listening: to the murmuring, to the mellowness — in order to find the real tone of that beauty, its rhythm, its essence. . . .

I think your analysis of *Voyage* is excellent. What makes me furious is the insensitivity of men; the world's sickness is insensitivity! I do what I can to shake off that haunting thought. "The world is led by its guts" — here, at least, Rabelais is *precise*.

If critics are 90% vanity, writers (vain, narcissistic monsters practically by definition) are still way ahead. Make it 150%! But that's not the question; you're right — what counts is the work, the results. Byron, Chateaubriand — certainly more vain than any critic — are nevertheless admirable writers. Sainte-Beuve, Taine — a lot more modest — are fine critics. . . . The spirit bloweth where it listeth. . . .

September 10, 1947: Pico della Mirandola (a Jew) held down a chair something like yours. He'd have been perfect for the University of Chicago since he "knew everything there was to know and a few things besides."

Really, your speciality is the *Encyclopedia*, like Voltaire, Diderot — a chair for "Great Minds". . . .

Pirandello was a wizard too. He's certainly (along with Gordon Craig) the master of the theatre of our time. Still, he missed being born in one of the "Great Centuries" — like Shakespeare, Cervantes — closer to the real thing — and even Molière. Great Centuries *sing* above all. Pirandello (here I think you're right) — too geometrical.

September 15, 1947: I'm working at *Féerie* night and day now. But with that sadness and timidity of a man who's had four manuscripts stolen, destroyed. . . . So now I tell myself that all this effort will get sucked down the drain too, like all the others. There'll be some "liberators," crusaders, barbarians — buffoons from West, North, or South to screw up all my work and me with it. Like Sisyphus with a paper rock! Grotesque, as we have to be in these grotesque times.

September 20, 1947: Giono's worth reading, seems to me. Lots of hamming, very calculated pantheism — Jean-Jacques Rousseauism gone mad. A bard delirious over nature with lots of contrivance. All that has a false ring—un*earned*—but he does have a certain gift for poetry. He'd have scored a triumph in English, I think—deliberately lyrical naturist. Makes you snicker a little in French—a lot even. Puts your teeth on edge.

September 24, 1947: Sartre's a maniac of the self-in-delirium. I'm a maniac of the self, too, like all authors. So should I go around beating him down for it? He's useful—popularizes certain "audacities"—does what he can. Now he's even desperately philosemitic, though a trifle slow at it. He had his first successes in Paris while she was under the German Heel, the ingrate! A little paper puppet, all excited at finally finding himself a big man in one leap, through the miracle of the "Purge." Same thing for Aragon and a hundred others. But they'll never be sent another windfall like that. All their head men in prison! What lucky people! "Lucky People" are idiots that others take seriously—pretentious idiots.

After the other war, another Sartre emerged, committed several plays on us (now completely forgotten). Along the same lines but better— *Têtes de Rechange*[30] —a whole new school. Ideological cynicism—unearned and without music—the old naturalism minus its epic aspect and the ingenuity of a Zola. Only a grimy little scrap left—and these gentlemen cornered the market in it. You do what you can. . . .

October 17, 1947: Among French humanists, I recommend Chamfort,[31] the quintessence of *l'esprit de finesse*. Schopenhauer gets everything from him without ever admitting it.

About "style" and "the stick"—I still don't think I've made myself clear. It's the "blossom" of the nervous system, spontaneous melody, the music of the soul that I try to capture and turn into writing. In reality, there are more "flashes" in *spoken* language; I try to capture them, and to artificially remake, in writing, an *ideal* spoken language—what men are working at quite naturally when they talk, in their natural attempt at poetry. To reach this goal, I move by a *trick* into the very soul of spoken language; by breaking into it, you might say, I steal its secret. It's a completely different thing from what you seem to have understood. I'm peddling "living diamonds" of spoken language. We'll have to talk about it again, in person.

December 15, 1947: I don't have a bit of trouble conceiving a novel, and I always follow the same procedure. I don't make an "outline"; it seems everything's already done, in the air. . . . Thus, I have 20 castles in the air I'll never have time to visit—but they're complete, everything's there. They're *mine. But*—and there's a very serious "but"—when I approach the castles, I have to free them from a sort of deposit[32] of fuzziness and rubbish—get it out of them. And I carve into this deposit, hollow out and sweep away all of it: a kind of tough cotton which protects those castles the second I try to touch them, to put them down on paper, to write them down, describe them. The process of transmutation from mirage onto paper is painful, slow — Alchemy! But everything's there; I don't really create a thing. I clean off a forgotten medallion, a statue sunk in the clay. My impression is that *everything already exists*. When everything's cleaned off — spic and span — then the book is finished. The housekeeping's done. . . .

Mirage, digging, then cleaning house: that was the way with *Voyage, Mort,* and *Guignol's.*[33] I've still got around 20 like that. They'd rise up out of the darkness if I could only live for two centuries: *La Volonté du Roi Krogold, Casse-Pipe, La Bataille du Styx,* etc.

All this talk about outlines seems insane. Everything's already written outside the man, in the air — sculptured. You have to clean off, sweep around it, make it come out into glaring daylight: *you have to be strong.* It's a question of *strength* — to force the dream into reality — a question of cleaning house.

Out of *yourself?* Out of your *outlines?* You'll get just a lot of foolishness. Everything's made outside you, maybe in the ocean depths. No vanity in all this; it's a common laborer's task. . . . A laborer in the depths. . . .

December 15, 1947 (enclosed in previous letter): Yes, sure I think W. Whitman was in the true American tradition. But he should have digested all that mechanical progress, Freudianism, etc. . . . that racial fusion. . . . I think it could have been done with a little more paganism — straightforwardly and not hypocritically. He caught the body but not the soul; his daring is superficial. . . . Music alone — jazz was really daring. But in literature, even in philosophy — zero!

March 31, 1948: Mon dieu, I'm really flattered that you think I'm related to La Rochefoucauld. Alas! I just have a certain free and easy way with the instincts of life. Not a pleasure seeker or a sensualist: I'm detached, serious, classic in my delirium — constructive. Maybe in that way I come near the "greats" — but that's all. I don't have the extraordinary power of conciseness of these people, who are still so much closer to nature than we are — to the country people, to the working classes. The unerring skill of a man like Bossuet confounds and crushes. The grandeur, the natural majesty of these great minds! Set off against Shackspeare's illuminations, you feel silly, shitty, struggling: laboriously piling up painful little heaps of lusterless dust.

Oh sure, compared to Sartre or Miller — or Passos. *Mon dieu* why not? Among the blind, "the one-eyed man is king." What a sorry consolation!

May 5, 1948: Oh Sartre's not really an unusual phenomenon. "Sartres" line the whole course of Art History. And they invariably reap all the profits, all the honors, all the patronage — inevitably! The public likes what's false—the elite too, for that matter. The phony always wins out. What's genuine is persecuted and butchered. That's the story of the world. And worst of all, they butcher up the people who fail, too. Everything's mixed up. The skillful ones (Sartre's a fool but skillful too) always win in this ignoble lottery.

In exile, what kills you most of all is the moral isolation. What a bunch of idiots, grocer's sons all of them—a real desert! Ah Main Street! But the whole world is Main Street! If I call to mind the true spirits I've met—the Ariels during these four years (terrible!—yet so eventful, so adventurous!)—in so many thousands of beings I find only two: Abel Bonnard, former Vichy Minister of Education (in exile in Spain); and Merion, the old Vichy Minister of Information (in prison, Paris). All the rest, the worst sort of Calibans. . . .

Notes

1. Donoël was assassinated on a street corner of Paris after its liberation from the Germans in a crime which has never been cleared up.

2. A translation of *rendu émotif*, one of Céline's most frequently used expressions.

3. From the French *truc*, another key term for Céline.

4. The title of the English translation is *Journey to the End of the Night.*

5. Céline's word is *intimité.*

6. Léon Daudet (1868–1942), one-time violently antisemitic French writer who founded the famous *Action française* with Charles Maurras.

7. I had sent him a quotation from an article by Trotsky in the *Atlantic Monthly* of October 1935, entitled "Novelist and Politician," which Céline's initial American publisher, Little Brown and Company, has used: "Louis-Ferdinand Céline walked into great literature as other men walk into their own homes. A mature man with a colossal stock of observations as a physician and artist, with a sovereign indifference toward academism, with an extraordinary instinct for intonations of life and language, Céline has written a book which will survive, independently of whether he writes other books, and whether they attain the level of the first."—M. H.

8. Aristide Bruant (1851–1935), French chansonnier and playwright.

9. Henri Barbusse (1873–1935), French novelist and poet, author of the controversial *Le Feu* (1916) which came out of his World War I experiences and which won him the *Prix Goncourt.*

10. Paul Morand (1888–), French novelist and diplomat, best known for his novel *Ouvert la nuit* (with an English translation, *Open All Night*) published in 1922.

11. The prescription for Sartre is based by Céline on his own experiences, for he served in the first world war, was wounded in the head, trepanned, and declared seventy-five per cent incapacitated.

12. Céline's own footnote to this passage reads: "This is the source of their diseased politics—e.g., Lamartine, Byron, Zola, etc."

13. By Jean-Victor Pellerin, who called his plays "the theatre of the unexpressed." A literal translation of *"Têtes de Rechange"* would be "spare heads."

14. Restif de la Bretonne (1734–1806), whose multi-volume "memories" *Monsieur Nicolas or The Human Heart Unveiled* were published between 1794 and 1797. The author's

strange ideas and uninhibited style earned him the titles of "the Chambermaid's Voltaire," and "the Rousseau of the Gutter."

15. The Théatre Libre was founded in 1887 by André Antoine who used it to introduce naturalism into French theatre.

16. Jules Vallès (1832–1885), a French novelist known chiefly for his three-volume autobiographical novel *Jacques Vingtras*. *Le Bachelier* is the second volume.

17. Céline's French term, *délire*, has a stronger connotation of "frenzy" or "ecstasy" than its English cognate.

18. Presumably Jorge Guillén-Alvarez, the Spanish lyric poet (1883–) whose work is sometimes compared to that of Valéry or Mallarmé.

19. The Dutch mystic (1293–1381) known as the "Ecstatic Teacher." This reference to him is interesting in the light of the recent tendency of certain French writers to find elements of mysticism in Céline's work.

20. Harpagon is the title character in Molière's *L'Avare*.

21. *Le Grand Meaulnes* (1913) by Alain Fournier (1886–1914). The title of the English translation is *The Wanderer*.

22. The reference is to my preface to the 1947 reissue by New Directions of Céline's *Mort à crédit (Death on the Installment Plan)*. — M. H.

23. It was at Médan in 1933 that Céline gave a talk published under the title *Hommage à Zola*.

24. In an episode from *Voyage* about which I had specifically inquired because it seemed to justify more than any other invention in the book Gide's observation: "Céline paints not reality but the hallucinations which reality provokes." — M. H.

25. Charles Mauriac Braibant (1889–), French novelist and scholar.

26. Elie Faure (1873–1937), French art historian and critic.

27. The Marquis de Vauvenargues (1715–1747), French moralist.

28. Ramon Fernandez (1894–1944), French novelist and literary critic.

29. The reference is to my 1947 New Directions preface to *Death on the Installment Plan* which I had jokingly called a *post*-face, since it should not be read before the book but afterwards. — M. H.

30. See note above.

31. Nicolas Roch de Chamfort (1741–1794), French writer and critic.

32. *Gangue* is the word Céline uses.

33. The full title of Céline's original French work and the title of the English translation is *Guignol's Band*; however, it is sometimes given in French as *La Bande de Guignol*.

Louis-Ferdinand Céline:
From the *Paris Review*

Claude Sarraute, 1 June 1960*

CÉLINE: What can I say? What would appeal to your readers? I don't know. They're the kind of people you've got to be nice to, we can't hit them over the head. You've got to amuse them without offending them. Never mind . . . I'll talk. A writer hasn't got so many books in him. *Journey to the End of the Night* and *Death on the Installment Plan* would have been plenty if my disaster hadn't hit me . . . that gave me new subject matter. Curiosity got me into it. Curiosity can be costly. I've become a chronicler, a tragic chronicler. Most writers look for tragedy but don't find it. They remember little private incidents that aren't tragedy. The Greeks, you'll say. The Greek tragic poets were under the impression that they communed with the gods . . . so you see . . . hell, it's not every day that you get a chance to ring up the gods.

INTERVIEWER: And what in your opinion is the tragic element of our epoch?

CÉLINE: Stalingrad. There's catharsis for you. The fall of Stalingrad was the end of Europe. There's been a cataclysm. Its epicenter was Stalingrad. After that you can say that white civilization was finished, really washed up. Well, a cataclysm makes a lot of noise: bubblings, rockets, cataracts. I was in the middle of it . . . I got something out of it. I made use of that material, I sell it. Sure, I got mixed up in doings — stuff connected with the Jews — that were none of my business. I told the story though . . . in my manner.

INTERVIEWER: A manner that created a scandal when *Journey* came out. Your style shook up a good many conventions.

CÉLINE: It's known as invention. Take the impressionists. They took their paintings out into the daylight, they painted out of doors; they saw people really eating lunch on the grass. The musicians worked in the same direction. It's a long way from Bach to Debussy. They revolutionized sounds and colors. My line is words, the position of words. I'm going to give you a little lecture on French Literature — don't get sore. The religions brought us up, the Catholic, Protestant and Jewish . . . well, let's say the Christian religions. For centuries French education was directed by Jesuits. They taught us to make sentences translated from the Latin, well balanced, with a subject, a verb, an object and a certain rhythm. In short, a mess of sermons. People say of an author: "He forges a fine sentence." I say: "It's unreadable." They say: "What splendid dramatic language!" I

*Reprinted with permission from *Writers at Work: The Paris Review Interviews*, 3d ser., translated by James Sherwood (New York: Viking Press, Inc., 1967). © 1967 The Paris Review, Inc., and Viking/Penguin Inc.

look, I listen: it's flat, it's no good, it's nonexistent. What I've done is to put the spoken language into writing. Just like that.

INTERVIEWER: That's what you call your "little music," isn't it?

CÉLINE: I call it "little music" because I'm modest, but it's a very difficult transposition, it's hard work. It looks like nothing at all but it takes know-how. To turn out a novel like mine you've got to write eighty thousand pages by hand and boil it down to eight hundred. Speaking of me, people say: "That's natural eloquence. He writes the way he talks . . . everyday words . . . almost in the right order . . . you recognize them." Only, you see, everything is "transposed." You don't get the word you were expecting or the situation you were expecting. It's transposed into the realm of reverie, between true and not-true. A word used in that way becomes at once more intimate and more precise than the same word as it is ordinarily used. A writer makes himself a style. He's got to. The trade is simple, it can be learned. A skillful worker has no use for ready-made tools. The same goes for style. All it's good for is to bring out of you what you want to show.

INTERVIEWER: What do you wish to show?

CÉLINE: Emotion. Savy, the biologist, said something very apt: In the beginning was emotion, not in the beginning was the Word. When you tickle an amoeba, it retracts, it has emotion; it doesn't speak but it has emotion. A baby cries, a horse gallops; one has to learn how to talk, the other how to trot. But to us and us alone the Word has been given. The result is the politician, the writer, the prophet. The Word is monstrous, it stinks. But translating that emotion is inconceivably difficult . . . it's horrible . . . superhuman . . . it can kill a man.

INTERVIEWER: But you've always felt the need to write.

CÉLINE: Nothing you do is free. You've got to pay. A story you make up is worthless. Only a story you pay for is any good. Once it's paid for you've got the right to transpose it. Otherwise it's bad. . . . That's what they all do . . . I mean, the guys that have everything: the Nobel prize, the Academy, the press, the gold medal for charlatanism. If I had money, I'd let them stew in their own juice. I can't listen to the radio any more . . . every week they discover a "genius," every two weeks a Balzac, every morning a George Sand. I haven't got time to keep up with them, because I work. I've got a contract, I've got to meet it. Only this is my sixty-sixth birthday and I'm 75 percent disabled. At my age most men have retired. I owe six million to Gallimard . . . So you see I have to go on. . . . I already have another novel in the works: more of the same [*Nord*, sequel to *Castle to Castle*]. One thing leads to another and you can't stop. I know something about novels. They were still being made in my day. Novels are something like lace . . . lace is an art, too, an art that went out with the convents. The novel can't compete with cars, the movies, television, and liquor. A guy who's had a good feed and tanked up on good wine gives his old lady a kiss after supper and his day is over. Finished.

Jean Guenot and Jacques Darribehaude, interview later in 1960

INTERVIEWER: Do you recall a literary shock or enthusiasm that left its mark on you?

CÉLINE: Oh no. Certainly not. I started out in medicine, medicine was what I wanted and definitely not literature, hell no. Sure, some writers struck me as talented. . . . I saw talent in . . . always the same names: Paul Morand[1] . . . Ramuz[2] . . . Barbusse[3] . . . those fellows were made for it.

INTERVIEWER: When you were a child, did you think of becoming a writer?

CÉLINE: Never. No, no, no. I had an enormous admiration for doctors. Medicine really fascinated me. It thrilled me.

INTERVIEWER: What did a doctor mean to you as a child?

CÉLINE: A man who came to the Passage Choiseul to see my sick mother or my father. . . . To me he was a miracle man who cured people, who did amazing things with a body that was out of order. I thought it was marvelous. He seemed so wise and learned. That's what I thought, absolutely, a magician.

INTERVIEWER: And what does a doctor mean to you today?

CÉLINE: Bah! Nowadays the social setup is so rough on him, everybody competing with him, he's lost his prestige. He lost his prestige when he stopped . . . once he started dressing like a garage mechanic, he began, little by little, to give the impression of a mechanic. He has nothing much to say any more, the housewife has the *Larousse Médical* and even diseases have lost their prestige, there aren't so many of them left. . . . Think it over . . . no more syphilis, no more clap, no more typhoid . . . antibiotics have taken half the tragedy out of medicine. No more plague, no more cholera. . . .

INTERVIEWER: What about nervous and mental diseases? Aren't they rather on the increase?

CÉLINE: But in that line we can't do a thing. Some cases of madness are fatal, but not many. But Paris is full of small-time lunatics. Some people have an individual tendency to look for excitement, but with all the pairs of buttocks you see around town, it's naturally going to inflame the sex urge . . . think of the school children . . . it'll make them all whacky . . .

INTERVIEWER: When you were working at Ford's were you under the impression that the mode of life imposed on the workers made for mental disorders?

CÉLINE: Not at all. No. There was a head physician at Ford's, my boss. Here's what he used to say: "I'm told chimpanzees can pick cotton. I'd be glad to see a few of them working on the machines here, it would be much better." Mental cases are better workers, they're much more attached to the factory than normal people, the normal ones are always walking out, the mental cases stick to the job. But today the human problem isn't medicine. Most of a doctor's patients are women. Women are always worried; they have every known weakness. A woman's got to . . . well, she wants to stay young . . . she's got her menopause, her periods . . . the whole gynecological shooting match . . . it's very delicate and makes her a martyr. Oh yes, she's a martyr but she goes on living, she bleeds, she doesn't bleed, she goes to see a doctor, she has an operation or she doesn't . . . another operation . . . in between she has a baby, she loses her shape, and that's bad . . . she wants to stay young, to keep her figure . . . she doesn't feel like working and actually she can't . . . no muscle . . . it's an enormous problem . . . that's been too much neglected . . . it supports the beauty parlors, the quacks . . . and the druggists. But it presents no medical interest whatsoever; a woman falling apart is simply a fading rose, you can't call her a medical problem, or an agricultural problem either for that matter. . . . When you see a rose fading in the garden, you resign yourself. There'll be another . . . but a woman . . . she doesn't want to die . . . that's the rough part of it. I'm well acquainted with the problem because I've spent my life with dancers . . . women aren't favored when it comes to muscles, we are . . . we're more muscular than women . . . a woman has to take care of herself, she doesn't like to. Okay, there's your medical routine, it gives a doctor his living. . . . But when it comes to real sickness, you don't see much of it, the young students today don't see the diseases I saw as a child. They don't even see corpses any more.

INTERVIEWER: Your work as a physician brought you certain revelations and experiences that you put into your books.

CÉLINE: Oh yes. I spent thirty-five years at it; after all, that means something . . . I covered ground as a young man . . . I climbed a lot of stairs in those days, I saw a lot of people . . . yes, plenty of people . . . but it did me a lot of good, in every way . . . oh yes . . . in many ways . . . yes, it did me a lot of good. But I didn't write medical novels because they're another abominable bore . . . take Soubiran.

INTERVIEWER: Your medical ambitions came to you very early and yet you started out in life very differently.

CÉLINE: Oh yes. And how! They wanted to make a buyer out of me! A salesman in a department store! . . . We were poor, my parents didn't have the wherewithal . . . I started in poverty and, well, that's how I'm ending. . . .

INTERVIEWER: Tell me something about the small shopkeeper's life around 1900.

CÉLINE: Horrible . . . horrible . . . I mean that we had hardly anything to eat, and we had to keep up appearances. For instance, in the Passage Choiseul, we always had two showcases, but only one of them was lit up because there was nothing in the other. And he had to scrub the Passage before going to work . . . my father, I mean . . . anyway, life was no picnic. . . . My mother had earrings. We took them to the pawnshop at the end of every month to pay the gas bill. Don't ask. It was terrible.

INTERVIEWER: Did you live in the Passage Choiseul a long time?

CÉLINE: I'll say. Eighteen years. . . . Until I volunteered. . . . A life of poverty . . . worse than poverty, because when you're just poor you can let yourself go, get drunk, lie in the gutter. This was the kind of poverty that keeps up a front, dignified poverty, and that's awful. For instance . . . all my life I've eaten noodles. Noodles, because you see, my mother used to mend old lace. And one thing that everybody knows about old lace is that odors stick to it forever. And the customers, well, you can't bring your customers smelly lace. So what didn't make any odors? Noodles. I ate whole washtubs full of noodles, my mother made them by the washtubful . . . I ate boiled noodles, oh yes, oh yes, my whole childhood, noodles and bread soup. Those things were odorless. As you know, the kitchen in the Passage Choiseul was on the second floor, it was as big as a clothes cupboard; well you went up by a winding staircase, see, like this, and somebody had to keep going up to see if it was cooking, if it was boiling or not boiling, well, it was hopeless, my mother was crippled, one of her legs didn't work, and she had to climb those winding stairs twenty-five times a day. . . . Life was impossible. . . . My father was a clerk. He came home at five. . . . Then we had to deliver the merchandise. Oh no, it was misery. Dignified misery.

INTERVIEWER: Was your poverty a source of suffering when you went to school?

CÉLINE: It was public school. . . . We weren't rich. So I didn't have much of an inferiority complex . . . they were all like me, all poor kids. . . . Oh no, there were no rich people in that neighborhood. . . . But we knew some rich people, there were two or three of them. . . . We revered them! My parents told me those people were wealthy . . . the neighborhood drapers. . . . They'd moved there by mistake but we knew them and revered them. In those days a rich man was revered. For his wealth! And at first we thought he was intelligent, too.

INTERVIEWER: When and how did you become aware of the injustice of such things?

CÉLINE: Late, I've got to admit, after the war. When I saw the war profiteers. The slackers who made money while other people were dying in the trenches. That was my first clear sign, something I could see with my own eyes. Later, I was with the League of Nations and that wised me up once and for all, I saw that the world was governed by the Golden Calf, by Mammon! Not a doubt! Implacably. Anyway, my social consciousness came late. I didn't have it . . . I was resigned. . . .

INTERVIEWER: Would you say that your parents' attitude was one of acceptance?

CÉLINE: Frantic acceptance! My mother used to say: "You little wretch, if there weren't any rich people (because somehow I already had my little ideas), if there weren't any rich people, we wouldn't get anything to eat. Rich people have a sense of responsibility. . . ." You see, my mother revered the rich. So hell . . . I took a leaf out of her book. I wasn't exactly convinced. No. But I didn't dare to have an opinion, oh no. . . . My mother who was up to her neck in lace would never have worn any, it was for the customers. Never. It wouldn't do. Even the jeweler didn't wear jewelry and neither did his wife . . . I was a jeweler's errand boy, I worked for a lot of jewelers, Robert on the rue Royale, Lacloche on the rue de la Paix. . . .

INTERVIEWER: What about Gorloge? And the Gorloge family?

CÉLINE: Oh yes! That's Wagner on the rue Vieille du Temple! Yes, that's him. I worked for him all right. . . . My job was toting the sample cases and going . . . you know those big leather cases they carry the models in . . . the models were made of lead, so you can imagine . . . we toted the cases from house to house, and I covered, we covered, the territory from the rue du Temple to the Opera. We did every jewelry store on the boulevard, and then we got together, all the errand boys got together on the steps of the Ambigu, you know, those steps that go down. So we got together and we all had sore feet because our shoes . . . I always had sore feet. Because I didn't get a new pair of shoes very often, so my nails were crooked, hell, they're still crooked. We did the best we could, our shoes were too small, kids grow. My, oh my! . . . I was very active in those days, I did everything so fast that I beat the Metro. . . . I ran all my errands on foot. . . . Oh yes, social consciousness. . . . When I was in the cavalry, I was present at the hunting parties given by Prince Orloff and the Duchess d'Uzès. . . . We held the officers' horses. I remember the Duchess d'Uzès well, on horseback, the old bag, and Prince Orloff who hobnobbed with all the officers in my regiment, and my job was holding the horses. . . . That's as far as it went. We were treated just like cattle. It was taken for granted, nobody expected any different.

INTERVIEWER: And anti-Semitism was drafted onto this social consciousness of yours?

CÉLINE: Yes, I caught on to another exploiter. At the League of

Nations I saw where the big deals were being made. And later, in Clichy, in politics, I saw . . . yes, I remember, there was this little louse . . . I saw all I needed to see. . . . The answer is yes. . . .

INTERVIEWER: Did your mother have much influence on you?

CÉLINE: I have her character. More than anything else. She was a hard woman, she was impossible . . . I can't deny it, her temperament was something special . . . she just didn't enjoy life. Not in the least. Always worried and always throwing a fit. She worked up to the last minute of her life.

INTERVIEWER: What did she call you? Ferdinand?

CÉLINE: No, Louis. She wanted to see me holding down a job in a department store, the Hôtel de Ville, or the Louvre. As a buyer. That was her ideal. My father felt the same way. Because he hadn't got anywhere with his degree in literature! . . . Or my grandfather with his doctorate! . . . They'd made out so badly they thought maybe I'd make a go of it in business.

INTERVIEWER: Wouldn't your father have been better off in the school system?

CÉLINE: Of course he would have, poor man, but here's what happened. He'd have needed a teaching degree, and he only had a general degree, and he couldn't take it because he had no money. His father had died, leaving a wife and five children.

INTERVIEWER: Did your father die late in life?

CÉLINE: He died when *Journey* appeared in 1931.

INTERVIEWER: Before the book came out?

CÉLINE: Yes, just before. He wouldn't have liked it. . . . Besides, he was jealous. . . . He couldn't see me as a writer, neither could I for that matter. On that point at least we agreed. . . .

INTERVIEWER: And what was your mother's reaction to your books?

CÉLINE: She thought they were dangerous and nasty and would make trouble. . . . She expected things to end very badly. She was a very cautious type.

INTERVIEWER: Did she read your books?

CÉLINE: No, she couldn't, they were over her head. She'd have thought them very vulgar. Anyway she didn't read books, she wasn't a woman to read books. No, she had no vanity. She worked till the day she died. I was in prison. I heard about her death. . . . No, I'd just got to Copenhagen when I heard about it. . . . An abominable trip, stinking . . . yes, the timing was perfect. Abominable. . . . But don't forget, things are only abominable from one angle. . . . Well, you know . . . experience is a muffled lantern that throws light only on the bearer . . . it's incommunicable . . . better keep these things to myself. . . .

The way I feel about it, a man was entitled to die, to go in, when he had a good story to tell. You told your story and you passed on. Symbolically speaking, that's what *Death on the Installment Plan* is. The reward for life being death . . . seeing that it's not God who governs but the Devil. . . . Man . . . or nature stinks, just look at the lives of the birds or the animals.

INTERVIEWER: When have you been happy in your life?

CÉLINE: Damn well never, I think, because getting old, I'd need . . . I think if somebody gave me a lot of dough so's I wouldn't have to worry — I'd like that — it would give me a chance to go away somewhere and not do a damn thing and watch other people. . . . Being all by myself on the seashore with no one to bother me — that would be happiness. And to eat very little . . . that's right . . . next to nothing . . . I'd want a candle. I wouldn't live with electricity and gadgets. . . . A candle! Give me a candle and I'd read the paper. . . . Other people, the way I see them, are all steamed up, most of all they're prodded by ambition. The life of the rich is a circus, they invite each other back and forth to keep each other's spirits up. . . . I've seen it, I've lived with society people. . . . Ah, Gontran, he actually said that to you? . . . Ah, Gaston, you were really brilliant yesterday! The way you put him in his place! Yes, really! He mentioned it again only yesterday. His wife said: Oh, Gaston was amazing! — It's a circus. That's how they spend their time. They chase each other around, they meet at the same golf clubs, the same restaurants. . . .

INTERVIEWER: If you could start all over again, would you seek your pleasures outside of literature?

CÉLINE: I certainly would! I don't ask for pleasure, I don't feel any . . . the enjoyment of life is a matter of temperament, of diet. You've got to eat well and drink well, then the days pass quickly. If you eat well and drink well, take an automobile ride and read a few newspapers, your day will soon be over. . . . You read your paper, you have a few people in, you drink your morning coffee, you take a little stroll, hell, it's time for lunch. . . . In the afternoon you drop in on a few friends . . . the day passes. At night, bed as usual, you fall asleep. And there you are. Especially as you grow older . . . because then the time passes faster. When you're young, a day is interminable, but as you grow older . . . it doesn't take long. When you're an old man living on your pension, a day's a flash; when you're a kid it passes very slowly.

INTERVIEWER: How would you choose to occupy your time if you were retired on an income?

CÉLINE: I'd read the paper. I'd go for a little stroll some place where nobody'd see me.

INTERVIEWER: Can you take walks here?

CÉLINE: No, never. Better not.

INTERVIEWER: Why?

CÉLINE: First because I'd be noticed. I don't like that. I don't want to be seen. In a seaport you can disappear. . . . In Le Havre. . . . I don't think a man would be noticed on the docks in Le Havre. They don't see a thing. A retired naval man, an old fool . . .

INTERVIEWER: You like boats, don't you?

CÉLINE: Oh yes! Yes! I like to watch them. To see them coming in and out. Sure, give me a jetty and I'm happy. . . . They leave a trail of foam, they go away, they come back, and they've got nothing to do with you, see? Nobody asks you anything. Sure, and you read *Le Petit Havrais*, and . . . and that's all . . . that's all there is to it. . . . Yes, if I had my life to live over, I'd do it entirely differently.

INTERVIEWER: Can you think of any individuals whom you look up to as examples? Men you would have liked to imitate?

CÉLINE: No. Because people like that are grandiose, and I have no desire to be grandiose, none at all. All I want is to be an old man nobody pays attention to . . . not . . . people like that have their names in the dictionary, I don't go for that. . . .

INTERVIEWER: I was thinking of people you might have met in everyday life. . . .

CÉLINE: Oh no. No. They're always putting on an act, other people give me a pain. No. I've inherited a kind of modesty from my mother, a total insignificance, and I mean total. What interests me is to be completely ignored. I have a propensity . . . an animal propensity, for crawling away. . . . Yes, Boulogne would suit me all right, Boulogne-sur-Mer. Place where nobody ever goes. I've spent a lot of time in Saint-Malo, but it's not possible any more. . . . I'm kind of known there . . . I went to medical school in Rennes. . . .

André Parènaud, 1 June 1961, Céline's last interview

INTERVIEWER: Does love occupy an important place in your novels?

CÉLINE: No place at all. It shouldn't. A novelist should have a sense of shame.

INTERVIEWER: And friendship?

CÉLINE: Let's skip it.

INTERVIEWER: Then you prefer to talk of the less important feelings?

CÉLINE: Let's talk about work, the job of writing. It's the only thing that counts. And even that calls for a good deal of discretion. Too much publicity in the way people talk about these things. We're objects of publicity. It's revolting. It's high time people took a cure of modesty. In literature as in everything else we're befouled by publicity. It's disgraceful. I say: do your job and shut up, that's the only way. People will read it or they won't read it, that's their business. The only thing for the author to do is to make himself scarce.

INTERVIEWER: Do you write for the pleasure of writing?

CÉLINE: No. Certainly not. If I had money, I wouldn't write a word. That's my first principle.

INTERVIEWER: You don't write out of love or hatred?

CÉLINE: Of course not! It's my business if I experience those sentiments, it doesn't concern the public.

INTERVIEWER: But you take an interest in your contemporaries?

CÉLINE: Oh no, none whatsoever. I took an interest in them once, I tried to prevent them from making war. As it happened, they didn't make war, but they came back laden with glory. And then they threw me into the clink. I should have concentrated on myself.

INTERVIEWER: Still, certain feelings come through in your most recent novels?

CÉLINE: A writer can make anything come through. There's nothing to it.

INTERVIEWER: Are you trying to persuade us that your latest books reveal nothing of your inner life?

CÉLINE: Inner life? No, absolutely nothing. Maybe one thing, and only one, the fact that I don't know how to enjoy life. I don't live. I don't exist. That gives me a certain superiority over other people who stink, you can't deny it, because they're always enjoying life. To enjoy life is to eat, drink, belch, fuck, all those things that make hash out of a man or a woman. I don't go in for dissipation and that's lucky for me. I know how to choose. I'm capable of savoring things, but as some Roman said, debauchery isn't going into a whorehouse, it's not coming out. All my life I've gone into whorehouses, but I've come right out. I don't drink, I don't care about eating. Those things bore me. It's my right, isn't it? I have only one desire. To sleep and be left alone, which isn't the case.

INTERVIEWER: In what writers do you recognize real talent?

CÉLINE: My feeling is that there were three writers in the great period. Morand, Ramuz and Barbusse were writers. They had a feeling for it. They were made for writing. The rest of them aren't made for it. Hell, they're imposters, the whole lot of them, and the impostors are on top. If the critics don't watch out, literature will be devoured by charlatanism. But that's already happened, the critics are up shit's creek.

INTERVIEWER: You seem to dissociate yourself from those things. And yet you were one of the most passionate men of the century.

CÉLINE: Yes, but no longer. They've bugged me too much. I'm fed up. I used to be pitiful, but not any more. Now I'm indifferent. They bore me.

INTERVIEWER: Would you say you were embittered? Philosophical? Contemptuous?

CÉLINE: No, no. Not at all. That's a lot of words, my encyclopedia is full of them. Pure shit. I know how to turn tables. Other people don't.

INTERVIEWER: Do you still regard yourself as one of the greatest living writers?

CÉLINE: No, not at all. Great writers. . . . What do I want with adjectives. First you've got to croak and when you've croaked they classify. First you've got to be dead.

INTERVIEWER: Are you convinced that posterity will do you justice?

CÉLINE: Hell no, of course I'm not convinced. Hell no! Who knows if there'll even be a France? Maybe Chinamen or Berbers will be digging out the archives, and they won't give a good goddam about my dopey literature, my fancy style and my three dots. . . . It doesn't take a genius. While we're on the subject of "literature," I was through a long time ago. After *Death on the Installment Plan* I'd said everything I had to say, which wasn't much.

INTERVIEWER: You hate life.

CÉLINE: Well, I can't say I love it. No. I put up with it because I'm alive and I have responsibilities. Otherwise I'm pretty much of the pessimist school.

INTERVIEWER: Does any man on earth have your esteem?

CÉLINE: My esteem? Nobody asks for my esteem. By what right would I hand out certificates of esteem or no esteem? What does it mean? Nothing. Scientifically speaking, not a thing. Why would I hand out certificates of good conduct? It's absolutely none of my business.

INTERVIEWER: But your feeling is rather one of despair?

CÉLINE: Why, not at all. What is this business about despair? It would imply that I hope for something. I don't hope for anything. I hope to die as painlessly as possible. Like everyone else. That's all. And I hope nobody suffers for me, on account of me, or near me. Just to die quietly. If possible to die of thrombosis or maybe I'll finish myself off. That would be the simplest. Things are going to be rougher and rougher. It's much harder for me to work now than it was a year ago, and next year it will be still harder than this year. That's the whole story.

Notes

1. Paul Morand (1888–1976), French diplomat and writer, and member of the Académie (1968). He was famous for impressionistic stories and novels on the night life of postwar Europe. He wrote *Ouvert la nuit* (1922) (editor's note).

2. Charles Ferdinand Ramuz (1878–1947), a Swiss writer who lived in Paris from 1902 to 1914 and wrote novels on French-Swiss country life. He was the author of *La Beaute sur la terre* (1927) (editor's note).

3. Henri Barbusse (1873–1935), French journalist, novelist, pacifist, and socialist whose novel *Le Feu* was awarded the Goncourt Prize in 1916 for its realistic description of life in the trenches during World War I. He authored a critical study entitled *Zola* (1932) (editor's note).

Mrs. Céline Publishes the Last "Ballet" of Louis-Ferdinand: *Rigadoon*
Jean Chalon*

If you marry a writer and you have problems, address them to Mrs. Louis-Ferdinand Céline, to whom we owe the Gallimard publication of the last posthumous work of her husband, *Rigadoon*. She will certainly give you the secret of the twenty-six years of marriage which she describes as "extraordinary." Here it is: "A writer," says Mrs. Céline, "is someone you have to let alone, undisturbed."

And she adds, "He wrote the whole day long. I danced. Dance was our common passion. Céline loved dance as well as literature. Look at his way of forming words and cutting sentences. It's rhythm. It's movement. . . . We never left each other. We were both, or rather I was like his double. We didn't see many people, except Marcel Aymé, who dropped by to spend a moment on Sundays. Céline couldn't get along with anybody. He was too obscure, too difficult. It was like oil and water. So we had to glide along; we never separated except for prison. Afterwards he often said to me, 'We should have committed suicide in 1940.' When I met Céline, he'd just finished *Death on the Installment Plan*. We met again everyday at Blanche d'Alexandrie's place. At the time she was the great mistress of ballet. He came to gather material on the dance. What? You didn't know that Céline wrote ballets? He brought his ballets together in *Ballet Without Music, Without Words, Without Anything* (Gallimard). He would have wanted me to dance them. I would have had to put together a troupe, to meet people. I think that after all I was as savage as he was. . . . The day he died he said to me, 'Now that I've finished *Rigadoon*, I want to

*Translated by Jóhanna Eiríksdóttir Hull for this volume from *Figaro Littéraire*, 24 February–2 March 1969, 25. Reprinted with permission of *Figaro*. © 1986.

write your book.' It was to be a book on my methods, the ones I have practiced for thirty years, and which are rather famous nowadays, such as the elongated bar, and doing horizontally the movements you would do vertically. The whole body vibrates with the abdominal muscles as if they were little motors. I teach my students the classic steps, along with oriental gestures. The arms are too often neglected."

The Rocketing Locomotive

She mimes and talks of dance as if to justify the red sign leaning against the door of her house, "Lucette Almanzor, Classical and Expressive Dance." Or rather what is left of the house. It burned down last May. . . . Mrs. Céline lives in peaceful Meudon. She sought refuge at once in the aviary. I mean that with the help of a bricklayer, she built another house, made of wood, around the aviary, where her crowded, personal Noah's Ark lives: two dogs, a parrot, other birds, rabbits, cats, and what have you. A bent for disorder puts furs alongside a tea set and a college thesis brought by a student: "The Fragmented Sentence in *Journey to the End of the Night.*" Material problems that separate so many couples, if we are to believe the Miss Lonelyheart columns, apparently haven't bothered the Célines very much.

"Food, for me, you know, is yogurt, an egg, some tea," she said. "Céline was even more temperate than I. When he was hungry he ate a piece of bread. And he drank tea like I do."

With this diet Mrs. Céline keeps an extraordinarily slender figure. She has a large forehead, a little turban, eyes that are very blue, a sweater that's very pink, and a pair of black slacks. She's also astonishingly lively. She has to be. She gives dance courses from morning to night. And come evening, she has for seven years reworked the manuscript of *Rigadoon,* with the help of François Gibault.

"I was certainly used to my husband's handwriting, but at the end of his life he produced real hieroglyphics. He didn't finish his words. He also used expressions that weren't ordinary. Listen, in *Rigadoon,* in the manuscript, there is a rocketing *(fusante)* locomotive. The proofreaders preferred to use smoking *(fumante).* If we reedit I'll correct it."

You can see how carefully Mrs. Céline watches over the works of her husband whose complete works we're far from seeing published:

"*Bagatelles pour un massacre* and *L'Ecole des cadavers* belong to me," she explains. "These books can't be found and I'm against their reissue. There's been enough scandal as is. I don't want to renew the pain and the gossip."

The Strange Case of Dr. Destouches and M. Céline

John Updike*

One would like to write of Céline without touching upon his anti-Semitism, his Facism, his collaboration with the Nazis, his political loathsomeness. The three book-length "pamphlets" — *Bagatelles pour un Massacre* (1937), *L'École des Cadavres* (1938), and *Les Beaux Draps* (1941) — with which the great novelist made himself a scandal were simply excluded from the collected words published by André Balland, and have never been available in English. Even fragmentary direct quotations from them are hard to come by. George Steiner, writing in these pages eight years ago, claimed that "it is nearly impossible to quote from them without physical revulsion," and Mavis Gallant recently in the *Times* offered a sentence (the ellipses of course not her own but integral to Céline's unique style): "Jewish bluffer . . . Dirty *con*, layabout . . . pimp of the universe . . . parasite of all time." Patrick McCarthy, in his biography and critical study *Céline* (Viking), devotes an entire chapter to "Céline the Pamphleteer," but here the wording and reasoning of the pamphlets are softened by his careful psychoanalysis of the author, and by a perhaps unavoidable note of pleading. Mr. McCarthy is at pains to point out where the anti-Semitic frenzy becomes almost confessedly absurd: "In *Bagatelles* he exaggerates to the point of creating disbelief. Léon Blum is Jewish, he tells us correctly; Masaryk and Beneš are also Jewish, so are Gide, Maurras and the Pope; the entire English nation is Jewish. At this point one stops: clearly Céline does not want to be believed." In the next pamphlet, *L'École*, "there is still exaggeration: the Pope is Jewish and his name is Isaac Ratisch . . . the Jews are responsible for the 1843 treaty of Verdun which separated France from Germany." Comical or not, the pamphlets amount to a call for the extermination of the European Jews a few years before such an extermination was all but completely carried out. In 1943, while the Nazis were mercilessly removing Jews from France, Céline allowed his publisher to reprint *L'École des Cadavers* and, with illustrations, *Bagatelles pour un Massacre*; a year before, he had written to the organizers of an anti-Semitic exhibition professing to be "surprised and a little hurt" to find neither *Bagatelles* nor *L'École* on display. Mr. McCarthy, for all his equanimity and tact, cannot help but reveal that Céline's views were more odious than one had dared suspect — more odious, it might be urged in his defense, than they needed to be for any sort of personal advancement or convenience. In this, he rather resembles Hitler, who carried forward the Final Solution to the detriment of the German war effort. Céline late in 1941 wrote, in a letter, of Hitler's anti-

*Reprinted with permission from *Hugging the Shore* (New York: Alfred A. Knopf, Inc., 1983). © John Updike. This first appeared in the *New Yorker*, 13 September 1976, 154–61.

Semitism, "It is the side of Hitler that most people like the least . . . it is the side I like the most."

Mr. McCarthy advances what mitigating factors he can. Anti-Semitism pervaded Europe between the wars, and was very strong in the shopkeeping class, from which Céline sprang and whose meannesses and anxieties he retained to the end of his life. Céline composed his notorious pamphlets within a specifically French tradition of violent rhetoric and theatrical exaggeration; other pamphleteers, like Daudet and Maurras, Bernanos and Bloy, wrote with similar extremism. Like other reactionaries, Céline was repelled by modern materialism and was nostalgic for the supposed pre-industrial virtues. A genuine dread of the impending war between France and Germany, rooted in his traumatic experiences as a soldier wounded in 1914, led him to a frantic pacifism and a desperate need for a scapegoat. His brief career as a League of Nations functionary had disposed him to see Jews as the nationless manipulators of the modern world. He was truly patriotic and believed (like the Norwegian Knut Hamsun) that his country must in its weakness submit to Germany. Céline, under his real name of Louis-Ferdinand Destouches, was a doctor, who preferred to work among the impoverished, who filled his life with acts of personal kindness, who said of himself that "there was no suffering to which he was indifferent." He loved animals. He was abstemious, and a meticulous reviser of his apparently dishevelled prose. Most interestingly, Mr. McCarthy portrays Céline as a terror-ridden man of many impersonations, and the somewhat clownish political hysteric as being, in Céline's mind, one more role, which had little serious connection with Dr. Destouches humanely practicing medicine among the Paris poor or with Céline the prose genius aspiring to the ranks of Rabelais and Ronsard. In his role of anti-Semite, "Hydra-Céline is putting only one of his heads on the block. He is still evading, still showing fear. He has fallen into a *délire*, just like one of the minor characters in his novels. The *délire* may be defined as the other, separate world that the maniacs and exiles invent when the normal world becomes impossible." This amounts to a plea of insanity, and certainly Céline's brain, battered ever after his war injury by headaches and insomnia and a roaring in his ears, flickered on a variety of wavelengths. His pamphlets are repetitious and irresponsible even by the standards of gutter literature, and amid their murderous nonsense is some harsh self-mockery ("a poor imbecile," he calls himself), including the gibes of his "Jewish friend Gutman" (who tells him, "You are delirious, Ferdinand"). One of the twists of the pamphleteer's tortuous tirade is a kind of identification with Jews, and *Bagatelles* contains a curious invitation to the Jews to kill him as a sacrifice, so that the Germans may not slaughter the French. At the war's end, an execrated exile, he went so far as to include the Six Million in comradeship with his own sufferings: "The Jews have paid like me." But he never distinctly recanted, merely shifted to Asiatics the focus of his crazy terror of "mongrelization;" once back in France, under an amnesty of 1951, he revelled—via interviews and the autobiographical explosions of his later books—in his vituperative isolation. One may add, in feeble defense of the resolute malevolence of his public personality, that Céline culled few favors from the Nazi establishment of the Occupation, and that his anti-Semitism taints surprisingly little of his fiction. The character of Bloch in Proust is a fuller Jew *qua* Jew, with more construably anti-Semitic overtones, than any portrait in Céline's novels.

Nevertheless, knowledge of Céline's bizarre and barbarous convictions disturbs one's appreciation of his art, all the more in that he anticipated so many qualities of postwar fiction. Thirty years before *Catch 22*, he wrote of the military life as sheer craziness and of cowardice as the only sanity. Long before *One Flew Over the Cuckoo's Nest*, he found the mentally ill a superior sort of society. Before William Burroughs, he sensed behind the electronic apparatus of modernity an enemy promoting spooky derangements and sudden deaths. Before Kerouac and the Beats and the tell-all Beatrices that have come along a generation later, he perceived that a good long monologue is novel enough, if the names are slightly scrambled and the events are linked to a nebulous "search." If not the inventor, he is the classic promulgator of the nouveau picaresque, with its comfortable paranoia, its pleasant assumption that the world is uniformly zany and corrupt and therefore cannot be analyzed, only experienced at random. Events without precedent, behavior without motivation, characters who come and go like strangers in an elevator—Mr. McCarthy almost names these as flaws in his description of *Journey to the End of the Night* but concludes that the disconnections have a philosophical function: "By this technique Céline destroys cause and effect." It has been a technique fruitful at least of verbiage; discarding cause and effect absolves the novelist of any duty to keep his mock-world coherent, and has made fiction as easy to write as free verse. Like the removal of metre and rhyme from poetics, this discarding throws upon the writer a continuous challenge to surprise and astound. Without any consequential development linking events, the reader is led along by the writer's voice alone, and its promise of ever-new prodigies of horror or style. These prodigies Céline was better equipped to provide than most of his successors; he did not flinch from the chasm of possibility he had opened up, and showed in his later work how truly *anything* can go into a novel—personal exhortations, fantasies, stories within stories, all sorts of confusions and noise. Has any writer ever been as fascinated with noise, with bangs and buzzing and shouts and rattling that fill the world, so that it seems, like the Detroit factory to *Journey*'s hero Bardamu, a "vast frenzy of noise, which filled you within and all around the inside of your skull and lower down rattled your bowels, and climbed to your eyes in infinite, little, quick unending strokes"? Céline's style, with its famous three dots replacing all logical punctuation, became a hammering of "little, quick unending strokes," driven with maniacal monotony toward a single point of deafness, of nothingness, of futility. If cause and effect are discarded, the world has no hinges for disassembly; nothing can be demonstrated save futility. This Céline was inexhaustibly eager to do. His novels, like Beckett's, are testaments of defiance, gratuitous breakings of silence, a numbed survivor's snarled testimony to catastrophes that are scarcely distinguishable. Agglutination and dissolution characterize the Célinean event; where a rationale might be perceived, it is suppressed. What Bardamu and the Pordurière Company of Little Togo are attempting to achieve at their trading outpost in Bikomimbo totally deliquesces in the nightmare of rain and fever—"Everything was melting away in a welter of trashy goods, hopes and accounts, together with the fever, itself moist too." The nightmare is compounded when Bardamu manages to set this sodden mass afire, kindling perfect physical anarchy, with a ball of crude rubber smoldering and stinking in the middle. This reductive vision, the glutinous confusion of dreams imposed on daylight as well as night, runs strikingly counter to the doctor's function, which is to diagnose and correct. In fact, Dr. Destouches prescribed few drugs, and advised his patients simply, "Drink no alcohol, exercise regularly." Except for his mastery of some technical terms, the doctor-hero of Céline's fiction appears a helpless witness, sullenly listening—in one dreadful episode of "Journey"—to his patient's blood drip away, drop by drop, to the floor beneath the bed. When Bardamu's friend Robinson dies, he describes the process with a cold medical eye, and in a kind of ultimate of Gallic psychological acuity observes that even in dying the man is dislikably human:

> I would even, I believe, have more easily felt sorry for a dog dying than for Robinson, because a dog's not sly; whereas, whatever one may say, Léon was just a bit sly. I was sly too; we were all sly. . . . All the rest of it had fallen by the wayside and even those facial expressions, which are still in some use by a deathbed, I'd lost as well. I had indeed lost everything along the road, I couldn't find anything of what you need when you're pegging out, only maliciousness. My feelings were like a house you only keep for the holidays. They were barely habitable.

Céline really did what Camus wanted to do—anatomize the emotional emptiness of modern, Godless man. Within the explosions and brawls of his prose there occur, like hollows in a sponge, haunting islands of emptiness: hotels miraculously undamaged amid the rubble, or the deserted landscape of the opening battle scene of *Journey*, abandoned to the contending armies like a room to a newly married couple—"We're by ourselves like newly married folk doing dirty things when every one's left." In the noise of Detroit, some sounds are "so violent that they spread sort of silences around themselves which make you feel a little better." A strange perverse grace glimmers here and there in the infernal mess this author makes of the world. In the last novels, the trilogy based upon Céline's remarkable journeys through the collapsing Europe of the Second World War, bombs fall, filling the page with their noisy emptiness and giving every sentence the texture of a flying shard. Yet these novels are not depressing. The wayward beauties and accuracies of Céline's style give delight; his sheer destructiveness and mordancy are exhilarating; he has the gift (like no one in modern English so much as Bernard Shaw) of irresponsible exaggeration; and the constant company of his first-person voice shelters us from the kind of confrontation with massive, inexorable reality that the great third-person novels provide. A first-person narrator is a survivor, or he wouldn't be there on the page. This minor technical fact mutes the sense of death that Céline ostensibly evokes, and tinges with frivolity the kind of autobiographical novel of which he is patron saint.

Mr. McCarthy, an English scholar who now teaches French at Haverford, has done a fine, firm job of bodying forth a man who habitually obfuscated the facts about himself, who was obscure for the first forty years of his life and a recluse for the last ten. Chapters of ascertainable fact juxtaposed with critical chapters describing the major works rather successfully solve the recurrent problem in literary biography of giving both the external life — the life of record — and the internal life, the author as refracted in his own verbal creation. Céline, like many another, wrote worse of himself than he was. Bardamu, the first of his alter egos, enters America illegally and finds farcical employment as an official fleacounter; in truth, the young Dr. Destouches was sent to this country by a body no less august than the League of Nations, in order to conduct a study of the health conditions of the Ford workers in Detroit, a study he creditably carried out. At all the junctures of his often irregular life, Céline sought out opportunities to practice medicine. Amid the debacle of his flight from France into a collapsing Germany, he ministered to the community of wretched French collaborationists at Sigmaringen, and upon his return from exile, pardoned but far from forgiven, he hung out his shingle ("Dr. L.-F. Destouches of the Paris Faculty of Medicine, 2–4 P.M. except Friday") in the Paris suburb of Meudon. Mr. McCarthy, though his book is nowhere near the gargantuan size of the lives that are now being devoted to even minor writers, moves steadily through the welter of Céline's adventures, and his calm methodical manner spares us much idle speculation. His level prose at worst becomes trite telegraphy: "[Léon Daudet] was so famous a critic that he could make or break a book with one article. He read "Voyage" and wrote a glowing review. Success, both literary and popular, followed. The novel made an enormous impact." On the other hand, his critical discourse displays many fine discriminations and, in connection with Céline's increasingly murky plots, a powerful gift of synopsis; as he describes them, generally unadmired, and in English unavailable, works like *Féerie pour un Autre Fois* sound exciting. He can write a sentence of such witty compression as this, of the

French journalists who espoused collaboration: "In one sense their cause had been doomed from the start: it was impossible to convince the French that their real enemies were not the Germans who patrolled the streets, but the English who had killed Joan of Arc." His sketch of the collaborationist community, which included, besides Céline himself, sensitive writers like Robert Brasillach and Lucien Rebatet, is vivid enough to make one wish for more. And more, too, might be told of Céline's women, other than that they tended to be dancers and that he waxed rapturous over long-legged American beauties. Elizabeth Craig, who had lived with Céline during the composition of *Journey,* was pursued by him all the way to Los Angeles, where she in the course of disputing her father's will had married one of the lawyers—an episode as surreal as Philip Roth's fancy that Kafka came and taught Hebrew in New Jersey. Céline died, we learn, the very day he had completed a draft of *Rigodon,* the third book of the trilogy that to some extent had rehabilitated his literary reputation. He died swiftly, of a brain seizure, and in his wife's arms—a peaceable, workmanlike death for a man who had taken so much of our century's violence into himself.

In Support of Céline   Anthony Burgess*

Céline's novel *Voyage au bout de la nuit* appeared in Paris in 1933. The only English version I know—*Journey to the End of Night,* done by John H. P. Marks—came out in London in 1966. I wrote a very laudatory review and was attacked in a book on the Moors Murders by Lady Snow, who seemed to allege that writers like Céline contributed to the murderous decadence of our age. That Céline is, to many, a dangerous writer seems confirmed by the paucity of translations of his work and the delay in apperance of such translations as exist.

Even in France he is touched with gloves or fire tongs. He died on the same day as Hemingway but got far less space in the French newspapers. Of course, he had all the wrong ideas about life. It was bad enough for him to prefer the dirty and diseased to the healthy bourgeoisie, finding, like Beckett but without Beckett's willingness to cleanse through melody, the truth about life in *la merde universelle.* However, it was totally unforgivable for him to be praised by the Nazi *Stürmer* and then, with a kite tail of anti-Semitic pamphlets attached, fly off to Hitler's Germany in 1944. If Ezra Pound was wrong-headed, Céline was a monster. That at least two of his books, though long ignored by the academic literary histories, are among the most important that modern France has produced

*Reprinted with permission from *Harper's Magazine,* August 1976, 76–82. © 1976 Harper's.

is now being grudgingly admitted, or readmitted, but Céline has not yet been totally forgiven for his treachery. Time, that pardons Paul Claudel, has still some way to run before the dead patriots and defectors alike can, in Eliot's words, be folded into a single party and accept the constitution of silence.

. . . Louis-Ferdinand Destouches, to give him his true name ("Céline" was his grandmother's), is revealed as a man of a complexity not easily unraveled, heroic soldier in the first war, pacifist after, saintly doctor who finds reality in disease and man's lot totally tragic, voice of shopkeepers as well as of whores and pimps, adorer of the human body, worshiper of women, physically strong but far gone into melancholy, utterer of *mots* like "Look closely at the cemetery. It contains everything you can say or feel."

The *Voyage*, with its relentless pessimism, must not be taken as autobiography, but it is built out of the author's own experiences — war, French colonialism, the industrial hell of Detroit, the *cauchemar* of New York, journeys which all end in self-destruction. Yet the adventures of the hero Bardamu are shorn of the "motivation" which the films of the Thirties used to persuade us was attached to every human act. Things happen aleatorically; life is meaningless. Death is certain and we try to wait around for it, being pushed minimally by events in the meantime; but death, unlike life, bestows the brief gift of choice: one can at least elect, if one is lucky, how to die. Man is not an animal; he is capable of knowledge even wider than that of the approach of his own end, but the knowledge is of no value, since it cannot lead to the changing of the human condition. Here, as McCarthy points out, is the difference between Céline and Sartre: "For Sartre, as for Marxists, knowledge involves change. The realisation of one's place in the universe brings with it the commitment to revolt. For Bardamu it was 'only inside me that things were happening.' "

Solipsism, perhaps, is the word. *Mort à crédit* (Paris, 1936; translated by Marks as *Death on the Instalment Plan*, London, 1968) was attacked by the orthodox Marxists — led, imposingly, by Ivan Anissimov in the U.S.S.R. — because it demonstrated the miseries of capitalist society without displaying their cause or presenting, even with the obliquity appropriate to a work of literature, a program for their destruction. The wretchedness of the Paris life Céline knew as a young man, and from which he escaped into the cavalry, is depicted with a naturalistic technique that goes beyond Zola (excretion, stink, the working-class pigsty), but it lacks Zola's insights, his balance, above all his underlying philosophy. There is nothing outside the phenomena the narrator observes, either in the drive of the Schopenhauerian *Wille* or in the engines of history. Naturalism should, after all, be a metaphysic as well as a technique, but Céline can only give us the flux without its springs, the entropy without the thermodynamic law.

This is as much as to say that Céline reads to us like a man of faith more than an existentialist or Marxist. Faith without faith, indeed, but there is a smell of Newman's "terrible aboriginal calamity" in all the meticulously detailed images of decay. This is what human life is like, and nothing can be done about it: there is no political nostrum, no redemptive avatar. And yet the verbal flow, the richness of the vocabulary with its neologisms and argot, suggests an embracing of the condition with a kind of relish. We think of Joyce, but even more of Rabelais. Here is the old paradox of art. The denial of human joy is made through language which is itself a joy. And there is, of course, the Célinian humor, blacker and more bitter than Beckett's.

There is also the Célinian dynamic, a world away from the *chosisme* of the antinovelists, who fill their world with solid bodies and deny solidity to the human observer. Again, we miss the old-fashioned cinematic motivation: things are live and swift-moving, but without cause. "All the dishes are in smithereens, spinning, crashing, hurtling through the air." English sailors "lurch and frolic along. Already tight and ever so happy. They skip and romp and guffaw. . . . They can't make any headway, their jigs collide around a lamp-post. They get entangled." But the dance is always one of disintegration; there are no true solid bodies to the solipsist, only a more or less solid observer.

Céline's literary gifts were evidently not cognate with an ability to think coherently. This unpolitical man, making literature out of the materials of the social reformer, atheist with a kind of religious sensibility, was given to the irrational choosing of scapegoats for his own wrongs and, by an inevitable transition, the wrongs of the persecuted world he knew best. He didn't want reform, he wanted merely to blame. As McCarthy says, he wanted to feel persecuted, and, as an author, his chief persecutor had to be his publisher Denoël. He wished to be cheated, and so there had to be cheaters, even imaginary ones. Like any small Paris shopkeeper of the Dreyfus era, he was bound sooner or later to pick on the Jews. We can see the progress of his anti-Semitism in 1934, when he visited Los Angeles. Beginning with his friend Mahé's paraphrase "No! we are not anti-Semitic. . . . But unlike the rest of the goys we can distinguish a Jew from a goy. So we are perfectly well aware of the great Jewish international solidarity" we can move on to "The Hollywood Jews . . . know what a pretty girl is" (Céline had an almost manic admiration for American female beauty) and "Ah! Goldwyn Mayer! I would have given ten years of my life to sit for one moment in their armchairs. All those goddesses at my mercy." The anti-Semitism is not yet serious, but it soon will be.

Add to this Céline's fascination with low life, his tendency to see the degraded side of a city like London or New York or Berlin and be indifferent to its beauty or creative vitality, his pleasure in being appalled, his tendency to impose his solipsistic vision on the outside world, and it soon becomes possible for him to believe that fascism is better than democracy. In the late Thirties he began to write pamphlets. War was coming, civilization was going to be destroyed. Blame the Jews, said Céline.

One has to see his *Bagatelles* — not included in the *Oeuvres complètes* because of the embarrassment of the publisher Gallimard — as being set very firmly in a French polemical tradition compounded of Gallic hot air and Gallic logic. You take a scapegoat premise for the wrongs of France — the British, the Americans, the Freemasons, the capitalists — and you work it to death. The Jews were just one of several available organized villainies, and Céline, who thought, remembering his mother's shopkeeping days, he knew what the Jews were like, went to work on them in a spirit closer to fantasy than to informed reason. He sings a note uncommon in the other pamphleteers of his day: the Jew is uncreative and an enemy of beauty. It is an attitude which only a word-spinning fantasist of Céline's talent could hope to make plausible. Plausibility is, however, conspicuously lacking. Life could be a dance, says Céline, society could be a ballet if it were not for the Jews. This, with so much of Richard Wagner's anti-Semitism (who could tolerate *Parsifal* if he took note of its philosophy?), can be laughed off, like Béraud's pamphlet recommending that the British be reduced to slavery. But unfortunately Céline went over to the Germans in 1944.

Forgiveness and rehabilitation are perhaps coming faster to this remarkable writer than his shade has any right to expect. But the work of his that may be expected to last as a genuine, if highly subjective and idiosyncratic, vision of life is not tainted by overt pro-Nazism, though Patrick McCarthy insists that the *oeuvre* be taken as a whole. Those who read Céline in English are unlikely ever to get the whole *oeuvre*; in the meantime it is in order to regard the *Voyage* and *Mort à crédit* as representative of his genius. He remains a dangerous writer, as does any writer who delves into evil — like the Marquis de Sade and, for that matter, William Shakespeare. He lacks Sade's logic and Shakespeare's compassion, but he has his own quality, not easily imitated. McCarthy's book is to be recommended highly on both its biographical and critical sides, reminding us as it does that important writers must not be ignored merely because they make us feel uncomfortable. Literature, as they say, has many mansions.

Céline on the Installment Plan   Patrick McCarthy*

Last week—July 26 to 30—Céline lovers gathered in Paris for a conference. Thirty scholars from France, Britain, Belgium, Germany, North America and Australia met to hear papers on all aspects of Céline's work—novels and pamphlets. The conference opened quietly but dozens of photographs of Céline were looking down ironically from the walls. He knew there would be trouble.

Sure enough, one M. Robert Faurisson had already started it. He was suspicious of the political slant of the newly-founded Société des études céliniennes. He feared that Céline was falling into the hands of communists who would slander and revile him. This fear came as a particular surprise to the American members, who knew that in New York anyone interested in Céline is still suspected of being a neo-Nazi. True, Céline does have left-wing French admirers who see in his work the destruction of "bourgeois" writing. But this hardly amounts to communist infiltration. Still, M. Faurisson, who himself has a pamphleteer's temperament, plunged on. First he issued diatribes about leftist conspiracies, then he decided to read a paper on the pamphlets, then he decided not to. But he did make many interventions to declare that *Bagatelles pour un massacre* is in fact a joyous and gay work. He also proposed a new reading: Céline was attacking the Jew as colonizer; he was thus taking the same stand as the Algerians had taken against the French. So all those who had supported the FLN should be on Céline's side. This strange piece of reasoning—worthy of Céline himself—met with scant sympathy. Henri Godard, who worked on the Pléiade volumes of Céline, was rightly determined that the Société should not become a haven of the ex-Algérie Française or of the extreme right in general. He rejected the FLN interpretation out of hand, but there was tension in the room. Céline, who once said "the communists have always hated me and so has the right," would have been delighted.

It took a Welshman, Merlin Thomas to calm things down and then the conference went back to its work. There were solid papers on the use of language and narration in Céline's novels. Speakers found a subversive element in the storytelling which led Céline to break down character and plot. The young hero of *Mort à crédit* does not mature; he is desensitized—stripped of his inner life. By juggling his narrators and by fracturing his syntax, Céline criticized traditional fiction. With deliberate and often comic ambiguity, he undermined the so-called real world. He then went on to write a new kind of novel. His tone of delirium was analysed as a conscious artistic device which enabled him to transform his subject. He was trying to communicate his vision of fear and death in a more direct,

*Reprinted with permission from the *Times Literary Supplement*, no. 3882 (6 August 1976):984.

jealously personal way than had been done before. Although his world is a strange one, it is always coherent; on this speakers were agreed. Céline was using madness, myth and legend to depict war — since war was for him the one great fact of life. Stress was laid on the later, very difficult novels where the process of transformation has been taken much further: on *Guignol's Band*, where London has become a giant puppet-show, and on *Féerie pour une autre fois* where ballet and cinema become part of the text.

Parallels were drawn between Céline and other modern artists. The hallucination that triggers off *Mort à crédit* was compared with Proust's theme of unconscious memory. The same paper noted that Proust's depiction of the Zeppelin raids on Paris anticipates the way Céline uses music and dance to describe the Allied bombing. Further comparisons were made with the French cinema of the 1930s: with Vigo, Duvivier, who thought briefly about filming *Voyage au bout de la nuit*, and with Marcel Carné, whose favourite actress Arletty was Céline's friend. It was remarked that Céline may well have influenced Godard, who also moves directly and rapidly from one level of reality to another.

The psychoanalysts had their moment. They brooded over Céline's strong but dubious sexuality. They talked about latent homosexuality and they attributed his liking for obscenity to anal-aggression. They were fascinated by the episode in *Mort à crédit* where the young Ferdinand tries to murder his father with — appropriately enough — a typewriter. Yet they sensibly refused to be dogmatic. They could not be drawn into saying that Céline was mad or ill or abnormal. They agreed that he *himself* saw his life as a disastrous failure and that he created other selves in order to escape from or overcome it.

In general the conference showed courage. One speaker had run three of Céline's books through a computer in order to study his use of direct and indirect speech. Another was endeavouring to translate him into German — an awesomely difficult task — and was preparing herself by reading Günter Grass whose language is rather like Céline's. The Société's energetic secretary Jean-Pierre Dauphin outlined plans for a dictionary of Céline's language, publication of his letters, a journal and a volume of criticism on the puzzling *Féerie*. All this is to be done with the cooperation of Gallimard who, having turned down *Voyage* in 1932, is now hoping to make money out of Céline. Céline, who royally abused Gallimard, would not have been surprised and indeed prophesied that this would happen.

The tone of the conference was austere and serious — perhaps a little too serious. During a very earnest discussion of comedy, a delightful French girl suggested that, instead of talking about absurdity in Céline's novels, one should talk about "l'esprit de foutaise." This happy formula was considered frivolous and was not accepted. Still, the most important thing to emerge is that Céline is now being studied in a calm, thorough way. Readers are no longer frightened by the virulence of the pamphlets or bewildered by the originality of the novels. They are not blindly rejecting Céline and they are not forcing him into narrow, simplistic categories. They are coming to grips with a fascinating, difficult writer. And that must happen, if Céline is really to live on.

Céline's Last Jeer   Pierre Audinet*

The last time I saw Céline was a long, muggy spring evening drenched by a heavy shower, a short time before his death. Bardamu [Céline] was waiting for me, surrounded by his pack of enormous dogs, dressed in his familiar rags, and waring his very gentle smile — infinitely sad despite the irony disguising it. His big blue eyes bore that childlike gaze which would never see the end of its journey into night, a journey that had started nearly three-quarters of a century before. One felt as if he were surprised at still being here among us, as if he were conscious of having become more and more a phantom to the coming generations — for whom his experiences of life would mean less and less — and, above all, to himself. . . .

In a corner of the garden, a large bird cage was being built for his parrots. We were looking out at the rain. Céline kept up a bantering conversation.

"They come regularly to consult the oracle. Why I write, why I'm not dead yet, that's what interests them. I don't write for the same reasons they do, neither for the Academy nor for the gardener's ass: that's the way it's been and that's the way it still is. I simply write to make *them* unreadable. Madame Valéry, Monsieur Collette, they can be imitated. There is a way: a cheap hand-knitted sweater, if you want, the embroidery of a young miss, but it's not the needle-work which takes everything out of a man . . . lace cathedrals but not stones dug from the quarries of life. That job constantly tears at your guts so that all you can do is go to bed at night. But since I don't sleep, I keep right on picking and scraping at the material. It isn't possible to write and at the same time," — he disdainfully purses his lips — "to go cocktailing, to have a *cinq-à-sept*, the movies, a little orgy, to take Rover out for a walk, with stops at a few *pissoirs* to stimulate the imagination. . . . Promotions, Social Security, Legion of Honor, pederasty and running errands. No, they'll never get out of school . . . forever glutting themselves in the dining hall, tucking each other in or overturning the bed after night prayers in the dormitories, always abiding by school rules, the nasty tricks played by the head kids. . . . The world of silence: a slyly intentional but quiet fart. So the notion of heroism is

*Reprinted with permission of World Press Review from *Atlas*, 12 July 1966, 51–52. Translated from the Paris weekly *Arts*.

associated with the burst of a well-aimed fart: Western civilization is anal; the one who makes his mark, who doesn't disown his ass, and who assumes responsibility for it, he is Man, Big Joe, a hero, Roland: the song of Roland: No, they'll never outgrow their childhood, it's obvious. . . ."

At that moment, as we were exchanging rather pessimistic views on life, I surprised myself by murmuring to him—however trite it may appear—Shakespeare's famous definition: ". . . a tale told by an idiot, signifying nothing. . . ." Céline agreed and continued:

"It's also their masked ball, like those dirty silent movies of before the 1914 war, with their big orchestras, brass and percussion, in the cellars: 'Fantomas-Tantouze,' 'La Main qui étreint,' 'Le Baiser qui tue' . . . in serial. They all went right from the lycée to the ivory tower without any transition, so that there they could fart and make like Proust at their leisure, for all eternity. . . . A pretty grim delight. . . . All those messages came right out of there, all those love stories which burst to overflowing the bins of Hachette, La Bibliotèque Nationale. . . .

"In the Tower they don't expose themselves. They never expose themselves except in the right place, to make things easy. Those are the people who are in the know. . . . They always have a sense of history, but only when it serves their purpose. Mind you, I'm not criticizing. That's the way they are. You can't fight it. . . . Right now they're in between acts. After being buggered by the Krauts, the English, the Russians, the Yanks, their only hope is in the yellows, and they're waiting with an impatient prostate. It will come, all they need is a little time and vaseline will no longer be needed. They've got a female nature. Those burly guys never really satisfied them. That kind is too slow, too heavy, too inclined to doze off. The black man, he might do the trick, but it's really the yellows they must have. Frenzy, steel nerves, blood-thirsty hysteria: Chinese torture, the garden of tortures. Ah, mother. The advent of our greatest rectal delights prepares itself behind the Urals. From Moscow to New York the White man will be buggered in shuddering delight. The A-bomb will burst in his ass." . . .

Madeleine Jacob, Jean-Baptiste Sartre, François Mauriac, La Callas, as far as I'm concerned, they're in the foreground, you don't need a magnifying glass to see them. But the innumerable anonymous progeny, the fraternal embrace of the ectoplasms—I have a staggering distrust of these. . . .

The conversation turned to contemporary literature, a topic which always made him burst out laughing.

"This time this is it . . . it seems they've discovered a new type of novel. . . . You've heard of it? I let them tell me that the last masterpiece was *La Robe sur le Gril* . . . or *La Robe grillée?*"

Robbe-Grillet!

"Yes, *Robe grillée.*[1] Undoubtedly it has to do with witchcraft, good for shadowy dealings. Cauldron, broomstick, a kiss for the devil's ass and the lepers. The deserts, that's their business also. The great art of Western folklore: the desert of the buttock, of love, of life . . . sobs, swoons, pain, grief, the grill, the stake, melted lead. Don't be mistaken about it, we haven't left the Middle Ages yet."

We began to speak of the beauty of women:

"That's the miracle. Between fourteen and sixteen years old, the time when they give you great religious emotions, the divine call. It doesn't last long, a woman's beauty. The Romantics are right. It lasts just as long as it takes a flower to bloom and then fade: from two to four years for the human species . . . the glory of the species: the dancing girl at sixteen."

"They come around from time to time, they send reporters to see how far gone I am, to see if I've really begun my death agony, if I will soon be dead. Let me tell you in confidence, and you'll be the first to know it. The end is coming very soon. Everyone will be very happy, and I most of all. You can proclaim that there will be no one at my funeral. Here is a satisfaction to savor all alone: one's finally taking off for good. I probably won't have time to finish *L'Ambassadrice*."

L'Ambassadrice?

"Yes, that's death . . . and you?"

I can still see his attention, the beauty of his totally desolate look, twinkling with an irony set off by my answer. When I had finished expounding my beliefs, he took a piece of paper on which, I surmised, he was writing something meant for me. The message he handed me said: "Monsieur Pierre Audinet, if one were to say about life what one knows of it, one would never get out of prison."

It started to rain twice as hard. Céline was silent now, as if his inexhaustible monologue had been suddenly dammed up, forced inward.

"Everything depends on one's mug. Mine doesn't turn people on. Got to get used to it. The other day, for example, I stopped at a bistro, a very unassuming place, where streetwalkers were leaning on the bar. I didn't really think I could be the cause of a scandal in such an unassuming place, but I was wrong. The bartender approached me, taking me gently by the arm, and asked me to leave. He led me to the door. 'No, not here,' he said. And I wasn't begging. I wasn't making any noise, I had a shirt on and my pants had no holes. The curse is not a legend, it's not imaginary nor a question of superstition; it's always existed and always will, it's physical: one carries it in the skin, it's there to be stared at, like leprosy or scurvy."

These were the last words he addressed to me.

Notes

1. Puns, perhaps suggesting the now infamous and therefore, in Céline's eyes, "saintly" or "priestly" profession of the modern French novel. Alain Robbe-Grillet (1922–), a leading figure in the French *nouveau roman*, whose *Le Voyeur* (1955) won the Prix des Critiques. His novels attempt to demonstrate the independence of fiction from reality. (editor's note).

INDEX

349